The Female Face of God in Auschwitz

The dominant theme of post-Holocaust Jewish theology has been that of the temporary hiddenness of God, interpreted either as a divine mystery or, more commonly, as God's deferral to human freedom. But the traditional religious image of the *Shekhinah*, as a female figure of divine presence accompanying Israel into exile, counters such theologies of absence. *The Female Face of God in Auschwitz*, the first full-length feminist theology of the Holocaust, argues that the masculinist bias of post-Holocaust theology becomes fully apparent only when considered in the light of both feminist perceptions of God and of women's holocaustal experiences and priorities. Building upon the published testimonies of women imprisoned at Auschwitz-Birkenau, including Olga Lengyel, Lucie Adelsberger, Bertha Ferderber-Salz and Sara Nomberg-Przytyk, Melissa Raphael interprets the relationships of care between women as an act of sacralization of Auschwitz: an invitation to God's presence into that place on earth which would most repel it.

God's face, as that of the exiled *Shekhinah* was not, says Raphael, hidden in Auschwitz, but revealed in the female face turned as an act of resistance to that of the assaulted other as a refractive image of God. For women's attempts to wash themselves and others, and to see, touch and cover the bodies of the suffering were not only the kindnesses of a practical ethic of care; they were a means of washing the gross profanation of Auschwitz from the body of Israel in ways faithful to Jewish covenantal obligations of sanctification. Women's restoration of the human, and therefore the divine, from holocaustal erasure opposes not only recent theories of divine absence, but also patriarchal theologies that accommodate absolute violence in the economies of the divine plan.

Engaging with Berkovits, Fackenheim, Levinas and other post-Holocaust Jewish thinkers, *The Female Face of God in Auschwitz* is a subtle meditation upon God's role and meaning in the world. Questioning the true nature of the Jewish God present in Auschwitz, and arguing for God's participation in its extremities of suffering and grace, it powerfully resists interpretations of the Holocaust as evidence of divine indifference or neglect.

Melissa Raphael is Principal Lecturer in Theology and Religious Studies at the University of Gloucestershire. She is the author of *Introducing Theology: Discourse on the Goddess* (1999), *Rudolf Otto* ̄ ̄ ̄ ̄ (1997) and *Theology and Embodiment* (1996).

Religion and Gender
Series editors: Ursula King and Rita M. Gross

Enchanted Feminism
The Reclaiming Witches of San Francisco
Jone Salomonsen

The Female Face of God in Auschwitz
A Jewish feminist theology of the Holocaust
Melissa Raphael

The Female Face of God in Auschwitz

A Jewish feminist theology of the Holocaust

Melissa Raphael

Routledge
Taylor & Francis Group

LONDON AND NEW YORK

To my mother, Lily Suzanne Raphael (*née* Shaffer)
1936–1978 and my sister, Caroline Sarah Raphael

First published 2003
by Routledge
2 Park Square, Milton Park, Abingdon, Oxon, OX14 4RN

Simultaneously published in the USA and Canada
by Routledge
270 Madison Ave, New York NY 10016

Routledge is an imprint of the Taylor & Francis Group

Transferred to Digital Printing 2006

© 2003 Melissa Raphael

Typeset in Bembo by Exe Valley Dataset Ltd, Exeter

British Library Cataloguing in Publication Data
A catalogue record for this book is available from the British Library

Library of Congress Cataloging in Publication Data
Raphael, Melissa
    The female face of God in Auschwitz: a Jewish feminist theology of the
    Holocaust/Melissa Raphael.
        p. cm. (Religion and gender)
    Includes bibliographical references and index.
    1. Holocaust (Jewish theology) 2. Jewish women in the Holocaust. 3. Presence of God.
    4. Femininity of God. 5. Holocaust, Jewish (1939–1945)–Personal narratives–History
    and criticism. 6. Aushchwitz (Concentration camp) 7. Redemption–Judaism.
    8. Feminism–Religious aspects–Judaism. I. Title. II. Series.

    BM645.H6 R37 2003
    296.3'1174–dc21   2002031819

ISBN 0–415–23664–9 (hbk)
ISBN 0–415–23665–7 (pbk)

Contents

Series editors' preface

Gender research has now become more gender-inclusive rather than just women-centred, a change of great theoretical significance. The Religion and Gender Series is dedicated to publishing books which reflect that change. It will feature innovative, original research which moves away from predominantly western to global perspectives, including comparative and interdisciplinary approaches where appropriate. Firmly grounded in religious studies, books in this series will draw on a wide range of disciplines, including gender studies, philosophy, theology, sociology, history, anthropology, as well as women's and men's studies in religion. By recognizing the limitations of previous, exclusively androcentric approaches to the study of religions, this series will help overcome earlier deficiencies in scholarship about religion and open new intellectual horizons in the field.

Although a relatively new area of enquiry, the materials relevant to the study of religion and gender are as old as humanity. They include the roles, lives and experiences of women and men, as shaped by diverse gender norms, stereotypes and symbols prevalent in different religious, cultural and historical contexts. Issues of gender – what it means to be male or female, and ultimately what it means to be human – are central to social, philosophical, doctrinal, ethical and practical questions in every religion, and gender symbolism is of great significance in all religious worship, spirituality and doctrine. The Religion and Gender Series publishes new research on these and all other aspects of gender and religion.

Ursula King
Rita M. Gross

Preface

This is a book about presence and absence, both human and divine, in an Auschwitz remembered by others. Born in 1960, into an Anglo-Jewish family that settled in Britain between the seventeenth and the late nineteenth centuries, my perspective is that of a generation and a community that 'sees upon its flesh the scar without the wound, the memory without the direct experience'.[1] While I remain uncomfortable with its presumption, if I have any personal rather than academic justification for writing this book, it is that, as Michael Berenbaum says of all reflection on the Holocaust: 'only a generation more distant from the immediate catastrophe could dare approach it. Like Lot's wife, survivors could not afford to look back while fleeing.'[2] My generation's increasing historical and critical distance from the Holocaust allows us to know the extent of the destruction and what can be retrieved from the debris. It is making a different sort of approach both possible and necessary if Auschwitz is neither to engulf liberal Jewish consciousness and become its (Americanized) civil religion,[3] nor be relegated by parts of Orthodoxy to a list of historical catastrophes that are largely irrelevant to faith and its observances. More immediately, many Jews feel unable to make an absolute distinction between the Jewish past and their own present. This is not to make a merely self-dramatizing incursion into times more tragically interesting than their own. Jewish spiritual collectivism - while not permission for boundless anachronism - is such that the temporal and ontological distinctions of personal identity are not drawn in the customary way. The Exodus, over three thousand years ago, is forever an annual experience and it happens to us, not a historical 'them'.[4] So too, as Cohen insists, for the Jew, all Israel is a 'real presence' in the death camps, just as it was at Sinai: 'the death camps account my presence really, even if not literally: hence my obligation to hear the witnesses as though I were a witness, to be with the witnesses as though I were a witness.'[5]

But the way in which theology witnesses with the witnesses will change over time. Auschwitz is both obscured and formed by its belonging to the history of another millennium. It may be that we will be healed of Auschwitz as much by the passage of time (as we have been of the Expulsion of Jewry from the Iberian peninsula of 1492 and the Chmielnicki massacres of 1648) as by theological persuasion. Suffering can be washed by time. (Gillian Rose found that the graves in the beech forests outside Tarnów, where 800 Jewish children and 1,000 sick and elderly Jews had been shot are now, by early spring, surrounded by 'masses of tiny, white wood anemones, wind-flower and bird-song, and the audibly rising sap of the pearly trees, as if a fairy tale had taken place [t]here.')[6] The Holocaust is something partially grown over. As I grew up, its legacy of absence and (occasionally) presence was only apparent to me abroad and in passing: in a hot, crowded bus travelling from Tel Aviv to Jerusalem, sitting next to a woman whose arm was tattooed with small blackish numbers; in central and eastern European towns and villages, looking into the faces of anyone old enough to have been at least complicit in atrocity; among broken Jewish gravestones lying in the fallen leaves in a wood outside a German town.

By the time my daughter has grown up the Holocaust will have receded, thankfully, into a world of visual and literary texts but almost beyond her direct knowing. The holocaustal self-revelation of God can now only be perceived in the act of reading (a very Jewish sort of religious experience). But I should like some of what she might read to be mediated in ways less flawed by androcentrism than those books that have been available to me. It was partly in the interests of Holocaust education, then, that I wrote this book. I found myself unwilling to enlist the assistance of those Holocaust theologians of my parents' generation whose work seems to me to be spiritually and politically inadequate to the task, and perhaps even part of its problem.

This book is dedicated to my mother and sister, but written, in some ways, for my daughter, as a way of telling her how the Holocaust might be, not redeemed, but qualified; that is, not entirely a fall from hope - as it once was for me. For like any other discourse, theology is never wholly disinterested. Again, Cohen: 'It is always the matter that theologians come to save others having first saved their own faith, wringing from their own unease a respite which conviction and hope move them to transmit to others as teaching.'[7]

Acknowledgements

Warm thanks are owed to Ursula King and Rita Gross who invited me to contribute this book to the Routledge series of studies in Religion and Gender, and to Roger Thorpe and Clare Johnson at Routledge for bringing this book to publication. I would also like to thank Fred Hughes and Peter Scott in the University of Gloucestershire's School of Theology and Religious Studies for agreeing the periods of research leave which allowed me time to prepare substantial parts of the manuscript. I am grateful to Ursula King, Stephen Barton, Janet Soskice, Pam Lunn, Sue Morgan, Lisa Isherwood, Beverly Clack, Peggy Morgan and Keith Ward, Kevin Scott, Susan Frank Parsons, and Margie Tolstoy whose invitations to lecture on my research have given me opportunities to present and discuss the work in stimulating company. Carol Christ and Dee Carter have also offered critical insight and friendship. I have greatly valued my father, Arnold Raphael's, interest in the progress and argument of the book. He, and Dee Carter, Sue Morgan, Beryl Francis, Una Blackmore and Harry Cowen have all generously supplied me with related books, newspaper cuttings and articles over several years. I am also grateful to my sister, Caroline, for not letting me visit Auschwitz alone, to artist and friend David Behar-Perahia for reworking part of his sculptural installation in the restored synagogue in Chania, Crete, into the enigmatic image of a mikvah that graces the cover of this book and to the members of the Women's Association of the Cheltenham Synagogue for their warm interest in this study. Above all, I owe immeasurable thanks to my daughter Verity for her ready understanding of the demands of academic life, and to my husband Michael for his emotional, intellectual and practical support throughout.

Parts of this book have been published in earlier and different forms. An earlier version of 'The Princess and the City of Death' was appended to my 'When God Beheld God, Notes Towards a Jewish Feminist Theology of the Holocaust', *Feminist Theology* 21 (1999), pp. 53–78, reproduced by permission of Sheffield Academic Press Limited. Parts of Chapter 1 appeared in a shorter form in 'Is Patriarchal Theology Still Patriarchal? Reading Theologies of the Holocaust from a Jewish Feminist Perspective', *Journal of Feminist Studies in Religion* 18 (2002), pp. 105–13; parts of Chapter 3 appears in 'Holiness *in Extremis*: Jewish Women's Resistance to the Profane in Auschwitz' in Stephen Barton (ed.), *Holiness Past and Present,*

Edinburgh, T. & T. Clark, forthcoming. Some of the argument of this book appears in preliminary and summary form in Susan Frank Parsons (ed.), *Challenging Women's Orthodoxies in the Context of Faith*, Aldershot, Hants and Burlington, VT, Ashgate Press, 2000, pp. 73–87 and Dan Cohn-Sherbok (ed.), *Holocaust Theology: A Reader*, Exeter, Exeter University Press, 2002, pp. 245–8.

Unless otherwise stated, all biblical quotations are from *Tanakh: The Holy Scriptures*, Philadelphia, The Jewish Publication Society, 1985.

Introduction

Despite a substantial and growing literature of women survivors' testimony, only since the early 1990s has Holocaust Studies' customary inattention to gender begun to be rectified.[1] Feminist scholars have challenged the assumption that the normative 'Jew' of religious and social discourse (who is actually a male Jew unless specified otherwise) also represents all victims of the Nazis. It now seems clear that the Nazis' killing operations were not gender-blind; women's experience of the Holocaust cannot be subsumed into that of men, and the gender-specific differences in the ways women suffered, survived and died in the Holocaust must be acknowledged and addressed. Without in any sense dismissing or competing with male suffering, in the interests of a more comprehensive and nuanced understanding of the Holocaust, feminist historians – notably Joan Ringelheim and Myrna Goldenberg – have asked both how women's spiritual, ethical and political resistance to Nazism was gendered and how Nazism placed Jewish women in 'double jeopardy' as objects of both its anti-Semitism and its misogyny.

As mothers of future generations and physically ill-equipped for most forms of slave labour, women and their children were the immediate targets of genocide. Gender-specific factors would also have weakened, exhausted and killed women. Not only were women already socially and spiritually disadvantaged in their own Jewish communities, in the ghettos it was wives and mothers who had to fight for the release of fathers and sons imprisoned by the Gestapo, to soothe and calm distressed, ill and hungry children. Often they combined slave labour with running ghetto households in ever-smaller living spaces and on ever-diminishing means (usually feeding children and men before or in place of themselves). They were also likely to have felt most keenly the loss of family heirlooms such as silver sabbath candlesticks and kiddush cups: the tangible symbols of inter-generational continuity and the security and sanctity of the homes they had laboured to create. In Auschwitz, if women survived 'selection' by looking youthful and fit on their arrival and by being unaccompanied by young children, they were usually forced, as in other camps, to undertake hard labour beyond their muscular strength. Their sexual identity was eroded by starvation, the cessation of menses, and sometimes forced abortion. The fear of rape and sexual abuse, and the anguish of separation from babies and young children for whom they had been the primary carers were emotional traumas to which women were especially vulnerable.[2]

If the historiography of the Holocaust has not been attentive to or normative of women's experience and response, no more has post-Holocaust theology. This is not to say that men's experience is of no theological account. To ignore the male half of Auschwitz's victims would merely reverse the error and injustice this book critiques. To polarize masculine and feminine Holocaust experience may in any case be misleading. Jewish studies of Ashkenazic masculinity have long demonstrated that its traditional ideal, embodied in the pale, dreamy scholar, is not that obtaining in more macho Gentile cultures.[3] While Holocaust theology's interests, values and imaginary are undoubtedly masculinist, its masculine God is, nonetheless, a vanquished God; the male Jewish theologians who reject or hold fast to him represent Jewish victims who have been feminized by their helplessness before the forces of hyper-masculine Nazism. To be a Jewish man in the ghettos and camps was in almost all cases to be stateless, unarmed, and left in a state of alterity and uncleanness more customarily ascribed by gynophobic religious ideologies to women.

In short, Steven Katz is right that Auschwitz 'will not yield to any conceptual oversimplification'.[4] Using gender as a category of analysis will neither explain nor solve the Holocaust. But as at least a corrective to the almost universal scholarly assumption that women's Holocaust experience tells us something important about Nazi savagery but not about God, it will show that much that is theologically significant about women's experience has been overlooked in the production of post-Holocaust theology and in exclusively masculine models of divine agency during the period in question.[5]

That women's Holocaust experience has been theologically overlooked is hardly to be wondered at. Susan Starr Sered has observed that 'a pervasive problem' in studies of Judaism is its tendency to treat formal, communal practice in masculine spaces as 'more noble, beautiful, important, eternal, primary or true' than private female religious practice.[6] Rejecting this androcentric and often ethnocentric assumption, Sered notes that, by contrast, the religious practices which have typically attracted women are those 'characterized by a preference for expressing ultimate concerns in the language of relationship' and that the personal, concrete ethical values (rather than halakhic priorities) associated with such practices should not be regarded as detrimental or substandard.[7] For within women's 'profane world' religiosity is interwoven with all other aspects and dimensions of their lives.[8] Sered's general distinction between traditional male and female interests and obligations, together with the more particular feminist studies of the Holocaust, have led me to question whether women's relational behaviour in Auschwitz,[9] absolutely the sphere of the profane, should not also be the object of theological enquiry, rather than historical or sociological alone. Sered's criticism of the way Jews and Judaism are studied raises questions for the way Jews and Judaism during the Holocaust are studied.

In order to see how women have been written out of post-Holocaust theology (by which I refer to theological reflection on the Holocaust written after 1945) we need to appreciate the degree to which (like most other religions) traditional Judaism casts women as the secondary objects of male agency, rather than the subjects and agents of their own experience. From the rabbinic period to the present, and despite some recent changes to a degree permitted by men regarding women's opportunities to study and pray, Orthodox male discursive, interpretative and practical dominance privileges masculinity as the primary likeness of God. It is masculinity that has been and remains generative of religious and historical knowledge, and authority and leadership in both the domestic and public religious spheres.[10] Until very recently, women (even those in relatively liberal circles) have known Judaism and Jewish thought from the perspective of the marginal, silent other. Consequently, it is men's spiritual and religious resistance to the Holocaust – including their anger and despair – which has generated and defined an authoritative body of religious knowledge and protest about the catastrophe. Women, never having been speaking Jewish subjects, remain the silent objects of the genocidal assault and subsequent discourse upon it.

Jewish feminists have now made a contribution to Jewish theology whose significance is disproportionate to their small number. Yet for reasons I suggest at the beginning of Chapter 1, there remains a glaring lacuna in Jewish feminist theology: to date there has been no full-length feminist critical dialogue with Holocaust theology or constructive feminist theological engagement with women's experience during the Holocaust. It is crucial that this be initiated. For if no Jewish theologian can believe or write as if the Holocaust had not occurred,[11] the rise of emancipatory theologies will make future theological discussion of the Holocaust seem a relic of an outmoded and unscholarly androcentrism if it is not at least conversant with the growing Jewish feminist literature and the religious practice it informs. It is not, as Orthodoxy fears, that Jewish feminism intends to supersede tradition. Orthodox anti-feminist rhetoric fails to understand the diversity, moral seriousness and, above all, prophetic Jewishness, of the Jewish feminist project and routinely mistakes it for that of secular modernity. Rather, it is that in late modernity the locus of discursive authority has shifted; others have spoken in ways such that post-Holocaust theology, as it reaches the end of its span and canon, requires resources which do not only supplement our theological reading of the Holocaust with women's writing and testimony, but change it. Gender difference – both that of writers and readers of Holocaust testimony – can, I believe, produce a different account of the enormity. If women, by choice, law or custom, perceive and situate God's presence differently to men, so too will a female account of God's presence and absence in Auschwitz.

Gender difference and inequality were significant factors in women victims' experience and their collective remembering, and remain significant in the possibility of contemporary Jewish women making an authoritative theological response. Yet Jewish feminism's own assertion of the full humanity of women and its broad affirmation of the legitimacy of female theological imagery has already prepared the ground for such a response. The Orthodox theologian Irving Greenberg urges that the renewal of Jewish life after the Holocaust will come about by the restoration of human dignity in the image of God: the image of God is the 'best, most indelible testimony to God in a world where total evil has triumphed'. And more than that, 'So savage was the attack on the image of God that the counter response of affirmation must be extraordinary. Any models or behaviour patterns within the tradition that demean the image of God must be cleansed and corrected at once.'[12] It is significant that in later pieces, Greenberg summarizes Jewish feminism as the movement that 'seeks to realize the Torah's dream' that every human being will be honoured as made in the image of God.[13] That Jewish feminism has undertaken what should be the post-Holocaust task of Jewry as a whole suggests that there is something about Jewish feminist theological revision that is crucially both at the heart of Judaism and at the heart of a properly Jewish theological response to Auschwitz, the effect of whose assault, if not its stated intent, was a degradation and erasure of the divine image that at once justified and hid its crime.

With these critical and constructive purposes in mind, I have written this book so that the first two chapters establish a critical context for the four subsequent chapters' constructive theology. These four latter chapters describe three movements: God's approach to, passage through, and departure from Auschwitz into an open future. In both parts, women's holocaust memoirs are used to produce and illustrate my critique as well as to revisit post-Holocaust theology and the tradition it engages. I end the book with a theopoetic postscript: a short tale in the traditional form of the *maaseh* that summarizes and concludes the book without merely rehearsing its argument. Although the critical discussion of post-Holocaust theology contextualizes my own constructive project, both can be read independently of the other.

The argument of this book

Any attempt to write a theology of the Holocaust on the basis of its historical recollection faces a number of methodological and theological challenges. It might therefore be helpful to outline the central elements of my argument and anticipate some of the objections it might properly raise.

Aware of the serious shortcomings of blunt, polarizing terms like feminist and patriarchal,[14] the first chapter examines the gendered factors of difference in mediating and reading the Holocaust, as well as the patriarchal values and priorities which underpin theological construals of the Holocaust where the masculine voice is authoritative and heard, and God is very often, and women almost always, silent. Offering the preliminaries of a feminist response I argue that post-Holocaust theology has been a thoroughly gendered enterprise. It has been produced by and for men on patriarchal premises of what constitutes morally and theologically acceptable divine means and ends, and what experiences constitute a theologically authoritative witness and what do not. In 1919 the radical Yiddish poet Kadia Molodowski wrote: 'My life is a page ripped out of a holy book and part of the first line is missing.'[15] With Molodowski's words in mind, I go on to use the opening chapter of a well-known introduction to post-Holocaust theology to demonstrate that there are connections, yet to be fully explored, between the male authority to pronounce after Sinai and to pronounce after Auschwitz. The halakhic inadmissibility of women as most forms of witness, or as scholar or judge, as well as the exemption (or exclusion-in-effect) of women from most time-bound religious observance is closely connected to the way in which they experienced, remember and bear witness to the Holocaust, and how that is heard, or failed to be heard.

What lies behind this first chapter and the next is a sense that much, though not all, post-Holocaust theology is disquieting not just because it relates catastrophe, but in what it permits of God's will and purpose and how, by ultimately vindicating the sovereignty of God's name, it once more secures masculine religious and territorial honour and standing. Although Holocaust theology has at least partially indicted God on account of his holocaustal absence, silence or (in more recent and vogueish idiom) his abusiveness, it has not questioned its own basic *model* of God, only certain failures of its attributes. It is my contention that it was a patriarchal model of God, not God-in-God's-self, that failed Israel during the Holocaust. Although the critical interrogation of God is not foreign to Jewish tradition, and indeed constitutes much of the intimacy between God and Israel, my critique is not directed at the finally unknowable God-in-God's-self, who neither can nor cannot be said to have failed Israel. It is rather directed at a model of God which was reliant upon an idea of masculine power that simply could not withstand the actual masculine patriarchal power that confronted it. Theological analyses of the Holocaust that persist in using patriarchal categories of understanding are not identical, but are continuous with, the ideological conditions that produced the Holocaust and therefore cannot persuasively move beyond them. By contrast, it is Jewish feminist theological revision of the immanent God as Shekhinah (the traditionally female image of the indwelling presence of God) which helps us to trace God's redemptive presence in Auschwitz in ways which do not entail divine or theological complicity with evil.

This book is not thereby unique. Generally antitheodical in tone and content, academic theological reflection on the Holocaust has not sought to absolve God from at least a degree of blame. This book does not, then, simply jettison or dismiss all previous Holocaust theology. (Knocking other theorists out of the field is a masculinist academic sport and is especially tasteless in the present anguished context.)[16] By the very scale of their object, post-Holocaust theologies are conscious of being only partial and limited responses to the questions raised by the radical evil of Auschwitz.[17] Indeed, my own theological proposal is far from immune to criticism and has no pretension to being the terminus of discussion; the missing words with whose insertion everything falls satisfyingly into place. To incorporate women's Holocaust experience (which was diverse) into theological discourse may no more succeed in reconciling human suffering with the existence of a good and loving God than can patriarchal theology. The feminist theology offered in the present study is but one construal of God's presence in the events of the Holocaust and it may raise as many questions as it answers. But it does not, at least, multiply or transcendentalize terror.

The second chapter engages the central preoccupation of post-Holocaust theology: God's apparent failure to intervene in the Holocaust, a failure accounted for by the trope of hiddenness. God's hiddenness is a possibility of the divine mystery and it is, above all, a way of saying that God may have to withhold his power for good reasons, in this case, so as to allow the consequences of a definitively human free will to take their course. But feminist philosophical criticism of patriarchal conceptions of autonomy as the privilege or licence of a masculine elite can obviate the theological and anthropological requirement for God to have been hidden. Indeed, the hiddenness of God's masculine face in Auschwitz no longer looks like the reluctant withholding of interventionary power, but a dereliction of love, an abusive complicity, a permission for violence or a tacit admission of his non-existence.

However, in so far as God's female face has always been occulted by the refusal or subjugation of the female dimension in God, the trope of hiddenness is not entirely dispensable. It helps us to ask how God might have been present but concealed in Auschwitz because her female face was yet unknowable to women. Likewise, women, as an assembly of Israel in Auschwitz, were also present to God even while their own faces – as both images of the human(e) and of the divine – were disappearing. The female face was hidden by its profanation: both as that which is set outside public religious view (not fully in the sight of God) and, differently, by its genocidal erasure. Moreover, the female face could barely reflect the glory of God into the world for God's face was itself profaned or covered over. Yet hiddenness implies (undetectable) presence. And to be present is transitive; it is always and only a positioning of one to the other. So that Israel's God is nonetheless an accompanying God whose face or presence, as Shekhinah, 'She-Who-Dwells-Among-Us', goes with Israel, in mourning, into her deepest exile, even if Israel cannot see her in the terrible crush.

While Judaism does not identify the world with God, neither does it countenance the vacation of the world by God. In Chapter 3 I ask how God could have been present in Auschwitz whose defining property was that of making the world, in Jewry, repellent to God. The Jewish concept of holiness, although criticized by some Jewish feminists as being inherently separative and therefore inimical to feminist relationality, is, I believe, the heuristic key to the mystery of God's presence in Auschwitz. For a woman to see, touch and cover the other was a form of washing which set her apart from Auschwitz ('do not come closer', 'the place on which you stand is holy ground' Ex. 3: 5). Washing restored her – however notionally – to the sphere of the holy as one of a covenanted nation holy to God (Ex. 19: 6; Lev. 19: 2). The face is the sign and medium of presence; only where Auschwitz is 'washed' from Israel's face can it be fit for divine presence; that is, only where Israel can see the face of Israel can it be seen by the God whose image it bears. To be clean is to be visible to God and therefore not to be forgotten by God. It is to be, in all senses, re-membered or re-assembled: a resurrection of sorts. Transposing the religious meaning and intention of Jewish women's traditional domestic and familial obligations into the (prohibited) times and spaces of relational care in Auschwitz figures how gestural cleaning, and the touch that is a form of cleaning from the profanation of contempt, could recapitulate some of the spiritual functions of the Sabbath: a foretaste of the world to come; the world in all senses before and after Auschwitz.

Auschwitz has been cast as the '*tremendum*': as an event that 'annihilates the past of hope and expectation [and which] confronts us as abyss'.[18] But because (after Rudolf Otto) the *tremendum* is analogous to and expressive of the awesomely dreadful and of overwhelming power and force,[19] too much has been conceded to the numinous horror and abyssal mystery of Auschwitz and not enough to the holiness of what it sought to destroy. Focusing on the holiness of Auschwitz's victims and their covenantal obligations to God and each other, rather than on the numinosity of its terrifying spectacle, (re-)establishes the Jewish continuum and refuses Auschwitz's self-proclaimed power of closure. Because both Israel and its God are one, what can be known of each before and after Auschwitz can also be known in Auschwitz. Yet the preoccupation with the non-rational dimension of the sacred, at the expense of the ethical mystery of the holy, permits an obliterative theology which, like the Holocaust itself, consumes everything in its path, including those whose presence as inmates within Auschwitz was not numinous but holy. Rudolf Otto's complete formulation of the holy as *mysterium, tremendum et fascinans* reminds us that the much neglected *fascinans* element of the holy can suggest that the mystery of the holy is also that which approaches or draws near, even to what is defiled. Those whose manner of living and dying countered Auschwitz's erasure of presence signalled towards the *fascinans* element within God, where God beckons to us and we beckon to God in the mutual attraction of a shared likeness whose glory Auschwitz could not, finally, extinguish.

While Chapter 3 asks how post-Holocaust theology can read (even notional) acts of moral and material purification as having upheld the covenant and invited God's exiled presence back into the world, Chapter 4 suggests how relations of care could welcome God into the world, even the world as pit. Rachel Adler's feminist theological method proposes that 'a story is a body for God'.[20] The stories of women's relationships in Auschwitz-Birkenau and other camps can be read and told as narrative bodies for God: media of the revelation of her presence. Here, women's holding, pulling and pushing the other from death back into the slender possibility of life – so often the very substance of their holocaustal narrative – were means of carrying God into Auschwitz under a torn shelter (not a fortification): an improvised Tent of Meeting in which women could meet God in the face-to-face relation.

Experientialist theologies such as this one find human agency translucent to divine agency: indeed a theology of image entails an aesthetic epistemology whereby it is only through observing the religio-ethical demonstration of staying with the other, of not leaving her in solitude, that we can discern the divine person – God – as a definitively good will and agency in the world. Disputing post-Holocaust theology's (quite understandable) predication of an averted face to God, I conjoin a theology of image with Emmanuel Levinas' theology of the ethical demand of the naked face to propose that where women in Auschwitz, each in God's image, turned (in whatever sense) to face the other, they refracted God's face or presence into the world from the light of their own. Compassion was transfigurative. When a woman saw or looked into the face of the suffering other (and that other's filthy, beaten, vacated face, was not easy to see and to look upon) the divine humanity of that face could be traced through the thick scale of its physical and spiritual profanation. Because what has been traced has appeared it also becomes knowable. What could be seen, but may not have been recognized, was God as Shekhinah – the presence of God among us in our exile. While God is never a visible material form she is figurable in experience. Within or without Auschwitz (and Arthur Green is speaking of the latter): 'knowing the invisibility of God and seeing the face of God everywhere', God is both wholly other to the world and yet God's face '"peers out from the windows, peeks through the lattice work." That face contains within it all the faces of humanity and each of them contains the face of God.'[21]

There are, of course, those who, like Lawrence Langer, would dispute both the memoirs' record of sustained relation and its theological reading on the grounds that in a situation of 'choiceless choice',[22] 'episodes of sharing and support and even of self-sacrifice, all of which occurred in rare favorable circumstances in the usually hostile camp environment . . . feed the legends on which the myths of civilizations have been built'; 'spiritual possibility turns out to have been a luxury for those not on the brink of starvation'. Langer insists that most survivors' stories 'nurture not ethical insight but confusion, doubt, and moral uncertainty.' For this reason, 'we must learn to suspect the effect as well as the intent of bracing pieties like "redeeming" and "salvation" when they are used to shape our understanding of the ordeal of former victims of Nazi oppression'.[23] Langer finds oral testimony to be the most educative form of testimony as it 'resists the organizing impulse of moral theory and art' (and presumably theology). The very form of the written Holocaust narrative lends it to self-deceptive, analgesic reassurances of order, dignifying the humiliations of powerlessness with a literary sequence and reflective voice.[24] But Langer insists that art, philosophy and the language of moral duty have no place in an authentically remembered Auschwitz. When the moral or aesthetic dimension 'intrudes' upon any survivor account 'we risk forgetting where we are'. In a breathtaking generalization and with scant attention to either the role of gender or Jewishness in the production of experience and meaning, Langer claims that when victims remember their ordeal authentically, memory is grounded in 'its own historical reality, and nothing more'. These survivors 'cannot link their near destruction to a transcendent or redemptive future'.[25]

Although commentators have noted that there were in fact many who felt that the 'supreme proof that God was with them in the bitterness of their suffering' was that they were enabled to exist during this period without 'losing their humanity',[26] one should not reject Langer's thesis out of hand. That is why I have chosen to present it here, at the beginning of the book, rather than leaving its discussion to a chapter ahead. Certainly, I have found that where Auschwitz is read through its survivors as literature it begins to look like an ordeal to be got through, even though for the vast majority it was the end, not an episode. And I could not but begin Chapter 4 by fully acknowledging that there is both evidence and – perhaps more – counter-evidence for the maintenance of a relational posture in the women's camp in Auschwitz-Birkenau. There is no doubt that, as in other camps, 'solicitude alternated with frustration or despair, as the challenge of staying alive under brutal conditions tested human resources beyond the limits of decency.'[27] Many women were hardened or simply deranged by loss, fear, brutality and starvation.

Yet despite the anti-redemptive assumption that underpins Langer's work and Holocaust Studies as a discipline, the memoir literature, feminist history of the Holocaust and theological reflection on the Holocaust (its androcentrism notwithstanding), have together convinced me that, for theology at least, Langer's claim that Holocaust testimonies are entirely a 'discourse of ruin' is insufficiently nuanced. Theology is not a purely evidential project and must attend to a distinctive and ancient patterning of signs. Theology must also listen carefully when women like Lucie Adelsberger, who was deported to Auschwitz from Berlin in 1943, testify that many women 'cultivated a compassion for others out of their own misfortune.'[28] Even assuming that the memoirs have edited out much that they consider is not to Jewish women's credit, their predominant theme, and one which the theological reader must take seriously, is that a necessary, though not sufficient, condition of physical and spiritual survival was to have forged and sustained practical relationships of friendship and care with other women. Separated from men, these could consist in relationships between family members, friends, or 'camp sisters' (*Lagerschwestern*) – groups of women who were not only divided but also bound by ties of nationality, religious observance, camp labour, political affiliation or friendship alone. Of course it is possible to explain camp sisterhood away as the mere instrument of survival, whether that of self or loved others (an imperative which can hardly be underestimated). But very often women cared for one another in modest but spiritually, symbolically and practically significant ways that were continuous with their relationships outside Auschwitz and not all to the detriment of others' survival. Moreover, they often continued to do so right to the end in the full knowledge that neither themselves or the other were likely to survive.

The accounts of camp sisterhood need not, then, only be weighed historiographically against their counter-evidential opposite, but can be read theologically as *midrashim* or narrative commentaries on the presence or face of God in Auschwitz. Here theology synthesizes the ethical and the aesthetic, linking the experience of divine presence to human ethical vision (not as choice, but as having acted because one has seen and known). This is not, however, to idealize women victims. To do so would be, as Esther Fuchs notes, to remove them all over again from religious and political discourse on the Holocaust.[29] Nor is it to exclude from the theological scheme those Jewish women who met their wholly undeserved torments without moral, spiritual or intellectual distinction.[30] Precisely because those torments were undeserved and forbade ordinary choice, normal ethical standards and expectations did not obtain in Auschwitz, nor can do so today in its study. These women were not better or worse than us. To ignore the 'wrong' kind of victim and idealize the 'right' is to forget how spiritually, psychologically and physically damaged all of them had been. It is not, in any case, those who were brutalized who count against the theological possibility, but relationality which counts against Auschwitz.

Arthur Cohen once remarked of the twentieth century: 'There can be no Jewish theology in this most terrible of centuries unless it is prepared to ask: what do we know *now* about the creator God in whose universe such horror is permitted?'[31] After Cohen, I not only want to ask what do we now know about God after the Holocaust, but more specifically, what do we now know about God in a world in which contemporary mothers – and as far as possible, mothers of the holocaustal past – are, through Jewish feminist historiography, art and liturgy 'heard into speech'? Chapter 5 again challenges theologies of absence by predicating (as the Hebrew Bible does itself) some of the relational, uterine qualities of motherhood to the divine personality.

For motherhood is, *par excellence*, a relation of active immanence or presence to the other and God's immanence, as Shekhinah, can be known (even in the tradition) in the curvature of the maternal posture. This latter: a capacity to bend over and cover, stroke, warm, feed, clean, lift and hold the other, was an embodied resistance to Auschwitz which had institutionalized the exposure, breakage and waste of bodies. Yet there, mothers had mothered daughters; daughters, mothers; sisters, sisters; friends, friends; and mothers, other mothers. That mothering was in many senses futile and pitifully ineffectual to the scale of loss, terror and deprivation. But in none of the memoirs I have read for this study were its comforts incidental or peripheral to meaning and hope, then or now. On the contrary, many women's sheer bodily presence to one another, carrying her burden at whatever its cost, mirrored and sustained the deathless promise of covenantal love between God and Israel, knowable in God's presence as a suffering Mother in Auschwitz.

However, the capacity to invite divine presence by the reordering of a disordered world is not a biological property exclusive to women and nor are women always inclined to mother or to be mothered by others. No doubt there will be those who regard any account of behaviour as 'female' or 'maternal' to be unhelpfully essentialist or as stereotyping women as innately caring, or better at caring, than men. That would be too easy. I am emphatically not assuming any transhistorical, transgeographical essence of womanhood. This study represents femaleness as a performative moral orientation and quality both specific to its cultural, religious and ideological milieu and as a universalizable morally good will without which femaleness would cease to merit the term but which may be equally attributable to men.[32] Janusz Korczak's care for the orphans in his Children's Home, was exemplary in this regard. Despite the children's and his own poor health, the Home was regarded as an 'oasis' in the Warsaw ghetto, with 'everything running according to the normal, long-established routine, everything exuding order, calm, good management'.[33] Korczak's mothering of the orphans until their death in Treblinka is but one demonstration that care is a function of all Israel – men and women – as itself a sanctified familial community.[34]

Femaleness, then, is a social environment that may or may not be biologically occasioned by motherhood and which has been articulated as a 'world of nurturance and close human relationships':

the sphere where the basic human needs are anchored and where models for a humane alternative can be found. This world, which has been carried forward mainly by women, is an existing alternative culture, a source of ideas and values for shaping an alternative path of development for nations and all humanity.[35]

That 'alternative culture' was evident in the holocaustal care of bodies which can be described as maternal, first, because its practices were and are associated with mothers (Jewish mothers' care for the physical and spiritual well-being of the family is a practical sanctification that has traditionally taken priority over opportunities for prayer). Second, and more important, if women live covenanted lives fully in God's image this entails that there is something about divine activity and covenantal agency which can justly be described in terms of maternal competencies: purification, refuge, and other forms of attention to the urgent need of the other that compel reconsideration of the maternal figures of the period, especially that of the at once derided and sentimentalized *yiddishe mama*.

That my argument is founded in the observation of bodily gestures and postures, rather than rational will and agency, is, I suppose, typical of the late modern or postmodern refusal to elide ethics and rationality; to cast the human and divine will as ordering *logos*, reason or word. But it may also be that the gesture is all that Auschwitz leaves to us. A substantial and cautionary literature attends to the holocaustal rupture of language. Judaism is a religion that hears, transcribes and reads ever-multiplying words (though not women's words). But like that point of night when it is so late that it is early, the pain of Auschwitz – a multilingual pandemonium of voices inchoate with distress – is too loud to hear. If Auschwitz destroys, or should destroy, the capacity for considered, measured speech,[36] some may instead want to look there, as I do, for a mediation of God's presence that is (necessarily) signalled before it is deliberated and spoken.[37]

The premise of Chapter 6 (divided into two distinct but interconnected parts) is that revelation and redemption cannot be deferred until after Auschwitz because divine activity is by its nature continuous and uninterruptable. A theology of presence must also be a redemptive one because eschatological restoration (*tikkun*) means that what has been taken away has been returned or put back there again. In part I of the chapter I discuss how the retrieval of Jewish presence from absence can characterize Holocaust and post-Holocaust writing and art and how women may have their own means of re-collecting and re-storing relationships with the dead. In both parts of the chapter, the restoration of presence through holocaustal relation is taken up into the redemption of God from patriarchal, and most particularly, holocaustal dis-appearance. Whatever their historical predicament, where women are fully and normatively female subjects, and God is known in God's fullness as a divine personality revealed in both female and masculine modes, these are together prerequisite to and prefigurative of *shalom* – the peace or completion of a world and a God that is to come. (The poststructuralist celebration of the death of the unified subject surely pays insufficient heed to Auschwitz's will not only to kill but to destroy any sense of the worth of self and agency, and the better future these might bring to fruition.)

Mystical Judaism, especially but not only in its Buberian neo-Hasidic strain, contends that each one of us bears significant responsibility for *tikkun olam* – the redemption, or better, restoration or mending of the world. The divine spark, banished, dispersed, and lost by sin, can be retrieved in this world in the most modest of ethico-spiritual actions and encounters. Transposing Jewish mystical theology's redemptive scheme into a feminist one, part II of the chapter argues that where, in Auschwitz, God was visible to God in the 'cleaned' female face, those elements of divine personality that might be characterized as female were returned to her by a refractive sighting of a reconciled world to come. God was no longer in exile from her personality and could be fully God. For God to be reunited with God is the completion of God and therefore the inauguration of a new time of divine and human peace. God and the world would come to experience unity and justice because it is in the moment when the human spark, even dimmed to the point of extinction in Auschwitz, can light the human face and hold up a mirror to God, then the world knows God and God knows the world. Everything is lost by and in Auschwitz. No one who died will be magically restored; God did not redeem or buy us back out of slavery and death. Auschwitz as an institution is not and will never be redeemed. And yet nothing is lost when its inmates are eternally known and present in the act of eternally seeing.

Neither Auschwitz nor the fathomless suffering it inflicted was in any sense the sacrificial instrument of redemption. What was redemptive was the capacity of many of its inmates to resist its cause and limit its effect. Female attention to the need of the other may have made little or no appreciable difference. But it is the divine quality of self-giving love between those subject to absolute hate that is as significant as its quantitative instantiation. Restorative acts bespeak the presence of a healing, mending God in spite of conditions which, although they cannot destroy God, appear to destroy the conditions by which the divine might be manifest. In so far as it could not do so, Auschwitz was not wholly obstructive of the restoration of God's exiled presence to the world as its blessing. For the restorative process was already long at work in the community of Israel and continued in spite of its deportation into the world of the gone. To restore, even momentarily, the dignity of persons made in the image of God was, thereby, to restore God's image in the world. A restored or redeemed world is one that is translucent to its creator. And the restoration of the humanity of the suffering female face in the act of seeing was, at the same time, a restoration of a (suffering) seeing, reflectively female, face to God. God's seeing and knowing was and is prerequisite to justice. This is an eschatological justice because it is endlessly deferred by a history of self-legitimating patriarchal discourse and practice that has turned away and hidden its injustice from God's sight and, comprehensively, by Auschwitz, which blinded God with mud, smoke and ash.

As a death camp, Auschwitz-Birkenau was the terminus of Israel's and therefore God's exile. But the redemptive trajectory of its inmates carried Israel into, through and out of Auschwitz towards Jerusalem: another end of exile. The holocaustal anticipation of *tikkun* was an ethical and aesthetic moment that recapitulated the moment of our creation and anticipated our redemption: the state of meta-patriarchal possibility; a world without the sins of alienation. In women's demonstration of the humane, in their acts of separate resistance to the engulfing profane, God's presence, as that of the exiled Shekhinah, mends and cleans the world of Auschwitz and takes Israel out to meet its future.

From Jewish women's history to Jewish feminist theology

This last should not belie the times when I was not sure that this book could be written. Theology presents a generalized, unified scheme, but it is inadvisable for theory to generalize about women and the Holocaust. The Holocaust had different phases and locations which placed variable strains upon women depending on their health, affluence, marital status, spiritual, emotional and moral sensibilities, and the numbers dependent on their care. The women who wrote their Holocaust memoirs were of a well-educated middle-class background not representative of all Jewish women in Auschwitz. Jewish women in Auschwitz were not a unitary body, but were of different generations, Judaisms and Jewishnesses. Not all of them had the same view of what it meant to be a woman. Some were rural and some were urban Jews; they were from different parts of occupied Europe and were not of one social class. Some women had suffered considerably more severe privations than others before their deportation to Auschwitz; those from southern Europe were more afflicted by the harsh Polish winters than those from northern and eastern Europe.

Jewish theology may be produced and enriched by difference, yet in theorizing Israel it moves towards the collective mode. I have tried to balance historical difference and the theological subsumption of difference. But in the interests of the former, while I have read and used numerous memoirs (mostly, but not exclusively, Jewish) I have drawn on a core literature of five women's memoirs listed below, all of whose authors were deported to Auschwitz between January and December 1944. The relative comparability of their recollections has limited any tendency to generalize about intra-gendered difference: the various periods, locations and resources of women who died in and endured the Holocaust. Sara Nomberg-Przytyk was a communist of Hasidic background. She was sent from Stutthof to Auschwitz in January 1944. Olga Lengyel had worked as a doctor with her husband Miklos Lengyel in the hospital in Cluj, the capital of Transylvania, that they had built in 1937. She was deported to Auschwitz with her whole family in May 1944. Of her immediate family, Lengyel was the only survivor of Auschwitz. Isabella Leitner was sent to Auschwitz in May 1944 from the Kisvárda ghetto in Hungary with her four sisters, brother and mother. Her mother and youngest sister were killed on arrival. Giuliana Tedeschi, a classicist from Turin, was sent to Auschwitz in April 1944. Although her two daughters survived the war in hiding, her husband, an architect, did not. Bertha Ferderber-Salz, from Krakow, an Orthodox Jewish wife and mother, was sent from Plaszow to Auschwitz in December 1944. Her husband Moses soon perished in Auschwitz but her two daughters, hidden with Polish Gentiles, survived.[38]

Even having limited my range of sources, there remained historiographical and philosophical reasons to question in what different ways even comparable women's memoirs were true and what the relation might be between historical testimony and its theological interpretation. Theological truth claims can transcend a great deal of the detail of history, but it must ask in what history consists before it can accommodate it within its own scheme. The memoirs were not written by historians. They constitute historical evidence but also represent the slippage between history and art. Survivors' remembering, like history itself, must take a narrative form if it is to be remembering at all. Charlotte Delbo knew that her experience of Auschwitz was turning into literature in the act of writing it down. Although she needed no reminding that Auschwitz is not a place in a story (it is now an imagined, though not imaginary, place), sitting writing in a café one day, she became conscious that telling suffering makes it something that will be pictured rather than known.[39]

I have had to be faithful to the substantive testimony of the memoir literature, but am aware that much of it has been written in a novelistic, sometimes epic, style assisted by professional writers, and has usually been translated into English. Some books seem almost to have been written by committee.[40] Sara Nomberg-Przytyk's memoir consists of a series of stylized vignettes in the manner of the Yiddish tale. Her recollections may also be skewed by the political situation at the time of her writing: that of communist Poland in the late 1960s when a celebration of the solidarity between socialists in the camps was allowable but that of Jews was not.[41] Reading the memoirs of women of a generation more reticent than our own also requires sensitivity to their gaps and omissions. Much has been written about the selectivity of Holocaust remembering and, when the pain is too sharp or the experience simply unassimilable, forgetting. Some of the memoirs were written two decades or more after 1945;[42] before which time the events had remained too painful and humiliating to record. Bertha Ferderber-Salz, writing twenty years after her liberation from Belsen, is aware that she is not always certain of her chronology; names slip her memory. Kitty Hart's *Return to Auschwitz* has run to several editions. Which one of these might be the most accurate an account of her experience is uncertain since memory can dim and understanding sharpen as time passes.

Gradually, though, I have come to realize that the methodological difficulty of classifying and judging the historicity of the memoir literature as a deposition of evidence is not entirely mine. This book is, above all, an imaginative work of constructive theology and its argument should be informed but not overwhelmed by irresolvable historiographical considerations. This study is not a historical reconstruction of women's experience in Auschwitz and it makes no claim to speak on behalf of women victims of the Holocaust; the memoirs are not used as 'proof-texts' for a theological position, but as textual pieces read from the vantage point of present faith. Indeed, I read the memoir literature through and alongside biblical and talmudic texts, Jewish feminist texts, post-Holocaust creative writing and art, and a varied Jewish theological corpus that is androcentric and patriarchal in some of its assumptions and exclusions but also beautiful and, read 'against the grain', indispensable to Jewish feminist reflection. Neither autobiography nor scripture are evidential proof for my argument. Rather, just as rabbinical students offer one text for another, each text is a responsive antiphonal commentary on the other.

As I wrote this book, one further question, an ethical one, continued to trouble me: At what point does a historical testimony without religious interests become a text available to religious reading? Can autobiographical, private texts about historical events also serve as collective, public, metahistorical texts, and if so, by what editorial process and by whose consent? What is the ethical propriety of changing the function of women's autobiography to that of (in effect) a theologically instructive story? To some extent, I refused to let this trouble me. I was, after all, using published texts in the public domain, not oral testimony. Ironically, perhaps, for one proposing a theology of the face-to-face relation, I had deliberately conducted no interviews with survivors to whom it would have been at least discourteous had I shifted my analytical focus from their history to my theology. Rightly or wrongly, I was reading books separated by their publication from the women whose experience they narrated. (Indeed, I found myself in some sympathy with postmodern critics who have been preoccupied with texts rather than their authors' purpose.)

But to suggest that the reader becomes the author and the meaning the reading would be to go too far. The truth and facticity of the Holocaust cannot be surrendered to those who would deny it. And even as a reading, the problem of colonizing, commodifying or sentimentalizing (mostly dead) women's experience needed to be faced even if, by nature of the project, the first two could not be entirely avoided. That these women were religious and, still less, feminists, could not be assumed. (Most, for example, would have objected to the use of the feminine pronoun for God.) David Blumenthal is right that the theologian must be 'a binder of wounds, one who comforts.'[43] Yet to propose a feminist theology which is sharply critical of a masculinist theological tradition to which so many who died would have been loyal may be precisely to open wounds. Such a theology is in danger of what Emil Fackenheim would call 'blaspheming against the God of the victims' and perhaps, in conducting a theological argument at their expense, against the victims as well, including those who would have refused the consolations of religion. To theologize as if on their behalf could be to subject them to a further, final indignity.[44] (It is ignominy enough that much of their suffering is relegated to the footnotes of the post-Holocaust literature.) For one like myself who was not there – not even born – to postulate God's presence in a death camp where God seemed most notable by his absence; where it seemed to make little practical difference whether he was present or absent, might be to bury its victims a little deeper; to silence the silenced.

I am aware that the dead have no defence against my argument, no voice to deny it as the cultivation of an illusion. But this is true of all and any post-Holocaust theology. On the one hand, a post-Holocaust theology must not seek to make it all alright again, taking up the abjections of history into the grander sweep of eternity. But on the other, for a post-Holocaust theology to claim that

God was present to Jewry in Auschwitz is not logically dependent on the human perception of that presence at the time. Of that vast majority of victims, some of whom are mentioned in this study, who did not survive to object, I can only hope that they would not have wanted to see Jews condemned to perpetual despair on their account. Conversely, since in some senses Judaism is the sum of what all Jews think and do, we should not have to forever defer to (some of) them to the extent that the only God and the only Judaism we can speak of in connection with the Holocaust is that of Orthodoxy. We have no way of knowing precisely how the vast silenced dead came to, or refused to, come to terms with their suffering and death. I do not know if any of those who endured would read this book and say, yes, that's how it was, now it makes sense to me. I doubt it.

But mine is not an entirely free reading. To whatever degree texts have been given over to their readers' interests, and to whatever degree their authors' experience has itself been culturally, conceptually or religiously mediated, the text was final; I had not been given, nor wanted, any licence to re-write it, correct it, or attribute words to women that were not their own. (This book may be presumptuous, but it is not, I hope, impertinent.) To interpret these texts theologically is not to claim their authors as theologians or feminists. It is not, in any case, possible to construct a feminist theology of the Holocaust from what the women who survived the Holocaust do or do not say about God. And it would not have been possible for a woman in Auschwitz to have formulated a theology of Auschwitz in so far as Auschwitz was unthinkable, unprecedented in their experience. Thus Maya Nagy: 'Maybe at a certain time I knew I was in Auschwitz, but I didn't know that Auschwitz was *Auschwitz*'.[45] I make no attempt to suggest that women who died in the Holocaust held protofeminist views of God; some of them might well have done, the vast majority would not and many of them were, in any case, secular Jews. This is a theological construal from a contemporary Jewish feminist perspective which does not use the memoir literature as its evidence but its illustration. The best Jewish theology has no pretensions to normativity: 'tentativeness is a virtue in theological thinking and if speculation is the more suitable word so be it.'[46] This, then, is a retrospective theological view; a contemplation of Auschwitz. (Contemplation is not always serene but its element of detachment has alone been an unsettling experience: I became the knowing, seeing but unobservable observer, hidden by time and space in ways not wholly dissimilar to the positioning of the patriarchal God. Even feminist theology must be vigilant against the hubris it condemns.)

To have written this theology is not at all to have transferred authority from women victims to myself or to the discipline. Rather its writing accepts that there is no unmediated experience. All narrative, oral or otherwise, is continuously rehearsed and interpreted in so far as it has become a part of the subject's consciousness. My own theological mediation may add another interpretative layer to their witness, but, as James Young would point out, it is not the first. The moral dilemma over the use or (mis)appropriation of women's experience is not resolvable unless one accepts, as I do, that testimony is already multiply mediated. While it would play into the hands of far-right revisionist historians to question

the historical facticity of the Holocaust, it must also be accepted that its transmission as history is a reconstructive, narrative interpretation. Young, noting the
'inescapably literary character of historical knowledge', finds the boundaries
between Holocaust literature and history to be blurred. Facts and their conceptual
matrix are interdependent.[47] In which case, against Langer, theological truth claims
are not as qualitatively different from the historical as might appear.

However naturalistic and realistic their style, the Holocaust memoirs do not, in
Young's opinion, 'literally deliver documentary evidence of specific events'; facts
have been assimilated into and reconstructed by conceptual schemata. Just as
rabbinical history does not record the minutiae of catastrophe but interprets it in
accordance with its own redemptive paradigm and promise, for 'as long as events
continue to enter the languages of the Jews, they continue to be incorporated into
a Jewish continuum and to be understood in inescapably Jewish ways'.[48] Each
survivor's testimony is shaped by his or her own biography and religious and
political orientation; it is a personal interpretation of events, not a set of raw 'facts'
or final truths.[49] For Young, the representation of Auschwitz in language is
metaphorical because language itself is metaphorical and figurative in character.[50]
'Governing mythoi' shaped Jewish experience during the Holocaust, the '"poetics"
of literary testimony' shaped post-Holocaust understanding of that experience,
and the tropes and selected details of the published memoirs in turn shape the
reader's understanding of the Holocaust.[51] A text's authenticity should not, then,
be confused with its 'authoritative factuality'. It is the narrator's interpretation of
events that is authentic, not its 'putative factuality'.[52]

Jewish memory and understanding of the Holocaust (the processes are effectively one) is more than ever multiply organized and produced by social and
religious ideology, by the autobiography, fiction, art, cinema and architecture of
the Holocaust, and by the metahistorical myths and paradigms of Judaism that
segue into the historical process even as it unfolds. The Holocaust is far too much
of the extremes to teach good moral or historical lessons. But that is not to say
that its scale and ultimacy are not theologically instructive, for theology is
precisely concerned with historical seizure and its accommodation within an
ordered scheme. To faith, Judaism's history is that of a covenant. Theological
history must select its evidence, construing history from a covenantal perspective.
Without selection and construal it would be neither theology nor history. The
interpenetration of history and theology produces insights which emerge from
both of these disciplines and neither of them alone. If Young is right that the
'listener's story is part of the teller's story'; that post-Holocaust art and discourse
are themselves 'part of the history that is being told after the fact',[53] this is the
point at which it becomes possible to negotiate between what has been told and
what has been heard.

Without adopting an offensively hortatory tone (Jews are traditionally hesitant
to justify God's justice when they themselves have not suffered the injustice in
question),[54] Jewish history, memory and the midrashic imagination are not
separable.[55] A post-Holocaust theology cannot do other than correlate witness,
interpretation and tradition. Faith does not comprehend Langer's 'untransfigured

actuality' because there is no actuality that is not always transfigured by an aesthetic sense of the presence of God and its moral demand. The face of the other as a perceptible image of God is always before us. In 'The Later Addresses' of 1939–51, Martin Buber claims that everything is 'essentially a divine pronounce-ment (*Aussprache*), an infinite context of signs meant to be perceived and understood by perceiving and understanding creatures.'[56] If Buber's 'everything' is not merely rhetorical, then Auschwitz, as a counter-eschatological ingathering of Israel, also sets the exegetical task of the chapters to come.

1 Reading post-Holocaust theology from a feminist perspective

> Before we can repledge our troth to the ancient God or present him with our complaint . . . we must make certain that it is still the ancient God whom we seek.[1]

From the post-war period to the present, Jewish women have not offered a sustained theological response to the Holocaust, feminist or otherwise. Jewish women's private theological reflections on their own holocaustal times and experience are not, of course, unknown and the two best known sources of such reflection are the writings of Etty Hillesum and Anne Frank, both of whom perished in the camps. Yet Frank's writing was that of one who was barely more than a girl; both were Jewish more by birth rather than religious identity. They knew little of their religious heritage and were each in their own way attracted to Christianity. These two women, who may well represent other Jewish women of the same class and temper, were the products of the liberal, humanistic, universalistic spirit of emancipated, often assimilated, Western Jewry, not of the Jewish scriptures or rabbinic tradition. As Rachel Feldhay Brenner notes in her recent study, although each sought consolation and support from God, it was not that of the Jewish God or the Jewish tradition.[2]

These women's apparent obliviousness to the possibilities of Jewish theological insight into their predicament is not surprising. Despite the distinguished history of Jewish philosophical theology, it has long been the popular view that theology is an un-Jewish and unnecessary apologetic enterprise, sufficient practical knowledge of God being generated by law and its communal observance. A complacent opinion prevalent among Jews (rightly condemned as 'misinformed and naive' and as a form of religious behaviourism)[3] is that they do not have to struggle with faith, but simply to *behave* as if they have faith: 'if you observe the law whose very existence is predicated upon the existence of God as giver of that law, whether you actually believe in God is irrelevant.'[4] And if observant men of the Holocaust period rarely theologized, still less did women whose legal exemption from study amounted to a prohibition. Even were the liberal Judaisms of the time to have developed women's religious intellects (which they largely did not) Jewish women of Hillesum and Frank's spiritual temper were in any case far more attracted to

Christianity perceived as a religion of love and compassion in contrast to the 'apparent rigidity and severity of the Jewish Law'.[5] Their more gracious (female) religion was a humanistic one which placed sacred value on goodness, kindness, empathy, beauty, inner strength and self-giving to others.[6] Although Hillesum set herself at the heart of the suffering Jewish people in its particular historical situation, hers was a religion of mystical love, suffering, and intimate prayer situated 'at the centre of all human suffering'. When challenged as practising 'nothing but Christianity', she replied, 'Yes, Christianity, and why ever not?'[7]

A Jewish feminist theology is now in its relative infancy but has still not substantially engaged with the Holocaust,[8] probably because there is much less Jewish feminist theology than there is Jewish feminism.[9] This is for roughly the same reasons that there is little Jewish theology. Despite Judith Plaskow having consistently argued that Jewish women's status as 'Other' to the male norm is grounded in a masculinist theology of which halakhic inequalities are but a symptom, most Jewish feminists regard women's role and status as first and foremost a matter for halakhic and thereby social reform. A theological reconceptualization is often (wrongly) regarded as foreign to the tradition and irrelevant to women.[10] Jewish feminist theologians are very few in number and are to be distinguished from women rabbis whose interest in theology may be more practical than theoretical, and from the relatively numerous feminist scholars of the Hebrew Bible.[11] Although it by no means suggests indifference, even in the two full-length, single-author volumes of Jewish theology that go by that name (Judith Plaskow's *Standing Again at Sinai* and Rachel Adler's *Engendering Judaism*) the Holocaust is not discussed and barely even alluded to. It may be that post-Holocaust theology has been perceived as a project undertaken by and for men whose aim is either to vindicate or berate an absolutist God who has passed from feminist interest or celebration.

Jewish feminists have played a significant role in the post-war reconstruction of Jewish cultural life and identity (indeed the second wave of Jewish feminism broke at much the same time as post-Holocaust theology began to be published). Yet with other contemporary liberative theologies, Jewish feminist theology would regard the non-natural suffering of the relatively innocent as the result of social, institutional and economic injustice that is undeserved and not, in itself, redemptive.[12]

Since the early 1960s, and gathering momentum after the publication of Richard Rubenstein's highly controversial *After Auschwitz* in 1966,[13] theological enquiry into the Holocaust has been principally undertaken by Ignaz Maybaum, Eliezer Berkovits, Emil Fackenheim and Arthur Cohen.[14] Their books were to form the 'classic' corpus of post-Holocaust theology; the canon most commonly studied and critiqued. As Dan Cohn-Sherbok points out, this corpus has not been significantly added to. These writers remain the 'major figures' in the field.[15] A sixth writer may now be added to this list: David Blumenthal. He alone engages with the feminist critique that has become a prominent element of the academic milieu, even while choosing to persist in faith with a God whom he knows to be sometimes, though not always, oppressive.

Writing women out of (and into) post-Holocaust theology

Cynthia Ozick's lament for what she sees as history's invisible 'holocaust' of Jewish women is illustrative of a Jewish failure to perceive its own capacity to silence and erase persons from history, even if without violence. She writes that Jews rightly grieve for the tragic losses of the Holocaust but are indifferent to, or simply have not noticed, the cultural and intellectual debilitations that Judaism's sexism has produced. There has been a 'wholesale excision', 'deportation' and isolation of women; half of world Jewry has been 'cut off and erased' from the 'creative center' of 'Jewish communal achievement' for centuries upon centuries. And yet of this catastrophic loss of countless poets, artists, writers, scientists, doctors and discoverers, 'Jewish literature and history report not one wail, not one tear'; indeed 'we have not even noticed it'.[16]

The cultural exclusion of women from the tradition is reproduced in and by its texts, including those of the Holocaust which, as themselves narratives of isolation, deportation and disappearance, subject women to a double invisibility: that of their historical annihilation and that of their subsequent theoretical erasure. It is not only that post-Holocaust theology has been a thoroughly masculine discursive space; it has also been markedly androcentric in its outlook. Using gender as an analytical category, this claim can be defended and developed by examining the introductory chapter of a widely-used text – Dan Cohn-Sherbok's *God and the Holocaust* – which exemplifies the gendered bias characteristic of almost all theological discussion of the Holocaust.[17] Entitled 'The Horrors of the Holocaust', the chapter presents the reader with a series of distressing accounts of Nazi atrocities interspersed with contrapuntal narratives of the survival of (male) Jewish spirit and practice against all odds. Cohn-Sherbok's chapter is indispensable to his book in setting his subsequent discussion of Holocaust theology in historical and religious context.

While women all but disappear in the theological bulk of the book, they are an identified presence in this historical section of the text and one whose innocent victimization is a readily apprehended index to the moral depravity of the perpetrators. However, although unintentional and reflecting the masculine bias of his sources, in the eyewitness accounts Cohn-Sherbok has chosen for his own text, women are without voice or reason. The first woman to come into sharp focus is a pathetically child-like 70-year-old from the Krakow ghetto. Her hair is loose about her shoulders and her eyes are glazed; she is in her house slippers, and has arrived for deportation without any luggage, carrying only a small puppy close to her breast. Next, 'laughing, inarticulately gesturing with her hands' appears, 'a young deranged girl of about fourteen, so familiar to all the inhabitants of the ghetto. She walks barefoot, in a crumpled nightgown.'[18] This text also contains accounts of a mother, 'crazed' by the murder of her new-born baby and women suffering the humiliation of being stripped and shaved. These narratives of female abjection are juxtaposed with stories of heroic Jewish resistance which the reader either knows or assumes to be male in character since women largely disappear from their narration.[19] In fact, women were active in the Jewish ghetto underground, in forest partisan groups and one, Gisi Fleishmann, was the courageous leader of the Slovakian Jewish community.[20] But in the text in question, resistance in the Warsaw ghetto is summarized in a now famous man: Mordecai Anielewicz, whose declaration that 'He who has arms will fight. He who has no arms – women and children – will go down into the bunkers',[21] removes women from textual view. Of course it may seem as if the present feminist study will approach post-Holocaust theology precisely as traditionalists might hope and expect it to do, namely, by affirming and focusing upon women's familial and social experience which has also been essentially private. However, the difference is that in the present study women of the past and present are speaking subjects whose experience, read and valorized from a feminist theological perspective, is affectively, morally and intellectually productive.[22]

Over the following pages of his chapter, Cohn-Sherbok presents striking accounts of how masculine religiosity can transcend the most harrowing of material circumstances. And these accounts are placed between narratives in which, again, women are not represented as religious subjects. We read how, at Yom Kippur, 1943, one Atlasowicz stood before a makeshift lectern in the Pawiak prison and spoke of the moment as 'our continuation. Here we take up the golden tradition of sanctity handed down to us by generations of Jews before us'.[23] This peculiarly Jewish hierophany among men who still inhabit sacred time is immediately followed by a sharply contrasting account of a large group of women in Auschwitz-Birkenau, who, having been starved in their barracks over some days, met their death on Christmas Day, 1943. The description of this event merits close attention:

> The victims knew they were going to the gas chamber and tried to escape and were massacred. According to an account of this incident, when the lorry motors started, a terrible noise arose – the death cry of thousands of young women. As they tried to break out, a rabbi's son cried out: 'God, show them your power – this is against you.' When nothing happened, the boy cried out, 'There is no God.'[24]

Of these thousands of young women's faith in (or denial of) God, history knows nothing. If the women cried out to their God, no one remembers it. In the text, as in Jewish tradition and in holocaustal life/death itself, the religious authority and significance of speech belongs to the male line – the rabbis and their actual and metaphorical sons.[25] Here, the women are background noise; only the boy, the voice of Judaism as distinct from victimized Jewry, is heard above their din.

The narrative moves on and Cohn-Sherbok relates another dreadful set of events – this time the snatching of children from the streets of the Kovno ghetto and from their mothers. Again, unlike the men, the women have (or are accorded) no theological voice. Once more they are screaming. Their quasi-animal reaction to the loss of their children renders them, in this context, not so much Jews, as the male figures in the text have remained, but biological mothers alone. It is not that women would *not* have been demented with shock and grief, nor is it the recounting of the events themselves that is problematic; on the contrary it is incumbent on Jews to do so. Rather, it is the *positioning* of gendered experience in texts as that of subjects or objects which determines its theological significance, or lack of it. In this text, women, as the objects of terror, scream; men, as subjects, can both grieve and pronounce. Women might well ask, 'Has the Lord spoken only through Moses? Has He not spoken through us as well?' (Num. 12: 2), but if he has, men have not been accustomed to listening.

It is for historians to decide whether it was only men who delivered great prophetic speeches of the sort made by, among numerous others, Rabbi Elchanan Wasserman in the Kovno ghetto, Rabbi Yerucham Hanushtate in Treblinka or the Ostrovzer Rebbe, Rabbi Yehezkel Halevi Halstuk who, in 1943, garbed in his prayer shawl and kittel, faced the German guns in Zusmir with the words: 'For some time now I have anticipated this *zekhut* [privilege] [of *Kiddush Ha' Shem* – the sanctification of God's name]. I am prepared.'[26] Certainly, only such men were given the roles, costumes and lines of a religiously performative death. The Jewish ideology of femininity as properly private and modest and whose glory, according to the halakhic maxim 'is to be out of public view', was such that public religious utterance of the prophetic kind was culturally and religiously alien to women in the gendered division of religious labour.[27] By contrast, at sites of mass execution it was possible for observant Jewish men to dance and sing, rejoicing in their opportunity to die for *Kiddush Ha' Shem*, 'completely ignoring' the Germans surrounding the graves who were preparing to shoot. Indeed, as Eliezer Berkovits comments: 'At that moment [when the men jumped into the pit] they lived their lives as Jews with an intensity and meaningfulness never before experienced.'[28]

If Berkovits is, or can be, right, it is not immediately apparent how a Jewish woman at just such a site of execution, perhaps holding a baby in her arms and with terrified children clinging to her legs, could have died that fully Jewish death. How, after all, would her body have been marked by God as a covenantal partner where it bore no religious mark or clothing (circumcision, sacral facial hair, and the fringed garments – *tallit* and *tziziot*) that help male Jews remember the covenant? How would her body protest its Jewishness when, in short, that body was required to do no more than look like a woman (that is, to refrain from wearing male garments)? Much of the present study will attempt to answer this question. But on the basis of *existing* historical and theological texts it is almost impossible to answer how, if at all, it might have been possible for a woman's falling into the pit to have been an intense and meaningful Jewish experience of the sort at once mourned and celebrated by Berkovits.

Mordecai Anielewicz wrote in a letter smuggled out to Palestine that he and his comrades would die a death of historical meaning and inspiration to future generations. Theirs was to be an owned, honourable (if secular) manly death.[29] In historical consciousness at least, Jewish men did not simply die in the great Jewish mass; like the Ostrovzer Rebbe, they *met* their own deaths authoritatively and in their own names. By contrast, the *mehitzah* or screen that keeps women out of sight and at a modest distance from the holy is also, figuratively, a feature of Cohn-Sherbok's text where women are a nameless throng,[30] viewed at an ontological and spatial distance and who, even at close quarters, are without the dignity of an audible, reasoned voice.

After the distressing 'white noise' of female panic, Cohn-Sherbok permits his reader to experience a dramatic release of emotional tension by offering several accounts of services held by men incarcerated in camps or prisons during the Holocaust and whose solemnity and dignified bearing at least partially redeems the Jewish people from total degradation. Two of these accounts make striking use of the numinosity of devotional silence: that culminating or expectant sacramental instant in worship where God is palpable in stillness and silence as *numen praesens* – the divine in our midst.[31] The text conveys to the reader that among groups of religious men who had been utterly separated from everyday conditions of life and cast into a place of terror, squalor and extreme violence, worship could still occasion numinous experience. (Perhaps, given the masculinist nature of the numinous as the sense of the dreadful sublimity and otherness of the holy,[32] men's separation into an/other place of the radical suspension of the ordinary was precisely productive of the numinous.)

Here in Cohn-Sherbok's text, masculine suffering does not preclude either religious experience or powerful theological articulation. During one service, Atlasowicz intones a psalm and after a moment of numinous silence makes a speech expressing his heroic faith in the assembly as a covenantal event and testament to the humanity of those assembled there (compare the two women assembled for deportation in the Krakow ghetto – half-dressed, alone, and without reason). Of a service on the eve of Yom Kippur in Auschwitz, 1944, Cohn-Sherbok notes that it sounded 'a note of religious exaltation despite the horror of the camp'. The dreadful silence was suddenly,

> broken by a mournful tune. It was the plaintive tones of the ancient '*Kol Nidre*' prayer. . . . When at last he was silent, there was exaltation among us, an exaltation which men can experience only when they have fallen as low as we had fallen and then, through the mystic power of a deathless prayer, have awakened once more to the world of the spirit.[33]

Men's access to the technical forms of worship (although forbidden) allows them the same production of the numinous that they had controlled before the Holocaust and, more than that, allows a form of resurrection. However degraded they may be, the Jewish sublime, 'the world of the spirit', remains accessible to men in masculine spaces, even in Auschwitz.

Describing another Day of Atonement, this time in Dachau, 1944, Cohn-Sherbok's male protagonists are again drawn by his source with poetic – almost painterly – luminosity and clarity. Unlike the women in the text, these men are tragic but not abject. With the cantor, 'a young Hungarian lad', stands 'Warsaw's last rabbi, his face yellow, hairless, wrinkled, his aged body bent, his hands are rocking like reeds in the wind; only the eyes, sparkling stars, look out towards the cold sky above, and his lips, half open, murmur softly.' And next to the cantor stands Alter der Klinger, a cab-driver from Kovno, not praying to God, but demanding justice from God in the face of the loss of his wife and children.[34] This describes both a historical moment and a theological tableau. In the coming together in worship of the boy and the old man covenantal continuity is affirmed. The old man, surely a hypostasis of the ancient tradition itself, transcends Auschwitz: he is translucent to the cosmos itself. Finally, in a manner characteristic of the masculine intimacy between Jewish men and God, Alter der Klinger protests God's ways. Trust in God is tempered by a masculine sense of betrayal that the Father or King of the Universe has proved himself not quite King or Father enough.

It is not that a feminist reading is not moved – profoundly moved – by the images of masculine transcendence these and many other such accounts evoke. The textual, more than spiritual, problem with this arrangement of memory is that while the men on *Kol Nidre* in Auschwitz–Birkenau in 1944 redeemed their physical degradation when they 'awakened once more' to their masculine 'world of the spirit' and to the power of masculine congregational prayer to engage God, women fall outside the range of audibility because of what they do not or cannot say, or are not recorded or assumed to have said. Although women did, in fact, improvise ways of marking the festivals, the textual processes of exclusion leave contemporary women apparently bereft of theological resources from which to produce a Jewish response that would be theirs.

Cohn-Sherbok's choice and arrangement of narratives effectively reproduces his sources' religio-cultural stereotypes of women as essentially secular or profane in character and activity, as acted upon, not actors, emotional rather than rational, as associated with the bodily (*gashmiut*) as opposed to the spiritual (*ruhniut*); as, in short, an undifferentiated category like children or the very old. This latter would come as no surprise since halakhah places women in the same legal category as children and Canaanite slaves. (Male children and slaves are at least full Jews *in potentio*, whereas a woman by virtue of her sex can never leave this category.)[35] The form of Cohn-Sherbok's chapter and much of its content is continuous with the bias of a (here undeclared) tradition in which women technically occupy the status of chattel for most of their lives and with the rabbinic defamation of women as light-minded, secondary beings whose access to revelation is through her husband.[36] The text is a prologue which effectively filters women out of religious discourse on the Holocaust. Perhaps, in view of the general inadmissibility of women's witness in a Jewish court of law, such texts suggest that they are second-class witnesses to – let alone judges of – the Holocaust. So that by the time the theological purpose of Cohn-Sherbok's book unfolds, the reader is prepared for – would indeed *expect* – women's subsequent absence.

Lest the reader think the text I chose for analysis is atypical, the writing-out of women from post-Holocaust religious discourse can also be illustrated by an example from post-Holocaust Jewish ethics. In a recent contribution to a study of contemporary Jewish ethics, Michael Morgan rightly takes issue with Jewish moral thinkers' 'fundamental assumption' that Jewish ethical imperatives are 'immune to historical considerations',[37] and considers how the Holocaust can be interpreted in ways that are morally helpful to contemporary Jewish life. Taking a

Fackenheimian approach, he asks how, if God's commanding voice spoke at Auschwitz, Jews can still hear it today, and if God was present there, how Jews can still participate in that encounter today.[38]

The questions are the right ones, but the answers are more than limited. For again, the characteristically Jewish covenantal process of 'reception, tradition, and transmission' is mediated from the Holocaust to the present day entirely by the male rabbinical voice: here that of Rabbi Ephraim Oshry of the Kovno ghetto. Morgan argues that it is through the halakhic decisions of rabbis such as Oshry that the moral obligations that arose during the Holocaust can be interpreted and taken into the moral consciousness of the contemporary Jewish community. Oshry's collected halakhic responsa amended Jewish law in order to oppose the Nazis' annihilatory purposes and he is cited as one of the many rabbinical authorities who,

> wrestled dignity and nobility from chaos itself. If anyone heard the [divine] voice, it was they, and if anyone's response ought to guide and direct our own, it is theirs. Indeed, *it is only because of them that we can respond at all*, and *only through them* that we can begin to see how to interpret the meaning of the divine presence for ourselves.

Morgan continues: 'Only through the actions and words of people [the context indicates men] like R. Oshry do we hear the voice that spoke at Auschwitz, and beyond that do we hear the dim but certain echo of that same Voice in its original encounter with the Jewish people.'[39] Rabbi Oshry's judgements are profound and humane. Again, for a feminist, the problem is not with the judgements as such but with the exclusionary absence of female subjecthood from the secondary and primary texts (Morgan's and Oshry's respectively). The male voice is authoritative because it replays the Sinaiatic male voice of divine self-revelation. In Morgan's words there is an insistence – and it is not that of rhetorical hyperbole alone – that the Mosaic-rabbinic line is Judaism's only epistemological, moral and theological resource. If that were so, it would exclude women's experience from religio-ethical discourse *a priori*.

Morgan presents the reader with several of Oshry's responsa, one of which was the decision to permit abortion in the ghetto. His was a wise decision as the Nazi edicts were such that to have ruled otherwise would have been to condemn both foetus and mother to death.[40] Yet here women's bodies are once more the silent objects of competing male rulings (the one good and the other evil). And if women are not speaking subjects in Jewish law, neither will they be in the authoritative religious mediation of the Holocaust. It is only the male voice of halakhic authority which, for Morgan, is the 'paradigmatic opposition to Nazi purposes' and is 'our only link to the divine commanding presence'. Rabbinic (masculine) ethical authority is binding, he says, unless 'something supersedes it, that is, unless we have some good reason for thinking that Judaism today can survive without any respect for *halakhic* decisions and the legal tradition.'[41]

But something *has* superseded the authority of the halakhic tradition and that is the prophetic feminist claim that the whole of Torah is distorted (or as Judith Plaskow puts it, 'poisoned') by its foundational assumption of the lesser humanity of women.[42] Judaism is founded upon a systemic injustice manifest as an ethical lack. That is, it suffers from a scandalously 'missing commandment that sits in judgement upon the world': the eleventh commandment, '*Thou shalt not lessen the humanity of women*'.[43] This superseding commandment summarizes the moral impetus of Jewish feminism and is implied by prophetic Judaism as a whole. But it is not one without respect for or interest in the legal tradition (on the contrary, the Orthodox feminist Blu Greenberg has demonstrated that Jewish feminism can be more than compatible with the halakhic process).[44] Rather, the eleventh commandment argues for Judaism's revolutionary transformation; one on a scale comparable to Judaism's post-biblical transformation from a religion of cultic sacrifice to that of rabbinic law.[45] It is Jewish feminism's eleventh commandment that informs the present study's account of women's holocaustal witness – a witness which testifies against all patriarchal assaults upon the humanity of women, whether religious or secular.

The patriarchal characteristics of post-Holocaust theology

Any feminist criticism of post-Holocaust theology must be prefaced by noting that it cannot be casually dismissed as patriarchal. Feminist criticism must take seriously post-Holocaust theology's refusal of the traditional theodical resolution to the problem of innocent suffering. Whereas biblical and rabbinic Judaism saw suffering as the divine punishment for Israel's transgression or disobedience, with the exception of rabbis such as Joel Teitelbaum and Menachem Harton, it has not been customary for theologians of the Holocaust to claim that the catastrophe was *mipnei hataeinu*, 'on account of our sins'.[46] On the contrary, as Zachary Braiterman has recently argued, post-Holocaust theological sensibility has been dominated by what he calls antitheodicy: a refusal to accept or justify the relationship between God and innocent suffering. Persevering in a 'stubborn love' for God, post-Holocaust theology is distinctive in granting antitheodic traditions a normative status; victims are not blamed for their suffering.

Although the postulation of a post-mortem reward for loyal suffering has been an important response to suffering in historic Judaism, this has also been a surprisingly muted theme in post-Holocaust theology (Berkovits and Cohn-Sherbok have only briefly appealed to the eschatological, post-historical dimension where suffering is redeemed by God).[47] As well as refraining from the attempt to compensate the victims with the promise of a better life in a paradisial world to come, theology after Auschwitz has focused on the renewal of Jewish religion, culture and community; 'justifying God barely enters into the equation'.[48] Rather, the post-Holocaust theological project has been something of a literary and rhetorical exercise, articulated through what Braiterman aptly describes as 'hyperbolic slogans', 'polemical overkill' and 'gross overinterpretation' whose purpose is less to address the philosophy of religion than to 'rally solidarity' and foster new Jewish identities.[49] One Jewish theologian, Richard Rubenstein, outraged the community by rejecting the sovereign Lord of history altogether. In the radical idiom and spirit of the 1960s, Rubenstein pronounced this God to be dead and instead celebrated Israel's post-Holocaust 'return to the soil, and liberation from religious guilt and inhibition'.[50]

The best of Jewish theology, including that of the Holocaust, does not seek to establish explanatory systems but poses 'conflicting midrashim [stories about stories], the goal of which is not how to explain God but how to live with Him'.[51] Post-Holocaust theology responds to the catastrophe rather than justifying it or explaining it (away). A religious response is both impossible and necessary.[52]

While it is clear that any use of the adjective patriarchal to describe post-Holocaust theology must be carefully qualified and that its readers cannot fail to be moved by its sublimation of emotion into argument, it is also broadly the case that theological discourse on the Holocaust has been characteristically patriarchal in at least five respects. Firstly, where it has postulated a God for whom history is the subordinated or sacrificial instrument of his self-aggrandizing purposes; when its function is to secure the sovereignty of God's name. Second, Holocaust theology may justly be termed patriarchal when it promotes the interests of a male military and religious elite over all others. To regard the acquisition of the land of Israel as a territorial recompense for the destruction of European Jewry and as a providential sign of ultimate divine favour and beneficence has been a central element of post-Holocaust theology. Third, post-Holocaust theology is patriarchal when it assumes that (masculine) free will is the essence of human personhood; that it cannot be compromised and may be safeguarded by God's choosing to turn away from the holocaustal suffering that is the product of free human will. Fourth, as we have already seen, the post-Holocaust theological corpus is markedly androcentric in its model of God and its historical focus. A fifth, and final, way in which post-Holocaust theology has been characteristically patriarchal is in its protesting God's failure to be patriarchal *enough*.

I shall return to these points in this and subsequent chapters. Suffice it to say here that the common theological determinant of most post-Holocaust theology is the valorization of masculine power crucially when accounting for a time when masculine Jewish power was being systematically humiliated and destroyed. Despite the holocaustal abjection of God and his people, God must be shown to have world and cosmos at his masculine command and in the name of the men to whom he has promised land and power. Theologies of protest have equally assumed God's sovereign power and will: but in God's failure to exercise them he is found guilty by his subjects.

Some popular theology has postulated a God who stakes out territory and even consumes his Chosen for the sake of his pre-eminent name. God's name is sanctified in the martyrdom of confessing Jews. The representation of God as akin to Moloch (a Semitic deity to whom parents were said to sacrifice their children) is not foreign to contemporary Jewish liturgy. A current 'Memorial Prayer for the Victims of the Holocaust' reads: 'O God, Who art full of compassion, who dwellest on high, grant perfect rest in Thy Divine Presence to all the souls of our holy and pure brethren . . . who were killed, strangled, burned and buried alive for the sanctification of Thy Name.'[53] Here the pre-eminence of God's masculine name is secured by a blood sacrifice, though the degree to which it is offered by its victims or demanded by God is not clear. Jonathan Sacks approves a similar theology of sacrifice in a text which is taut with contradiction. Here God weeps motherly tears but also, greedily, both offers and takes his children as a sacrifice to his own glory:

> God did not die at Auschwitz, they [the ultra-religious] said. He wept tears for His people as they blessed His name at the gates of death. Their bodies were given as burnt offerings and their lives as a sanctification of God's name. 'The fire which destroys our bodies', said Rabbi Elchanan Wasserman before he was killed, 'is the fire which will restore the Jewish people.'[54]

In both of these not untypical passages Orthodoxy sanctifies both God's name and human life, the extinction of which latter is transcendentalized as the fuel of divine life. Divine and human life is sanctified by death and the destruction of bodies (as if Israel can be not-body). The present study will argue that it is the presence – now – of the one to the other which purifies because it continually restores the other from the erasure of objectification and consumption as the means to a powerful agent's own end. Yet in the passage above the valorization of fire as an agent of national purification is distressingly common to both Nazi ideology and Jewish martyrology.

And nor are patriarchal caricatures of God confined to Orthodox rhetoric. Arthur Waskow, well known for his progressive views, attributes the Holocaust less to human hubris than to the numinous, quasi-ejaculatory, force of God's own being:

> Even the Holocaust – it is all right for you to tremble as you read this, for I am trembling as I write it – even the Holocaust was an outburst of light. Those who say we cannot blame God for the Holocaust are only partly right: it was the overflow of God, the outbursting of light, the untrammeled, unboundaried [sic] outpouring of Divinity, that gave us Auschwitz . . . and may yet consume the earth.[55]

Post-Holocaust affirmations of the sovereignty of God

Significantly, the Holocaust first came to sustained theological attention after Israel's 1967 Six Day War when the Jewish determination to never again be cast as victim began to be articulated throughout Israel and the diaspora.[56] Emil Fackenheim's thought typifies this defiant posture. In his early work, *God's Presence in History*,[57] Fackenheim drew a parallel between the decisive transformatory 'root experiences' of God's self-revelation in the Exodus and at Sinai, and 'epoch-making events' such as that of Auschwitz which challenged the very substance of the 'root experiences'. In Auschwitz the 'epoch-making event' was God's self-revelation in the giving of a 614th commandment: the commandment that Jews must survive and die as Jews. Even secular Jews are subject to the quasi-religious imperative to survive as (secular) Jews. God both commands endurance and gives the power of endurance.[58]

There is no doubt that Fackenheim's account of survival is morally serious. Those who survived must now earn their survival by fighting against evil; they must not succumb to despair but precisely because they have known Auschwitz they must work in solidarity with all of the world's oppressed for a humane world. But the point I wish to make here is that God as 'the Commanding Voice of Auschwitz' brings the theological project into dangerous proximity to that of Hitler. Here, God's command is not only prior to Hitler's command, it is also a countermand subsequent to and in competition with Hitler's command. That is, Fackenheim's God is one who, as 'The Commanding Voice of Auschwitz' has not been deposed by history and has not been robbed of his monarchical prerogative because his command, though good, can match the form and type of oppressive commands. Fackenheim's position typifies the patriarchal refusal of divine abjection and its affirmation of a God whose expectation of Jewish obedience to his beneficent will refuses Auschwitz as the imposition of another powerful, but evil, masculine will. In being subject to God's will, Israel could be subject to no other and was, in that sense, free.

Yet if we are considering the mode and possibility of divine presence in Auschwitz from a relational perspective, did its inmates want, and do we now want, to hear another commanding voice in or from Auschwitz, where women and men were continuously berated, shouted and sworn at by their *Kommandant* and those who did his bidding? Does a Jew want to feel that she is still under orders, subjected to another overbearing masculine will? Fackenheim styles his God the 'Commanding Voice of Auschwitz', but the Jewish people were surely subject to enough raucous commands in that place. The commanding voices of its atrocious hierarchy were infinitely more than enough. A German *Kommandant* who knew and watched suffering and did nothing to stop it bears too close a resemblance for comfort to a God who commands Jewry to remain Jewish but does not command Germany to call a halt to the agonies it has commanded. On the one hand, Jews were 'forbidden to despair of the God of Israel, lest Judaism perish'.[59] And on the other hand, the discriminatory laws issued by Germany and like-minded nations facilitated their perishing by forbidding Jews to be Jews. Jewry was caught in a deafening cross-fire of command and countermand – the one bearing a disquieting formal similarity to the other.

While Fackenheim's position is still frequently aired (often without acknowledgement of its author) it has not gone unchallenged.[60] But the point at issue here is what the divine commandment of which Fackenheim speaks can mean for Jewish women. What does it mean for a woman to hear and obey God's commandment in the second Sinai of Auschwitz when she was not there to receive the revelation of Torah at the first? Judith Plaskow has rightly suggested that an important instance of 'the profound injustice of Torah itself' is that at Sinai Jewish women were invisible because Jewish men had been commanded by God to keep themselves apart from women (Ex. 19: 15). Men were to keep themselves 'pure' for the holy *tremendum* of God's self-revelation on Sinai. Plaskow remembers how, for this reason, Rachel Adler asked of Jewish women: 'Have we ever had a covenant in the first place? Are women Jews?'[61] Consequently, we must ask *how* are women *there* and *where* are they positioned to receive the epoch-making self-revelation of God in Auschwitz? Are women in contemporary Judaism subject to socio-biological factors continuous with those the Bible narrates? The continuities between biblical, rabbinic and contemporary Orthodox interpretations of revelation would suggest that they are.

Orthodox Judaism is masculine by default. Prayer and study define a normative Jewish life that is masculine by virtue of a set of gendered exemptions which have amounted to prohibitions.[62] Although the Orthodox female private realm is undoubtedly a place of familial sanctification it is also a supporting one. Because Jewishness is gendered, to survive as a Jew, as Fackenheim's command would have it, first and foremost refers to the survival of the male Jew. If, as Fackenheim urges, the post-Holocaust Jewish people respects the image of God in all persons precisely because of its holocaustal degradation, then it should set an example by its just relations. Yet the most punctiliously Jewish, as it were, of the Jews – those most obedient to Fackenheim's commandment – refuse to do so and the divine image is obscured once more. Only where the Jewish God is also called by her female names and pronoun will her voice be heard by all Jews because a God made exclusively in the masculine image is always calling over women's shoulder to someone else. If God calls to women in Auschwitz it is as a God hidden by the profanation of God's image unto death and in the tradition's exile of God-She from its discourse and practice. This profaned God does not and cannot command women but calls to them in anguished love, in the midst of their *common* profanation, to restore God to God's unity in the image of the women in their suffering midst. She does so because her own restoration to wholeness is at once that of the women made in her image. And the same God still calls to us to restore God's glory by re-calling that God of Auschwitz in ways that are open to a far better future.

In almost all post-Holocaust theology the degradation of European Jewry has been corrected by the triumphal (re)possession of a holy land promised by God. In his demonstrable lordship of history – that is, in the reconstruction of Jewish life in the United States of America and nationhood in the State of Israel – God's good name has been restored. In their different ways, most post-Holocaust thinkers – whether conservative or liberal – have offered the establishment of a Jewish state as (effectively) a substantial compensation for the Holocaust. While the Holocaust was not its precondition, almost all major post-Holocaust theologians regard the founding of the State of Israel as decisive evidence of the faithfulness of God to the Jewish people. Fackenheim is of the view that 'the heart of every *authentic* response to the Holocaust – religious and secularist, Jewish and non-Jewish – is a commitment to the autonomy and security of the State of Israel'.[63] This is not to say that the establishment of the State of Israel is regarded as the dawning of the Messianic age. Nonetheless, for Berkovits, while God may have been absent in the camps, he is present in the establishment of the State of Israel. Without this presence or reappearance faith could not be sustained; here God is finally revealed as a saving God.[64] He has finally shown his face in the establishment of the State of Israel: 'The state of Israel came at a moment in history when nothing else could have saved Israel from extinction through hopelessness.'[65] Even if Israel is God's suffering servant, it cannot forgive God's abandonment. God must therefore earn his people's forgiveness, discharging his obligation in the gift of the land of Israel. In this act, according to Berkovits, 'we have seen a smile on the face of God. It is enough.'[66]

But it is not enough. Even if Jewish feminism supports at least the principle of Israel as a homeland for Jews, it would not, particularly from an early twenty-first century perspective, invoke territorial acquisition and the conflict and suffering it has spawned as a providential sign, compensating for the depthless suffering of the Holocaust or redeeming God from unbelief. The moral and political conditions obtaining in Israel have not supported the weight of theological expectation set upon it. Most Jewish feminists have been justly critical of the State of Israel's perpetuation of gendered and intra-ethnic inequalities and its unjust and oppressive policies towards the Palestinians. In turning his face back to Israel this God may have turned away from the Palestinians with whose oppression Jewish feminists may identify both as women and as Jews. Although sensitive to the anti-Semitic undertones of the pro-Palestinian stance of the wider feminist movement, most Jewish feminists, in solidarity with history's present victims – the strangers we are biblically commanded to care for – give powerful voice to the aims of the Israeli peace movement.[67]

It is well known that many Holocaust survivors have struggled with a sense of shame and humiliation at their radical disempowerment during the Holocaust period. Even so, and perhaps because of this, triumphal models of God have not disappeared from contemporary Jewish theology where (in a ceremonial gesture aped by Hitler) God finally displays his authority in the biblical manner by the raising of his hand against his enemies. It is *this* point which is basic theologically; not where Jewish feminists may or may not stand in the debate over the moral issues attending military, civic and religious life in contemporary Israel. The problem, then, is where post-Holocaust theology safeguards masculine honour by postulating a masculine God who will not share in or carry his people's abjection. An argument from Michael Goldberg's *Why Should Jews Survive?* illustrates my point. Rejecting Rubenstein's assertion that the Holocaust dealt a deathblow to the biblical God, Goldberg's argument exonerates God through a computation of his victory: 'While over one-third of the world's Jews were butchered, the empirical fact remains that Hitler's minions were unable to exterminate the world's remaining Jews, and that reality must count as heavily, if not more heavily, for talk of God's survival than of his death.'[68]

Quite properly, Goldberg argues that the Exodus story, not the Holocaust, must constitute contemporary Judaism's theological 'master narrative'. However, in Goldberg's argument, the Exodus does not so much tell a story of liberation from oppression as teach us that the Holocaust must be viewed from a long-term strategic perspective: 'we can see God's justice if we view events from the right angle of vision. From such a standpoint, it matters that the German nation was defeated. From that perspective, it means something that the country that had sought to exterminate the Jews was itself virtually wiped off the map by the advancing Allied armies.' There remains, for Goldberg, 'only one true Lord with whom the world can dependably join ranks to save it from every Pharonic attempt to enslave it – whether Ramses II's in ancient times or Hitler's in our own'. Jewry must not renounce its faith in the interventionary God of tradition, but must 'keep following its Commander's lead, its marching orders for the campaign ahead'. And wherever Jews remain alive, 'God's promise to sustain the Jewish people has not died'. In answer to the question, 'Where was God during the Holocaust?', Goldberg is able to answer, 'With every Jew reading these words, *now*'.[69]

Of course Goldberg has hardly resolved the issue. Those who miraculously escaped death, or managed to escape from occupied territories should not constitute evidence for God's interventionary power because that leaves the – apparently expendable – men, women and children who *were* shot, burned or gassed as those who could be strategically sacrificed to God's final vindication and victory. How far can such arguments go? On Goldberg's logic, one could even argue that God used the Jews to save Europe from Germany, because the success of their military campaign was impaired by the diversion of resources from the conduct of war to that of the 'Final Solution'. But it is not just that Goldberg's argument, and others like it, are morally and theologically intolerable; they also demonstrate that supremacist patriarchal thinking seriously injures the credibility of divine love.

Perhaps the theology which most typifies what is objectionable about those masculinist interpretations of the Holocaust which feel compelled to take it into the environs of divine will in order to preserve divine sovereignty is that of Ignaz Maybaum. Maybaum's most important contribution to post-Holocaust theology was his *The Face of God After Auschwitz*.[70] Despite his mother having died in Theresienstadt and his sisters and other relatives in Auschwitz, his theology inherits the *haskalah* (Jewish Enlightenment) confidence that cultural progress is to be achieved by the westernization of Judaism. His liberal, Viennese Reform background – that of a wider nineteenth-century progressivism – led him to argue that the Holocaust was providential. The ghettos and shtetls of old Jewish Europe, along with their irrational, archaic observances, were to be sacrificed in order to bring Jewish medievalism to a close. Auschwitz was a *mophet* or dreadful portent marking the passage of Jewish history into a modern, emancipated post-Holocaust era for Jews and for Europe as a whole.[71]

Maybaum might have looked in hope towards the horizon of modernity, but his account of history rolls slowly forward on a groaning wheel of apocalypse. He delineates three catastrophes that have befallen the Jewish people, each a *churban* (national tragedy) whose destruction inaugurates the renewal that takes Jewry from one era of their history to the next. The first *churban* was the destruction of Solomon's Temple, providentially ensuring that the Jews would become a diaspora people, carrying the word of God to all nations. The second was the destruction of Herod's Temple, bringing in its wake the establishment of the synagogue where

God could be worshipped through prayer rather than the violence of sacrifice. And the third *churban* was the Holocaust: a demonstration of God's awful holiness. Auschwitz was the redemptive 'Day of the Lord' in that while one-third of the Jewish people world-wide were sacrificed as martyrs and witnesses, two-thirds miraculously remained as God's Saving Remnant.[72] Maybaum brings Auschwitz and the Exodus together: both were characterized by numinous horror, but both took Jewry out into the future. Where *haskalah* had tried and failed, Auschwitz was to pave Jewry and ultimately the whole of humanity's way towards the Holy Land of justice, mercy, peace, democracy and, it must be noted, sexual as well as civic equality. To this end, Hitler did God's will to 'cleanse, to purify . . . a sinful world'. Hitler is to be understood as the prophet Jeremiah had understood Nebuchadnezzar – as God's chosen servant; the instrument of his will. Maybaum's God apostrophizes Hitler thus: 'Hitler, My servant!'[73]

Maybaum's thesis is indefensible on almost every front. In fact, Auschwitz destroyed Jewish faith in *haskalah*, paving the way for precisely the kind of religious conservatism Maybaum wanted to abolish. The classic age of the shtetl was in any case over before the war began. And since the war, a world-wide ultra-Orthodox community has proved itself able to preserve Jewish 'medievalism' within a sophisticated technological, capitalist environment. Moreover, barbarism has continued almost unabated throughout the post-Holocaust period. Neither the Holocaust nor modernity (a patriarchal attempt to both ameliorate and master) have achieved what Maybaum thought they would.[74] Indeed it might be said, with Zygmunt Bauman, that the Holocaust was symptomatic of modernity.[75]

In one sense his critics have said all that needs to be said about what was simply mistaken or sub-ethical in Maybaum's argument; more (feminist) ethical criticism is merely otiose. But what is important from a feminist perspective is to see what Maybaum's God tells us about the patriarchal construal of divine and human power. Namely, that the domination of history by violence can cast suffering as an evolutionary cause and that masculine power is made the strong arm of God. If God sanctioned the violence of the Holocaust and made it his instrument then he is present in and through Hitler – which is intolerable. According to Maybaum, God's will is such that it can parasitize upon the will of Hitler; what allows this symbiotic relation is a towering will to abstraction and totality. Masculinist projects, whether the Reich or modernity, come to take precedence over the care of persons within socio-economic structures that will nourish persons and which will of themselves bring about the post-barbaric, rational world Maybaum envisages. Yet in Auschwitz, depicted by Maybaum as another Golgotha, God panders to the lowest patriarchal common denominator to make himself understood: he offers the spectacle of violence. Maybaum assumes that violence is the only language power understands. It is surely self-contradictory to postulate an archaic, overbearing God in order to end the irrational 'medievalism' that has constructed precisely such tyrannical models of God in the first place. To postulate a God who countenances the destruction of relation, who will do evil in order to do (what Maybaum considers to be) good, has already signalled the failure of rationality. In fact, relationships are conserved by the sort of law and ethics that are truly rational because they are truly relational.

God's failure to be patriarchal enough

One rather different way in which post-Holocaust theology has been demons-trably skewed by masculinist assumptions is in its protest against God. Such a protest (and Elie Wiesel's early writing falls into this category) is patriarchal in so far as it consists in anger at God's failure to meet the patriarchal expectations of which he is in large part a projection. That is, the classical attribute of omnipotence and mercy is still predicated of God and the protester is angry that God chose to refrain from its exercise. Were God less supremely powerful, the protester might feel compassion for God; as it is, he feels betrayed. Conversely, if God cannot, after all, be confessed as a saving God but has proved ineffectual, then while he cannot be blamed for his desertion, his humiliation and exposure as unequal to the demands of history render him a God not worth professing; humanity is left eternally vulnerable to its own maleficence. A less apparent way, then, in which post-Holocaust theology has been shaped by the patriarchal valorization of conquest and dominance has been that it has found itself unable to cede God his victory and so must reproach his defeat.

It is arguable that in the Mosaic God, the incomparable glory of God's holiness became the political instrument by which the territorial ambitions of the Hebrews were fulfilled.[76] But by the time of the Holocaust the tables were long turned and Israel was, impossibly, both the victim of history and the standard bearer of its omnipotent Lord. In Auschwitz, the terrible risk of the patriarchal God as (in scriptural and rabbinic idiom) a 'Man of War' was made evident. For when theology allows divine power and political terror to approximate one another it can be, as it was here, the undoing of God. His power, being only *an idea* of masculine human power, was there for the taking. Once the Jews were dispossessed of their God he could not turn around to save them because he had been dis-appeared; emptied of his numinous power by its arrogation by real people with real power. (Wiesel notes the irony that only Hitler kept his promise to the Jewish people. The Nazis assumed God's power and he was impotent in the face of it.)[77]

Theological fault lines develop along historical ones when the exercise of God's power is not defined as wholly other to that which fuels men's colonizing ambitions. In modernity, where divine claims, as much as any other, are subject to empirical verification or falsification in the eventualities of history, the dissonance between a God who promises protection and then, empirically, fails to deliver it will make theology ever more incredible. God can no longer be trusted. In other words a modern critical theology looks to see if God could and did behave like a (meta) man. And if he did not it seems logical to some to reject God as having either unjustifiably withheld his power or as being merely ineffectual.[78] (As the Yiddish folk saying goes, 'If God lived on earth, people would break His windows.')

Although the monarchical God has not always set his creation a good moral example, it would be far too large and bold a claim to hold the patriarchal model of God responsible for the Holocaust. And I am not, in any case, persuaded that there *is* a single, morally unambivalent patriarchal model of God. Rather, I want to say that when one masculinist model of power is pitted against another it will usually prove its competitor unequal to its appointed task. This occurred when the Reich was set against the reign of God. The sovereign power of the Jewish God over history was in some respects too close in kind to the world domination sought by Nazi Germany, which therefore sought to destroy it. And, for a while, Nazi power prevailed, especially in spaces like Auschwitz where absolute power was exercised without restraint because God's putative absolute power did not intervene to deliver its victims.

Richard Rubenstein once argued that the God of Jewish tradition would not have let the Holocaust happen and that as it *did* happen, *that* God cannot exist. And even if that God did exist, if 'it was God's will that Hitler committed six million Jews to slaughter' it would be immoral to believe in such a God or in Israel as the chosen people of God.[79] Holocaust theologians' problem is that their God is omniscient and omnipotent and his power and control over the world are therefore absolutely valorized.[80] But since such suffering *did* continue then the God who would *not* have allowed it to continue does not exist. Or to put it another way, the God who did allow it does exist, which returns us to the original problem.

Perhaps there is no way out of this impasse because it is one of human devising. The Master of the Universe whom patriarchal Judaism has made (up) is a golem: a soulless clay servant of its own secret making and naming, conjured by patriarchy's own will to usurp or exploit the power of its creator.[81] According to legend, the golem made by the sixteenth-century Elijah Baal Shem, Rabbi of Chelm, eventually became too big and tall for him to control any longer, and when it dissolved back into the mud the rabbi was crushed and submerged under its weight.[82] This is a parable of the monarchical God in Auschwitz.

A feminist version of Rubenstein's argument might then run as follows. Since the God of the masculine Jewish tradition has a violent and abusive element in his character which *might well* have let the Holocaust happen, this golem/God is either the product of the idolatrous projection of masculinist patriarchal values and therefore *should not* exist, or if this God could not stop the Holocaust happening he *need not* exist in this conceptual mode and form and can be replaced by a model of which we may have different expectations. Rubenstein felt that the Holocaust demonstrated the death of the God of Jewish tradition; that we were 'totally and nakedly alone. That we could expect neither support not succour from God nor from our fellow creatures.' The world was, for him, a place of pain, suffering and alienation.[83] If, as Rubenstein believed, a 'void [. . .] now confronts man where once God stood',[84] then this void can occasion a spiritually and morally regenerative plerosis whereby the lineaments of God assume a form more permeable to an eirenic female imaginary.

In sum, where post-Holocaust theology persists in using masculinist categories of understanding, it is not identical but continuous with the ideological conditions that produced the Holocaust and therefore cannot move beyond them. To varying degrees, post-Holocaust theologies are unsuccessful solutions to the problem because (to borrow a phrase Phyllis Trible used to describe certain oppressive texts in the Hebrew Bible) they are 'texts of terror'; they are not just about, but part of, the problem. Some (not all) post-Holocaust theology holds a common patriarchal view that supposed creative ends (whether those of God, 'man' or Nazi Germany) may deploy or permit absolutely destructive means (Maybaum). Although it must not be forgotten that the patriarchal God is *also* a God of justice and liberation, this God is prepared to suspend his power and permit atrocity in order to preserve an essentially masculine free will to do good or evil (Berkovits and Cohen), or in the case of the Nazis, to pursue the end of their free will which was to make all non-Aryan wills unfree. This latter insistence that Auschwitz is a necessary possibility of human freedom is particularly ironic where, by virtue of its established standing, Orthodox theologies of the Holocaust share with other oppressive ideologies the assumption that some human beings – here, women – should not be accorded the dignity of full subjects as agents rather than recipients of the legislative process.

I wonder, then, if Michael Goldberg is right when he says: 'there is only one fully truthful answer we can give as to why during the Holocaust such bad things happened to such good, God-revering people: *We do not know*.'[85] Granted, God is not an ordinary object of knowledge. From a theoretical point of view we cannot know enough about God to know whether God acted during the Holocaust or not.[86] And it may be pointless to court unfruitful if not ethically and emotionally repellent debate over the logical possibility that God did in fact intervene in the Holocaust to make it slightly less catastrophic than it might have been. Certainly theology must remain agnostic in so far as we cannot penetrate divine consciousness (or even know quite what we mean by divine consciousness). But we can penetrate human consciousness to the extent of making claims about the ways in which theo-political structures of power and authority permit bad things to happen to good people.

To put it another way, we can claim that patriarchal theological discourse on the Holocaust may fail to persuade or interest feminist theologians because it is predicated upon a model of God whose will and character shares significant elements of the alienated patriarchal worldview of its perpetrators. It does not and cannot mount a significant moral critique on the world that produced and inherited Auschwitz because it enjoys discursive and religious privileges within that world.

Re-figuring divine power

In the light of these comments, there seems little point in making yet another assault on the rockface of the classical theodical problem: that of reconciling God's omnipotence, justice and perfect goodness with the suffering of his creation. To attempt to reconcile the patriarchal God's omnipotence and supposed moral perfection with the facts of the Holocaust would be futile when religious feminism considers that model of God and its ideological aspiration to omnipotence to be morally flawed from the outset, irrespective of the Holocaust.

Yet it is no easy task to deny or even modify the attribute of divine omnipotence and space does not permit me to do so in any detail here. Although it is not unknown for Jews to have argued that God's power is finite, most Jews, in so far as they reflect systematically on the divine attributes at all, regard God's omnipotence as a non-negotiable, definitive attribute of an infinite God who will, finally, vanquish evil. Judaism's hope has been in the God of the Exodus who, before Israel's 'very eyes', 'ventured to go and take for himself one nation from the midst of another by prodigious acts, by signs and portents, by war, by a mighty and an outstretched arm and awesome power' (Deut. 4: 34). It is not that philosophers have claimed that God's omnipotence is unlimited by reason, morality and the logical operations of natural law. God cannot do any conceivable thing. Nonetheless, doctrines of omnipotence figure God as the ruler of all, including those who practice evil. Because God is omnipotent he could have prevented the Holocaust if he had been inclined to do so. But for reasons of his own he did not. The Holocaust ran its course and God's triumph over evil was once again deferred to an eschatological dimension.

The traditional assumption of God's omnipotence, coupled with the evidence of his holocaustal non-intervention, prompts a variety of post-Holocaust responses. Rubenstein rejects God on that ethical count. Berkovits more or less submits to the 'injustice absolute' of God's withholding his omnipotent power, while Blumenthal and the early Wiesel are profoundly angry about it. Maybaum, however, sees the Holocaust as precisely a function of God's omnipotent will and Cohen does not deny God's omnipotence but denies that it is the sort of immanent power that intervenes in the course of evil. Fackenheim's God, as the 'Commanding Voice of Auschwitz', shouts over it. But few can find it in themselves to deny God's omnipotence; no one wants to claim that God's power tried and failed.

In his discussion of post-Holocaust theology, Oliver Leaman comments, 'How we expect God to react to our sufferings represents how we want to think of God, what his relationship with us is going to be'.[87] Feminist theology, aware that God's omnipotence is as much a political value as it is a religious hope, must question whether omnipotence is a necessary attribute of divinity and prerequisite to redemption. It must ask whether God can be infinitely powerful without also claiming that God is omnipotent, that is, controlling everything that is, was and will be the case. Being methodologically committed to speaking from women's experience, a feminist theology of the Holocaust must also question whether the concept of divine omnipotence would have played any significant role in women victims' experience of suffering.

If knowable at all, this latter is a matter for historical enquiry. But by far the most prevalent response to suffering in the women survivors' memoirs is not one of a sustained call for deliverance upon the God of Israel, but upon the assistance of Israel itself in the bodily form of the women around them. Broadly speaking, for secular Jewish women, familial, national and political connections were of paramount importance as sources of practical and emotional sustenance. For liberal Jewish women, philanthropic and ethical resources of a broadly Christian as well as Jewish kind would also have predominated over supernatural consider-ations. For Orthodox women, the maintenance of religious observance as well as familial affiliations were central; theological manoeuvre and the consolations of theology (such as they were – few Jews at the time practised anything by that name) were not normally accessible to women and are rarely so today.

Women survivors' accounts are not preoccupied by theology but with conveying the immediate struggle to survive as an individual or as part of a family or group of friends. Sara Nomberg-Przytyk, for example, was committed to secular socialist politics, not Judaism. Indeed, in Auschwitz, Jewish faith 'irritated' her in the face of the 'unavenged murder of the whole Jewish people'.[88] Other memoirs testify to a loss of faith or trust in the redeeming God of Israel, but (perhaps because Judaism has not been much detained by the question of the existence of God) this loss is not a torment comparable to that of their comprehensive loss of family, friends, and home. It is this locus of suffering which indicates that their relationships are of ultimate concern. In other words, for Jewish women and men whose worldview is a relational one, existential meaning is not dependent on the possibility of divine omnipotence. Providence comes in the form of the brave men and women who help them to survive or ameliorate their end. Bertha Ferderber-Salz, a woman of conventional Orthodox background, found that in Auschwitz and Belsen she could not tolerate theological reflection on the God whom she claims had tortured her for long enough. In Belsen in 1945, half delirious and lying in a bunk among the dead and dying, she screamed at God, (addressed, perhaps ironically, as 'Lord of the Universe'): 'Leave me alone. I don't understand anything. I don't know anything. My head is bursting! . . . Leave me alone!' After the war she carried on going to synagogue, but not to pray. Instead the synagogue congregated the dead; it evoked a relational presence that may not have been that of the God of masculinist tradition but was none the less a real and necessary presence. That is, the synagogue functioned (as it should) as a place of Jewish assembly, but here one which enabled her to 'meet [her] dear ones once more'.[89]

This prioritizing of relation over philosophy should inform a post-Holocaust conceptualization of divine power, not because Jewish theology is a product of private religious experience (which it is not) nor because what women experienced was the whole and final truth about God (which it could not be). Rather, if post-Holocaust theology is true to women's experience as well as to men's it will be more comprehensively and attentively Jewish. Above all, it will correlate with the personalistic, embodied character of Jewish theology itself, where election is a matter of corporeal, not ethically or philosophically elective, descent. In a feminist context, the argument of Michael Wyschogrod's *The Body of Faith* is highly significant: God enters the world 'through a people whom he chose as his habitation. Thus there came about a visible presence of God in the universe, first in the person of Abraham and later his descendants, as the people of Israel.'[90] It seems to me that the consequence of Israel's corporeal election is that where God is among us as an assembly of suffering bodies, God's power, *there*, is limited by the conditions of embodied finitude and, God being wholly good, is manifest in the exercise of the beneficent power of *hesed* or human love and kindness within that assembly.

The attribute of divine omnipotence must in any case be suspect after Nazi Germany's totalitarian celebration of the unbridled power of the Aryan male individual and the political structures he established to achieve the power of life and death over subjected others. This view of moral evil as a political rather than ontological problem was articulated early in the history of second wave radical feminism. In the light of these claims, some on the left of the Jewish feminist movement have made connections between the postulation of an omnipotent male God, the consequent valorization of masculine power, and the Holocaust. Aviva Cantor, a co-founder of the Jewish feminist magazine *Lilith*, wrote to the Jewish feminist artist Judy Chicago, expressing a view of patriarchy that was to underpin Chicago's own figurative representation of the Holocaust:

> What made the Holocaust possible (and some may argue inevitable) is the fact of patriarchy, and the fact that patriarchal values dominate our society. . . . Patriarchy is rooted in the elevation of power to the highest value and in the struggle for it among groups of men and by individual men. Men seek power over each other, over women, over children, over animals, over the natural world, and justify this on grounds of utility. It is these values which have made the Holocaust possible.[91]

Chicago also claimed that because men believe themselves to have been directly created in God's image, a burden of omnipotence is placed upon them. The Holocaust can then be understood as the 'logical outgrowth of the rule of force, dominance and power'. Chicago cites both Robert Lifton's study of Nazi doctors as evidence for how endless killing requires a 'hardening of the self' that 'is related to cultural principles of masculinity' and Rianne Eisler's view of the Nazi elite as 'living exemplars of "manly" virtues' who won 'glory, honor and power by unleashing destruction and terror'.[92]

Theological reflection on the Holocaust has been within the frame of a traditional theological anthropology that assumes the value and necessity of hierarchical masculine power and its transcendental correlate of divine omnipotence. But Jewish feminist theology, like Christian feminist theology, wants at least to question the attribution of omnipotence to God on the grounds that of all the divine attributes of classical theism, omnipotence seems most a patriarchal fantasy; a projection of the ultimate patriarchal aspiration onto God. In asserting that the way dominant men attempt to dominate and control history may have nothing to do with the way God should act in history, feminist theology is compelled to attend to the human structures of power, often buttressed by religion, that have created the conditions for atrocity.[93] At that point – at the perception of a causal connection between the modelling of human and divine activity – it could be asked whether morally flawed masculine power structures should still structure theological responses to demonic power, one of whose purposes is to articulate resistance to such.

Writing on the Holocaust, the Catholic theologian Mary Jo Leddy denied that feminist criticism of the coercive patriarchal power that produced the Holocaust compels it to espouse a 'feminine' theology of the powerlessness of goodness. Powerlessness can amount to little more than ineffectiveness or complicity. It is possible, Leddy says, to reject post-Holocaust theological assumptions of national dominance and control, while still advocating a theology of power that is oppositional to evil. Religious feminism celebrates the relational power-in-between persons; the different power she finds speaking in the 'different voices' of women in the Holocaust, which also speak of a redemptive God. Leddy postulates a powerful God, but one whose redemptive power is vested in non-coercive relation and therefore vulnerable as well as creative and enduring. Referring to those women who continued to give birth to and to care for children in the 'long and dark night of the Holocaust', Leddy affirms that creation is always the answer to destruction.[94]

A maternal, relational model of God which modifies divine omnipotence – perhaps to the point of repudiation – might be said to create as many problems as it solves.[95] As Leaman remarks: 'were I to have a choice between a comforter who could share my distress and a technician who can end it, I think I should choose the latter.'[96] This is understandable; there could be no good reason to refuse divine deliverance were it to be proffered (which to all appearances it was not). But it is not to design God to a set of human specifications to claim that God was present in and through relationship for such is true to the covenantal nature of Jewish history and to its future. A covenantal, relational theology acknowledges that God's power was not such as could stop the destruction of relationship, but it affirms the infinite flow of God's power to renew it. Later in this book I will argue that God's presence, as one who creates, loves, orders and sustains the world, is revealed in the act of welcome. The transcendent God is immanent in the aperture made between the one seeing and opening to the other. That is the redemptive moment. It is not an interventionary fiat which overrides history and persons. If that does not seem enough it is because love has been made secondary to sovereignty and because what we may see as God's limitation is a part of how God is known: namely, as the transformatory power of love labouring to break into history as its redemption. Love and power are a necessarily unitary moral reality. To be reconciled to a God whose nature is not such as to marshal historical forces in our defence is a part of spiritual maturity. (Thus Elyse Goldstein: 'I felt safe and secure with God the Father, the rabbi and my own father mysteriously intertwined. Then I grew up. I found out that the rabbi was human, my father was flawed, and God could not take care of everything.')[97]

It might be countered that the 'feminization' of God in Auschwitz will introduce the disequilibrium between God's mercy and God's justice that rabbinic Judaism sought to avoid. But while the self-revelation of the metapatriarchal God does not require conditions of numinous terror, there is no reason why a feminist conception of God need reject the possibility of God's wrath. The female face of God is not to be cast in the bland image of passive femininity. To insist (with Rudolf Otto) that wrath belongs to the sublime *tremendum* of God's holiness,[98] is to respect the inviolability of the human person made in the image of God.[99] If God's presence is produced in and by relation it is in experiencing the sanctity of relation that evil is named as its degradation and as the criminal expulsion of God from the world. The social transformation of human relationships by love and justice is the means by which God's judgement is manifest. God's return is enabled by religio-political structures that legislate the correction of injustice, exploitation and victimization within the historical order.

Relational care, rather than quasi-military intervention or the miraculous suspension of the laws of cause and effect, is the sign and medium of God's power within the world. In the chapters to come, I figure God, with mystical tradition, as the exiled Shekhinah. This is already to acknowledge the tragedy of God as one whose torn garments trail after us in the dust; it is to deny that God has the patriarchal power over history that might simply intervene to arrest its course. Yet God's love and ours in its image, *is* unlimited and omnipotent in that it is experienced as all-conquering by those who love and are loved absolutely, even if its effect is not one of victorious deliverance. God's power is invested in the power of interpersonal and social relation to mediate its blessing and to institute justice and judgement on those who violate it.

God was not real-ized in Auschwitz by might and Israel – shocked, hungry, and almost entirely without military means – was rendered more or less physically powerless. Divine power was not that proclaimed by the wonders of the exodus from Egypt. On the contrary: the lintel of every Jewish household in Nazi Germany and occupied Europe was smeared with the blood of its occupants. And the angel of death did not pass over but folded its wings over the roof like a great bird settling on its nest. If God's 'outstretched hand' was there it was to hold not to smite. This could not be experienced as deliverance because God – *HaMakom* (the Place) – is with Israel in the place where Israel is: here a place of powerlessness. And because God is in (though not incarnated by) Israel, and Israel is always a body in a place, here God, with Israel, lay wounded in the mud.

God's power takes its historical chance. But as everlasting life, *Chai-ha-Olamin,* God does not die (or resurrect). To claim that God was there in so far as Israel was there (to the other's need) is not to develop a quasi-Christian incarnational theology in which God's redemptive presence *is* that of the marked bodies of the victims, as if they were her garment of suffering flesh. God did not take the brunt of Jewry's suffering or die on its behalf. The memoir literature makes it more than apparent that the load was not lifted from human shoulders. The Jewish God is indivisibly one so that to say God was present among women in Auschwitz is not at all to say that God has ever *become* a suffering woman. Rather, she is revealed in moments of welcome; of one going out to meet the other. By such acts of hospitality God and humanity are united. That restoration of presence – where one has gone to the other – may only allow a momentary affirmation of the infinite dignity of each Jew as Israel: God's beloved. And that restoration – a mere glance or nod – may also be undertaken on behalf of those who no longer have the strength or reason to do so.

2   The hiding of God's face
in Auschwitz

Announce to the cities of Judah:
'Behold your God!'

(Is. 40: 9)

Although properly hesitant to explain God's looking away from Auschwitz, a number of Jewish philosophers and theologians have, in effect, justified God's silence, inaction or absence by weighing the necessity of human moral freedom against the suffering it can cause. If humanity is to be truly human, that is, free, God must be, in some senses, less than God. God must give way to human (normatively masculine) freedom and becoming by withholding his omnipotent power to override human choice. The good would not be the good, and therefore pleasing to God, had it not been willed and chosen. Human morality therefore entails the strong possibility of its failure. Auschwitz is the price of human becoming and, indeed, human morality itself. At the same time, God's freedom is secured by his being mysteriously unknowable in his ways and, according to some philosophical traditions, a God who is ultimately apathetic or unmoved by the conditions of finitude. All of these operations can be indicated in the trope of divine hiddenness. As we shall see, the most authoritative exponent of the post-Holocaust free will defence of God's holocaustal non-intervention has been Eliezer Berkovits. In *Faith After the Holocaust* he argues that had God exercised his power in preventing the Holocaust he would have impeded 'man's' becoming: the project to which even divine justice and happiness must be subordinated. God's love for our freedom effectively exceeds his love for those who suffer its consequences.[1]

But as I have argued elsewhere, God no longer has to stay his hand or remain hidden if autonomy is acknowledged to be an elitist masculine project that is not the first or only prerequisite of human dignity and becoming.[2] And if the divine attribute of omnipotence is acknowledged to have a contingent political as much as a redemptive function as the projection of patriarchy's own aspiration, then neither is divine power necessarily required to give way to human freedom and becoming. Subsequent chapters of this study will seek to demonstrate that, during the Holocaust, and to the point of death, freedom was not necessarily the guarantor of human dignity; human dignity could consist in the capacity, however vestigial, to honour communal or familial obligations.

Judith Tydor Baumel's research on Jewish women's structures of mutual support in pre-war Nazi Germany and during the Holocaust suggests that, historically at least, Holocaust theology need not turn on the axis of freedom. Tydor Baumel has shown that the catastrophe strengthened 'women's spheres' of influence: the philanthropic and educational patterns of leadership that had been developing since the nineteenth century. These activities were no longer the means of middle-class women's self-expression, but cooperative strategies for survival that fostered sisterhood and solidarity. Tydor Baumel concludes that 'long-term crisis situations may strengthen women's communal identities and power by negating the masculine ideal of the autonomous individual'.[3] Women seem to have invested their dignity less in freedom as such than in the degree to which they were needed and bound to others by ties of love and obligation.

So too, the women's memoir literature gives little evidence either for a female equation of dignity and freedom *per se*, nor for women calling upon God's interventionary power to save them, but far more for their calling upon one another's presence to their need. What this literature relates is not resistance to degradation by the exercise of freedom as an abstracted choice or as an existentialist manifesto; rather, to be free was to maintain a capacity to respond to the need of the other which was continuous with that of relationships outside the camps. Responsiveness to the other was not, and could not be, a bid for freedom but for the conservation of love against the gross profligacies of hate. There, love, both human and divine, was not omnipotent but it could be indestructible. Relationship was covenantal in character: to protect the familial or quasi-familial other was often expressed in the language of promise. Human dignity lay in the preservation of the capacity to love, not in the freedom to love.

The holocaustal dis-appearance of God

The covenant of presence elaborated in this book responds to a patriarchal negotiation between God and men that trades divine absence for human (read masculine) becoming. This latter is more to patriarchy's advantage than God's since human autonomy effectively makes God not merely hidden, but redundant. Although God's redundancy summarizes the impetus of modern patriarchy, the move is not peculiar to modernity. Within a narrative theological framework, the philosophical argument that God can only honour human freedom if he does not intervene in particular human predicaments requires that God must absent himself from that predicament; that he must not see it and that he must remain silent. In biblical idiom, God must 'sleep' through the slaughter (Ps. 44: 24) or 'stand aloof, heedless in times of trouble' (Ps. 10: 1). Philosophy and theology come together in popular faith and in post-Holocaust theology – in particular that of Berkovits, Buber, Blumenthal and to a lesser extent Cohen and Levinas – to dis-appear God from holocaustal space and time (just as Nazi Germany had done, though for entirely different reasons).[4]

While theological discourse may construe the absence or hiddenness of God as that which preserves human freedom, in actuality, numberless Jews would have experienced the absent God as not-God in Auschwitz. Divine self-restraint in the name of human becoming may have been experienced as a divine desertion of post; the silence left by his absence would have been taken as a licence for Nazi atrocity. If Auschwitz was the evident vacation of God from the world, then it seems offensive to reason, God's goodness and Auschwitz's victims to sanctify Auschwitz by the postulation of God's presence. Speaking for many Jews, Menachem Rosensaft therefore finds it a conceit of theologians 'even to suggest that God was somehow present at or a participant in Auschwitz'. Worse, the postulation of divine presence is an act of blasphemy against the victims as well as against God.[5] Of course, Rosensaft makes the common mistake of confusing God's presence in Auschwitz with its orchestration. Even so, divine presence and absence are the central tropes by which Jews both understand and contest God's holocaustal will and responsibility. Because hiddenness encompasses both God's presence and God's absence, trust in God and in a Jewish future can be sustained at precisely the same time as protesting God's role in the Holocaust.

This move has been most notably elaborated by Berkovits in his *Faith After the Holocaust* which is, thereby, the most traditional and scripturally grounded of the post-Holocaust theologies.[6] Berkovits' God must, in order to protect human free will, hide his face; must turn away: 'That man may be, God must absent himself; that man may not perish in the tragic absurdity of his own making, God must remain present. The God of history must be present and absent concurrently. He hides his presence.'[7] God's mightiness, then, consists in 'self-restraint' and 'self-control'. So that 'while He shows forbearance with the wicked, He must turn a deaf ear to the anguished cries of the violated'. Both 'man's' freedom and his suffering are, indeed, an index of the divine love for him: 'God's very mercy and forbearance, his very love for man, necessitates the abandonment of some men to a fate that they may well experience as indifference to justice and human suffering.'[8]

Because God is not an object among other objects, the boundaries between divine presence and absence are not merely blurred but unknowable. For Berkovits, the two must be held together by the dialectics of faith: God's presence is necessitated by his self-revelation and it is the condition of human hope. The survival of the Jewish people, its sanctification of God's name and its repossession of the land of Israel, are a witness to God's saving presence. Yet because God must absent himself, the innocent suffer human evil. God will not restrain this evil because he must give way to the greater good of human becoming (though if severe trauma arrests the self's becoming, it is hardly to its own good). This turning or hiding of the divine face is known as *hester panim*, a paradoxical function of God's self-revelation well known to rabbinic Judaism. Furthermore, God's self-hiding is not a historical incident but, after Isaiah 45: 15, is an attribute of the divine nature: 'Such is God. He is a God who hides himself.'[9] But because God must also, eventually, be present to Israel there is the assurance that goodness will prevail. That Jewry has survived all assaults upon it and has not been annihilated is proof that God is not only hidden but present as Saviour in its history.

Emmanuel Levinas delivers a yet harsher theology of 'the God Who Veils His Face'. His is a God who offers 'no reprieve, no consolation of presence'. There is to be no expectatation of 'warm, almost palpable communion with the Divine'. God is not revealed 'like an image in a darkened room'.[10] On the contrary, God renounces succour and calls on 'man' to realize his maturity and responsibility. (Again, it is notable that for God, 'man's' coming of age takes priority over the care which Levinas demands of persons.) God abandons the righteous, but is yet known in the Word mediated by Torah. It is in the divine word, not the divine presence, that Israel achieves intimacy with its God. The holy is mediated by reason, not presence or touch: 'God manifests Himself not by incarnation but by absence. God manifests Himself not by incarnation but in the Law.'[11] God's face is veiled precisely so that he can ask the 'superhuman' of 'man', that is, to love God in spite of God's turning away. Yet in a dialectic with which we are now becoming familiar, to accept that God's face is veiled is to give one the right to demand its unveiling: to demand justice. It is this dialectic which establishes a kind of equality between 'man' and God; 'man's' dignity is assured.[12]

Rather differently, in *The Eclipse of God* Buber interprets Isaiah 45: 15, 'You are indeed a God who conceal[s] Himself' as a necessary means of preserving the mysterious living God from epistemological or doctrinal domestication as an It instead of a Thou. God is hidden because he is not a mere object of knowledge. Perhaps because of his temporal proximity to the events, Buber does not write at any length about the Holocaust (nor, according to some of his commentators, in much depth). However, it is clear that Buber also feels that God's presence may be sought in suffering and not found, and that this must be endured until such time as dialogue and communion is restored.[13] In *On Judaism* Buber speaks of the God who 'allowed those things to happen'; who had 'withdraw[n] utterly from the earth' so that the believer 'is fated to spend his life in a time of His hiddenness', still awaiting the voice of the Lord who is both merciful and cruel.[14] Less conventionally, just as feminist scholarship is unwilling to ontologize a flaw that first pertains to human political structures and their ordination, Buber wants to say that the catastrophe was a function of the primary betrayal and alienation of relation he characterises as I/It: the reduction of the other to an object.[15] This alienation puts our dialogical capacity to call to God and experience God's presence in question.[16] Where Buber connects the causes of the Holocaust to humanity's exile of God from the world this is properly distinct from the notion that by turning away God let 'man' do his worst. There can only be healing when we turn to one another in love, the turning being an authentic *teshuvah* or repentance.[17] Buber's approach to the question of God's hiddenness during the Holocaust is variously nuanced, but it is a trope he nonetheless wishes to use.

Again, not everyone has been satisfied with these discussions. It is not, after all, clear whether God was hidden in the processes of the Holocaust or hidden, somewhere else, for its duration. Nor is it clear whether God's hiddenness was the cause of the catastrophe or whether it was a turning away from what had already begun. The former can imply a vindictive and undeserved punishment, the latter, a desertion.[18] None of these possibilities casts God in an attractive light. As Sacks points out of Berkovits' theology, God was actually 'neither present nor absent at Auschwitz: He was hidden. The line of thought was barely comforting, for it argued an exile of God from the human domain that was little short of complete eclipse.'[19] Morally, if God was capable of doing so, he should have intervened.

To say, as Berkovits and Levinas do, that God is present precisely in his absence is something of a rhetorical trick. It is, in Wieseltier's words, 'not a paradox, it is a contradiction'; it is 'an idea in need of an explanation'.[20] (Compare Athos's riddle in the novel *Fugitive Pieces*: 'How do we know there's a God? Because He keeps disappearing.')[21] What can it mean to say to the child abandoned on the ghetto street, his parents dead, dying or deported,[22] that God is present because he is absent? Admittedly, God is not the same thing as a mother or father and Jewry is not a child. Even so, the fatherhood of God is deeply embedded in the Jewish imaginal repertoire, and therefore Israel's relation to that God is analogous to that of his child. And it would be no comfort to a child to say, in effect, I love you so I will let you suffer alone; I am with you because I am not.[23] (Now compare the biblical text: 'When You hid Your face I was terrified', Ps. 30: 8.)[24]

In the Warsaw ghetto Manya Zygelbojm would not part with her son Artek, even for his own safety. Refusing to send him over the ghetto wall onto the 'Aryan side', she said, '"Without me, he would perish."' If they were to die, at least they would die together (as they did). Or again, when the two 10-year-old twin sisters Nellie and Vlodka Blit were housed with a Gentile family on the 'Aryan side' of Warsaw, their mother (who was to die in Majdenek) found out which windows her daughters would be able to see her from. Thereafter she 'haunted Wolowa Street every day, and making sure that she was not being watched, she would walk slowly up and down, looking up intently at the closed windows of Dubiel's house. The little girls would wait for her and peep through the curtained windows'.[25] Presence, a keeping watch, is a function of love. A present God paces back and forth, circling the object of her concern; an absent God seems to have walked away.

A God who looks away

In recent years one of the most significant contributions to the discussion of holo-caustal divine absence has been that of David Blumenthal in his 1993 book, *Facing the Abusing God: A Theology of Protest*, which again describes the presence of a hidden God. This book is central to our discussion not only because it formulates the theme of God's holocaustal hiddenness in the more contemporary currency of abuse but also because it debates feminist objections to its argument.

Blumenthal interprets God's turning away as his turning a blind eye to Jewry's abuse and so not only letting it happen but being complicit in its happening. Blumenthal cannot justify God's hiddenness in the way Berkovits (finally and reluctantly) can. Blumenthal judges God's absence as a non-interruptive presence that was, as such, abusive. He does not seek to excuse God or to deny that as victim, Jewry was innocent: '*God is abusive, but not always. . . .* In this [abusive] mode, God "caused" the holocaust, or allowed it to happen.'[26] Scripture portrays

'God as an abusing person' and history reveals human beings to have an abusive side to their personalities. As God and humanity are co-responsible for the Holocaust, we must come to face and accept the abusiveness in our humanity as much as we have to face the abusiveness of God.[27] This is the '"difficult" side of human and divine being' and it is, indeed, part of the bond between humanity and God.[28] We must acknowledge God as 'the Other Who is present to us in fear *and* in kinship, in terror *and* in presence . . . we will affirm the God Who has worked wondrously through us, just as we acknowledge the God Who worked aw(e)fully against us.'[29] If we wish to understand God or ourselves, there should be no 'ethical censorship' of unpalatable texts and traditions whose 'serious religiosity' lends us knowledge of a dimension of God's personality that is simply a cosmic given.[30]

In both judging God and feeling himself bound to God, Blumenthal allies himself with a distinctive Jewish tradition of theological protest mediated through scriptural, rabbinic and modern literary texts (including those about the Holocaust) in which (male) Jewish writers judge and sometimes reject God, while not denying his existence.[31] A trust has been broken and a great love betrayed; the divine–human relationship is now an agonized one. The early work of Elie Wiesel, for example, protests God's non-intervention in the Holocaust, shuts God out and refuses Israel's election. Blumenthal supports such a move: after the Holocaust 'distrust is also a proper religious affection'; 'sustained suspicion is a religiously proper faith stance toward God'.[32] Just as children's bonds with parents who abuse are such that they can rarely simply reject them, so too Jewry can accuse and question God, but cannot reject him. (Blumenthal is not alone in this: Berkovits also accuses God of countenancing monstrous evil yet must be loved and trusted nonetheless.)[33] We are created by God, his presence is irreducible and our bond or covenant with him cannot be nullified. Rather than reject him, we have to learn to 'cope with God and God's actions'.[34] God, however, must also repent. In a closing prayer to the abusing God Blumenthal writes 'may God share with you His anguish and His shame at His own hateful actions'.[35] Blumenthal does not, then, demand rational and moral perfection of God. God can act in error and sin.[36] Rebuilding a relationship with God entails learning to resist evil and learning to open yourself to 'the good side of God'.[37]

Blumenthal's book is particularly interesting in that its methodology is a perspectival, reflexive, dialogical one. His thinking is involved, self-critical, non-linear and affective. He draws upon the texts and theologies of Jewish feminist prayer and is willing to make theoretical and experiential connections with the Holocaust and other abuses of power. In short, his work bears the marks not only of a postmodern but also of a 'post-patriarchal' way of doing Jewish theology (which may have been there all along).

And yet his pessimistic anthropology: 'the ugly fact' that 'there is an abused child within all of us, just as there is an abuser within us all'[38] ontologizes patri-archal alienations of power and distorts his theology of divine and human person-hood and its correlated theology of image by forcing it into an eternalized cycle of violence. From a feminist perspective, even though the catastrophe *did* occur in the world created by God, what is to be distrusted is not God but a particular model or figure of God. It is certain notions of power that are abusive, not God, who, if he is abusive is demonstrably not God. That is why Jewish feminists recovering from abuse have rejected the masculine God who not only failed to protect them from men, but also sanctioned and hypostasized some of the latter's privileges and powers.[39] As Blumenthal's own (Ottonian) discussion of the holy recognizes, God's *sui generis* holiness is what defines God as God and so as wholly other to alienated human values and practices. Without acknowledging the distinction between God in God's-self and God as an ideological projection, post-Holocaust protest theology is knocking its head against a brick wall of its own making.

It is Blumenthal's correspondence between himself and Diane, an adult survivor of childhood abuse, and Wendy Farley, a Christian feminist systematic theologian, which crystallizes what most religious feminists would regard as the central flaw of Blumenthal's theology. To his credit, this correspondence is published in the book and forms a significant part of its structure and immediacy. In her letters to him, Diane examines his analogy of the post-Holocaust Jewish people as an abused child. For her, whether the omnipotent God was the author of the abuse/Holocaust, or was so negligent a parent as to let it happen, God must atone for what he did. And even should he do so, healing might not be possible because that God has been an abuser and, in fact, nothing can atone for what he did. On 30 January 1990, Diane wrote to Blumenthal: 'God, omnipotent and uncaring, is someone whom I would never wish to encounter again. I would stay as far away from Him as possible, forever. He would not be deserving of my company, comfort, praise, and love.'[40]

Farley takes the critique further and criticizes Blumenthal's rendering of the relationship between God and Israel as a hierarchy of powerful parent and powerless child. This, she argues, belongs to a patriarchal notion of covenant which, as an expression of sovereignty, does not nurture compassion towards others or inspire a sense of mutual obligation. Authentic covenant is, by contrast, intrinsically non-hierarchical and premised on mutuality and solidarity.[41] Writing to Blumenthal on 6 April 1989, Farley argues that Blumenthal's account of God as Abuser is truly a 'text of terror' – a text that is about terror and which itself terrifies – where the God to whom one looks for protection from the terror of abuse is, nightmarishly, the ultimate source and reality of abuse.[42] Farley recognizes that Blumenthal might not have intended nihilism, but he has nonetheless composed a 'serious prayer for an un-world in which one prays to God who is the un-God, the deification and justification of the lust for humiliation and torment'.[43] In her letter of 26 May 1989 Farley refuses to worship an abusing father. It is immoral and idolatrous to absolutize one element of human experience and, theologically, it is 'the crudest form of anthropomorphism'. By sanctioning injustice and evil, the Holocaust is removed from the sphere of ethical and theological discourse and praxis.[44]

Abuse can occur when the one who could and should intervene will not even witness to the evil. The silence of God is a cognate metaphor of disappearance also commonly used in post-Holocaust theology and this too, as Cohen notes, is 'a metaphor for inaction; passivity, affectlessness, indeed, at its worst and most extreme, indifference and ultimate malignity'. It is a reproof and a punitive withholding of mercy and justice.[45] In intra-human relationships the one who has been betrayed will often say that she or he cannot and does not wish to see or speak to the faithless other. So too, within the divine–human relationship, as soon as God's hiding is understood less as a theological mystery than as an abandonment or withholding of mercy, then theologians are compelled to seek some human betrayal or transgression as its explanation. Most post-Holocaust theologians have, however, refused to find one. It is true that human silence can be the only possible response to enormities of a scale that exceed the ambit of linguistic response. Numerous commentators have counselled human silence as a properly reverent answer to the ultimately unanswerable questions Auschwitz raises. But God cannot refuse to listen to those who call upon God in their innocent suffering. God's loving word cannot be exhausted by history as ours might be. And, in any case, the God of biblical and rabbinic tradition is not predominantly silent and withdrawn, but has been present in the Jews' great redemptive moments at the Exodus and at Sinai. Jews have always turned to God in faith on the assumption that he, in his great love for Israel, would save Israel in its hour of need.[46]

In fact, God's hiddenness is not to be crudely equated with absence but may be more an elusive form of immanence (hence Berkovits' insistence that God is present in his absence). God is there, somewhere, but he is hidden. Rabbi Rafael of Bershad told how his Rebbe used to say that God's hiding 'ceases to be a hiding, if you know it is a hiding'.[47] But what matters is that a well-hidden divine presence can be experienced as God's taking cover; as a dereliction of love quite alien to the loyalties instituted by God's act of redemption from Egypt and by the several biblical covenants. Certainly, Judaism is not a faith in so far as it does not proceed as if God were one whose existence could be disproved. But it does have trust, *emunah* (sometimes weakly translated as 'faith'), in God. God answered Moses' 'Oh, let me behold Your Presence!' with the words: 'you will see My back, but My face must not be seen' (Ex. 33: 23). But in Auschwitz to have seen only God's back as it receded into the distance was to see God walking away from suffering because only the face turned to the other acknowledges the desperate need of the other. In Auschwitz, to have seen only God's back was no longer to witness a God whose power and glory is too mighty to behold, it was to see a God whose humiliation and sorrow was such that he could not face us; could not bear the sight of us.

Presence, absence and gender

Terhri Utriainen's anthropological study of female presence and the dying found that her research subjects needed no more than for the other to be *there*. Presence is the key to a good death. *In extremis*, passive presence (rather than the efforts of doctors or other skilled practitioners) covers the spiritual and material nudity of death and dying. This mode of being and holding is a significant part of the

practice and iconography of mothering for the mother is a liminal figure mediating both life and death. Women take care of the intimate processes of dying and
death where men, at a distance, govern the rituals that publicly sanctify death.[48]
Of course, in the camps it was a matter of the dying caring for the dying. The
dying were not watched over in grieving tranquillity from the bedside. But the
point remains that the trope of divine hiddenness from suffering may fail to
engage women's experience of holocaustal (or any other) death. Women would be
more likely to postulate the presence of God over and above God's power over life
and death. As the memoir literature repeatedly testifies, it was only the presence of
a caring other (herself in acute need of care) who made the living/dying (only
just) survivable.

The problem with theologies dependent on the trope of hiddenness is that while
there is only one God, there is more than one model of God. By nature of their
attributions, some of these conceptual models allow God's presence to withstand
Auschwitz and others do not. For example, contrary to those who believe him to
have turned his face, the excessively patriarchal god called God could have been – as
numen – very much present in Auschwitz. In that apocalyptical place of fire and
smoke, of terror and ultimacy, of the *tremendum*, where the Bible's most severe
prophetic warnings of desolation and abomination were realized, the patriarchal
God was indeed almost at home. Auschwitz was *his place* in so far as the conditions
of numinous horror were graphic illustrations of his threats to bring punitive disaster
upon the House of Israel. But this (sometimes, not always) vindictive, savage God of
Joshua whose conquest drives all before him, is but a scarecrow, a paper tiger, a
Wizard of Oz. This God of smoke and consuming fire before whom all but his
technicians cower is merely one aspect of an idolatrous projection of patriarchal
hubris, cast in the likeness of its own aspiration.

The tradition also proposes very different non-anthropomorphic models of
God and, by contrast, these would be too transcendental in form and quality for
him to make any incursion into history. Traditional Jewish philosophy – which in
its negative theological turn refuses to allow anything to be predicated to God
except his (at least grammatical) masculinity – would be loath to countenance the
possibility of divine presence within the conditions of finitude. The God of Jewish
philosophical theology whom George Steiner refers to as an 'unbearable',
'immeasurable absence', 'blank as the desert air',[49] has not given much ground for
hoping that he will take his suffering people to his bosom. He is already absent
and silent. The God of Jewish philosophers is one who,

> despite happy anthropomorphisms and intimacies, is construed as a God of
> immense distance and immaculate isolation, without qualities drafted from
> the observation of nature, bereft of any attributes of diminution or constraint,
> without limit or condition, without temporality and affect. A supreme and
> awesome integer of abstract grandeur and magnificence is our God.[50]

But this metaphysical diremption of God and world is far from the whole of
Jewish theology. Most believing Jews have devoted their lives to making the world

fit for the divine presence and many have espoused a prophetic theology where Jewishness is above all expressed in a commitment to social justice. Moreover, not all Judaism is as aniconic as its more austerely philosophical practitioners would intend it to be. While the impassible God is a legacy of medieval Jewish anti-anthropomorphism and the negative theologies that drove an ontological wedge between divine and humanity, Jewish tradition has always enjoyed a bipolar theology where God is at once supra-personal and transcendent and personal and immanent in the world. So that, in tension with the wholly inaccessible God 'without temporality and affect', is what Cohen calls 'the incarnate God of study': a guardian and participant of Jewish learning and halakhic argumentation. This God, he claims, was destroyed by the Holocaust, leaving only 'the extreme monopolarity of Jewish theism'.[51]

This is not quite right. God's intimate presence is not only accessible to learned men and the conditions of God's presence were not destroyed by the Holocaust. To the contrary, as we shall see in later chapters of the present study, the conditions by which Cohen's 'incarnate God' could be present were maintained by women's relational labours that are themselves a part of Jewish history and therefore of the tradition. It was the 'supreme and awesome integer of abstract grandeur and magnificence' who disappeared during the Holocaust because he never could have appeared.[52] That God's inaction or hiddenness in the Holocaust was not so much a sign of his betrayal as a sign of his non-existence, though his non-intervention was such as to make little or no practical difference whether he existed at all.[53]

I want to suggest that if God is one who abandons us and is silent in the face of our suffering (as in Ps. 22: 2–3) there can be little to experientially distinguish this God's silence from his non-existence. God's silence in Auschwitz was the silence of an omnipotent God-king who was never there in the first place, but was one who reigned in the minds of those who required divine sanction for their own hierarchical rule. He was not hidden in Auschwitz; he was simply deposed and, abjected, had fallen from view. The Psalmist cries out that God has turned his face from him and he is 'numbered with those go down into the Pit'; he is 'abandoned among the dead, like bodies in the grave of whom [God is] mindful no more' (Ps. 88: 5–7). In Auschwitz, the patriarchal God was numbered with those in the pit for in those 'darkest places, in the depths' evoked by the Psalmist, God's patriarchal face disappeared and his power was extinguished. But the metapatriarchal God was also, differently, numbered with those in the pit for she never left their side. What is perceived as divine absence may, then, approximate more closely the displacement of a particular model of God which, being only fictive, had only fictive power. Robert Jan van Pelt, the Dutch architectural historian, once referred to 'the singular, numinous and kerygmatic reality of Auschwitz'.[54] Could the kerygma of Auschwitz proclaim the disgrace, dispossession and exile of God by patriarchy itself?

Theological discourse on Auschwitz turns on the presence or absence, silence or speaking of God, but I have indicated that the meaning of these turn on whose God and which God we are speaking of.[55] Gender difference in women's and men's experience of Judaism may produce difference in the way they construe the characteristic dialectic of God's presence/absence on which post-Holocaust theology turns. The history of Jewish marital relationships (on which Israel's relationship with God has been so often modelled) could, for example, suggest that women may have had lower expectations of a divine interventionary presence during the Holocaust period than men. In pre-war Eastern Europe in particular, Orthodox Jewish life was homosocial in character. There were large numbers of men who, freed by their wives or parents-in-law from economic responsibilities in order to pursue their religious studies, would 'abandon' their families on a daily basis, sitting in the bath and study houses, discussing matters of religious and political interest for most of the day and long into the night. Such husbands might often spend long periods with their Rebbe, often at some distance from their wives and children.[56] A form of masculine desertion, then, was already integral to many Jewish women's lives.

Without dismissing the strengths and virtues of Jewish marriage, it is possible that during the Holocaust many Jewish women would have perceived God's apparent desertion and punishment for unknown sins differently to men. Perhaps the hurt was less. They were used to coping without male presence and were sometimes familiar with male violence. The assumption of the masculinity of God had further acclimatized them to experiencing him at one remove. In the creation story in which woman was fashioned by God from the body of man and then given back to him as a gift (Gen. 2: 18–24),[57] the almost ineradicable marks of gendered separation and subordination Judaism bears had been, from the very beginning, cosmologically inscribed.

Some women's sense of exclusion from the immediate presence of God was also already affected by their exemption-turned-exclusion from the study of Torah. Orthodox women of the Holocaust period would not have enjoyed the same sort of proximity to and intimacy with the male God of the Torah as would have the men who daily communed with him in study and prayer. Conversely, boys' achievement of spiritual maturity in *cheders* and seminaries at the expense of separation and ever greater distance from maternal care could have contributed to some Jewish men's sense of God's presence in the camps and ghettos as a disciplinary power not entirely discontinuous with that exercised by those administering (often punitively) the childhood religious education of the period.[58]

That women may have a sense of living to the side of divine presence; of living with male attention trained elsewhere, is not uncommon in female Orthodox circles today. As one woman tellingly remarked in a discussion group: 'You see I'm very happy with the woman's role in the home. I don't need the spiritual side, but I'm very lucky that I haven't had a crisis when I've needed to turn to God.'[59] If experience of God's presence/absence is gendered, who, in the holocaustal situation, is hiding who from whom? If the face of the monarchical God was turned from Israel, might the face of an-Other God have been turned towards it, even if it were one Israel could not recognize? Rabbi Barukh of Mezibizh told that God hides himself, but no one wants to seek him. Similar could be said of God-She.[60]

Israel, present to God

There has been too much asking '*where* was God in Auschwitz?' and not enough '*who* was God in Auschwitz?' An answer to the second question is also an answer to the first. Jewish feminism has been asking 'who is God?' for several decades and much of the movement wants to name the God of their experience Shekhinah.[61] The Shekhinah traditionally marks Judaism's faith in God's immanence. As the attribute of presence, Shekhinah's does not make God identical with the world. God's transcendence ensures that the divine will and purpose are unconditioned by human evil, while God's immanence ensures that humanity can become God's partner (*shuttaf*) in bringing God's purposes to fulfilment in the immanent realm.[62] Wyschogrod is right that 'if there is no need for sacrament in Judaism, it is because the people of Israel in whose flesh the presence of God makes itself felt in the world becomes the sacrament'. Without in any sense deifying Israel, it can be said that it is 'the collective existence of the Jewish people that is the dwelling place of Hashem'.[63] If, wherever they may be, the people of Israel are presentative of God we can begin to see that God is not only or even predominantly a God who conceals God-self.

The Shekhinah is a manifestation of God defined by her presentness. While the conditions in Auschwitz were wholly non-ordinary, God-She may have been so 'ordinarily' present among women whose personhood was getting ever less perceptible that she was herself imperceptible. But that is not to say that she had deliberately hidden *herself*. If she seemed hidden it was by virtue of the non-numinousness of the medium of her presence, the depth of evil into which she was plunged, and her very soft tread. It may then be the case that God's presence in the camps was hidden only in that it was not ordinarily perceptible. In a religious feminist context the phrase *hester panim* could connote not so much the hiding of the face as its disguise, and one which brought God deep into the broken heart of Auschwitz. She remained among us, perhaps unknown and unknowable, but not hidden. (Much as in the women's camp at Auschwitz-Birkenau when one of Charlotte Delbo's friends has pulled her safely from the flailing clubs and lashes of the SS, Delbo is asked '"Who were you with?" "With me, we were together,"' interjects Yvonne. Delbo says, '"She had never stopped being by my side. I had not seen her."'[64])

While some women had to turn their face from others' suffering because they were too horrified to watch or too exhausted and numbed by their powerlessness to stop it,[65] Shekhinah did not hide her face, they – the desecrators – hid her face just as they hid women's behind the accretion of filth that was integral to the holocaustal assault. But even from the pit, among the dead of whom the patriarchal God seemed mindful no more, she could still see and hear Israel because she loves and knows Israel like a mother loves and knows her children from near and far; she is, as parents are, moved by their affliction to the point where she would willingly suffer it for them. God was among us, not as us, but as the figure of our assembly. The Shekhinah indicates the real presence of a suffering God but, not herself a person, is not a quasi-Christian incarnation of God crucified in

Auschwitz.[66] Jürgen Moltmann, in a Christian depiction that is close but not identical to this one, characterizes the Shekhinah or the spirit of God as one who 'wanders with Israel through the dust of the streets and hangs on the gallows of Auschwitz'.[67] In Jewish understanding, the suffering of the Shekhinah is that of one who, being among us, suffers with us, but does not suffer vicariously *for* us.

The argument, then, is this: that the divine presence *is* the assembly of Israel. And in that the assembly of Israel was there and no longer there God's presence was continuous with her absence. The face of Shekhinah was hidden only in so far as the Jewish faces that imaged her were de-faced by their profanation; burned and dispersed as ash. In so far as God had been turned away because Jewry had been turned away by Christian Europe, God could not see us and if God could not see us, still less could we see God. Yet in women's care for the other – emblematized in the wiping of filth from a face – God's face was revealed as present and visible to the eye of spiritual perception in the facing image. But this is a God whose face is *already* partially hidden, not because she chooses to withdraw for the sake of our freedom, but because the full revelation of the Jewish God whose oneness makes God both masculine *and* feminine in character – not half a God – has been eclipsed by the masculinization of theology and worship. This God has been profaned twice over: by the profanization of the female face in Auschwitz and by the profanization of her own face – that aspect of God that has been set outside the precincts of the holy for most of Jewish history.

If God is, as it were, completed by the creation of humanity in God's image and restored by the human recreation of humanity in God's image, perhaps, for some, it was less a question of how God might have been present to Jewry in the Holocaust, but how Jewry might have been present to God. Etty Hillesum, aware of the dangers of what she calls 'heroic illusions', writes in the midst of catastrophe:'I shall merely try to help God as best I can and if I succeed in doing that, then I shall be of use to others as well.' On another occasion she writes, 'And if God does not help me to go on, then I shall have to help God'.[68] Hillesum is as much present to God as God, through the reciprocities of love and service, is present to her. It is she who, close to her end, reassures God with the words, 'believe me, I shall always labour for You and remain faithful to You and I shall never drive You from my presence'.[69] Buber also regards God's fate as a human responsibility. We must offer ourselves to God as his 'helpers and companions'. Buber addresses his reader: 'Don't you know also that God needs you, in the fullness of his eternity, you? How would man exist if God did not need him, and how would you exist?'[70] There is an old and fragile narrative thread running through the tradition of a God whose heart will break if we do not mend it; if we do not take some of God's burden from him. If a non-omnipotent God weeps for his exiled children (Berakhot 59a), how can we *not* comfort God? Later Jewish mysticism is founded upon doctrines of creation and redemption where at creation God empties God-self of God so as to enter into a relationship with the world which will not absorb it into the totality of Godhead. And this God's creation will only be redeemed by the mutuality of divine and human labour; the world is mended not solely from above but also from below.

In so far as God is made present as much by our beckoning as by the initiative of God, the theme of hiddenness may not be entirely dispensable. In this sense post-Holocaust theology is right in observing that the conditions of presence and absence in Auschwitz must have coexisted in dialectical relation to one another. If the theme of God's apparent absence is to be of assistance to a feminist theology it may be more fruitful to look to narratives of divine hiddenness other than those of scripture where it is at worst a punishment and at best distressingly inexplicable.

In particular, the Ashkenazic legend of the *Lamedvovnik* or Just Man suggests a preferable model of divine presence-in-absence than that of Berkovits', admittedly more distinguished, scriptural theology.[71] The Jewish legend of the *Lamed Vav Zaddikim* or Thirty-Six Hidden Saints tells of the Just Men concealed in every generation upon whom the fate of the world depends. Without their shouldering the terrible burden of human suffering God's tears would drown the world.[72] Among one of them might be the Messiah but he is unknown and unrevealed because the people are not worthy to recognize him. Some Just Men are not even aware of their being of the chosen Thirty-Six. Often held in contempt, these men live without honour in humble anonymity; the essence of their saintliness lies precisely in such. Mysteriously, silently, appearing and disappearing, they journey through the shtetls of European Jewry, painfully singled out to see the face of God; to receive the Divine Presence. They disappear so that God can appear.

Mystical Judaism has seen God in the unassuming disguise of the Just Man. Like the *zaddik* (holy man) who, disguised as a humble pretzel seller, cured the blind daughter of a hasid of the Rabbi of Rizhyn,[73] the Just Man's secret care for the sick is a miracle of modest piety. Such stories will raise a wry smile among women. Since they are expected to conform to the codes of feminine modesty, their care for others is not a particular sign of the holy; it does not have to be carried out in secret; it is merely normal, public and assumed. Humility and anonymity are prerequisite for ordinary virtue in a woman but supererogatory, indeed, redemptive, virtues in a man. Orthodox women, then, can hardly assume the redemptive role of the Hasidic *nistar* or hidden saint when their discursive and religious 'hiddenness' is that of required modesty or, in effect, their erasure from the public religious sphere.

While the discursive and religio-social hiddenness of Orthodox women can be an affront to their intellectual and spiritual abilities, female hiddenness may bear different theological meaning in the holocaustal situation. For here God-She may have been known in, and her grief carried by, the many anonymous female 'saints' described in the memoir literature who appear and disappear on their own short journey of erasure through Auschwitz and the other camps and ghettos of the Holocaust.

I have asked elsewhere whether Jewish tradition has made a Just Man of God by hiding the female face of God behind the male face of God and in doing so left God's female aspect nameless.[74] God too is cast out, like the *Lamedvovnik* she wanders through Jewish history, all the while secretly sustaining the world by her care. And it is not only God, but the women created in her image who are, as it were, the other Just 'Men'; the hidden of the hidden. For in the shtetls, it was they, not men, who lived in ill-educated anonymity by virtue of their sex, not just their class. Women enjoyed none of the public honours of the religious life; as women their domestic and mercantile labours went on unremarked and screened off from the world of public religious devotion. Yet as we shall see in the following chapters of this book, from a post-Holocaust perspective, their labours, like that of the Just Men, carried the world through Auschwitz, redeeming it from chaos, and, declaring a Sabbath on its grinding cycle of destruction, returned to the world a sense of the renewed, cleaned dimension of its creation.

Contrary to the received view that the Jewish God is unrepresentable, God's face is visible and his love figurable as it passes across the face of the Just Man or (non-traditionally) Just Woman. Her modest care tells us something else about what is beloved of God and about the locus of Jewish revelation, namely that revelation may sometimes consist precisely in what is unrevealed, unnoticed and intellectually despised. If the Jewish God has long been a humble God of care got up in the heavy robes of monarchical patriarchy, then, stripped of its office, the under-face of this Other God may be revealed in the faces of women who, in every generation, have laboured to bear the exiled Shekhinah to wherever their exile has taken them, including the death and concentration camps. Here, without the supernatural finery of omnipotence, God can only do her restorative work in and with those whose care – even unknowingly – invokes, meets and labours alongside her.

In Bergen-Belsen, in the first months of 1945, Bertha Ferderber-Salz remembers listening to an old Hungarian woman softly intoning a Sabbath prayer as she lay in utter dereliction in the darkness and stench of a filth-sodden bunk. The dying woman then wished Ferderber-Salz '"A good week! A good week to you, to the family, and to all the House of Israel. Amen!"' When asked if she had been praying, the old woman replied 'in a weak, barely audible voice', '"It is our duty to praise God at all times and in every place. God hears our prayers even when they are said from the deepest pit. And even if He does not come to our aid, there are other Jews in the world for whom we should request a good week."'[75]

Had Ferderber-Salz not recorded this Just Woman's words in her memoir no one would ever know of that moment of God's hearing, at the bottom of 'the deepest pit' where she lay dying among the dying (compare again Psalm 88). The old woman's prayer was not for God to intervene on her own behalf and she does not decry her abandonment by God. She affirms her own and God's love of Israel. God's hearing in the pit allowed the woman to die celebrating and mediating the obligations of a divine love upon which she made no personal demand. It may even be that the prostrate God *could not* come to our aid and the old woman blesses Israel in God's stead.

Giuliana Tedeschi's memoir yields another such female hierophany (though she would not describe it as such). One night in Auschwitz, in a 'state of spiritual prostration an overwhelming desperation' took hold of Tedeschi. Cast out as a punishment from the barrack block into the freezing night wearing only a thin sleeveless night-shirt, in physical pain, her human dignity violated, forcibly separated from her husband and children, and with the flaming crematoria before her, she had never before had 'such a strong feeling of being a grain of sand alone in the universe'. Prostrate on the freezing ground she wept. It was then that she felt two hands lay a garment around her shoulders:

> I recognized her in the glow from the flame. A Frenchwoman, quite old, who worked in the *Schuhkommando* [mending shoes], one of those dull creatures, without life or intelligence, who in normal circumstances barely manage to get by, and who in the camps seemed mad and moronic. I threw my arms around the neck of this companion in punishment, while to console me she whispered: '*Ça va finir, mon petit, ça va finir; bientôt!*'[76]

Both of these narratives owe something to the European tradition of wise women: crones who, bent over by age, appear on the path from nowhere to guide and protect the good who are lost in the metaphorical forest. Of course the 'crones' recalled by Ferderber-Salz and Tedeschi are themselves the objects of Nazi fury and can protect no one. Abjection is not the condition of spiritual and ethical virtue. But while their protection is not deliverance, it is protection of a kind. I am reminded of a now almost iconic nameless old woman with 'hair white as snow' who is remembered for holding in her arms a motherless 1-year-old child as she stood at the edge of the communal pit, about to be shot with the rest of her village by Nazi troops. The old woman sang to the child and tickled him under the chin until he laughed with joy. Then they were shot.[77]

These women's (disappearing) faces bear traces of the female face of God, dimly glowing as when the face of the moon is eclipsed by passing clouds in the night sky. And when there was no one at all, inanimate natural objects could take on the functions of divine presence for women. Victor Frankl remembers a young woman in Auschwitz who, as she lay dying, told Frankl (who at first thought she was hallucinating) that she could see one almost bare branch of a chestnut tree from the window of her block. There were two blossoms on the branch. The girl told Frankl that the tree was the only friend she had in her loneliness and that she often talked to it. When asked by Frankl if the tree replied she answered, 'It said to me, "I am here – I am here – I am life, eternal life."'[78] If God has chosen Israel as God's vehicle of self revelation then the suffering of Israel must tell us something about the nature and posture of God's presence among us. It may seem little more than a tree stripped of its leaves by an untempered wind.

3   Feminist intimations of the holy in Auschwitz

And let them make Me a sanctuary, that I may dwell among them.

(Ex. 25: 8)

The covenantal sanctification of Auschwitz

There are those who would regard the conjunction of the words holy and Auschwitz as blaspheming against both Auschwitz's victims and their God, especially when conjoined on behalf of, rather than by, the victims. Yet it is surely possible to suggest, as will this chapter, that Jews could establish sacred space and time within Auschwitz without claiming that Auschwitz – a palpably demonic institution – was itself holy, a place appointed by God for the exercise of God's will and purpose.

Even were that qualification to be granted, I open this chapter conscious that its framing is not unproblematic. Religious feminists have been sharply critical of the binary dualisms that have established a hierarchy of values and experience, producing contempt of things natural (read female) as profane, and reverence for things transcendental to or abstracted from nature (read male) as sacred or holy. Religious feminism is distrustful of the grading or distinction of the holy and the profane, claiming that it has sanctioned injustice against women and the God whose image they bear and a religious choreography which is inimical to female social environments and the relational spirituality characteristic of these.[1] Although the Jewish concept of holiness is not notably ascetic in character, there is little doubt that the will to holiness has often entailed a struggle against the natural inclinations and passions that has not favoured Jewish women.[2] Drorah Setel, advocating a feminist Judaism centred in relational connection, intimacy and diversity within a communal unity, has identified the 'obsolete' separative, hierarchical dualism of the Jewish concept of holiness as a principal locus of contention between Jewish feminism and the patriarchal tradition.[3]

Bearing these points in mind, this chapter finds that the Levitical command that Israel 'must distinguish between the sacred and the profane, and between the clean and the unclean' (Lev. 10: 10) entails separation from profane historico-political forces that are destructive of the identity and integrity that are a precondition of relationship. It is precisely the separation of the holy and the profane that will, finally, make that distinction redundant. Women's relationships with one another could set themselves apart from Auschwitz while still inside it; they could 'wash' Auschwitz from themselves in ways that were presentative of divine presence and that are generally overlooked by androcentric religious and historical studies of the Holocaust. Women's acts of care for bodies – washing, holding and covering them – were acts of separative purification that not only fulfilled Israel's covenantal obligation to make the world fit for divine presence, but also, and more immediately, separated women from the engulfing profanation that was Auschwitz itself. These purificatory practices belong traditionally, but not exclusively, to female gender performance and correlate with the traditional as well as feminist Jewish account of the maternal work of Shekhinah – the female figure of the indwelling presence of God.

It is doubtful that Judaism is as spiritually reliant on women's domestic labour as Orthodox apologists claim it to be.[4] But in the *holocaustal* situation, care for the personhood of self and others was a *mysterium tremendum*. Care revealed the likeness of God's personality that Auschwitz corroded and erased and it (re)covered the body from the gross rigours and indignities of its regime. Female care was a sign of an order of value that is known in the immanent realm but is other or transcendent in quality and origin. In which case, the particularities of Auschwitz seem to me to precisely demand a dual ordering of the world. Duality, but not dualism, is a necessary element of any theology of Auschwitz because Auschwitz's profanization of the world made the world unfit for divine presence. To refuse Auschwitz is to resist the radical pollution of its accommodation in the world which, as God's creation, is holy. Israel, set aside by God as a holy people, makes the world fit for God's presence by virtue of being Israel and by virtue of its religio-ethical labour. Therefore Israel is already situated eternally over and against Auschwitz, as the holy is to the demonic.

As we shall see, the memoir literature demonstrates that women in Auschwitz – Jewish and non-Jewish – resisted their degradation by gestural and notional washing. From a post-Holocaust Jewish perspective such acts re-established, even momentarily, the sphere of the holy, so that the covenantal obligations of Israel were being honoured and Auschwitz remained fit for, and indeed invited, God's presence. Two key theological points inform this argument. First, Abraham Joshua Heschel insists that the immanent presence of God is dependent on human partnership with God: 'The presence is not one reality and the sacred deed another; the sacred deed is the divine in disguise.'[5] Second, Emmanuel Levinas has argued that God is revealed 'discretely' only as 'Trace' discernible in the face-to-face interhuman relation: that confrontation with the other that is a fundamentally ethical moment revealing the holiness of the face as that singularity which must not be harmed.[6] Now the face is a traditional metonym for divine presence in Jewish theology and in its human form, the presentative image of God. So if Levinas and Heschel are right, it can be argued that the cleansing of the body – especially the face – is a restoration of the obscured face of God; for the sake of God as a means by which God can behold God in the world, and for the sake of humanity as a revelation of God as an accompanying God whose nature may not be to quasi-magically alter our historical conditions, but who does not abandon us.

In Leviticus Moses speaks to Aaron of the God who had told him 'Through those near to Me I show Myself Holy, and gain glory before all the people' (Lev. 10: 3) (sometimes translated as 'Through those near to me I shall make Myself holy'). In Auschwitz, God's glory was so diminished as to barely illuminate the begrimed Jewish face. The darkness of Auschwitz was therefore experienced as a sign of the withdrawal of God. At this moment God and Israel were in equal need of redemption from the pit. God could hardly find her way through the darkness – but the darkness was not her disappearance. However momentarily, the spark generated between the seeing and seen face was analogous to a Sabbath candle inviting God's presence – Shekhinah – into Auschwitz. Even the most infinitesimal spark of light was enough to illuminate – if only momentarily – the grey face of the other and so refract God into the toppling world.

The idea of covenantal sanctification is indispensable, then, to a theology of divine holocaustal presence. For the intimation of the holy in human communities is a signal and manifestation of the presence of God in the world: Judaism's very purpose. As Arthur Cohen has put it, 'The Holy is not simply a cognomen for God . . . The Holy is the dimension of God's presence; the presentness of God is his holiness'.[7] This chapter will argue that it seems possible to discern a causal relationship between the holiness of women's relational acts in Auschwitz and God's self-manifestation or presence. Buber helps us to understand this causal relation. In his Preface to the 1923 edition of *On Judaism*, he wrote: 'We ought to understand that to "realize God" means to prepare the world for God, as a place for His reality – to help the world become God-real (*gottwirklich*)'.[8] Likewise, in the attempt to resist their degradation by the notional cleansing of the face and body, Jewish women prepared the world for God, even in Auschwitz.[9] The trace of God would be visible in the 'clean(ed)' human face; it would be knowable in the dim reflection of her image so that the redemptive process of divine/human (re)union could be sustained. For to clean the self and the other is a sign and medium of welcome: a readiness to receive the other – human and divine – into the ambit of one's obligation.

The presence of Israel and God to one another is mutually redemptive, but it is a presence whose blessing consists not in miraculous saving interventions but in its own reward of having done that which Jews were covenanted to do, namely to mediate the blessing of God's love, justice and beauty to God's creation and to experience its effect. God's ineffable presence should not be merely instrumental to the human purpose. But should it be asked why humanity should seek the presence of God, a minimal answer is that a world that is fit for God will be abundantly fit for human beings. In other words, God's willing us to sanctify her world is her willing that we should be blessed; the holiness of the world is intended by God to be a gift to humanity at the same time as it is our gift to her. Because God is definitively holy, her personality defines the love, justice, peace and beauty by which the holy is intimated in the world. The moral, spiritual and material cleanness of relationships are the ethical and aesthetic means by which the conditions of God's presence are preserved. On these grounds, we can intimate the holy in Auschwitz wherever, and however tenuously, these relational values and practices were enacted for the sake of human dignity and therefore (intentionally or otherwise) for the sake of God in whose image the dignity of persons is founded.

This is an essentially ethical approach to the separative production of holiness which is embedded in biblical and rabbinic tradition. It is not to reduce Judaism to ethics in a manner typical of the nineteenth-century Reform movement to argue as Buber does that Jewish holiness consists in 'true community with God and true community with human beings, both in one'.[10] Irving Greenberg's view that the urgent command rising out of Sinai and now out of Auschwitz is for humanity to be active partners in the covenantal relationship and honour the image of God in the human face,[11] prompts my suggestion that it is in so far as the relationality of home and family was sustained in Auschwitz (as it was in the groups of mutually supportive, quasi-familial camp sisters that we shall return to in the next chapter)[12] that we can call Auschwitz-Birkenau holy without blaspheming against the dead. For one woman, not debilitated to the point of absolute incapacity, to care for another with deeds of loving kindness (*hesed*) was to perform what Rabbi Yitzak Nissenbaum (following Maimonides) called at the time *kiddush ha' hayim* – the sanctification of God's name in everyday life rather than in death. (Hannah Senesh makes much the same point in her diary on 23 April 1941).[13] Not suspended by Auschwitz, this is the Jewish obligation to the God who says to Israel: 'You shall not profane My holy name, that I may be sanctified in the midst of the Israelite people – I the Lord who sanctify you' (Lev. 22: 32). If Jews could observe no other particular commandment they could still seek to honour, in whatever and however notional a way, their foundational covenantal obligation to God to be holy as God is holy. And in doing so, they fulfilled God's creative purpose which was to have made humanity in such a way as to assume God's own image (Gen. 1: 27).[14]

Auschwitz-Birkenau has been defined as a city intending to 'negate the intelligibility of meaning, orientation and personhood, the basic properties of the design of the ancient city'.[15] Within the boundaries of the camp the extraordinarily horrific quickly passed into the ordinary to which many gradually became accustomed. Sara Nomberg-Przytyk, for example, soon became accustomed to stepping over corpses as if they were 'pieces of wood'.[16] Women, like men, who had been in Auschwitz for even a relatively short space of time became emotionally detached from the mounds of corpses around them.[17] There, in a place of disease and ceaseless destruction; where death and (the end of) life were at once arbitrary and rigidly controlled and often barely distinguishable, the separative possibilities of the holy were in every sense displaced. But it is precisely in Auschwitz's displacements of time and space – the customary coordinates of the holy – that both the flow and obstruction of God's presence in the world can now be mapped. Differently, for both victim and post-holocaustal witness, Auschwitz is a sign of what the world looks like – its utter moral and material dereliction – when God is damm/ned or turned back from the world by the demonic. But where the acts of its inmates invited God into Auschwitz, Auschwitz, as the sum of its victims, at least signalled towards the covenantal and redemptive possibility.

The profanization of women in Auschwitz

I am conscious that to use the terms 'profane' and 'profanization' (the process of making profane) to describe the nature and function of Auschwitz may appear to give a rather weak account of the Nazi assault. The profane need mean no more than the ordinary or non-sacral: that which has not been set apart. And yet if Auschwitz was a spectacle and experience of the most horrifying transgressions of the ordinary or customary,[18] what is under discussion here is not merely the non-cultic or a gradation of the freely available, but the active forces of destruction which theologians have traditionally referred to as the demonic. Nonetheless, I wish to describe Auschwitz as a profanization unto death because profanization was the means by which unchecked patriarchal power made all things available (that is, profane) for its own use, having forcibly removed them from the protected sphere of the holy. Here, the profane was, in its strongest sense, not merely equivalent to the secular, but both the quality and product of a kind of patriarchal domination that colonizes, breaks, spoils, wastes or uses up what is holy to God and appropriates it for the expansion of its own power and sphere of operation.

It has been instructive to read the Levitical injunctions to holiness alongside the Polish Catholic Pelagia Lewinska's account of her experiences of degradation in Auschwitz.[19] The (in all senses) repulsive character of these experiences suggested the phrase 'excremental assault' to Terrence Des Pres as a way of summarizing the Nazis' attempt to destroy the Jews even before their death and perhaps more comprehensively than by their death. For Berkovits, too, the Nazi crime commonly regarded by Jews as the 'most difficult to forgive or to forget' was their crime against the humanity of the Jews and their self-respect. In the camps and ghettos, and under the conditions of ban preceding these, 'whatever a human being ever cherished was degraded'.[20] This degradation was enabled by a history of virulent Christian anti-Semitism and anti-Judaism, but was, in this instance, instituted by racist ideology, not religious doctrine. However, Jews can and did understand that degradation on their own religious terms. When a soldier attempted to cut off an observant Jew's beard the Jew shouted at the soldier: '"Don't touch me with your defiled hands." He was shot.'[21] In 1947 Simha Elberg expressed his disgust at Germany's profanation of its own body with soap made from the bodies of Jewish children. Germans 'washed their . . . bodies with our souls': 'With how much "filth" must Hitler have "dirtied" the German people forever.'[22] Berkovits understands the Nazi profanation of Jewry non-politically as 'the deification of the diabolical; the religious befouling of all innocence'. Jews, he notes, understood the Nazi assault as that of '*Kohot ha Tumah*' – powerful forces of impurity.[23] The comprehensive profanization of Jewish men and women was a precise index to the perceptible reality of their holiness; why else would they have been so *excessively* defiled?[24] Religious Jews like Rabbi Mendele Alter of Pabianice thus construed their degradation at the time. As he went to the gas chambers at

Treblinka, he is reputed to have picked up the bleeding body of a baby lying on the ground and turned to those with him saying:

> This is holiness, purer than all purity, a Jewish child. . . . These 'defiled' ones, when they see a Jewish child in the arms of his mother are immediately filled with the urge to murder . . . the forces of *tumah*, demonic defilement, cannot endure the sight of holiness, the spirit of purity that hovers over the face of a Jewish child.[25]

The profanation of Jews in Auschwitz was not, of course, instantaneous; it was a process operative long before most Jews' arrival in the camp. It was intended that Aryan Europe should be 'protected' from contamination by the Jewish 'virus'. Many Jews had already suffered the imposition of an exclusionary ban on the whole of European Jewry. From the Nazi party's accession to power German Jews were refused access to cinemas, certain shops, park benches and so forth. Gradually, Jews under their rule began to simply disappear from sight by hiding, emigration, or incarceration in transit camps and ghettos. Frida Michelson describes how, after the Nazi occupation of Riga, 'Latvians – acquaintances, friends, neighbors – quit talking to us. When we met on the street, heads turned away.'[26] By imposing a form of quarantine, it was intended that European Jewry, isolated behind ghetto walls and electrified fences, would become so absolutely cut off from the sanctuaries of domestic and religious normalcy and so enclosed by its own squalor and disease, that Jews would be perceived, and might come to perceive themselves, as a danger to the racial health of European civilization.

One girl in a ghetto camp lamented the lack of facilities for washing and disposing of picked lice: 'we used to squeeze the lice with our clothes, which caused the latter to become damp and stick to our bodies.' Significantly, she adds, 'We literally lost the image of God.'[27] Reading history from a religious perspective, Nazi Germany seemed to have arrogated all of the patriarchal God's taxonomic power over his creation, but none of his mercy. It is customary to translate the Hebrew *kadosh* (holy) to mean that which is set apart; reversing the separative functions of the holy, what was once separated for its protection was now separated for its destruction. The Reich (exemplifying the demonic numinous) cut off Jewry (the truly holy nation) and set them apart for 'special treatment' (murder).[28] European Jewry was exposed to the absolute violence and power of the Nazi numen: the Aryan *Volk*. It was, in effect, 'cut off' from the protection of God and from European Christendom's sphere of moral duty and responsibility.[29]

Though Jewry was the defiled, not the defiling, occupied Europe was made to believe the reverse: that Jewry polluted its soil. Frida Michelson remembers a Nazi's horror at Jewish women performing forced labour in the fields outside Riga, shouting to their guard, '"Who dared bring those damn Jewesses here? They'll contaminate anything they touch!"'[30] As in the Riga ghetto, where Michelson remembers becoming of the untouchable caste permitted only to walk in the gutters and under curfew,[31] Jewry was made morally and physically invisible and Europe could not see its face. Where the Jew is made in the image of God, the holocaustal ban left no Jewish surface by which God could be made present to the world. God was blocked out of the world, leaving the world partitioned and available to the occupation of demonic power.

The train journey to the camps was the most rapid deportation of Jewry from the relative cleanness of normalcy into the profane. In the freight wagons, crammed with between seventy and eighty bodies, with one slop bucket, women who were still menstruating had no way of changing sanitary napkins and babies suffered the chafing of their dirty nappies – sometimes for several days on end. Little was to distress the 13-year-old Judith Jaegarmann more than seeing her respected father suffering an attack of diarrhoea on the overflowing slop bucket in the freight wagon transporting her family from Theresienstadt to Auschwitz in 1943.[32] Olga Lengyel remembers how 'the corpses that had been with us for days [in the freight wagon] were bloated hideously and in various stages of decomposition. The odors were so nauseating that thousands of flies had been attracted. They fed on the dead and attacked the living, tormenting us incessantly.'[33] It is understandable that, with a certain theological poignancy, Charlotte Delbo anointed herself with a phial of perfume as she entered Auschwitz, pouring it slowly between her breasts.[34]

Upon arrival in Auschwitz, women's bodies were marked for destruction. After receiving hopelessly mismatched rags, Lengyel remembers that 'to complete the style, the Germans had an arrow of red paint, two inches wide and two feet long, on the back of each garment. We were marked like pariahs.'[35] Once inside Auschwitz, the absence of sanitary facilities in the women's camp of fourteen thousand women was, as Pelagia Lewinska observed, a deliberate way of erasing the humanity of women; condemning them to die in and as excrement. (The one water tap was forbidden to Jewish women.) The absence of sanitary facilities was perceived by Lewinska as a deliberate means of condemning the women to,

> die in our own filth, to drown in mud, in our own excrement. They wished to abase us, to destroy our human dignity, to efface every vestige of humanity . . . to fill us with contempt towards ourselves and our fellows. Such was the PURPOSE, the IDEA behind it all! The Germans made a perfect job of it; they knew we were incapable of looking at each other without disgust.[36]

Charlotte Delbo was first able to make a (prohibited) attempt to wash herself in a freezing stream sixty-seven days after entering Auschwitz. As she took off her clothes she found that her toe nails had detached themselves from her toes and stuck to the insides of her stockings. Her pubic hair and underpants were 'stiff' with dry diarrhoea.[37] Also in Auschwitz, Kitty Hart's skin became 'a mixture of dark grey and red'. Colonies of lice overran every inch of her skin: 'my whole body was blotched with scabs and boils, especially on my legs, which oozed pus. After a while I ceased to notice that they hurt; I squeezed them out regularly, but they wouldn't heal, and the holes they left got bigger and bigger. We were rotting to a slow death.' Fleas also swarmed beneath her filthy clothes.[38] Livia Bitton-

Jackson (born Elli Friedmann), who was taken to Auschwitz with her mother, brother and aunt in 1944, describes how her face – unprotected from harsh sun and insects – blistered and cracked: a 'brownish discharge oozes from the cracks and forms large crusts around the edges. Our faces look ridiculous and repulsive.'[39] Lewinska also remembers how 'the women scratched at their wounds and the smell of unwashed bodies suffocated us'. There was nowhere to wash clothing and women could not often wash themselves with snow as this further chapped the skin.[40] In the women's camp two barracks were eventually turned into 'washrooms', as the guards had come to fear the inmates' contagious diseases, but most of the time these supplied no water at all. The 'evil-smelling' women who 'swarmed outside the building' went there mainly to find (foul and discoloured) water to drink, as without tooth-brushes, combs or soap, attention to personal hygiene often seemed futile and came second to thirst. Because the latrine could only be used at set times, women were compelled to evacuate into their clothes and drinking bowl. There was a total lack of lavatory paper. Inevitably, as Olga Lengyel recalls, it became 'a struggle to overcome the disgust we felt for our companions, and for ourselves'.[41]

Cleanliness can be a sign of and invitation to the holy, but it is not the holy itself. Were that so, Nazi Germany, kept meticulously clean by the Nazi *Hausfrau*, would also have been holy. To the contrary, where household cleanliness was intended to demonstrate Aryan genetic purity and vindicate its right to cleanse Europe of racial 'uncleanness', it was no more than an accessory to erasure in the guise of hygiene. Cleaning should restore its object, not make it disappear. Judaism 'washes' its environment in order to restore or maintain a fit, ordered space in which to conduct its relationship with God. In preserving the cleanness or translucency of the world to God, Judaism also maintains that of the relationships between persons. Yet the physical debilitation, agony, and very often death wrought by punishment in Auschwitz de-faced and dis-appeared the divine image in women. (Thus Hart: 'As long as numbers tallied, nobody cared about faces.')[42] Beating and flogging tore the surface of the flesh and covered it in blood. The female body was so systematically assaulted that the image of God in her face – an image already made difficult to discern by Jewish patriarchy – could be lost to view.[43] Other punishments inflicted a similar hiding of the face (the literal meaning of the Hebrew theological term *hester panim*). On one occasion Bertha Ferderber-Salz and other women were punished for an offence against camp regulations by being forced to lie down and roll in the mud for about half a kilometre to the edge of a field. Those who did not die from this torture returned to the camp 'humiliated and covered in mud and filth'.[44]

While the cinema commonly represents women in Auschwitz as grimy but interestingly pale and gaunt, the memoirs record that the surface of the body was partially concealed by mud and filth and opened by suppurating sores, boils, insect bites, sunburn, frostbite and beatings. The body was also internally polluted by contaminated food and the putrid water from ditches and puddles that women were compelled to drink by their desperate thirst.[45] Additional to the physical erasure of her face, the loss of each woman's name and its replacement by a number erased her personhood; her stench and visage further prohibited approach, touch, relationship and knowability.[46] The camp administration was using genocidal defilement to isolate and set each Jew apart for the destruction of body and identity. Although the next two chapters will relate how relationship could survive its physical and moral degradation in Auschwitz, the smell and sight of filth alienated persons from one another by keeping them from, in the full sense of the word, *seeing* one another.[47]

Not only was the female Jewish body defiled (sometimes sexually – a violation far less susceptible to a notional washing than the affliction of dirt),[48] Jewishness itself was fouled. Auschwitz not only prohibited the media of the holy, it also desecrated them. Some women, for example, were given pieces of *talles* (prayer shawl) to wear as underpants.[49] Others were given strips of fabric made of torn prayer shawls to hold on their ill-fitting shoes. By this means the symbols and possibilities of (male) prayer were trodden into the mud and, for those many who suffered uncontrollable diarrhoea, literally shat on.

To repeat, Nazism was a secular, racist ideology rather than an intentionally religious one. However, the Nazis were virtuosi in the production of the spectacle of quasi-numinous power and force. In Auschwitz, the over-powering will and force of the SS would have compelled in most a terrorized abjection, a feeling akin to what Rudolf Otto describes as 'numinous unworth'; that is, a 'feeling of absolute "profaneness"', a self-abasement or 'submergence into nothingness before an overpowering, absolute might'[50]; a consciousness of the racial 'sin' of being a Jew. As well as being referred to as *Figuren* – mere shapes – the word *Sheiss* or shit was the guards' common mode of address to Jews in Auschwitz. Corpses were referred to as '*Scheiss-Stücke*' (pieces of excrement).[51] Europe was to be purged of its racial 'impurity'; Auschwitz was to consume and void the Jew (of God). Where women were pushed and fell into an abyss of self- (and other) loathing, the face of God disappeared from view and the darkness closed over Auschwitz altogether.

Washing Auschwitz

Without underestimating the sheer force of the 'excremental assault' – indeed because of it – the purificatory acts of some women in Auschwitz can be read as attempts to maintain the reflective quality of the face: the mark of personhood, both human and divine. Although a woman looking relatively neat and clean could court ever more sadistic notice from those who might infer that the regime was evidently not harsh enough,[52] some women persisted in their acts of purification as a way of setting themselves and others apart from moral and material chaos. The Jewish doctor Lucie Adelsberger, for example, remembers Miriam the indefatigable 'Shitkapo' who, in Auschwitz, volunteered to labour from four in the morning until nine at night to rid the infirmary floor – 'an undulating open sewer' – of its pools of diarrhoea.[53] Sara Nomberg-Przytyk knew that 'it was important to wash, even if it meant rubbing your face with a fistful of snow. The effort to wash your face is an expression of life.' The Dutch women on the block of the *zugangen* (new arrivals) lacked the will to do this and many of them died almost immediately.[54] Other women survivors have testified to the need to keep as clean as was possible in the labour and concentration camps, futile and tokenistic as the attempt might have been.[55] Some washed in their own urine, believing it to have disinfectant properties.[56] Women would often wash utensils, hands and faces in the 'horribly foul' green sewer water in the ditch running the length of the barracks, aware that to do so would aggravate their condition rather than improve it. That women washed with ineffective cleaning agents like coffee, urine or sewer water may suggest that cleansing could not but become a gestural or ritual act.

Of course, not all women were strong enough to find the means to maintain an even notional bodily cleanliness. Starving, cold and 'fatigued past all human limits', it was not surprising that 'the need to maintain one's toilet [became] a secondary matter'.[57] But according to Lewinska and others, the attempt was not primarily or solely a matter of achieving physical cleanliness: 'For some of us it was something more, an act of will to show ourselves we could defy Auschwitz. It was our part in an act of protest which said: We will not let ourselves be broken!' Lewinska's cleaning of her footwear, 'each evening, half-dead', boosted her morale, however pointless an effort it may appear to have been.[58] In Auschwitz, any gesture towards the bodily well-being of self and other could keep women from descending into the blank-eyed, expressionless state of the '*Muselmänner*'[59] in whom the divine spark had been extinguished.

In Levinas' ethical theology, the sphere of the holy opens up from the vision of the face. The Nazi assault was that of the demonic profane desecrating the holy by closing or erasing the face. But so long as there was the will, if not the capacity, to open or restore the face then the possibility of God's presence – as a sign of the infinite worth of human presence – was not lost altogether. Lewinska makes an explicit link between the attempt to remain clean and to remain human. Even if she were to die it would be as a human being: 'I would hold on to my dignity. I was not going to become the contemptible, disgusting brute my enemy wished me to be.' Although women's constant, almost simian, lice-picking may have appeared to degrade them, it also demonstrated to Lewinska that 'these were mothers, wives, young girls, *human beings* struggling furiously to hold on to their dignity in the most monstrous conditions imaginable'.[60] Indeed, women's determination not see themselves and others as the SS saw them is a common refrain of the memoir literature.[61]

The longing for liberation was often identified with the longing to return home: the place where personhood had been cherished. Significantly, the return home, and as such, to a past and future life, was often symbolized (especially for urban, middle-class women) by the dream of hot, perfumed baths.[62] For Giuliana Tedeschi, life outside Auschwitz was defined by its cleanness: 'the smell of soap and lavender, of clean linen folded in cupboards. I can smell the freshness . . . the freshness of laundered sheets around the body.'[63] Just as a woman's ritual immersion in the sacred waters of the mikvah after the 'non-life' event of menstruation is not a cleansing from literal dirt but a cleansing which marks a rebirth: a willed separation between life and death,[64] that which brings a woman into 'immediate contact with the Source of life, purity, and holiness – with the God who surrounds her and is with her always',[65] so too women imagining washing and attempting to wash in Auschwitz may have been a sign of their willing life over the death that had polluted their bodily surface.[66] This is not to ignore Auschwitz's psychological pollution of memory, consciousness and hope, but to say that the rituals of the body (which is not separable from consciousness) are a way of engaging these.

Merely to touch another was to clean her of impurity by a gentle wiping. The Hebrew term *kipper* is often translated as the verb to atone or expiate, but is more precisely a synonym of *mahah*, to wipe away or *hesir*, remove. *Kipper* is also cognate with verbs for purification and decontamination and in Israelite ritual connotes a 'rubbing off' of impurity. A stroking touch to the cheek was a moment of at-one-ment that signified the worth and restored the standing of the other. Lucie Adelsberger recalls that women and children in the infirmary in the women's camp in Birkenau could be cheered by a little extra food, but 'often enough, all that was needed was a gentle stroke, a comforting word, a tiny token of affection'.[67] Similarly, on a work detail, Charlotte Delbo's friend Lulu lovingly pushed Delbo behind her so that she could cry: 'Lulu goes on working and stays on the look out at the same time. Occasionally she turns around and with her sleeve, softly wipes my face.'[68] Cleaning was often a gesture of love before it was a practical task. A promise to lift up another woman if she were to fall, as so many did, into the deep, fetid mud that surrounded the barrack blocks (no easy task given the physical weakness of the inmates) was 'the ultimate proof of devotion' to another.[69]

To be washed could be to be resurrected. Livia Bitton-Jackson remembers how, during a brief respite from Auschwitz in 1944, a forced labour factory in Augsberg provided her with clean white sheets on her bunk, soap, showers whose flow of water could be controlled, and clean towels. The experience was more than merely pleasurable, it was a restoration of the holy to self and world. Her joy is couched in the language of Jewish mystical theology: 'As we get out of the showers, a secret spark of self-esteem is nurtured deep within. It's a divine message. A promise of redemption.'[70] Similarly, of the (admittedly relatively privileged) conditions of the infirmary dormitory in Barrack 13 of the women's camp at Auschwitz, where there was a basin and scrubbing brush, Olga Lengyel writes:

> No spectacle was more comforting than that provided by the women when they undertook to cleanse themselves thoroughly in the evening. They passed the single scrubbing brush to one another with a firm determination to resist dirt and the lice. That was our only way of waging war against the parasites, against our jailers, and against every force that made us its victims.[71]

A profound emotional investment was made in the labour of establishing a boundary against the chaos of the profane. There were no chairs in that dormitory and if anyone came straight into it from the verminous filth of the infirmary and sat on the bunks of 'Dr. G.' and the dentist, 'these two intelligent women, who had probably been excellent housewives, sobbed like children.'[72]

It must be said, however, that Auschwitz was also and more commonly typified by those like the women of Block 25 who, too ill to work, were kept waiting for days on end without food, water, sanitation or proper ventilation, to be gassed. These women, in physical and emotional *extremis*, were carried beyond the sphere of sanctifying touch. Neither they nor God could be redeemed from the abyss of impurity into which the divine spark had been cast, or at least the time for its redemption had not yet come. Adelsberger's account of one of her medical colleagues who had contracted typhus fever with the complications of diarrhoea and phlebitis can be read as an instance where the abandonment of persons also marks the irretrievability of God. The woman's legs had swollen to the knee and she could not get quickly enough to the latrines. She was mocked by all the non-Jewish inmates working in the infirmary and 'beaten half to death. In the end she lay in her own excrement near the latrine, craving potatoes and vitamins that no one could bring her, until she, too, perished miserably.'[73] This infinitely suffering, nameless woman, lying beaten and dying in her own filth, represents the point at which the world has been so voided of the holy that both God and persons have passed out of the range of intra-historical redemption. Or again, when a woman struck by an epileptic fit, fell to the ground, Tedeschi remembers that 'no one goes to help her'. Even in recollection, her naked, contorted, anonymous body is described in words devoid of concern as 'something miserably obscene and gross.'[74] Left untouched, these women (the latter no more than a 'something') became literally untouchable; they were abandoned and exposed utterly and only to violence. God cannot be known where there is no one who will turn their face to hers. To posit God's presence as Shekhinah in Auschwitz has nothing to do with the doctrines of omnipotent omnipresence that have given comfort to patriarchal theology. Hers is a power of transformation contingent upon mutuality and responsibility and is therefore dependent upon the presence and absence of conditions on earth that invite or repel the divine; that look out for the divine and human other, or turn their backs on them.

Women's sanctification of Auschwitz

There is no doubt that the women's camp in Auschwitz-Birkenau was primarily characterized by chaos and cruelty and that this was systematically generated between, as well as against, Jewish women themselves. But there were also women who, not selected for immediate death, sought to preserve some vestige of their former lives as Jewish persons in community. By this I do not refer only to observant women who tried to adapt domestic practices governed by halakhah to the camp situation: who smuggled *siddurim* (prayer books) into Auschwitz, lit candles on the Sabbath from anything which would burn, or made *matzot* at Pesach almost from air, literally marvellous as such acts were.[75] My discussion is intended to be inclusive of the considerable religious, cultural, social and political diversity of Jewish women in Auschwitz and other death and concentration camps who tried to reconstitute some of the purificatory and relational functions of the (Jewish) home. Clearly, Jewish women who had medical skills, or who had otherwise 'risen' through the Auschwitz inmate hierarchy, were relatively privileged and better able to purify their space than others. Those who worked in the infirmary had better access, for example, to washing facilities than other women in Auschwitz and those who worked in the depots of *Kanada* had access to clean clothes.[76]

But mine is not a quantitative theology, contingent upon circumstance. It is a qualitative, ethical theology concerned with the practical restoration of persons as created images of the divine wherever and to whatever degree that obtained.[77] Wherever women gathered together in the mutually supportive pairs or groups which I will interpret as a form of sacred assembly, parts of the camp then constituted a morally separate enclosure whose even temporary boundaries marked women's fundamental opposition to the profanity of their situation, beset as they were by moral evil, filth, disease and death.[78]

It should become clear that this way of reading women survivors' memoirs is grounded in concepts and schemata inherent in Judaism itself. However, because women's experience has not been religiously normative, the historical evidence does not invite such a reading. Religio-historical studies have described how observant Jews (largely and normatively, male) heroically refused to surrender the means by which Israel could remain a holy nation, but on terms presented and defined by men and in honour of essentially masculine religious modes.[79] This substantial literature, whose content is by now an Orthodox metanarrative in itself, is an impressive testament to male religious resistance to profanization. In the camps, and at risk of punishment and death, men sometimes found ways to put on *tefillin* (phylacteries), hold the three daily services with prayers learnt by heart or written out by hand, observe the Sabbath and festivals, study Talmud through the recitation and analysis of passages from memory, improvise *yeshivot* or seminaries using the same means, and engage in Talmudic dispute as they trudged to, from, and sometimes during, slave labour. But it was Torah-educated men, not women, who

> lived in the nightmare kingdom as if it were just another day, patiently confronting the never-before-imagined questions and finding answers. May a father purchase his son's escape from the ovens, knowing that the quotas will be met and another child will die in his place? May a Jew in the Kovno ghetto recite the morning benediction, 'Blessed are you, O Lord, Who has not made me a slave?' May one pronounce the blessing over martyrdom over a death from which there is no escape? What blessing does one make before being turned to ashes?[80]

There is no doubt that observant Jewish men's determination to ask and answer the question of the holy and to maintain the marks and practices of holiness was an affirmation of the transcendental meaning of Jewish life. But it is unhistorical and theologically partial to read male (usually Orthodox) holocaustal observance as if it summarizes the essence of Judaism and the experience of the Jewish people as a whole.[81] Secular feminist historians of the Holocaust have long insisted that the genocide was not gender-blind and nor should be its historiography. It is also the case that theologically and phenomenologically, the subsumption of female into male experience ignores the role of gender in the production of holiness during the Holocaust.

In the camps, the masculine production of holiness consisted in awesome feats of spirit and memory that were the fruit of dedication to study over many years. The male 'wandering Jew' (as Christendom disparagingly referred to him) had formulated a Judaism that was adaptable to migration. Very early on, the Priestly writers made use of a desert theology of divine presence where God does not so much dwell on earth in a fixed sanctuary, but settles where the tent is carried. The poles are not to be removed from the ark of the covenant so that it is always in readiness to go (Ex. 25: 15). Masculine Judaism remained (de)portable because it sanctified the world in ways that were separable from the limitations of the immediate situation: it was spoken, textual and theoretical before it was practical (as when engaged in complex deliberations on the appointment and functioning of a Temple no longer standing). For Jewish men a form of sacred space would have been established wherever ten Jewish men were gathered for prayer. The Rabbi of Lublin's disciples used to say 'when we were with our holy seer, we were in a little sanctuary. We lacked nothing, and we did not feel the sadness of exile, nor the darkness that lies over all.'[82] For Hasidic men in the camps sacred space would likewise have been concentrated simply where the Rebbe was or, in his absence, where his teaching was propounded (the *hozer* was one who could recite the teachings of the Rebbe). Most significant of all to the present discussion, rabbinic Judaism has taught that wherever men are gathered around sacred texts the presence of the Shekhinah is summoned into their midst.[83]

While masculine sanctification of the holocaustal world was subject to the practical demands of prayer, study and dietary purity, it was also far more cerebral than that of women, consisting not in a vestigial domesticity or the remnants of familial relationship, but above all in words and arguments committed to memory. In a barrack block in Buchenwald a group of Hasidim established themselves on the fourth and highest tier of the planks that served as beds. The height of their bunk was intended to keep them apart from the squalor and noise so that they could pray and study without disturbance. Their bunks were known as the *tahara bretter* (the boards of purity)[84] and it was in such spaces that 'the map of the camp received the impact of a humanizing purpose'.[85] By such means, for Torah observant men, the camps and ghettos could be at once sites of demonic degradation and 'the holy of holies on this earth'.[86]

Leviticus 19: 1–2 reads, 'The Lord spoke to Moses, saying: Speak to the whole Israelite community and say to them: You shall be holy, for I, the Lord your God, am holy.' The Jerusalem Talmud (Kiddishin 1: 7) remembers that women as well as men are of this nation holy to God. But in post-cultic Judaism women are sanctified by the holiness of their home and marriage. The tradition predicates the Shekhinah or divine presence to the home as a place of relational peace (Sotah 17a) and the performance of the commandments.[87] Yet Nazi Germany had destroyed the Jewish home and the worlds of communal prayer, study and halakhic dispute had never been theirs.[88] Bereft of the female media of the Jewish holy, how were women to be holy as God commanded? Where Rabbi Mendele Alter of Pabianice died in Treblinka, reputedly preaching and practising the meaning of Jewish holiness even as he entered the gas chamber, how did or could women invite and reveal the presence of the holy? The rabbis have said that 'over one who uninterruptedly studies God's word . . . even the angel of death can win no victory.'[89] But how could women, who did not study God's word, have won any sort of victory over the Nazi angel of death?

Orthodoxy allocates the task of physical and spiritual care of the home and family to women. A significant part of that labour resides in observance of two areas of purity laws: those concerning menstruation and those concerning the preparation of fit or kosher food. It is also women's responsibility to pass a sense of Jewishness and rudimentary knowledge of Judaism on to their children – especially girls. Yet if the female practices of purity and separation were forbidden, irrelevant or materially impossible in the camps, then how might the distinctively female means of sanctifying the world have been transported into the women's camp at Auschwitz-Birkenau where the Jewish family had precisely ceased to exist. It is not that women were entirely bereft of extremely limited means to pray, light Sabbath candles and maintain a rudimentary dietary purity. But these means to sanctification were not ontological and embodied. Women could not, for example, wear on their bodies as a sign of resistance the 'signs and remembrances' of *tefillin* (phylacteries) (Ex. 13: 9) and *tzitziot* (fringed garments) (Num. 15: 37–41) that are laid upon the male body as a reminder to observe God's commandments and 'to be holy to their God.'[90] The marks of the holy – the beard and head-covering – that observant men in the ghettos often refused on pain of torture and death to remove from their face and head also signify gender differentiation in the production of the holy. The resistant male Jewish face could still wear the holy. (After a beating during which the Germans had sought to remove his hat, the Zabner Rebbe defiantly walked to the train that would take him to his death covering his head with both hands.) [91] Circumcision had left a mark of covenantal inclusion that could not be erased.[92] But by what sign would women resist the demonic and remember and bear in and on their bodies their Levitical vocation to be holy as God is holy?

To answer this question we need to use the Jewish concept of holiness to develop a (counter-)reading of the Orthodox ideology of female sanctity that already assumes difference in the fulfilment of women's covenantal obligations. The Jewish concept of holiness indicates that there is a necessary relationship between holiness and the ethical will. If it can be demonstrated that Jewish women's domestic labours are not only halakhically governed but are primarily acts of the practical ethical will whose religious symbolism and intentionality extends beyond the confines of the home then such labours could also sanctify Auschwitz. The ethical dimension of Jewish domesticity is particularly significant to the theological contemplation of Auschwitz, not despite, but because of, its prohibition of the ordinary exercise of Jewish will. Eliezer Berkovits (whose thinking is tinged by the existentialism of his period) rightly notes that holiness is 'not about Being but Becoming'. That is, 'the sacred is not, but has to be brought into being as the result of someone's action or behaviour . . . Israel is made holy by God and becomes holy by sanctifying itself.' Holiness is a this-worldly 'challenge to Israel, a task, a responsibility'.[93] But 'if a man will sanctify himself a little, God will sanctify him more and more' (Menahot 43b). Whatever little Jewry could do to restore holiness to the world from inside Auschwitz, God did more.

Holiness is not, then, a definitive characteristic of persons (such a claim would be idolatrous). For Jews the task of holiness is to come to image but not to imitate God; not to be hubristically 'like unto God' (Gen. 3; 5), but to model themselves on the divine attributes of compassion and loving kindness by acts of *avodah halev* ('service of the heart'), or *avodah begashmiut* (service to God through the conditions of everyday life). Despite the semi-ascetic values and practices sometimes connoted by holiness in Jewish discourse, a predominant tradition is one in which the notably this-worldly concerns of Judaism sanctify the profane by taking all of life into the sphere of the holy.[94] And ignoring, for a moment, the sexual discrimination in this division of labour,[95] this is as much a female task as it is a male one.

God's presence abides with Israel 'even in the midst of their uncleanness' (Lev. 16: 16). A text from Giulinana Tedeschi's memoir conveys something of this. She and others in her work detail were ordered to clear excrement from the latrines and carry it in a cart to the pit: 'the work was humiliating, yet from it we discovered a new sense of dignity. The girls' movements were coordinated and graceful, the expression on their faces proud and severe.'[96] This spectacle has nothing to do with the virtues and pieties of the *baleboosteh* or bourgeois Jewish housewife. Wherever women maintained the even notional purity of Israel before God by relationship or the cleaning that is a function of relationship, they sanctified Auschwitz and carried on Israel's covenantal task of making the world fit for the indwelling of God. Indeed, they did not merely continue that task, for their acts were powerful in precise proportion to the demonic power those acts resisted. Therefore while an impression of tremendous non-natural power was produced by the sheer dreadfulness of Auschwitz as a human institution, the truly numinous spectacle was not the horror of the flaming chimneys but the mysterium of human love that is stronger than death, the *tremendum* of its judgement upon demonic hate, and the *fascinans* of its calling God back into a world which had cast her out.

Although not all commandments have a spatial focus, in general, Jewish 'sacred space becomes such through the performance of God's word'.[97] It is God's word that Jews purify the world; set it apart from evil. So that wherever there was the service of the heart in a place dedicated to its opposite it purified the world of Auschwitz. The service of the heart established a separate, bounded, wholly/holy other space inside that of the bounded camp of Auschwitz and made that fit for God.

Because holiness is not a material property of things or persons, the question of women and the mediation of the holy in Auschwitz is not primarily an historical question, but a practical theological one. Israel is commanded to be a holy nation.[98] That the holiness of Israel consists in its being commanded to be 'a nation of priests' is the basis of my argument. Defining priesthood broadly as the mediation of the holy, the art of consecration, women in Auschwitz, as women, continued to fulfil Israel's covenantal mission to mediate God's presence to the world (Ex. 19: 6) when they sought to remove from their and others' faces and bodies the marks of the profane – the filth that the Nazis commanded them to bear. In so doing, they purified themselves in preparation for divine presence and as a revelation of that presence. For ultimately God's presence is re-membered not by dressing the body in halakhically prescribed fabrics or by the fashioning of facial hair, but by any will and act that honours the body. Women's loyalty to this quintessentially Jewish task of mediating God's presence would have consisted in a necessarily minimal form of religio-ethical action: in effect – if not always intention – their protecting and tending of the holy image of God in themselves and those suffering with them.

Much Jewish theology would want to frame the discussion rather more halakhically. As David Shapiro notes, it is above all the observance of law that allows 'man' (as he puts it) to achieve 'the goal for which he was created: the attainment of his Godlikeness – the unfolding within him of his divine image'.[99] But the study and practice of halakhah does not and cannot 'unfold' women's divine image because women are not positioned in relation to that discourse as speaking subjects, agents or decisors. In their status as objects of the law – 'silent recipients, outsiders to the process';[100] 'silent, absent from the Jewish construction of the universe and God'[101] – they are not normatively Jewish; a screen of patriarchal prohibitions, customs and exemptions from study, prayer and judgement has been interposed between women and the halakhic mirror onto God's will.

Yet it is also possible to say that in spite of the Orthodox gendering of halakhic operations, and in some ways because of it, women can attain the 'Godlikeness' Shapiro refers to; even in Auschwitz. Because Israel is beloved to God, the Shekhinah dwells among them, even when they are unclean (Sifre Numbers 1b). And more specifically, it is the Orthodox ideology of femininity that suggests the possibility of women's resistance to, and sanctification of, Auschwitz. Granted, on the one hand, women's traditional vocation has been a practical, domestic path of care which some would justifiably construe as an alienation of religious labour.[102] But on the other hand, and more positively, in the corporeal election of all Israel and in women's domestic replication of the divine order, the practicalities of Jewish women's religious lives also allow those lives to infuse the practical with the transcendent.[103]

Although Jewish women's history has shown that women's spirituality has been largely spontaneous, private and reflective of their everyday domestic and familial concerns, that is not at all to say that they have not been actively engaged in a search for God, often expressed in the blessings, prayers and other devotional writings published by women since the sixteenth century.[104] And more germane to my own argument, it can be claimed that while in one sense the female sacred sphere is the realm of the everyday (the profane understood as the non-special), in another sense it is a primary (decentralized) locus of the sacred. For in Jewish sacred geography the home, known to the rabbis as a *mikdash maat* – a small sanctuary, demarcates the boundaries of peoplehood. It is a counterpart to the destroyed Second Temple, and is microcosmic of the land of Israel from which Jewry is in exile. The preparation of kosher food, celebration of the Sabbath and maintenance of family purity all sanctify Jewish life in the absence of the Temple cult. Representative of Orthodox opinion then and now, Hyman Goldin wrote in 1941 (in America) that the observant home is a 'sacred institution'. Every home can be 'turned into a shrine where godliness prevails' because holiness is not confined to any one class or place. God is to be found wherever places are made holy by acts and intentions and wherever we conduct ourselves as to invite God's presence among us; Jewish holiness is not the sole prerogative of scholars. Goldin concludes that 'all Jews, then, are priests and holy if they follow [God's] teachings: if they are God-fearing, merciful, kind, and peace-loving; if their homes have a Jewish atmosphere . . . Then every member of the family is a priest unto God; the home is a shrine; and the table is an altar of God.'[105] In Diaspora Judaism the family table – a space at the heart of the female sacral sphere – replaces the Temple's sacrificial altar as a central locus of the holy. Orthodox Judaism has not, therefore, rendered women (albeit married and heterosexual) irrelevant to the consecration of the world. It has taught that the 'female' home and indeed 'female' virtues are redemptive and model the proper human posture in relation to God.[106]

The intrinsic religious significance of the Jewish home may explain why nineteenth-century Jewish protofeminists, contemporary Jewish feminists and contemporary Orthodoxy as a whole, have all, if for different reasons and in different ways, affirmed the hallowing qualities of female domestic observance, especially as symbolized by the kindling of the Sabbath lights. Orthodoxy commonly cites the Talmudic dictum: 'It is women alone through whom God's blessings are vouchsafed to a house' in defence of the gendered status quo.[107] Of course, there is little doubt that much Orthodox rhetoric on the sanctity of the home, and its reassurance to women that study of Torah (that is, masculinity) is not the only prerequisite of Jewish holiness, performs an ideological function: that of compensating women for their lack of public religious authority. There are numerous reasons why a Jewish (and Christian) bourgeois, essentially nineteenth-century, conservative ideology of femininity cannot be uncritically affirmed. Jewish homes are, after all, diverse. As social institutions, Jewish families are historically conditioned and subject to cultural, geographic and economic factors of difference.[108] And the Jewish family, as much as any other, can institute servitude, wife-beating and abuse.[109] There is also no doubt that domestic labour as such should not be sentimentalized: at the time of the Holocaust preparations for the Sabbath would often begin almost as soon as the Sabbath was over and for poor women especially these could be little more than drudgery. The tradition itself knows the burden of domesticity. In a medieval midrash on Bereshit 59a, the tradition undermines its own ideology of femininity by making female domestic obligations, including those for the Sabbath, an atonement for the sins of Eve.

It should also not be forgotten that Jewish women are also traditionally cast as sources of ritual uncleanness.[110] Jewish naming of the Nazi calumny against Jewish personhood should therefore be morally reflexive. In the light of Nazi Germany's racist abuse of the religio-moral concept of purity, Israel – the body cast as the contaminant of Aryan space – must particularly revisit its own perception of the *niddah* (menstruant) as a contaminant.[111] In memory of Nazism's denial of the full humanity of Jews, Jewry should repudiate those gynophobic textual and practical inheritances that enshrine as Torah the defamation, derogation of, or discrimination against women.[112] Where the tradition is gynophobic it diminishes the Nazi crime, lending its isolation and destruction of Jewish bodies, especially women's bodies, the vocabulary and worse, the ontology, of religious purification. Never again should the rabbinic description of a woman as 'a pitcher full of filth [excrement] with its mouth full of blood' (Shabbat 152a) pass without censure.[113] Traditional Judaism must listen again to the words 'Women are a separate people' (Shabbat 62a) because after European Jewry was set apart for destruction in camps and ghettos those words cannot mean whatever they might have done before 1933.

Nonetheless, read 'against the grain' and without advocating its regressive sexual politics, Orthodox rhetoric can suggest a properly feminist construction of female sacrality within the particular conditions of Auschwitz. Religious feminists who wish to affirm female difference rather than erasing it in the name of equality with the male norm (the historic tendency of Reform Judaism), must take seriously the Orthodox contention that women have, in effect, through their own meticulous, halakhically governed purificatory and separative practices, the priestly power to mediate the presence of God. As such women's covenant with God is as much a priestly vocation as men's.

Of particular significance is the female invitation of God as Shekhinah into the Sabbath home through the domestic separation of holy from profane time and space. God blesses and hallows the Sabbath (Ex. 20: 11) as the means by which the world is recreated. In mystical understanding, women in their turn realize the recreativity of the Sabbath by the hallowing practices of purification: the washing and cleaning of bodies and objects in readiness for the holy event that is the arrival of the Shekhinah, the Sabbath Bride.[114] With mystical intentionality or interpretation domestic preparation for the Sabbath – making the house and its inhabitants gleam and shine – is a work of cosmological significance, not only preparing but also facilitating and participating in the inner meaning of the Sabbath: a sacred marriage within God, between God and Israel, and often enacted in love between husband and wife, that will recreate and restore the tired and damaged world to something of its first glory.[115]

The holy is that which God wishes to be set apart from harm. Cleanness – what has been both washed and re-covered from its exposure to destructive forces – is a signifier of the moral and spiritual health on which the blessings of peace and stability in the home, the House of Israel, the world, and the cosmos depend. Rabbinical Judaism teaches that the body is the vessel of the holy spark and so must be kept clean and healthy. It must not be neglected and one must wash daily as part of the glorification of its creator (Shabbat 50b). In which case, to say that the holy was present in Auschwitz is to say that it had something crucially to do with women cleaning (however notionally) their own and other bodies – their 'face' – from the afflictions of physical and spiritual defilement. To do so was to declare not only a bounded sacred space, but also a bounded sacred time: a momentary Sabbath on Auschwitz which by its nature restored the face of God to a world de-faced by the demonic exercise of patriarchal power. Remembering past Sabbath meals at home is a theme of the more observant women's memoirs. In Belsen, where, as in all such camps, there was no Sabbath from suffering and death, Bertha Ferderber-Salz's yearning for the restoration of life focuses on her early childhood memories of the Friday night Sabbath meal when her mother's labours, voice and affectionate touch created an 'enchanted world' suffused by the glow of her love for her children.[116]

The women's memoir literature can be read through traditional discourse on the domain and values of Jewish female sacrality as indicative of human transcendence and divine immanence among women in Auschwitz. If one transposes this domestically centred Jewish theology into Auschwitz, women's experience there takes on a different hue. Again, to take the case of Bertha Ferderber-Salz: after being taken from Auschwitz to Belsen, she, her niece, sister-in-law and another young girl were able to maintain what she calls their 'communal household' in Belsen. This Belsen 'household' is what she herself calls 'home'.[117] Throughout 1939, in hiding from the Germans, Ferderber-Salz had wound her baby daughter's wet nappies around her waist to dry them, and in the Krakow ghetto had struggled hard to keep her two daughters' underclothes, bodies and hair clean.[118] Here in Belsen, her young daughters left in hiding, she and the other women supported one another emotionally and helped one another to keep the filth at bay. They shared food, tried to wash one each other's hair with ersatz coffee, and used needles improvised from splinters of wood to knit and sew one another garments made from the unravelled threads of their blankets.[119]

Or again, Tedeschi writes that both among her friends in the camp bunks and sitting on her stool at work with the women of the *Schukommando* (mending shoes), it was as if she had 'rediscovered a tiny harbor'. When she was evacuated from Auschwitz by the Germans she found that 'departure from the torture camps became itself another painful leave-taking from families, homes, and native countries'.[120] Jewish and non-Jewish women alike found sustenance in sharing recipes and planning elaborate meals, though for Jewish women this consisted more in the remembered preparation for the Sabbath and other religious festivals.[121] Ruth Elias describes how women on the third tier of her bunk would 'cook' dishes from home after devouring their rations; it made them feel a little more replete and a little more human.[122]

Women also issued invitations and made promises to visit one another's homes. Those invitations were both a necessary fiction and a commitment to liberation. To labour outside the immediate boundaries of Auschwitz-Birkenau and see signs of ordinary domesticity: a house with white muslin curtains and a tulip growing in a pot on a windowsill, was to experience 'a moment of hope'; 'we utter "muslin" softly in the mouth.'[123] Delbo describes sheltering in an abandoned farmhouse during a rainstorm, where the women's bodily presence alone turned its empty shell into a temporary home. They imagined how they would furnish and decorate it and found that the cold, damp rooms have 'grown warm, lived in. We feel good.'[124] To stop 'conjuring up each and every detail' of home and to stop imagining their return was, for Delbo and her friends, tantamount to dying; going home was the trajectory of survival.[125]

The memoirs do not theologize their own re-visioning of space and time. But reading them from a theological perspective, in practically and imaginally covering and protecting the body by the practices and functions of 'home', these women also covered and protected the divine spark.[126] They made a sanctuary for the spark of the divine presence that saved it from being extinguished. That the maintenance of human personhood in Auschwitz through acts of covering and purification is essential to the production of holiness and hence divine presence is inherent in the moral relation Jewish tradition establishes between holiness and divine/human personality.[127] According to David Blumenthal, God has two essential attributes in Jewish tradition and these are holiness and personality. God is manifest in personality and holiness. Holiness and personality are respectively the attributes of relation and relatedness. A vision of God and of humanity that is rooted in both holiness and personality is one which is therefore particularly resistant to evil.[128]

The image of God (*tselem Elohim*) consists in both holiness and personality: those two defining characteristics of God and humanity are at the heart of the tradition and establish the possibility of mutual, dialogical relation between God and the world and between persons. While the image of God in humanity was once perceived as a capacity for moral judgement in the knowledge and presence of the holy, this view declined with the intellectualization of theology among medieval rabbinic philosophers. But it remains the case that the theology of image offers an epistemic and experiential principle by which humanity can come to fully embody the image of its creator.[129] Berkovits, also writing in the holocaustal context, likewise wants to say that the image of God is 'the secret of ['man's'] humanity. To guard that image, to live in a manner worthy of it, is his responsibility on earth'.[130]

It is this personalistic, ethical theology of holiness which, taken up into a feminist critical frame, is central to a post-Holocaust attempt to counter the holocaustal attack on persons and to counter the charges of divine absence or desertion discussed in the previous chapter of this study. In the holocaustal context, washing should not only be understood as the physical act of wiping away material dirt in the rare instances that that was possible; rather it could be an act of *seeing through* Nazism and seeing through the effects of Nazism to the divine image reflected in the darkened mirror of the suffering human face. (*Tselem* suggests a reflection or shadow of God in the human person. It is not the drawing of a likeness.) Here, washing can be read as an attempt to maintain the reflective quality of the material world (so well known to the theology of the Sabbath) in the reflective quality of the face that is above all else presentative of personhood, both human and divine. Just as a parent's careful attention to the bodily needs of his/her child is a form of *kavannah* or spiritual focus, in Auschwitz, where bodily needs were radically denied, remembering home and its purificatory, protective, nourishing functions, was a resistance to and a sheltering from Nazism's demonic assault on the body. This powerful symbology took quasi-domestic acts, or the longing to perform them, out of the realm of the ordinary or profane and into a realm of the reconsecration of the body. Ordinary acts like the attempted washing or wiping of a face were, here, in the radical disruption of normal categories of action and agency, transposed into a sacred dimension in ways that might not have been (or be) the case outside Auschwitz.

At the beginning of this chapter I wrote that there is a presumption, if not a perversity, in discerning the holy in Auschwitz, even if only in the texts of those who survived it. But it is precisely because Auschwitz cannot support a fastidious theology, but one that must begin with the gross indignities of bodily degradation, that the notion of cleanness takes on the hue of prophetic criticism and hope. The sheer scale and quantity of impurity beneath which the victims struggled and died is not to be dismissed if only because to underestimate the power of the demonic profane is also to underestimate the power of the holy to resist and thereby transform it. It is, of course, not possible to 'read off' the holy from the world as if it were a property or quality of things visible to the naked eye – it is rather the moment in which God and persons are connected through a particular act or medium. Eternity is in the historical instant. Just as early Jewish historiography was not primarily concerned with the facts of a catastrophe – 'what was remembered and recorded was not the factual data but *the meaning of the desecration*'[131] – here too, theological historiography and imagination are interpenetrated. In this sense, the meaning of women's practical ethics in Auschwitz resides in the notion of *Kiddush Ha' Shem* – a (female) sanctification of God's name. Yet it was a name that was not yet known because the domestic practices traditionally performed by women had not yet been recognized as telling us something about the female activity and personality of God. Even where the female face was restored by its notional cleaning, the female face of God had not yet been seen because it was not yet considered fit to look upon.

This is not to make the historical claim that all or even very many women interpreted the attempt to maintain a clean body as a religious experience. Extremely filthy, afflicted skin is simply very uncomfortable and for this reason alone women would have sought its alleviation. And for some, the care of the holocaustal body through washing may be better interpreted rationally or pragmatically as a way of avoiding contamination by harmful bacteria and parasites. It might be also objected that most Jews passed through Auschwitz by being gassed on or close to the time of arrival so that any putative process of restoring God to the world by cleaning would seem in quantitative terms to have been over before it had begun.[132] But this restoration or *tikkun* does not occupy a quantity of space and time; it is the theophanic possibility of a moment. Attention to the dignity of persons is a state of ontological and moral openness to the need of the other. That openness to the need of the other could remain a quality or posture of being until such time as a person passed into a state of terminal weakness and death, beyond which a historical theology cannot speak.

To those who have internalized the masculinist denigration of female domestic labour (civilization both disdains and depends upon it), female acts of purification which are not directly halakhically governed such as the improvized dressing of a wound or the affectionate and soothing touch, may seem a rather slender evidential basis on which to posit divine presence in Auschwitz. But valorized as sacral, indeed priestly, these acts can be interpreted without bathos as exemplifying the traditionally close alliance of cleanliness and divine presence. (Perhaps Nazi Germany had a demonic intuition of the truth of this in its will to 'cleanse' or wipe Jewry from the face of the earth so that it would itself flourish eternally.) The heart of Jewish theology is a practical one.[133] In Deuteronomy 23: 13–15 it is commanded that,

> there shall be an area outside the [Israelite] camp, where you may relieve yourself. With your gear you shall have a spike, and when you have squatted you shall dig a hole with it and cover up your excrement. Since the Lord your God moves about in your camp to protect you and to deliver your enemies to you, let your camp be holy; let Him not find anything unseemly among you and turn away from you.

In the twentieth-century anti-camp of Auschwitz, where typhus was endemic among inmates and excrement would run uncontrolled down their legs and could not be washed off, God knew Israel's 'unseemliness' but still moved about the camp and did not turn away. Indeed she was like a mother who will not be repelled by her child's 'unseemliness', but in washing her must come all the closer because of it. If God were merely the patriarchal numen who punished minor infringements of his cult (such as that of the ill-fated Uzzah) and who would not tolerate physical dirt, then God could not have been present under the conditions of Auschwitz, bereft as it was of all material means of preserving the immaculacy of the holy. That is why God had to profane herself there. If she had not, she would have ceased to be Shekhinah: God in the mode of immanence. As Shekhinah or God in exile, God voluntarily underwent a kenosis of the holy so that she might draw near as a woman of sorrows to her soiled creation. The divine is present as an image reflected in the human face. But an image is not the thing itself – there is an interval between the image and the imaged. This suggests that God was not immanent in any sense that would have bounded or exhausted God's being which is also transcendent and wholly other to the world. It was rather that Auschwitz, as the suffering face of Jewry looking up, into and sometimes through the smoke, could yet be a mirror to God's looking and seeing face.

The (de)portation of the holy into Auschwitz

It is difficult to conceive of God's presence – her looking and seeing face – in Auschwitz without some further consideration of the tradition's use of the name Shekhinah to denote God's accompanying presence in Israel's exile. In biblical texts the term 'shekhinah' is merely grammatically feminine and indicates the sense of being in a sacred place. 'Shekhinah' comes from the root *shakhan* – to be present or dwell as in a tabernacle, sanctuary or tent (as in Ex. 25: 8) and the term was often used to denote God's presence in the desert camp or Temple. Although the Shekhinah has a relatively minor role to play in rabbinic Judaism, nonetheless, rabbinic literature has an 'unshakeable belief' in the indwelling presence of God among the daily life of the people of Israel.[134] Even while Israel is unclean the Shekhinah is with them (Yoma 56b) and although evil drives her away, she watches over the sick (Shabbat 12b). When a human being is in pain the Shekhinah's head and arms ache (Sanhedrin 46a). In so far as the Shekhinah is a symbol of God's self-revelation and immanence in the everyday world, rabbinic theology is also a mystical theology. In the earliest midrashim (biblical commentaries in narrative form) the Shekhinah denotes less God's presence in a particular place, than the presence of God among the exiled community of Israel wherever they might be. God's Shekhinah was present in the exiled body of Israel and the body of Israel was God's dwelling place.[135] Often manifest as a shining light, she becomes an image of the female aspect of God caring for her people in exile. Most writers of the rabbinic period regarded the Shekhinah as a personification of God that was more than a literary device: God's closeness to the suffering Israel and her sharing its exile was central to the maintenance of faith, but, avoiding ditheism, the rabbis would not hypostasize her as a divine being in her own right.[136] Nor does the feminine gender of the term necessarily associate her presence with that of women. On the contrary, in Mishnaic, and again in medieval mystical texts, the presence of the Shekhinah is strongly associated with the gathering of men around the holy texts they study.[137]

Some rabbinic commentators assert that the destruction of the Temple was a sign of the Shekhinah's desertion of the Jewish people on account of their sins. More representative, though, is Rabbi Akiba's view that because God is compassionate and loving the Shekhinah is always present and shares Israel's suffering in exile.[138] In the absence of the Temple, the home is the place of her presence. It is in seeing where the symbolics of the (destroyed) home could be transposed into the anti-home of Auschwitz that it becomes possible to argue that the Levitical vocation to be holy as God is holy, and its redemptive effect, could be deported, with the Shekhinah, into the women's camp in Auschwitz-Birkenau. Of course, the symbolics of the (remembered) home do not exhaust the necessary or sufficient conditions for God's presence in Auschwitz and may also suggest more stable intimacies than Auschwitz could normally sustain. But that women who had suffered a series of deportations out of the sphere of the holy could nonetheless fulfill God's command to make God a sanctuary so that God could live among them (Ex. 25: 8) is a possibility inherent in Judaism because God, as Shekhinah, is a wandering God, and Jewish sacred space is mobile. In the early biblical period sacred space is established wherever Jews are encamped in the barren wilderness around them. And from the rabbinic period to the present God's presence is not limited to a specific place but is marked by God's people, Israel, who carry God's presence with them.[139]

If both the God of the wilderness and of the post-biblical period does not dwell in a fixed sanctuary but settles wherever, as it were, the tent is carried, it is the sheltering of the divine presence (the Shekhinah) in whatever wilderness Israel might find itself, that links the redemptive qualities of the home to those of the (assaulted, homeless) body(ies) of Israel in Auschwitz. To clarify: the Priestly documents of the Hebrew Bible describe the *mishkan* or 'Tent of Meeting' as the portable wilderness shrine where for Moses and the people the divine presence resided in its holy of holies (see Ex. 25–27). Within the *mishkan* was the shrouded chest that was the ark of the covenant of which unauthorized approach and touch was forbidden (Ex. 25: 10–22, 37: 1–9; I Sam. 6: 19; 2 Sam. 6: 6–8). Now it seems to me that the *mishkan* is also a metaphor evoking how women's holding or encirclement of bodies created a form of home or, if not that, a portable and temporary sanctuary for God;[140] a kind of *mishkan* in the holocaustal desert of blood, mud and excrement. Whereas the masculine *mishkan* consisted in the capacity of the memory to be a sacred chest in which to carry and mediate the presence of God in words spoken from inside the head, for women, exempted or prohibited from the sacral performativity of words, the holding body became a mobile sanctuary of the divine spark. And God sought to return, here, to this portable tent of meeting – the body/ark which in Auschwitz was carried 'in the midst of their uncleanness' (Lev. 16: 16).

While the image of the *mishkan* in Auschwitz is no mere linguistic conceit,[141] it must be emphasized that relational acts of service to bodies could not render the women's camp in Auschwitz-Birkenau a sanctuary qua place of protection. Such acts may have resacralized the Jewish body, but not Auschwitz itself. Auschwitz was not and never could be a city of sanctuary;[142] there was no place on earth where a Jew was more exposed and vulnerable to harm; no place on earth further from God's holy mountain of prophetic-eschatological imagining where none shall be harmed. The victimized female body was under attack: a ruined sanctuary that could offer little refuge to Shekhinah, and often none at all. The body/sanctuary was without immunity; it had been entered and defiled. Shekhinah was both exposed to the profane gaze and obscured by the covering marks of its profanation. Whereas the holy desert ark was protected from the contagion of unclean or profane touch by tented layers of animal skin and cloth, the exposing and consuming touch of Auschwitz tore all protection from the holy.[143]

But conversely, the profane can be transformed into the holy by the blessings of sanctifying touch. And, in the end, the Nazis' degradation of women in Auschwitz could not, in fact, desecrate them for holiness is not a quantity that can be found and destroyed. Just as the Torah scrolls are, in fact, too holy to profane, only God can dis-appoint the holiness of her own children.[144] Holiness is known in a perception of the personal and moral relation between created things and God. Because it is a category of willed relation, rather than being a material property of objects, holiness cannot be taken away from those objects by physical force. Those who forced rabbis to desecrate the scrolls of the law by, among other means, trampling or urinating on them were not aware that for Jews the scrolls are so holy they cannot be profaned by human command. Or again, the Nazis tattooed numbers onto skin, painted stripes and sewed fabric shapes onto garments to set the victim apart for destruction. But the ineradicable stamp of divine origin is how God sets apart persons, things, places and times as God's own and God's holiness is indestructible.

As Isidore Epstein notes, in the Talmudic dictum 'Shall you say that the world is *hefker* (ownerless)?', 'is announced the indomitable conviction that the world is not left with no one to care about what happens therein. There is no human action that is allowed to go by unrequited. There is no moment in human history over and against which God does not stand in judgement.'[145] The time and space in and on which Auschwitz was erected was, after all, that of God's creation. Its victims were not *hefker*; they were not available to be taken, used up and wasted. Therefore while it could torture and kill people, Auschwitz's institutional attempt to claim those Jewish bodies for itself was ultimately futile. For Jews, 'in their flesh, are God's possession; they belong to God. For exactly that reason, no one may abuse them or lay claim to absolute authority over them.'[146] That humanity belongs to God is not to say that it is a possession at the sole disposal of God, but rather that God's creation is the place where humanity belongs, namely in the particular place which was created, appointed and blessed by God to be fit for both divine and human presence.

In the Levitical codes the people of Israel are to be kept separate from their impurity lest they die by defiling the tabernacle or dwelling place of God that is in their midst (Lev. 15: 31). But we have seen that in Auschwitz the Jews could not be kept separate from their impurity; indeed the Nazis tried to make them ontologically and materially identical to it. And because the contagion of their uncleanness was dangerous, they did die from its diseases. But as God's tabernacle, the body as person and the body as Israel could not be defiled because the unclean is finally a moral and spiritual (dis)orientation, not material uncleanliness itself. As a disciple of the Baalshem Tov insisted, 'call nothing common or profane: by God's presence all things are holy'.[147] It is on the certainty of this that the argument of this chapter has rested. Namely, if the Jew, even the dying Jew, remained holy to God — within the precinct of God and therefore fit for God — then God could be present in Auschwitz, sanctifying and sanctified by her people. For wherever things and persons are sanctified Israel is not cut off from God or forgotten by God — a more total and final meaning of Jewish death than any Nazi Germany could conceive.

In sum, the recursive relation between God and humanity is such that the degradation that befell the Jews also befell God immanent as Shekhinah. But God is also too holy to be profaned so that as God overcame God's own profanation, Jewry also bore at least the shadow of the divine face passing over its own. Humanity was redeemed in God's redemption by humanity. Women's will to purify and their gestures towards purification set their face against Auschwitz; set their bodies apart from the profane so that God's face/presence could be traced in their becoming visible to the other by being 'cleaned'. In so doing, they both fulfilled God's will that Israel be holy (in human ways) as God is holy, and allowed God to be and behold God on earth. It was in this way that women, intentionally or otherwise, could realize God's presence in Auschwitz, refuting what was to be post-Holocaust theology's contention that God was hidden, absent or eclipsed by it. The redemption of persons (both alive and dead) from erasure by the profane is dependent upon the presence of God in conditions which, although they could not destroy God, could have destroyed the conditions in which the divine might be manifest. But I have wanted to deny that Auschwitz could entirely destroy the conditions in which God could be manifest and have instead suggested that where Israel in Auschwitz signalled towards a world fit for persons, Auschwitz was made fit for God. For God's presence is eternal and does not wait upon the future. As Shekhinah, God's presence in Auschwitz was that of a God whose power was such that she could consent to be defiled by virtue of her immanence and still be God, then, now, and in the times to come.

4   Face to face (with God) in Auschwitz

> [On] your behalf my heart says, 'Seek My Face!'
> O Lord, I seek Your face.
>
> (Ps. 27: 8)

We have seen that the dominant theme of post-Holocaust theology has been that of the eclipse or hiddenness of God, whether as a function of the mystery of divine activity or of human freedom. But Jewish theology has also wanted to say that its God is an accompanying God, going with the assembly of Israel, even in its exile. Theologies of divine hiddenness (*qua* desertion) do not keep faith with that wandering, deported God whose presence establishes and maintains community wherever Israel finds itself. Such theologies ignore how community was not only destroyed by the Holocaust but also sustained. Most particularly, such theologies ignore both new and traditional forms of community sustained by women.

In a letter to the Jewish feminist artist Judy Chicago, Vera John-Steiner, a survivor, wrote: 'Although I am reluctant to make great generalizations about women during the Holocaust . . . nonetheless, I believe that it is the rootedness in community that is ontologically fundamental to Jewish culture, and it is the effort to maintain community that can be specifically seen in the female Holocaust experience.'[1] John-Steiner's view is far from atypical: the evidence for sustained relationship constitutes a considerable literature in itself. It is the record of women's efforts to sustain relationships of care in Auschwitz and other camps (whether heterosexual or lesbian)[2] that offers the post-Holocaust theological reader a textual insight into the presence of God among them; of their having carried God aloft through Auschwitz. In the previous chapter I looked to see how women might have prepared the way for divine presence by keeping the world fit or ready for God. In this and the next chapter I look to see how that presence could be disclosed.

There is no doubt that sustaining or developing relations of care in Auschwitz could have been a survival strategy beneficial to both parties; an act of pragmatic solidarity rather than an ethical or spiritual response to the suffering other. But that this was often the case does not exclude the possibility that care also signified more and other than the survival of the self or family for its own sake.[3] By 'more',

I am not referring to moral disinterest where the other becomes an occasion for virtue. Neither the ascetic perfection, conquest or annihilation of the will through acts of supererogatory moral excellence nor the cultivation of a privatized inner strength by suffering are particularly Jewish motivations.[4] While these spiritual virtues are not to be lightly dismissed, I want to attend to a different, non-expiatory, non-heroic relationality which brings God and humanity together by the operations of ordinary self-giving love in circumstances which made non-ordinary demands on that love. Here the other is not reduced to an abstraction, a mere object of attention, but belongs within a nexus of more ordinarily human (and indeed more characteristically Jewish) reciprocities of care in so far as these could obtain in conditions which few expected to survive.[5]

This is not to speak of women's Jewishness as if it were an innocence beyond reason, anger and history. It is not to impose upon women's struggle to hold their families together a nineteenth-century proto-feminist view of women's religion as an affair of the domesticated heart, not of the mind. Both Jewish patriarchal ideology and first wave Jewish feminist theology made the continuity and survival of one generation of the family to the next a woman's principal biological and spiritual duty to the covenant. Though radical in many respects, first wave Jewish feminists such as Bertha Pappenheim regarded care for the family as woman's primary duty.[6] My founding a feminist theology of the Holocaust on the maintenance of familial and quasi-familial relations is *not* to say that these should be the priorities of all Jewish women everywhere. To read female care theologically is not thenceforth to confine women to a purportedly non-rational role of care. It is rather to urge that both men and women care in the image of a loving God whose covenant with us institutes relational commitment.[7]

In Auschwitz, where the covenant was under extreme duress, to hold and tend the body of Israel in its dereliction was at once a practically and ethically maximal undertaking of the Jewish obligation. Judaism has always had to be such as to preserve the covenant in times and conditions where its institutions have been destroyed. The covenant had to survive the transition from biblical to rabbinic Judaism, from the cultic worship of the Temple to the prayer-based worship of the synagogue, from prophecy to the study of Torah, from monarchy to the leadership of the sages.[8] Motifs of promise, commitment and hope have always constituted the dynamic structure of the covenant. Here, in the peculiarly catastrophic setting of the Holocaust, I want to interpret women's fidelities to relation not as a peripheral fidelity to the covenant but as binding up the covenant between God and Jewry against the forces of its historical dissolution. For in Auschwitz, little or nothing was to remain of covenantal practice but those relational structures that had long constituted the spiritual and practical substance of most Jewish women's lives.[9] Women's struggle to keep their promises of practical love to those whom they had committed themselves as mothers, sisters, daughters and friends, became the locus of faith in a future imagined in the form of familial reunion and of having or making a home to return to. By figuring the covenant as a divine/human maternal promise to an immediate family and to the greater family of Israel, discourse on Auschwitz can be truthful to its cruel foreclosures while holding within itself, perhaps unexpectedly, a dis-closure of the future.

Yet for the purposes of this book I have chosen to develop a theology of image, rather than a covenantal theology alone, because a theology of image precedes and underpins the mutuality and reciprocity of covenant. My contention is that, *in extremis*, to conserve the personhood of self and other by relation is also to conserve the framework and possibility of covenantal relationship. Covenantal relationship is, thereby, a witness to the theology of image that posits a relation of recursive presence between God and persons. The divine personality is ontologic-ally transcendent and other to human personality, but it is such that when human personhood is carefully tended so as to remain reflective of the divine personality it images, then the divine personality achieves immanence *by* its reflection. Within the recursive relationship of God and humanity, divinity is tended in the tended person. The image of both coalesces in a moment of (re)unification that recalls the moment of creation in and by God and looks forward to the reconciliation of redemption or *tikkun*.

God, in Auschwitz, was knowable in the moment of being seen in the face of the seen other; was produced in and as the inter/face between persons; the face between faces. Granted, in Auschwitz, the visible differentiation of self from the anonymous mass could attract dangerous attention. There were times when the erasure of the face could, in fact, assist its survival by helping an inmate evade notice.[10] Yet in the restoration and return of the human/divine image, a gift of presence and therefore love passed from persons to God and God to persons. For face-to-face presence is a declaration of loyalty and is the condition of love. So too, the commonalities between God's transcendent personality and immanent human personhood are such that God is present wherever personhood is honoured, for personhood is the locus and episteme of divine will and activity. Relational acts testified to the presence of the human/e in Auschwitz whose purpose was to destroy and consume it. Relational acts thereby testify to the presence of God who is the creator and meaning of humanity not so much as species but as a category of value and locus of revelation.

In proposing an integral relation between personhood (as 'face') and the divine presence (also 'face' in biblical idiom), the theologian must of course be mindful of the gendering of philosophical conceptions of personhood. As feminist philo-sophers have observed, modern notions of personhood are profoundly gendered and prove, upon examination, to consist not so much in an essential quality of humanness but in idealized, cerebrally oriented, projections of the autonomous, masculine agent. The personhood of women has, by contrast, traditionally consisted to a far greater degree in its production through her relations to others; confirmed in the extent to which she is loved and needed by others and can see and touch them. To patriarchal philosophers these dependencies are a sign of female abjection. To feminist historians and theologians of the Holocaust these dependencies may suggest the contrary.

That Nazism intended the destruction of Jewish personhood, of *both* men and women, is obvious and undeniable. Yet because personhood is culturally and biologically gendered, it becomes possible for historians to observe how men and women would have been vulnerable to different kinds of humiliation and physical and emotional deprivation. Ethically too, attention to gender difference makes it possible to see where the distinctive moral and emotional production and performance of female personhood, especially in the roles of mother and sister, withstood the Nazi assault (even if only unto death). Above all, for theologians, attention to the gendering of human personality makes it possible to see how the (even momentary) restoration of the human female face constituted not merely a random act of compassion but a restoration of the female face of God in whose image women are made. That is, the gendered labour of the restoration of personhood to assaulted (female) persons could restore God's presence or face to the de-faced world that was Auschwitz – the deepest exile she has ever endured for our sake.

This is not to say that there was a God for men and a God for women. Rather, to a significant degree, gender difference produces a Judaism for men and a Judaism for women and in this way the one, same God is differently known. Speaking theopoetically, to restore God's immanence to the world which has expelled it is to make God once more visible to God in God's transcendence. Where that immanence bears a countenance best evoked as female, the work of God's restoration to the world allows the obscured 'female' dimension of divine personality to be visible to God-self. It is a reunion in God of a kind long envisaged by mystical Judaism.

The degradation of relation

The circumstances of women in Auschwitz sharply challenges any theological construal such as that outlined above. I shall therefore go to some lengths to present its counter-evidence so as to rebut the charge that a constructive theology of Auschwitz must entail sentimentalizing or trivializing the conditions of holocaustal death and survival. There are also good theological reasons for presenting the counter-evidence: although theology is itself a counter-claim to forms of reductive reason, it is also tolerant of ambiguity and doubt. And even were it to be true that only a minority of Jewish women had the physical, spiritual and moral strength to care for others, as Wyschogrod affirms in another context, the bond between God and Israel is eternal, it 'cannot be severed by the deeds of Israel'.[11]

But the human bond is a more friable one. That the Jewish people has suffered a rupture in its line and form has recently been most hauntingly witnessed through architecture in Daniel Libeskind's fragmented, almost unbuildable, Jewish Museum in East Berlin. A Jewish feminist theology (like architecture, a (re)constructive project) must acknowledge the truthfulness of such representations but speak truthfully of *both* the brokenness *and* the connectedness of Jewish women's relationships during the Holocaust. That is, it must not merely withstand the truth but speak the truth(s). Although relation could save lives and hope, it was far more likely to offer little or no physical or psychological defence against the onslaught, and often no moral defence either.

Sara Nomberg-Przytyk is far from alone in her view that in Auschwitz, 'the *will* to compassion may have remained intact, but its power to oppose the ungoverned ferocity of the camps faltered before the sterile cruelty inherent in the system'.[12] For many women, the degradation of relationship by acclimatization to the suffering of the other had already begun in the ghettos. In Rabbi Shimon Huberband's censorious essay of the time, 'The Moral Suffering and Moral Decline of Jewish Women During the War', he is shocked by the callous indifference of 'thousands upon thousands' of elegantly dressed women of the Warsaw ghetto who, during 1941–2, were failing to show the compassion Judaism expected of them and were merely stepping over the frozen, half-naked bodies of dead and dying children lying on every street corner.[13] And outside the ghettos, other women decided not to sacrifice their own chance of survival by protecting others. Frida Michelson gave a small boy – a fellow survivor from the Rumbuli massacre – her remaining food. But, by her own anguished admission, she also went on without him, leaving him alone in the freezing night despite his pleas for her help. He did not survive.[14] Nor was the maternal instinct always inviolable: given the 'choice' at least one young mother, on arrival in Auschwitz, is reputed to have refused to go to the left (to her death) with her 10-year old daughter who, struggling in the grip of three SS officers, was screaming for her protection.[15]

Even before reaching Auschwitz, relationships between mothers and babies were placed under intolerable stress. In the freight wagons that took Adelsberger to Auschwitz there were babies who screamed continually from thirst because there was no water and the bottled milk had soured, and their dirty, chafing nappies could not be changed.[16] Genocide is the murder of a people not only by killing but by breaking its solidarities, erasing its past and terminating its future. Babies and children were not to survive lest they should either perpetuate the Jewish 'race' or grow up to be avengers of their parents' deaths. Mothers accompanying children under the age of about 13 were not selected for labour.[17] Like the sick and the elderly they were killed immediately upon arrival at Auschwitz. Adelsberger records that SS regulations determined that 'every Jewish child automatically condemned his mother to death'.[18] A woman simply standing next to a child, or looking after someone else's child could be sent to the gas. In short, although mothers, daughters and sisters within an approximate age range could enter Auschwitz together, a woman whose death was postponed by her selection for labour was intended to be a woman already divested of dependent relationships.

In an environment of unceasing bodily and verbal abuse, a strenuous effort of moral will and imagination was required for a woman to continue to see herself and others as persons. The Nazi reduction of Jewish personhood to mere quantity was inscribed onto the body, ineradicably tattooed into the skin as a number: 'It is impossible to estimate the effect it had on morale. A tattooed woman felt that her life had vanished; she was no longer anything but a number.'[19] This marking of the body was the initiatory moment when new arrivals to Auschwitz underwent a public severance of the connections between their personhood, agency and identity. On arrival, all vestiges of personal belongings were removed: letters, photographs, soap, toothbrush, clothes, underwear – 'Nothing remained but naked existence – and for most of us not even that for very long – and the thoughts in our hearts.'[20] Of all the objects appropriated by the Nazis on arrival at Auschwitz, Olga Lengyel was most distressed by the loss of her family photographs (another erasure of the face).[21] Many survivor testimonies observe how the confiscation of their toothbrush on arrival at the camp was one of the first significant steps towards their dehumanization; for Maya Nagy it was 'a dangerous moment for the loss of self, of identity'.[22] Although some women would come to wipe their teeth with a scrap of rag, with foul teeth, the mouth, and therefore the face, would close. Each woman's personhood, phenomenalized by the facial features or sur-face that signalled her identity, was to be quite literally eroded by the extreme rigours of the camp regime. Her neck would be bent by grief, fear and exhaus-tion; her face would disappear into the disappearing mass.

Maya Nagy remembers that one of the worst aspects of existence in the camps was the Nazis' 'interference, intrusion into the most *personal* things in one's life'.[23] In modern Western culture, the notion of privacy supplies the individual's capacity for relation as an emergence from solitude across an ontological and physico-spatial divide to see, hear and touch the other. This movement between the private and the public maps the contours and the pleasures of relationship. In Auschwitz, however, overcrowding could make women impatient and bad-tempered with one another – even to the point of mutual loathing.[24] Whether in the barracks, work details or when visiting the latrine (which was permitted only at certain times, and not according to need) there was none of the emotional and spatial privacy that has been the precondition and corollary of intimacy. The pande-monium: women screaming and shouting, not only in pain but in authority, interfered with the transition between private thought and public speech: 'How they could scream! Shouting was the symbol of leadership in the camp, so they were always screaming at the top of their lungs.'[25]

Depersonaliztion permitted gross assaults on persons, even between Jewish inmates. Nomberg-Przytyk observes of Auschwitz: 'Cruelty to the weak and humility towards the strong was the rule here.'[26] There were fights over bread and women often stole bread from one another, sometimes while the other was asleep.[27] Those without physical strength, who had 'no experience, no meanness, no selfishness' would, according to Nomberg-Przytyk, quickly perish. She remembers a girl in her first barracks ('tears big as peas ran down her cheeks') who 'missed maternal warmth in this terrible world that was entirely beyond her comprehension: she would perish for sure'.[28] Similarly, Lengyel observes: 'It seemed as though the Germans constantly sought to pit us against each other to make us spiteful, competitive, and hateful.' When the planks serving as bunks were filled to (literally) breaking point, 'violent and abusive quarrels would ensue over space'. Women who had been 'mothers of honest families, who formerly would not have taken a hairpin, became utterly hardened thieves and never suffered the slightest feeling of remorse.' She goes on, 'Perhaps the Nazis wanted to infect us with their own morals. In most cases they succeeded.' Only those 'endowed with exceptional moral stamina could remain honest and good'. It required 'an extraordinary moral force to teeter on the brink of the Nazi infamy and not plunge into the pit'.[29] Survival was often dependent on obedience to orders, and this could entail complicity in atrocities against other inmates, including children.[30]

The cross-hatch of live electric fences in and around the camp made loved ones literally untouchable. The fences fatally divided families and lovers into sub-camps between which communication was forbidden, and that cut off inmates from any previous relationship to the world beyond.[31] And nor were these separative boundaries always material ones. Of a woman whose name had been written down at the previous selection on the list of those to be gassed, Nomberg-Przytyk writes: 'I did not talk to her, though she lay no more than an arm's length from me. I was ashamed that I was to live.'[32] At a later date, the period of death marches and extreme privation between Lucie Adelsberger's evacuation from Auschwitz and her liberation revealed to her that 'there is no saving face when caught up in the whirling dance of death, All inhibitions are cast aside. There are other things the very memory of which makes me sick – things in myself that I cannot forgive so easily.' She remembers refusing to drag a girl through the snow, who, not strong enough for the march, was stumbling and holding on to her for support. Adelsberger herself had barely the strength to keep going, but wonders whether 'if it had been my sister or my beloved, would I have helped then?'[33]

And yet it is common sense that a person can only be subject to moral expectation and judgement when she enjoys moral choice. In a death camp, the notion of moral choice was in some senses meaningless because inmates were subject to orders delivered with at least the threat of the utmost violence, and most would die whether they helped one another or not. In the camps, 'things *happen* to you, you are *completely* out of control'.[34] Disorientation was induced by not being told or prepared for what was to happen next. The unpredictability of managed terror also served to destabilize personality and therefore its capacity for relationship.

Perhaps the strongest argument against the relational possibility is a physiological one. For as Lucie Adelsberger experienced (as both a doctor and sufferer) true starvation is not only a painful abdominal sensation, but 'an attack on the whole personality. Hunger makes a person vicious and undermines her character. Many of the things the prisoners did, things that rightly seem outrageous and monstrous to the outsider, become understandable and to a certain extent excusable when seen from the perspective of starvation.'[35] Thus Nagy, close to death at the end of the war: 'I don't remember myself being of comfort to anybody throughout this period. I was too run down.'[36] Isabella Leitner's memoirs show that she and her three sisters' determination to keep together at all costs not only supported but also physically and emotionally drained them by the sheer weight of its demands and obligations. A terror of separation began to exceed the fear of death. The relational bond could become just that: another heavy chain: 'I am tired. Let me go. . . . No we won't. . . . My darling sisters, you are asking too much.'[37]

Auschwitz's most systemic structures of alienation were its formal and informal inmate hierarchies. In the women's camp, German Jewish *zugangi* (new arrivals) often regarded the Polish Jewish women as 'rabble from the East' and imagined that 'the Germans would eventually remove them from the Jewish block and that the theory of *herrenfolk* would serve to elevate them above the Jews from other countries'.[38] All *zugangi* were 'at the bottom of the ladder. They were pariahs who were treated contemptuously by the other prisoners. They were beaten and kicked mercilessly and endlessly . . . they made themselves absurd by trying to defend their human dignity.'[39] As a *zugang*, Nomberg-Przytyk had been unable to reach the soup cauldron without being pushed away or having her portion grabbed from her. She admits that she would probably not have survived this period had it not been for a girl from Bialystok called Karola who shared with her whatever food she had.[40]

At the top of the formal inmate hierarchy, the *Lageraelteste* governed the women of Auschwitz-Birkenau, responsible only to the Germans.[41] According to Nomberg-Przytyk, the barrack blocks were generally ruled by Jewish women from Slovakia who had helped to build the camp in 1940. They 'were the real aristocrats of the camp'; 'they felt a certain pride in having built the camp' and resented having suffered while the other women were still 'sleeping in warm beds'. She adds, 'it seems strange, but in this congregation of misery, baseness, and fear, they sparkled with an unusual luster. . . . We existed only so that they might have someone to kick around, somebody to beat up on, somebody to serve as a background to their reflected glory.'[42] The *blokowe* or block supervisor could behave with a viciousness virtually indistinguishable from that of the SS. Nomberg-Przytyk remembers one *blokowe* who, catching an old woman relieving herself in front of the block instead of going to the latrines which lay at some distance from there, beat her without mercy. When she had finished, 'a rag of a human being', covered in mud, lay in front of the block and 'Madame *blokowa* returned to her warm room' furnished with pink silk eiderdowns, tables, chairs, dishes and glasses.[43] Additional to hierarchies of nationality and duration of incarceration, were those of occupation. Women who worked in the *Effektenkammer* where confiscated goods were housed were relatively well-fed and clothed and in a good position to 'organize' ('steal') and trade goods for food. Other inmates had 'a hard time believing that they [those in the *Effektenkammer*] were prisoners in the death camp of Auschwitz'.[44]

National loyalties very often superseded the solidarities of Jewishness. Tedeschi's memoir suggests that women's loyalties were national before they were Jewish. Greek and Italian Jewish women from southern Europe were socially and culturally distinct from those of central and eastern Europe: 'the groups had formed out of instinct, with each woman trying to find in those around her a tiny piece of her own land and family.' Nationality both preserved identity and invited hostility.[45] Political loyalties could also divide as well as unite. Nomberg-Przytyk's 'salvation', as she puts it, came from women of her own Communist sympathies who singled her out and gave her work in the infirmary as a clerk.[46] Others, without such connections, and often working in *Kommandos* (work details) in the far harsher conditions out in the open air,[47] were less 'fortunate'.

Philosophical as well as historical difficulties attend the development of a holocaustal theology of relation. For relation need not, of itself, connote a moral or practical good. Familial solidarity is not necessarily synonymous with care since it can amount to no more than an extended and highly exclusive form of self-interest. This was true of individuals who would inform on others not only to save themselves but also to save their families; the preservation of one set of relationships may have been at the cost of others.[48] Contemplation of particular relationships preserved at the expense of the relational *per se* is not theologically fruitful. There is an ethical point at which attempts to preserve relationship at any price has denied the relational values which make life worth surviving for. Neither is maternal care for the other always a self-evident good. As Tzvetan Todorov points out in his study of ethical choice in the Soviet gulags and Nazi death camps, mothers also need care, children do not need mothering for ever, and sometimes, during the Holocaust, the best way to care for children was to part with them, leaving them to the care (or otherwise) of non-Jews.[49]

As a consequence, ethico-religious discussion of inmate behaviour in Auschwitz, if appropriate at all, is clouded by issues of practical necessity and expedience. To take just one example: perhaps the most painful instance of moral disorientation among Jewish women doctors in Auschwitz was the treatment of women inmates whose pregnancies had gone undetected during the initial process of selection. The doctors were aware that as soon as the baby had been delivered both mother and baby would be gassed (or worse).[50] Not without a moral conflict whose torment did not cease after liberation, the doctors generally came to the conclusion that it was preferable to save the mother's life by killing her baby at birth.[51] As if subjected to the role of Lilith – the child-killing demoness of patriarchal imagining who was condemned by God to witness the death of one hundred of her own babies a day[52] – Jewish women doctors took the lives of babies by abortion, poisoning or suffocation at birth. Even though this saved the mother and child from the possibility of their both being pushed into the crematory ovens alive,[53] Lengyel (herself a mother of two sons who were gassed with her own mother on arrival in Auschwitz) still sees hers as a 'terrible' crime: 'the Germans succeeded in making murderers of even us.' She writes, 'I try in vain to make my conscience acquit me. I still see the infants issuing from their mothers. I can still feel their warm little bodies as I held them.'[54]

And yet, in spite of all she witnessed and was compelled to do, in the closing paragraph of her memoir, Lengyel is still able (or wants) to write of a goodness unvitiated by ambiguity:

> Yet I saw many internees cling to their human dignity to the very end. The Nazis succeeded in degrading them physically, but they could not debase them morally. Because of these few, I have not entirely lost my faith in mankind. If, even in the jungle of Birkenau, all were not necessarily inhuman to their fellowmen [*sic*], then there is hope indeed. It is that hope which keeps me alive.[55]

The persistence of relation

Rabbi Hillel's oft-quoted words summarize the ethical dilemmas of holocaustal relationality: 'If I am not for myself, who is for me? If I am for myself only, what am I?' (Pirke Avot 1: 14). These words also predict the fate of relationship, which (apart from its conclusion by death) could both deteriorate under extreme pressure and could also consolidate under those same pressures. Judith Tydor Baumel has conducted extensive interviews with female survivors and has analysed the gender dynamics of women's mutual assistance groups as a specific illustration of 'the depth of the communal bond in crisis'. She has concluded that 'the very [camp] framework that was meant to be an instrument of prisoner atomization and human fragmentation became the testing grounds for the true meaning of the term *human community*.' She, like others, has drawn scholarly attention to 'solidarity frameworks that the Nazis did not dream would ever be able to take shape in the morass of Auschwitz, Majdanek, or Bergen-Belsen'.[56]

Tydor Baumel's typology of female mutual assistance groups distinguishes types of holocaustal community which, though closely similar in function and operation, were more various than those deriving from biological relationship alone.[57] Some groups developed from sharing a barrack block or workplace, such as that of the girls and women working in the *Bekleidungskammer* (garment sorting room) at Auschwitz-Birkenau during 1943 and 1944.[58] Other groups were figured in familial terminology, with older and more experienced women acting as 'mothers' or 'older sisters' to the younger, less experienced 'daughters and younger sisters'. The 'camp sister' or 'camp brother', was one of the most important social units in the camp, second only to the biological relationships that could be sustained after deportation.[59] Still other types of mutual assistance groups in the camps had sometimes formed first in the ghettos. These were founded in shared educational and ideological affiliations and geographical origin. (Although these could as readily spawn animosities outside the group as solidarity within it.) Many of the women and girls of the Auschwitz factory *Union Werke* had, for example, been involved with the left-wing Zionist movement *Hashomer Hatzair*.

Of particular interest is Tydor Baumel's research into the ten 'camp sisters' known as the *Zehnerschaft* ('group of ten'), formed in the spring of 1943 in the Plaszow labour camp in Poland. The *Zehnerschaft* consisted of women between the ages of 16 and 26 and was founded upon the Orthodox values they held in common. All but one of the women were of common educational and religious background (that of Krakow's Beis Yaakov school for girls founded by the Hasidic educational reformer, Sarah Schenierer).[60] After Plaszow, the *Zehnerschaft* was sustained at great risk through Auschwitz and Bergen-Belsen. Significantly, the women of the *Zehnerschaft* did not limit their assistance to members of their own circle but, during the two years they were together, endangered their own lives to help other women by sharing food, a broken lice comb and other precious commodities, regardless of whether these other women were observant Jews.[61] Camp sisterhood was not, of course, peculiar to Jewish women. Delbo remembers of her French group: 'my friends never left me alone.' Fearing for her sanity, they firmly, but gently pulled her back from the literal and psychological edge.[62] Vita gives Delbo her own drink to save her from dying of thirst; Lulu swaps Delbo's heavier tool for a lighter one: 'only surrounded by the others is one able to hold out.'[63]

Writing of Jewry, Eliezer Berkovits is not alone in his view that volumes could be filled with the record of selfless care for others during the Holocaust.[64] It is not difficult to find moving testimonies of women in hiding and in the camps who were helped by the compassion and practical assistance of other women, often, but not always, their actual mothers and sisters. More memoirs and secondary sources than can be examined here recall friendships or familial or quasi-familial relationships that were a significant factor (among others including luck, attitude, skills and affiliations)[65] in their author's practical, spiritual and emotional survival.[66] Women's memoirs are not only well furnished with such examples, they are often constituted by them: keeping together *is* the holocaustal narrative. (Isabella Leitner's memoir is just one case in point.)

Adelsberger's memoir, among many others, provides evidence of a familial understanding of relation in the women's camp in Auschwitz-Birkenau. She describes the children and young women in the infirmary whom she and her colleagues had 'adopted' as 'family',[67] affirming that there were many 'families' in the women's camp and 'everyone had their own'. The formation of these 'families' was motivated by a

> genuine sense of solidarity among people who shared each other's grisly fate and felt responsible for one another. The very fact that people came together, stood up for one another, often putting their lives in jeopardy by denying themselves the very morsel of bread they needed for their own survival, and that they formed a family more tightly knit than many a natural one, was something exceptional; and not only for those who survived, but also for the many for whom such friendship and the love of their comrades eased the horrors of their miserable end.[68]

Adelsberger herself was adopted by two young girls as their 'camp mother'. This was not simply their means of enlisting her help. They reciprocated by also appointing themselves as her 'mother' and her 'grandmother', bringing her food and clothes and performing small kindnesses whenever they could. According to Adelsberger it was 'always the poor ones who did what they could to help others', not the privileged of the inmate hierarchies.[69] Or again, Sara Nomberg-Przytyk adopted a Slovak girl called Magda in February 1944 as her 'camp daughter'. Of Magda she writes, 'the camp degraded most women, but somehow it ennobled her. She was wonderful – very brave and also a happy girl.'[70] By 1945, in another camp, Ravensbrück, Nomberg-Przytyk found herself alone: 'I cried under the blanket at night. I was not used to being alone. In the camp the wall separating one human being from another was sometimes so thin that it was transparent.' When she realized that she was alone and without a child or other to care for, she became indifferent to her own survival.[71]

The women's memoir literature is substantially a narrative of the loss and the endurance of relationship. Ruth Adler's relative in Auschwitz, separated from her husband and having left her child with friends, formed a trio with two Frenchwomen 'and saved each other's lives, over and over again, each one at the risk of losing her own'.[72] Lengyel notes of the infirmary workers' dormitory: 'We shared everything, even the most trifling acquisition.'[73] In Bertha Ferderber-Salz's 'communal household' in Belsen, her niece and sister-in-law were later joined by an unnamed girl who had tended her through typhus and was also to survive Belsen. From the day of Bertha's recovery 'she never left my side. She joined our trio, and we shared every bite with her.' Ferderber-Salz also traded food she could have eaten herself for a coat for her niece, but in the camps, any girl who became attached to Ferderber-Salz would call her 'aunt'.[74]

In the light of such evidence, Holocaust Studies as a whole has shifted its focus from an examination of the mechanics of Jewish death to an exploration not only of the dynamics of physical survival, but also of the survival of the human spirit, thereby countering the stereotypical popular view of Jews having gone as passive 'lambs to the slaughter'.[75] Certainly, feminist scholars of the Holocaust engaged in historical or literary analysis of the role of women's bonding and care in women's spiritual and physical survival have differed in their conclusions, and Joan Ringelheim was to sharply revise her earlier relational emphasis.[76] Nonetheless, feminist scholarship has made a central contribution to the discourse on women's relational empowerment (not forgetting their 'ultimately being targeted for death') within Jewish voluntary and compulsory communal structures of the time.[77]

Although Tydor-Baumel observes that the onus of research has now shifted from the question of whether women may have been better at forming cooperative groups to how theirs differed from those of men,[78] Myrna Goldenberg is not alone in noting that there was more extensive and more durable bonding in the camps among women than men; virtually all women in Auschwitz formed surrogate families.[79] Certainly familial and quasi-familial groupings were not unknown among men in the camps,[80] but there is a broad consensus that men did not usually form the mutually dependent, protective, surrogate parent–child relationships that were found among women. Unlike men within mutual assistance groups, women rarely engaged in struggles for hierarchical prominence or command based on age or experience. Women's relational resistance was far more likely to consist in the sharing and networking more characteristic of women's leadership patterns of the time.[81] The practical, domestic nature of women's skills and their reactions to extreme physical and emotional deprivation also allowed their groups to develop more quickly and to be more stable than men's.[82] Mary Felstiner notes that men tended to formalize arrangements for sharing on the assumption that all would cheat, whereas women 'depended on a kind of inexplicit [*sic*] morality which constantly broke down in practice but was not seriously questioned'.[83]

Admittedly, the women's memoir literature should be read as much for what it has not said, as what it has. Women may have edited out the breakdown of some relationships. To spare their own and their readers' sensibilities they may have projected back into the past sensitivities and emotions which had been numbed at the time. And yet, despite their strict prohibition by the camp authorities, mutual assistance groups seem to have been less the exception than the rule and they yielded the kind of material and emotional support that could help a woman survive longer than might otherwise have been the case.

If relationship were only a pragmatic strategy for survival then it would be difficult to read it theologically. An exclusively reductive reading is not, however, warranted. Actual and surrogate mother/daughter bonding was informed by a maternalist ethic that was already important to women's emotional and intellectual development and had been celebrated by the central European feminism of the period.[84] From the turn of the twentieth century Jewish women across Europe had taken leadership roles in a variety of Jewish proto-feminist philanthropic, educational, Zionist and youth organizations for women, all of which had fostered leadership skills and a sense of responsibility and care for women and girls within and outside the organization.[85]

The notion of Jewish sisterhood would have been far from unknown to women in the camps. Jewish women's sisterhoods, grounded in explicitly religious ethical thought and practice, had been established by Jewish women for the social and educational advancement of Jewish women throughout Europe and North America. The *Judischer Frauenbund* (JFB), founded by Bertha Pappenheim in 1904, had attracted thousands of women in the thirty-five years of its existence, and like other such bodies at the time, believed not only in the equality of women but that the maternal instinct and female friendships would revitalize society in general and the Jewish community in particular. In the latter case, female solidarities would, it was believed, lead women into the very presence of God.[86] Later, in Nazi Germany, structures established by Jewish women for mutual aid and the welfare of the sick and elderly were translated from the essentially domestic sphere into a form of public female agency that enabled day-to-day survival in the ghettos and camps.[87] In the camps, mutual assistance groups represented the 'last vestiges' of the Jewish communal network that Nazi policy intended to destroy by means of the radical social atomization of their inmates.[88]

Joan Ringelheim has expressed the view that studies of women's mutual assistance in the camps must not be distorted by cultural feminist assumptions and values that end in the valorization of oppression and a crucial loss of perspective: mutual assistance, she argues, was incidental rather than central to women's experience and was, moreover, an ineffective mode of resistance to a psychological as well as physical assault.[89] There is, of course, some justice in Ringelheim's observations. There is no doubt that a scholar's spirituality and politics will dispose her to highlight aspects of the Holocaust that others would dismiss. But Ringelheim neglects the possibility that mutual assistance and the spiritual values it embodied may have mattered more to women than its material effect. Her argument is also framed from a secular, not a religious or ethical, perspective.

Ringelheim's argument that women's Holocaust studies may have devoted disproportionate attention to camp sisterhood has been most effectively countered in Judith Tydor Baumel's work whose strength is that it attends to the different dimensions of women's Holocaust experiences – including that of Judaism itself. Baumel notes that care was not merely expedient, nor wholly a product of oppressive gender ideology, but was integral to the whole of Jewish religious, political and cultural life, as underpinned by the values of *hesed* (kindness).[90] Among both secular and religious Jews, broad humanistic and biblical ethical precepts concerned with love, justice and kindness had already knitted social and spiritual values together, developing a strong Jewish sense of moral responsibility to self and community. The Levitical injunction to love your neighbour as yourself (19: 18) and the prophetic ethic summarized by Micah 6: 8 – do justice, love mercy and walk humbly with your God – are among the biblical precepts commonly cited in women's memoirs. Relational obligation remained integral to death and life in the camps. Thus Menachem Rosensaft, referring to Bertha Ferderber-Salz's memoir: 'defiantly, the humanist essence of Judaism elevated the victims of the Holocaust into a dimension of sanctity which can only be understood in the overall context of Jewish history.'[91]

Women's mutual assistance groups were evidently not wholly pragmatic but, in their sense of ethical obligation, broadly Jewish. Both proto-feminist and traditional ideologies of motherhood had established cultural patterns of maternalist nurture among women's extended families in pre-war European Jewish communities. Additionally, observant Jewish family life was permeated by the characteristically Jewish sense that the whole people of Israel bears responsibility for one another.[92] The Orthodox young women of the *Zehnerschaft*, for example, had been enculturated into both a Jewish ethic and into an educational community where pupils were encouraged to regard each other as sisters. From their youth, the women of the *Zehnerschaft* had internalized general ethical precepts concerning the sanctity of life such as the Talmudic dictum, 'He who saves a life, it is as if he saves the whole world' (Sanhedrin 37a and similarly Sanhedrin 4: 5).[93] To serve others was to serve God: for Rivka England, a member of the *Zehnerschaft*, 'life in Plaszow and Auschwitz was a test of our willingness to "sanctify God" by adhering to our faith, by assisting as many Jews as possible and by remaining decent human beings.'[94] When Rega Laub was asked how she – a secular Zionist – came to join the Orthodox *Zehnerschaft* she replied, 'Because of their devotion to morality in an amoral camp universe.'[95]

Also typical is the way in which Itka Frajman Zygmuntowicz took her family's (especially her mother and grandmother's) capacious Jewish ethic with her into Auschwitz: an ethic summarized by the Yiddish term *menschlekheit* – acting humanely. Her whole family were murdered; alone in Auschwitz, her mother's ethic gave spiritual guidance and a means of preserving the bond between them. Her mother had always sought to remind her, ' "Your *menschlekheit* does not depend on how others treat you but on how you treat others".' Or again, all that remained of Zygmuntowicz's relation to her grandmother was the latter's insistence on the paramount importance of justice and kindness; her lesson that '"you only have what you give away"'. After her liberation from Auschwitz, Zygmuntowicz's only relief from acute loneliness was this childhood legacy of maternally mediated ethical guidance which was deathless because it would be transmitted by memory to future generations.[96] (Likewise, the survivor Susan Kaszas has now passed on her Auschwitz ethic of divine presence – 'Lead your life as if there were nothing else around you but your conscience and God' – through the Internet.)[97]

In their different ways, then, Orthodoxy, liberal Jewry and the assimilated Western European Jewish intelligentsia of the time had all made broad, enlightened notions of human decency and dignity their own and had accepted the

imperative of ethical relation as a minimal definition of Judaism.[98] More specifically, Judaism teaches that its ultimate purpose is to elicit the presence of God and
that we are never nearer to God than when we respond in love and sympathy to
the need of others.[99] Whether religious or secularized, this ethic was a source of
relational values familiar and available to most Jews of the holocaustal period. It
was an ethic which could support a human(e) posture for as long as that remained
a physical and psychological possibility and whose resistance to the prevailing
order drew us closer to what the rabbis, in the language of tradition, called the
Messianic Age. And in the meantime, the ethico-relational counter-claim to
Nazism delineated here was and remains transformative. Sara Horowitz has
written that her work with women survivors has meant 'becoming a witness not
only to their lives but also to my own. It means importing into my life and work
their desire to act ethically in conditions that made this nearly impossible; the
sense that one's choices count, even (especially) under conditions that constrict
choice.'[100]

Facing God in Auschwitz

A holocaustal theology of relation has to elucidate the connection between God's
presence in Auschwitz and the religio-ethical response to the suffering other
accounted to many, though not all, women in Auschwitz. One way of elucidating
the connection is by reading that religio-ethical response of, in whatever sense,
staying by the side of the other, as *itself* the essence of presence. It was a presence
that exemplified the Jewish obligation of *hesed*, translated here not only as
kindness but also as faithfulness or 'gracious love'.[101] From a post-Holocaust
perspective, relationship in Auschwitz was a staying-there with the suffering other
that was an act of gracious love: a love infused with a mysterious energy that was,
in the circumstances, miraculous (though not, in the traditional Christian sense,
gracious because it was undeserved). *Hesed* was a way of seeing and recreating a
woman's full humanity. As such, it was an act of resistance: a faithfulness to the
image of God in her suffering face and a judgement on the gross inhumanity that
sought to make any person less than human. *Hesed* present-ed God by holding up
the image of God in the restored image of the human.

In which case, it would have been more than a summation of good deeds that
invited the presence of God into Auschwitz. A theology of presence requires a
stronger, more productive reading of relationality than an ethical one alone.
Martin Buber's thought is, of course, one of the most powerful statements of the
causal connection between divine presence and relationality (the practical
substance of ethics). For Buber, it is basic to Judaism that, 'true human life is
conceived to be a life lived in the presence of God'. The radiance of divine glory
or presence 'glows dimly in all human beings, every one of them; but it does not
shine in its full brightness within them – only between them'. Divine presence
may be revealed within the individual, 'but it attains its earthly fullness only where
. . . individual beings open themselves to one another, disclose themselves to one
another, help one another; where immediacy is established between one human

being and another'. Where this occurs – and the previous section of this chapter has explored the social and religious structures by which Jewish women *could* establish such immediacy between one another – 'the eternal rises in the Between'. It is in 'this seemingly empty space' that God and community are realized. For 'true community is that relationship in which the Divine comes to its realization between man and man.' Revelation 'resides within the deed itself; from within his own deed, man as well as nation hears the voice of God.'[102]

Arthur Cohen has doubted that Buber's existential, relational theology was, finally, anything more than an 'aesthetic doctrine, because a Judaism of *Erlebnis* and spontaneity cannot be transmitted'.[103] Perhaps the same could be said of my own theology of God's presence in Auschwitz (whose demonic nature is hardly such as to establish tradition). Yet the Jewish theology of image depends on the aesthetic, it should not apologize for it. When even one women in Auschwitz saw the neighbouring other and, moved by her seeing, refused to defect from the (obscured) humanity of that abjected other, hers was an ethico-aesthetic judgement made in the moment of not looking away. And the aesthetic is the theological in so far as it is grounded in a theology of image: the visibility of God (only just) present to experience.

Granted, images run the risk of becoming idols whose biblical prohibition has established Judaism as a religion more of heard and read words than of represented faces.[104] But an idol is not an image as such; it is an image which figures an arrogation of divine power and authority. The destitute Jewish face in Auschwitz, however, with nothing left to itself, is wholly and painfully translucent to the creator in whose image it is made. Such moments of aesthetic disclosure substantiate a holocaustal theology of God's presence in Auschwitz because the word *tselem* – image – connotes the visual. That is why the dignity of the divine image persists in death; the corpse remains holy because the image is not only spiritual but is primarily material.[105] The truly human bears a trace of the truly divine. It is only by the (re)creative energy of God's presence that we are or can be present. In Auschwitz, the revelation of the human(e) *as presence to the other* was entirely dependent upon the real presence of God as that to which the human other was agonizingly transparent. For the same reasons, the presence of God was entirely dependent on our showing ourselves to have been human(e). So to perceive the female face of God in Auschwitz *was* an aesthetic experience: that of seeing the other as a work of divinely created beauty and meaning and acting upon that judgement.

Feeling alienated from traditional masculinist images of God, Laura Geller once wrote: 'God is the Thou I discover through my encounter with the human thous in my life, people of whom I can say "for seeing your face is like seeing the face of God".'[106] Geller's theology points towards Emmanuel Levinas' conjunction of the ethical and the aesthetic, and it is this, at least as much as Buber's relational theology, that informs my reading of women's Holocaust memoirs.[107]

In Levinas' view Judaism rejects the overbearing, non-rational quality of numinous theistic experience. The *mysterium tremendum* or absolute otherness of the biblical God is instead revealed 'discretely' only as 'Trace' discernible in the interhuman relation. The face-to-face confrontation is a fundamentally ethical moment revealing the holiness of the face as that which must not be harmed. The face issues a call to justice. This is a kind of disenchantment of the world: an appeal to ethical freedom rather than the magic and violence of ecstasy.[108] In claiming that the experience of the Jewish holy is a fundamentally ethical rather than merely affective moment, Levinas proposes that Judaism, or at least the meaning of the Jewish Bible, is not about knowledge but about an *a priori* responsibility in the face-to-face relation. To be for the other is the meaning of subjecthood. Levinas writes that 'the Other becomes my neighbour precisely through the way the face summons me, calls for me, begs for me, and in doing so recalls my responsibility, and calls me into question.'[109] The epiphany of the other is in her having suffered offence; by her being the stranger, the widow or the orphan. Judgement is pronounced in my response to her summons.[110] It is our duty to give the bread from our mouth and the coat from our shoulders.[111] Understood by Levinas' philosophical reading of the biblical term *panim* (face), the face is the ground of the human concern for justice, not as a calculation of interests but as a revelation of the primary commandment: 'Thou shalt not kill'. The trace of God discernible in the neighbour reveals the command to expunge or assuage the humiliation or suffering of the other because 'God is a commandment to love. God is one who says that one must love the other.'[112]

Feminist critics would only cautiously recruit a Levinasian ethic to their cause. Simone de Beauvoir regarded Levinas as having deliberately taken the privileged male point of view and accorded woman the secondary status of mysterious Other to the absolute male Subject.[113] Others, including Tina Chanter, have noted that 'the domain in which the face of the feminine makes its appearance for Levinas is the realm to which woman has been consistently relegated; the relatively serene abode of the domicile, the dwelling as preserved by the "feminine touch".' He appears to 'sketch out the arena for the woman in the most traditional way (by identifying the woman with domesticity, keeping her at home), but he also deprives the feminine face of the facility of verbal speech.' Levinas' view of women appears reactionary. Lacking dominance and assertion, the feminine face seems to signify what he calls 'discretion'.[114] There is also no doubt that, as Grace Jantzen points out, Levinas' theology of the face provides an ambivalent and in many ways alarmingly masculinist symbolic for feminists for in its nakedness and vulnerability the face is fraught with the possibility of violence: it at once invites and forbids acts of violence against it.[115]

But it should be remembered that Levinas was a Russian Jew whose family fell victim to Stalin's regime and who survived a German prisoner of war camp. His work is permeated by a usually unstated consciousness of the Holocaust.[116] Suffused by a sense of the power of violence, Levinas' assumption of violence may be less patriarchal than historically conditioned by his having written 'in the shadow of Auschwitz' which, like other cataclysms of the twentieth century, raised attention to the Other to a supreme ethical principle.[117] In my turn, I am reading Levinas (as others have done) in the shadow of the re-membered/imagined Auschwitz.[118] And it is Auschwitz which lends a particular relevance to Levinas' ethic of the face, not the extent to which his sexual politics shaped his ethic. For Auschwitz could only be Auschwitz by not seeing the face. As Delbo writes in verse of another woman's young sister:

> You can't imagine how beautiful she was.
> They mustn't have looked at her.
> If they had, they would never have killed her.
> They couldn't have.[119]

It was not only the SS who would not see. Women themselves could not always look: 'each one stares at the others grown increasingly ugly, and does not see herself.' It was dangerous to look because to look was to see one's own fate.[120] Yet Delbo also knew that it was vital to carry on looking at and seeing the other. This is her refrain, addressed to herself, the women with her in Auschwitz, and her reader: 'Try to look. Just try and see.'[121] But it was very hard to look. Tedeschi, grieving that she could not remember the faces of her two daughters, also found that she could not hold a sharp focus on the faces around her. Others could no longer bear to remember the faces of those they loved. SS guards commonly referred to Jews as *Figuren* – shapes whose human form and meaning had been disassembled. The beating of faces with clubs, their encrustation with sores and filth, and the shaving of heads made individuals difficult to recognize: 'for each friend you have a double image; how they look now, and how they were before.' And more than that, in the 'inexpressive and clouded eyes' and 'crazed or absent expression' that met Tedeschi's gaze, 'something human' had been lost from the face.[122] Even after Auschwitz, the preoccupation with faces did not diminish. Delbo continued to look into people's faces to know if they were a friend; if they would help her or not.[123]

Levinas' ethical theology of the face is not intended to be a theological reflection on the Holocaust. But it seems to me to be *precisely* the defenceless destitution, the exposed nudity and absolute poverty of the open (because ruined) human face in Auschwitz which did indeed both provoke limitless violence from the Nazis and their collaborators and, at the same time, issue the ethical appeal Levinas describes. 'Deprived of everything' (to use Levinas' phrasing) the face issued a prohibition of murder that captures the authoritative, but non-coercive mode of divine self-manifestation whose purity intensified both violence and love.

In Auschwitz, the almost erased human face was indeed, to borrow Levinas' words, 'a demand', 'an open hand', which (like the God it reveals) could do nothing – was not a force, but an authority. For as Levinas notes, 'there are these two strange things in the face: its extreme frailty – the fact of being without means and, on the other hand, there is authority. It is as if God spoke through the face.' In speaking of the face as 'the frailty of the one who needs you, who is counting on you',[124] and as one who summarizes his entire philosophy as there being 'something more important than my life, and that is the life of the other',[125] it is not difficult to see how Levinas' theology of the face assists a feminist theology of the Holocaust where, as we shall see in the next chapter, mothers in particular were ethically positioned in just such an asymmetrical relation to the infinitely vulnerable, expectant faces of the children who, if for not much longer, remained in their care.

Relationship was a clothing of the naked; a re-touching of the divine image. And because 'the dimension of the divine opens forth from the human face',[126] this re-covering and re-touching is how we come to know God. By a practical aesthetic of the senses, sight and touch became the principal means by which women in Auschwitz could overcome their separation from each other, from the world and from the holy. In its absolute singularity, the body is both a separation of one from the other and a revelation of self and God as loved because seen and seeing. The loved and loving face turned to the other is itself a moment of reassurance. (It was said of Dov Baer of Mezritch that his followers were at peace when they looked into his face.)[127]

Certainly, the feminist project is not Levinas' concern. Yet his view that feminine tenderness is not determined by a purely biological set of characteristics and is therefore available to the whole sexual spectrum underpins this study. Tina Chanter has suggested that, despite evidence to the contrary, Levinas does not regard women as merely 'ancillary' to the male project.[128] Indeed, his philosophy is not incompatible with feminism as he posits the ethical relation of the face to face as primary and prior to traditionally virile logic and reason. For Levinas the 'vocation' of the feminine is as an antidote to the 'masculinity of the universal and conquering *logos* [reason]'; the 'ontological function of the feminine' is as 'the one who does not conquer' but, in contrast to reason's cruelty, is 'the origin of kindness on earth'.[129] Whether or not this is a reactionary claim depends on where it is made. In Auschwitz, Levinas' account of the feminine identifies a distinctive form of resistance and judgement. My contention that relationality and its practical functions rendered the wholly uninhabitable Auschwitz habitable to God (though not to humanity) derives from Levinas' view that women's secret presence, their silent footsteps, render the world habitable.[130] It is not that women's presence is always to be secret and silent. It is rather that in Auschwitz, where presence was erased by disease, disfigurement, death and the prohibition of moral choice, women's presence could not be other than, as it were, secret and silent.

Neither Levinas' ethic nor his narrative (aggadhic) rather than halakhic approach to the interpretation of tradition,[131] makes Levinas a prophet of Jewish feminism. Not unsurprisingly, Levinas remarks that in Judaism 'the feminine will never take on the aspect of the divine' and his discussion of the feminine element in Judaism rehearses a good deal of rabbinic hyper-misogynistic sentiment without noticeable censure.[132] But reading his work in the holocaustal context his (not entirely sexist) valorizing association of the feminine with welcome, shelter and tenderness far more significantly supports my contention that female kindness held open the gates (only just) wide enough for God to pass through. Levinas is right to insist that the feminine is other to the masculine and to erase female difference in the name of equality with masculinity is to defer to the priority and normativity of the masculine.[133] But while he regards the feminine as properly indwelling and self-effacing; as in some sense a secret remedy for the masculine, I regard acts of 'female' kindness in Auschwitz as an all too public judgement and transformation of once-persons to persons once more.

It is not the purpose of this study to give a detailed account of Levinas' theory of the feminine, nor does feminist theology need to be buttressed by male authorities. I make no claim that his work is entirely usable in this context or that he would have approved my use. But it is instructive to juxtapose Levinas' theology of the face and his account of the domain of the feminine. In his thought, the face, bearing the divine trace, commands that you welcome it and he also associates women with the act and orientation of welcome. This is significant. When a woman in Auschwitz saw the face of the other and went out to meet her she can also be said to have gone out to meet God. Auschwitz was a mirror onto the suffering face of God; God was seen and authoritative in the face of the suffering other. (The Hasidic rebbes were more literal than Levinas: the sign of the image in which God has created humanity is said to be on the forehead.)[134] Although Judaism understands itself as an aniconic tradition, Elliot Wolfson has justly described the Israel of mystical understanding as 'the one who sees God'.[135] What I refer to here is not the seeing of God's face as an act of ocular interpretation but an embodied experience in which the eye opens, receives and welcomes the whole need of the neighbouring other. In Auschwitz, the other's open(ed) face not only mirrored the appeal in the facing face but, as a sign of God and a sign to God, welcomed God into Auschwitz as if it were God's home. The open, naked face demanded of both the other and God, do not leave me alone here; be with me.[136] For contrary to those who would insist upon its alterity to the point of voiding it of intelligibility, Auschwitz was a place where, like any other, God could be, even for a very short while, safe in our care.

While it may be true that Levinas is interested in ethical obligation to persons, not their aesthetic contemplation,[137] I am also drawing on a Jewish theology of image to give a 'stronger' account of the theophanic possibilities of the face than might Levinas. I am arguing that there is a crucial link between God's being made present and the seeing and touching of faces and bodies that have been made unseeable and untouchable; that have disappeared. As Susan Handelman comments of Levinas, face is not only or even primarily a visual perception but a way of understanding the subject/object relation *as* a relation.[138] Theologically, this means that the immanence of the face-to-face relation, as an opening onto divine immanence, reveals that the divine/human relation is indeed a relationship between persons with its own imperative of mutual presence.

'Face' is, after all, a biblical metonym for divine presence. Israel yearns for God's face while its foes taunt her with God's absence (Ps. 42); she constantly seeks God's face (Ps. 105: 4) and experiences the lifting up of the divine face to shine upon her as the blessing of divine presence which grants friendship and peace (Num. 6: 25–6). In Auschwitz-Birkenau when a woman lifted up her cast down face to the summons of her mother, daughter, sister, or friend it caught the reflected light of the Shekhinah on its upturned surface, reflecting the glory or *kavod* of God's face back into the world – even a world which was, for them, over, and a world which, become Auschwitz, had turned God away at the gates.[139] The relational moment offered no more than a dedication to peace. Yet even the dimmest illumination of one suffering face by the facing, seeing, other produced the intimation of God's radiance (*kavod*) among them. Rabbinic midrash compares the Shekhinah or divine presence to light, to what shines. 'Washed' by ersatz coffee, urine, brackish water or love alone, the reflective face lit God's way into, through and out of, Auschwitz.

Women's resistance to the Nazi diremption of body and face was a great, necessarily public, cosmic sign of the redemptive process at work in Auschwitz among those who saw through its effect to the personhood of the abject other, returning what had been taken from them and re-calling Jacob's words to Esau: '[A]ccept from me this gift; for to see your face is like seeing the face of God' (Gen. 33: 10). Theirs was a gift not only to each other but to Israel, the one who, to enlarge on Wolfson, *must* see God, if God is to see us.

5 A mother/God in Auschwitz

'Comfort, oh comfort My people,'
Says your God. 'Speak tenderly to Jerusalem . . .'
(Is. 40: 1)[1]

Maternalist perspectives on post-Holocaust theology

Jewish feminist anthropology's central observation has been that Jewish women's perspective is derived from an 'alternative reality': a female 'subculture' or 'second world' to that of men. 'Cross-culturally', Susan Starr Sered observes, Jewish women who are excluded from the male systems that confer prestige have found 'other ways of striving to be moral beings'. Women's own religious modes, operative within the 'little tradition' as opposed to the sacred, written, masculine 'great tradition', are normative for themselves. Sered summarizes traditional Jewish women's religiosity as being 'more to do with love, death, and human relations, than with abstract theological concepts' (a religiosity which she has especially begun to respect since becoming a mother herself).[2] Consequently, 'in diverse cultural situations, women . . . modify theologies that ignore the suffering of children in this world.'[3]

I do not think that post-Holocaust theology has ignored the suffering of children. Fackenheim and Greenberg, to name but two, have been much preoccupied with it. For Greenberg, the screams of children thrown into the fire pits at Auschwitz-Birkenau in 1944 are the only index against which theological claims might be justifiable and sayable. What post-Holocaust theology *has* ignored is the experience of those children's mothers and the theological possibilities of maternalist language and values. Maternal experience and the ethical difference that produces has been an important focus of second wave feminist scholarship. It is this, and Sered's analysis of Jewish women's traditional concerns with 'love, death and human relations', that contextualizes my situating the experiences and tropes of motherhood at the centre of the feminist theological enquiry in ways that will challenge, modify, and finally alter the character and substance of the post-Holocaust project. In particular, I am convinced that a feminist theological reading of women's narration of broken (and sometimes preserved or restored) familial relationships during the Holocaust shifts our conception of God's presence among European Jewry between 1933 and 1945.

Jewish women's Holocaust testimonies are generally constituted by their record of the fate of close family members.[4] The survival of the Jewish people or the covenant as theological ideas are of less immediate concern than that of familial and social relationships. The tendency to filter holocaustal experience through a closely worked mesh of family connections persists among women survivors. Sara Horowitz recalls how her attempt to publish a record of the experiences of a woman she calls Judith in an anthology of women's writing on the Holocaust was much impeded by Judith's unyielding insistence on opening her contribution with,

> a long passage consisting of the names of her murdered relatives in Europe, with her family network laid out in elaborate detail, and reaching back several generations. These were the people who had constituted her intimate world as a child. Her beloved maternal grandmother, her maternal uncle, her mother's sister – all named, the relationships carefully traced.[5]

Like so many women who were (and in Orthodoxy, still are) charged with the duty of guarding the family identity; 'the duty of perpetuating *Yiddishkeit* from generation to generation'[6] – Judith's situating herself within a now dead family was not merely the preface to her story, but *the story itself.* The familial is the frame and fabric within which the narration of the fate of European Jewry is woven. This 'female' narrative is not transcendentalized: here, the history of Jewry is a local, domestic narrative of interconnected families. And it is not only biological mothers who tell this story.[7] As evoked in the poetry of Jane Jacobson, women may mark other women's (dis)appearance into history by those women's association with the times, spaces and objects that constitute a female environment that is both remembered and ever renewed:

> Not until I told my mother
> I was going to marry under a wedding canopy
> did she let me know that I had a great-aunt Anna
> who did the scene in the gold leaf frame
> a picture as familiar and secret as my own reflection. . .
>
> sent from Warsaw between the wars,
> [it is] all we have of her.[8]

Judy Chicago describes meeting a woman survivor who found it important to cook in the way her murdered mother had done; more problematically, the woman had tried to resurrect her mother by making her 9-year-old daughter dress up in her grandmother's clothes.[9] Jewish women of the post-Holocaust generations also reflect on the Holocaust in the light of shared women's experiences. Jewish feminist biblical commentary might, for example, be offered through the interpretative lens of Holocaust experience specific to mothers.[10] Similarly, even for Jewish women who were born after the Holocaust, the more emotionally charged aspects of contemporary motherhood can be filtered through the lens of Holocaust 'memory'. As one woman told a discussion group: 'The realisation of the Holocaust is very strong for me. I put my arm around my son when he goes on the train and I think of how other women then, during that time, must have put their arms around their sons.'[11]

In her commentary on an interview she conducted with the survivor Itka Frajman Zygmuntowicz, Sara Horowitz notes that Zygmuntowicz's spiritual inheritance is intertwined with and preserved by her memories of her mother and grandmother. And like other women survivors, her key memories of the Holocaust are also remembered differently – that is, mediated through their (often final) conversations with their mothers. Zygmuntowicz's mother, like so many others, urged her to 'retain her self – neither to imitate the Nazis nor to absorb the image they project of her'. Most significantly, for Zygmuntowicz and other women whose mothers perished, 'their spiritual legacy passes to them along a chain of women. A sense of continuity with the Jewish past and with Jewish meaning is embedded in their memories of mothers, and often grandmothers, rather than articulated abstractly.'[12]

Giuliana Tedeschi particularly mourned the loss of a small bunch of dried violets that her daughter had picked for her grandmother in the Italian spring of 1944 and which had been taken from Tedeschi with her other belongings on arrival in Auschwitz.[13] Here the female line was symbolized in the giving of flowers, by one generation of women to another. The dry, dead, crushed and, finally, vanished flowers evoke the withering, death and disappearance of countless maternal lines. But after the Holocaust, Charlotte Delbo could see a new baby as having been born on behalf of all those mothers who had died: 'You remember this peasant woman, lying in the snow, dead with her newborn frozen between her thighs. My son was also that newborn. I look at my son and recognize Jackie's eyes, Yvonne's pout. . . . My son is their son, he belongs to all of them. He is the child they will not have had.'[14]

Theologians cannot simply rule out women's relational perspective on the Holocaust *a priori*, as if it were not a properly Jewish place to start. To be faithful to the actual and particular suffering of *all* persons during the Holocaust and to the covenantal presence of God in the midst of that suffering, Jewish theology must reflect on the gendered variety of Jewish experience before or instead of its resolution of a set of formal (theo)logical problems whose framing is itself gendered. Post-Holocaust theology must also contest its customary subordination of imagination and historical particularity to the authority of approved texts – the 'little tradition' to the 'great tradition'.[15] After all, the 'great' tradition is capacious and can not only accommodate the 'little' one, in so far as it is that of the whole Jewish people, it is both product and productive of the 'little' tradition. Until now, for Holocaust theology to *be* theology, emotion and memory must have been sublimated into argument.[16] But that Holocaust theology might sometimes be undertaken from a subjective, involved and familial perspective need not connote an introverted, parochial theology that places the interests of immediate relationships before those of the wider human community. On the contrary, post-biblical

Judaism is in many respects a familial, domestic religion where the flourishing of families is a sign and precondition of the holiness of the human community as a whole. Indeed, the women survivors and feminist scholars with whom Judy Chicago made contact during the course of her research all wanted to make connections between the Holocaust and other historical genocides and atrocities. By contrast, she found that masculinist scholarship 'invariably' stressed 'the uniqueness and mystery' of the Holocaust. One survivor, Vera John-Steiner, wrote to Chicago claiming that arguments about the uniqueness of the Holocaust,

> cut away at our connectedness to other communities and other individuals who were also victimized by genocide and its legacy – mass murder. Focusing on the female experience of the Holocaust helps us move toward, rather than away from, an understanding of our human connectedness and helps repair the human fabric of community.[17]

A maternalist perspective reveals how the very mapping of the holocaustal territory – its scale, dimensions and boundaries – is gendered. For the relationships destroyed were, in the very nature of relationships, not temporally or spatially bounded. The six million who died were not us. But when interpreted from a maternalist perspective the crimes of the Holocaust are almost infinitely multiplied and assume yet more unmanageable proportions.[18] Not only were over a million and a half new beginnings lost in the children murdered by the Nazis and their accomplices, the 'maternal *continuum* that lies in the past of every human born, male or female; and the infinity of a maternal *continuum* that presents itself as a future possibility when a woman generates a daughter'[19] entails that there is no outer limit to their crime.

(Divine) motherhood and providence

For some women, the preservation of post-Holocaust faith may be only secondarily (if at all) about the hope that this or that proposition about God is still the case. The Holocaust was rather an absolute offence against the relational substance of a practical religion whose sphere of the holy was established where tradition engaged those relationships. And yet the methodological separation of questions about the nature of God and about the bodily assault upon the body of Israel can leave Auschwitz primarily a crime against an idea of God or an idea of the religious civilization founded in his name. This abstraction of Auschwitz neglects the victimized social and individual body: the first site of the catastrophe and the first site of the religio-spiritual problem.

If religious philosophy has paid any attention to motherhood at all, it has been as a natural institution standing (boringly) outside the public sphere of the historical world. But this is untrue. As feminist historians have pointed out, motherhood is a social institution as well as a biological connection and is subject to considerable historical and ideological change. (The bourgeois European notion of motherhood dates from the Reformation period and is, as ever, in a state of transition.)

Likewise, to cast God in a maternal mode is not to remove Judaism from its historical relationship with a God of history. There is no reason why a God who can be likened to a mother is not also a God whose will and whose suffering the consequences of her own immanence is revealed in history.

Were a feminist post-Holocaust theology to figure God's presence in Auschwitz as maternal in character, then the peculiar horror of, for instance, mothers' attempts to bring new Jewish life into the vast necropolis that was Europe under Nazi rule and hoping, against all hope, to nurture it, would tell us something about the occultation of divine presence by radical evil. But at present such a symbology could not be theologically accommodated for God's female face has been turned to the wall. Because the patriarchal model of God wills and speaks rather than births the world, the particular experiences of pregnant women in labour in the camps and ghettos have been incidental rather than pivotal in helping theologians to figure the meaning of the Holocaust. These experiences do not strike androcentric theologians as a special problem; they do not impinge upon their theological imaginary. Post-Holocaust theology has largely proceeded as if the suffering of mothers and children has offered a graphic illustration of Nazi barbarism, but not insight into God.

Yet where the metaphor of a Mother-God represents not merely an aspect of God, but a function of God that reconfigures the entire concept of God, then a pregnant woman in Auschwitz assumes a particular theological poignancy. For most Jewish feminists, 'The Holy One is *Gaol-tanu*, *Ima-ha-olam*, our Redeemer, Mother of the World. She is *Ha raham-aima*, Compassionate Giver of Life. She is *Makor hahaiim*, Source of Life. She is our neighbourly spirit, the Shekhinah.'[20] In Jewish feminist liturgy,

> Blessed is She who in the beginning, gave birth . . .
> Blessed is She whose womb covers the earth.
> Blessed is She whose womb protects all creatures.[21]

Auschwitz was above all a crime against what women and men had made from their bodily love and had nurtured to maturity from their bodily labour. These labours are both symbol and medium of divine presence; of how God is carried into the world and how God carries the world in God. They suggest a theology which is biblical as well as feminist. In Ps. 22: 10–11 the Jewish body is scorned, mocked, abandoned, 'less than human', yet the womb remains a juncture between divine presence and the world: 'You drew me from the womb, made me secure at my mother's breast. I became your charge at birth; from my mother's womb You have been my God.' Here God's agency is manifest within the birth process. Birth is the beginning of a relation not only with the mother but also, through her body, with God. Or again, in Isaiah 46: 3–4 God is one who, like a mother, has carried Israel 'since leaving the womb'. In this text God describes his relation to Israel in maternal terms: 'Till you grow old, I will still be the same; When you grow grey, it is I who will carry; I was the Maker and I will be the Bearer; and I will carry and rescue [you].'[22] In short, where the uterine is a significant medium of divine presence, the contractions of a woman in labour in Auschwitz become both locus and symbol of the vulnerability and abandonment of both God and Jewry to the Nazi desecration of the divinely created and creative order. The woman in labour (who will shortly be murdered with her new-born child or whose new-born baby will be killed by Jewish women medical orderlies in a customarily Jewish ethical attempt to save the mother's life)[23] becomes a real symbol of Judaism in convulsion; of how Nazism attempted to destroy Judaism from within its own future.

A theology of the suffering face is not, then, a decapitation of the feminist imaginary. The face, like the womb, is imaginally saturated in both feminist and patriarchal discourse but belongs to the fully embodied ethico-spiritual repertoire of motherhood. Whether or not the face faces the other as its mother, the face assembles the particularity of the body as person as it becomes, itself, a part of Torah.[24] The female Jewish body carries the historical process as an ark or tabernacle inside which is wrapped the story or Torah Jews have told about the relationship between themselves and God, and which unfolds and rolls on and out through time in the carrying and opening of the body to new life. And just as the Torah scrolls must be cherished, dressed, crowned with silver and cradled in our arms, so too must be each woman's (derelict) body in Auschwitz on which desecrated scroll is inscribed another (not the last) chapter of the story of the love between God and Israel. I shall turn now to some of these body-stories within stories as *midrashim* on the love of God for Israel, the utmost sign of which was God's presence as (a) Mother in Auschwitz.

There in Auschwitz, the body of Israel was being consumed by fire and starvation and Mother was not yet one of God's names. Indeed, her maternal presence had an elusive namelessness hauntingly evoked in a story told by Sara Nomberg-Przytyk of Auschwitz's evacuation in 1945 in the face of the advancing Russian army. After a long march away from the camp, the women were loaded into open wagons in the freezing January night. Sara was moments from dying of exposure when a nameless woman stretched out her hand from the next wagon along and gave her own camp blanket, saying she could share with her daughter. In reply Sara said:

> 'Ma'am . . . please give me your name. I really must know your name.' Silence. 'Can you hear me?' I called out loud. 'Please. Your name.' 'Your name, your name' was repeated in the echo of the wheels. 'Stretch out your hand.' I heard a whisper from behind the wall. I stretched out my hand. In my hand I found a dry crust of bread from the camp. I chewed it up and then let the dry crumbs dissolve in my mouth. 'Your name, your name,' I insisted. 'Your name, your name, your name.' The wind was blowing in my ears.[25]

Although the work of a secular Jew, this text now calls across time of a God whom women had not yet called upon in their own names but who was and is no less a feeding, clothing, saving presence. As Shekhinah (until now a female name for God's presence mediated by men and therefore a subjected presence), this was a not-yet-named God whose hands were stretched out to us even though they were too mired and it was too dark to see them; whose face was turned towards us even when the walls of our suffering were too high to see over. (Just as there were mothers who longed to touch the soft skin of their children, even though those children were no longer there to touch.)[26] As in Gen. 3: 9 where God moves through the garden in the cool of the day, calling 'where are you?', God seeks us, but does not always know where to find us, especially when, profaned, our faces disappear from view. Sometimes the exiled Shekhinah, going (in all senses) in Israel's train, fell behind. On the forced march out of Auschwitz in January 1945, among the sixteen and a half thousand women on the move, Tedeschi's camp sisters, would call to one another in the dark, checking that they were all there. But Tedeschi's friend Violette gradually became unable to move her swollen legs. Tedeschi remembers: 'I said something to her as she walked alongside me; when I looked for her a few moments later she was gone. The road had swallowed her up. In the morning five pairs of hands would reach out to help anybody who slipped on the ice; in the evening those who slipped lay where they fell.' Women tried not to trample on bodies but still went on without looking.[27] So too, God sometimes disappeared in Auschwitz, but did not turn her face from its suffering. God, among them, fell from view and women did not always know where or how to find this God among the vast throng of nameless dying for they did not know her name.

The moments when God might just have caught the whisper of the first and most comprehensive of her names were among women who offered care even when they had nothing left to give but the self they would soon cease to be. Across the not always bridgeable temporal and interpretative span between then and now, such women seem to be saying to one another, over and over again, the most enigmatically metapatriarchal and the most minimal of all God's names; perhaps the only one that *could* have been uttered in Auschwitz: 'Ehyeh Asher Ehyeh' (usually translated as 'I am who I am' or 'I will be who I will be').[28]

Nomberg-Przytyk's story evokes an elusive but providential divine female presence; in Judith Jaegarmann's testimony this divine presence comes closer, knowable in the traditions of maternal succour associated with Shekhinah. In 1943, at the age of 13 and from an Orthodox family, she was deported from Theresienstadt to Auschwitz. There her mother, described as a 'guardian angel', continued to give her the courage to live. She offered motherly comfort to all the girls who were alone: 'all the girls tried to stay near to her and felt sheltered by her.' In the women's camp in Birkenau, Jaegarmann's mother tore her own blanket apart and made bands to protect her daughter's legs from the frostbite wrought by winter temperatures of minus twenty degrees centigrade. On one occasion, transported out of Auschwitz to another work camp, Jaegarmann lost consciousness while labouring in the snow. As in the moment of birth she opened her eyes to a circle of female faces above her: 'Suddenly I felt as if someone wakes [*sic*] me and I saw the faces of many women over me. I overheard them saying "the little one almost froze to death." They let me lie down for a little while longer and then many girls started massaging and rubbing me, so that I started to feel my body, hands and feet again.'[29]

Or again, when Susan Cernyak-Spatz was recovering from typhoid fever her German-Jewish support group 'shlepped' her through the gate of the camp in the morning after roll call. They hid her, watched over her, and fed her what they could find – a live frog, some greenery.[30] These narratives of embodied, maternal care as *itself* the power of redemption and resurrection, belong with that of Charlotte Delbo (a non-Jewish French inmate) who recalls those women 'who [would] hold you up, or carry you when you can no longer walk, those who hold you fast when you're at the end of your rope.' Women's bodily solidarity was also a moral solidarity: 'We protect one another. Each wishes to remain near a companion, some in front of a weaker one, so as to be hit in her stead, some behind one no longer able to run, so as to hold her up if she begins to fall.'[31] Similarly, Tedeschi describes how the women whose job it was to drag cart-loads of slopping excrement in the cold heavy rain arranged themselves into a block, 'shoulder to shoulder, breast to breast'. Tedeschi's friend Zilly was weak and was allowed to pretend to be pulling. At the head of the draw bar a Polish woman, Bianca Maria, would cry '"Dalej, dalej – on, on!" Thus she helped us to drag the much heavier cart of our captivity.'[32]

Torture should never be gilded by romantic notions of its heroic endurance. It is not to glorify torture to observe that its burdens could sometimes (and only sometimes) be shared out among a group of bodies whose power exceeded the sum of its parts. From a post-Holocaust perspective this phenomenon suggests a female spirituality of holding and carrying; of being the one who rubs, holds, presses against or pushes women on: a repertoire of divine maternal succour and female solidarity also suggested by Maya Nagy's (non-religious) story. After Nagy's mother's death, and at the very end of the war when Nagy herself was close to death, she was found by an aunt who had lost contact with her own children. Her aunt began to mother her and find food for her. 'But the most important thing she did was when we were marching to Copenhagen; I kept falling because I was terribly weak by then. Though she had not the strength to *lift* me, she kept pushing me forward with her foot, and that saved my life.' Her aunt lives on in Nagy's memory 'as this woman who pushed me to freedom and survival with this gentle movement of her foot.'[33]

During roll-call – often lasting a day and a night without interruption – Lucie Adelsberger remembers how the women stood still, in rags, in all weathers, beaten whipped and lashed with pistols if they fell, with empty stomachs, often with diarrhoea and unable to move so that 'excrement streamed out of them like a waterfall'. And yet here too: 'furtively and inconspicuously they pressed up against one another to keep warm, and thus they supported their comrades when they began to reel.'[34] Charlotte Delbo too remembers how, at roll-call, each woman would both support and be warmed by another by placing her hands in the armpits of the woman in front of her. And when the legs of women in her work detail became too swollen for them to walk the others would try to carry them, terminally weak as they themselves were.[35] Some women maintained a maternal posture (that is, not necessarily one of biological motherhood) to the very end. One girl, Adele, flung into the trucks heading for the gas chambers 'turns to help those behind her. . . . She is not afraid. Her arm encircles a weaker girl whose knees are failing her.'[36]

Levinas recognizes that maternity is the immediately ethical relation between one who is under an obligation to nourish, clothe, house the other who is not an object of contemplation but of giving.[37] Feminist theorists, however, have challenged why mothers should enable others without the social and political reciprocation of opportunities for mothers. And yet women survivors' memoirs show that motherhood – whether as a socio-ethical posture or as a biological relationship – is not always an asymmetrical relation of care. During the Holocaust, care for children could give women themselves a sense of meaning, purpose and hope. When an orphaned, 4-year-old Jewish girl arrived at the house in Antwerp where Clara Isaacman and her mother were hiding, her mother's depressed, withdrawn face 'lit up when she held the child on her lap, singing to her and combing her curls'.[38] Often, the sustenance of children by mothers was reciprocated by children. Ghetto children sometimes worked for their mother's survival by finding food for them and tending them when they were sick (fathers and older brothers having been commonly separated from their families at an earlier stage of the genocide). Children could themselves become 'mothers' where their own mothers had numerous children to care for. Isabella Leitner mourns her baby sister Potyo, who was probably thrown alive into the fire-pits of Auschwitz on 31 May 1944, as if she had been her own baby: 'She was "my" baby.' Leitner had bathed and changed her nappies as if she were Potyo's mother. Speaking as her mother might have done had she survived, Leitner writes: 'She would be a middle-aged woman now, and I still can't deal with having lost her.'[39]

Female comfort was not always or even very often materially transformatory. In the 'infirmary' where Adelsberger worked, she and other doctors could not treat the starved, delirious inmates, but only 'comfort and encourage them. It didn't make them any better: they still died like flies.'[40] But at least the doctors were *there*. It is notable that the Talmud (Sukkah 49b) urges not only that we give charity but that we speak tenderly to those who receive it; this may mean more to them than the gift itself. Yet more significantly, the Talmud urges the imitation of God through compassion. Just as God clothes the naked, visits the sick, comforts mourners and buries the dead, so too should we (Sotah 14a). This Talmudic identification of God's activity with that of the carer is what should be affirmed of the women in the camps who were able to show compassion to those who were yet more broken than themselves, or who were as much objects of compassion to the tended other. It was their acts that were presentative of God for all women, for the imitation of God brings God among us.

To comfort another was to trace upon an afflicted body a sign of remembrance of a way of being in the world that was wholly other to Auschwitz and was also a promise of its (quasi-eschatological) restoration. Perhaps the redemption of love could be anticipated even on the way to Auschwitz. Maya Nagy remembers being in the freight wagon with her mother and grandmother:

> We were crowded, so crowded. It was a tragedy. My grandmother, who was a source of food and goodies all her life, took out from somewhere some sort of cold drinking-chocolate. I think it was just plain cocoa, with a little bit of

cold water poured over it. Heavenly! heavenly! I don't know how she managed it. It was in a glass jar. I mean, they had *really* taken away everything from us; we didn't have any luggage. Where she got it from I don't know. Somewhere.[41]

I would not want to say that this was enough. What of those in the wagon who watched the three women drink the cocoa but had nothing themselves? But signs are just that: indicators rather than the thing itself. This grandmother's provision could be read as a sign and remembrance of the divine female gift of life, not withdrawn but here carried in the folds of the body and its garments and produced to be shared with those whose faces were turned towards her and whose hands were open to receive it.

By contrast, the Father-God – the monarchical Man of War – was of little or no consolation or relevance to the women whose memoirs are the narrative ground of the present theological project (which is not to make a global historical claim about women's faith during this period). In Auschwitz Bertha Ferderber-Salz still sought an unfailing presence, but it was not that of the God she knew from the tradition. Here, unfailing presence was embodied in the maternal night watching of the smooth, round face of the moon whose soft beam became the symbolic antithesis of the merciless rays of the beating sun (the rebuke of her memoir's title). The face of the moon is always turned towards us, even if it is darkened by shadow and cloud. In Auschwitz, the empathetic, gently 'smiling' moon – a traditionally female symbol of divinity and one strongly associated in the mystical literature with the luminous light of the Shekhinah[42] – carries Ferderber-Salz to the daughters she has had to leave behind. In a place where the living were barely distinguishable from the dead, the distinction between animate and inanimate objects began to blur in some women's need for the consolation of a deathless, redemptive, transcendent presence. Ferderber-Salz addresses the moon as if it were a benign (though far from omnipotent) power that is both maternal and an object of petitionary prayer:

The moment it appeared, peeping through the window into the sleeping block, I said a silent prayer to it. The cool, pale moonlight did not harm or taunt us; on the contrary, it soothed and comforted us. Its light was as pale as we, who were considered dead during our lifetime. On nights when I could not sleep I would unburden my heart to it. 'Soon you will disappear from my window, travelling over the city,' I whispered. 'Please look in the windows of my little girls, caress their head with your cool light, because I cannot stroke them with a mother's loving hand. Be kind to me, and when you return to my window tomorrow night tell me about my children. Are they sleeping peacefully in the strange house in that hostile city?'[43]

Motherhood itself began to lose its usual relational contours as sisters took on the providential functions of mothers to one another, and mothers took on those of quasi-divine presence. Even in the days after liberation, Isabella Leitner's sister

Rachel remained what she calls the 'mother hen', sewing a cut-up blanket into a coat to keep her sister warm. Speaking for her sisters as well, Leitner writes to Rachel: 'The endless care. The endless concern. Our complete confidence that we could rely on you. We always blessed you. Did you know that?'[44]

The experience of a divine or quasi-divine power that did not redeem by mighty intervention but by care may not have been unusual among women of this period. In Rachel Feldhay Brenner's study of Anne Frank's and Etty Hillesum's writings, a theology of care and consolation emerges from the lesser rigours they endured outside the death and slave labour camps. We do not know if their spiritual resistance would have persisted *in extremis* because Frank was taken from Auschwitz to Bergen-Belsen in 1944 and died there at the beginning of spring 1945. Hillesum died within eight weeks of her arrival in Auschwitz. It is none-theless significant that Brenner finds that in their 'humiliating and degrading exclusion from humanity, the two women needed to reaffirm their humanity in the consoling presence of the Divine.'[45] Although Hillesum affirms that she 'will always feel safe in God's arms',[46] Brenner observes that both Hillesum and Frank have a concept of God who 'saves them *in* but not *from* the terror in which they live and die'. The God to whom both Hillesum and Frank pray 'is not a God revealing himself as [a] powerful redeeming God, but rather a God of loving attention and consolation. It is a God who does not rescue the lives of the victims, but one who sustains the sufferers in their struggle to maintain, as long as possible, a life of dignity and self-respect.'[47] Both Frank and Hillesum were protected and sustained by their God, giving the latter strength to be 'a mediator' to and of God to those around her.[48] Hillesum's care for others in their suffering extends even to the defenceless God whose survival depends on the work of human beings to defend the world from destruction.[49] Brenner's interpretation of Hillesum's theology is central to my own interpretation of the maternal dimension of the survivor literature. She writes of Hillesum's theology:

> God is the divine spark that constitutes the essence of humanity and must therefore survive. And as the divine spark in us, God is more powerful than ever, because the illuminating spark of the divine compels us to resist the dehumanizing logic of destruction and affirms our courage in the reality of the apocalypse. What emerges, therefore, is the absolute, irrevocable inter-dependence of God and humanity/humaneness. To remain human/humane, the individual must protect the 'God' part in her; to remain divine, God must be protected and guarded by the individual.[50]

Brenner's subjects assert spiritual freedom in the act of writing. But their kindness and attention to suffering also encapsulates the relational dynamic of the theology I have wanted to elaborate here, where kindness is not to be reduced to an ineffec-tual gesture or to a demeanour cherished only by children, but, *in this situation*, where all gestures against Nazism were more or less materially ineffectual, was the maternal quality of divine love. This is the love of a Mother-God, known to tradition as (the) Shekhinah.

That Frank's and Hillesum's was not a Jewish God (nor even, entirely, a
Christian one), but one represented by an 'ecumenical' ethic of 'dignity, self-
respect and responsibility' constituted by Judaeo-Christian and Enlightenment
values,[51] does not diminish the importance of their theological contribution. On
the contrary, there may not be *a* Jewish God. In the history of God's self-
revelation and its human reception the Jewish God has been one God with several
faces, one of which is a consoling face: that of Shekhinah beneath whose wings (as
numerous Jewish feminist poets, songwriters and liturgists testify) many women
have found shelter. Thus Sylvia Rothschild's liturgical adaptation of Psalm 143:
9–12: 'Be with me, El Shaddai . . . cover me in the shelter of your wings, hold me
to your breast and comfort me. . . . I run to your sheltering presence for you are
my God, your spirit is good.'[52]

The maternal face of God in Auschwitz

Neither Frank nor Hillesum were mothers. It may be that the mothering of young
children yields a different, yet more powerful, imaginary by which to speak of the
consolations of protective love that were a quality of divine and human presence to
the other in Auschwitz. To suggest such is not to break with tradition. It is well
known that the lineaments of a maternal conception of God can be traced through
the biblical literature. Yet, distorted by its own patriarchy, the biblical God is one of
bewildering contradictions. In Deuteronomy 33: 27, 'The ancient God' is affirmed
as 'a refuge'; 'a support are the arms everlasting.' In the next verse this is also a God
who 'drove out the enemy before you. By his command: Destroy!' In the Hebrew
Bible, the triumphal and the maternal aspects of the divine personality – the
awesome *tremendum* and the beckoning *fascinans* – are intertwined. The book of
Isaiah repeatedly holds these two elements of the holy together. In Isaiah 40: 9 God
comes in might and triumph but also, by verse 11,

> Like a shepherd He pastures His flock:
> He gathers the lambs in His arms
> And carries them in His bosom.[53]

In its liturgical reform and copious literature, Jewish and Christian feminists
have long sought acknowledgement of the religious, political, and intellectual
seriousness of construals of motherhood. Although many feminists are justifiably
apprehensive of maternalist philosophies (fearing their latent reproduction of
essentialist patriarchal socio-sexual ideologies) much religious feminism has
rendered maternalism of less ambiguous assistance than that of the Scripture
which inspires it. After the birth of her first daughter Penina, Amy Eilberg found
that she was no longer praying to the God of law and commandment who had
become so familiar to her during rabbinical training. Instead she was calling

> to God as the giver of life, the God of mothers and children, of love and care
> and nourishment, a God who would understand that there was sanctity in

nursing and diaper changing and rocking and comforting as surely as there was sanctity in my encounter with the *siddur*. That night [on the second Shabbat of her daughter's life] I encountered a feminine image of God, who rejoiced in the birth of my daughter and my own rebirth as a mother. This is a gift that will be with me forever.[54]

So too, when Penina Adelman recently wrote the liturgical words 'I give praise to you, *HaMakom*, the Place of Power. *Shekhinah*, in the darkness of Your Womb we find comfort and protection. *Rakhameima*, Mother of Compassion, in the Darkness of Your Hidden Place we find the Source and the Power',[55] she recognized that to be a mother is to be presentative of a mighty love which, as refuge, holds its object within itself.

Of course, it can be difficult for Anglophone Jewish women over the age of 40 not to read Jewish motherhood through the stereotypes of their own times, especially that of Jewish-American caricature (the most excessive being that of Sophie in Philip Roth's puerile 1967 *Portnoy's Complaint*).[56] Even after the Holocaust had consumed so many of them, the Ashkenazic *Yiddishe mama* was something of a comic turn. An ambivalent object of both derision and sentimental yearning, she was a smothering, over-protective, over-feeding emasculator of sons; a woman who was ageing gracelessly into the interfering 'old' woman for which Yiddish has numerous derogatory terms: *yidneh, yenta* and *yachne* being some of them.[57] The contemporary Jewish mother is no longer caricatured as the (now somewhat dated) *Yiddishe mama* but – if she is prosperous enough – a grown-up, materialistic, flashy, over-dressed Jewish Princess who would be faintly contemptuous of the *mama* who did nothing to arrest her own ageing.[58] The cultural stereotype of the Jewish Princess (Anglo or American) is, in fact, both aspirational and self-deprecating; it is self-subverting. Far more theologically interesting, however, is the *mama* of the eastern European *shtetl*, who, taken seriously as a necessarily resourceful woman who often earned the wages to feed and clothe her family, can become a symbol of strength and responsibility: a very good image of divine providence.[59] Etty Hillesum describes one such mother in the desperate conditions of the Westerbork transit camp. The woman's husband and two elder sons had been deported. Herself starving, the mother had seven children left to care for as she made ready for her own deportation from Holland to Auschwitz:

> She bustles about . . . she's busy, she has a kind word for everyone who goes by. A plain dumpy ghetto woman with greasy black hair and little short legs. She has a shabby, short-sleeved dress on, which I can imagine her wearing when she used to stand behind the washtub, back in Jodenbreestraat. And now she is off to Poland in the same old dress, a three day's journey with seven children. 'That's right, seven children, and they need a proper mother, believe me!'[60]

During the Holocaust, motherhood was, in Katharina von Kellenbach's view, as much a form of resistance as armed revolt. Those seeking to understand Jewry's struggle for spiritual and material survival should not overlook women's reproductive labour. In hope and faith couples partook in a tradition of resistance to genocidal persecution dating back to the time of Moses: they chose to have children at the least auspicious of moments.[61] By the time she had come to term, a mother may have lost her husband. Mothers and children often faced starvation and deportation without their husbands, fathers and older brothers since men were commonly separated from women in the ghettos for the purposes of slave labour. Other families were separated on arrival in Auschwitz.

In women's memoirs of Auschwitz relationships with men generally become *textually* incidental. Relatively little reference is made by their authors to absent or dead husbands and fathers. This is not, of course, because men and women were indifferent to each others' fate or because varying degrees of sexual segregation were already a feature of women's lives by virtue of the economic and religious demands made on men and women's time. It is rather that in the immediacy of the crisis women were very often forced to manage and survive on their own. The capacity of the mother/daughter relation to withstand the catastrophe often becomes the most important story to be told of their holocaustal experience. In the many women's memoirs of the Holocaust published in recent years (one thinks of those of, say, Trudi Birger, Sara Tuvel Bernstein, Rena Kornriech Gelissen, Kitty Hart, Clara Isaacman and Schoschana Rabinovici)[62] it is the author's relation with her mother (whether living or dead) which gives meaning, purpose and substance to her survival and thence to the narration of her experience. Sisters, especially in the absence of a mother, similarly anchor meaning and hope. (Kornreich's memoir, for example, is shaped by the promise she made to her mother to protect her sister Danka, who, the physically weaker of the two, also helps Kornreich herself to survive Auschwitz.) It is as if within the story of Israel's relationship with the male Father/King God, is another (untold) story: the story of the female bond of protective love between the Mother-God and the daughters of Israel *in extremis*. If love is stronger than death (Song of Songs 8: 6) then so is maternal presence – a phenomenalizing of divine and human love.

The narratives of more memoirs and testimonies than can be cited here are almost constituted by the story of the turbulent passage of the mother and daughter, or sister and sister relationship which, whether actual or adoptive, either survived or ended in the holocaustal period. All of the brief survivor narratives that can be found on Judy Weissenberg Cohen's web-site on the subject of women and the Holocaust demonstrate that maternal or quasi-maternal relations with other women were of ultimate concern. For example, alone in Bergen-Belsen, the 16-year-old Weissenberg Cohen herself asked the Feig sisters to adopt her as their *Lagerschwester*. They did so and proceeded to share all that they had. For Cohen, these women assumed some of the functions of a mother: 'it was very important to know that someone cared whether you woke up in the morning.' Elisabeth de Jong's account of surviving Auschwitz's human experimentation Block 10 also focuses on how the female doctor there would 'gently wash and dress our wounds and try to console us' and how she herself struggled to keep her sister Lilian alive. Judith Rubenstein's two entries speak of little more than two women: the tragic manner in which her mother sacrificed her own life in Auschwitz to save that of Judith, and of the kindness and compassion of Ethel, a *Blockälteste* who 'attempted to ease the pain' and also saved her life. Irene Csillig, a Hungarian dressmaker, tells her story in such a way that all other experience is omitted from her narration except that of the preservation of her relationship with her mother and sister. Having survived a period in Auschwitz, her mother died in Stutthof; after liberation Csillig went back on a fruitless journey to their home town to find objects – a wedding ring and a petit-point embroidered cushion – that would remind her of her mother, or more, re-present her mother to her. Although these were not returned to her, like those of other women survivors, her account is at least partially resolved by its closing reassurance to the reader (common to the genre) that she has married and has had children and grandchildren.[63] The maternal line, a covenant of trust between mothers and daughters, goes on into the future.

Because classical theology generally postulates an omnipotent God who subjects history to the mysterious purposes of his will, Holocaust theology to date does not (and perhaps *cannot* in the counter-evidential light of bottomless human suffering) take the love of God as its determining theme. To imagine a Mother-God in Auschwitz is to envision a different covenant of divine/human love. Here the love of God for Israel is no longer, as in prophetic tradition, likened to a patriarchal marriage where the husband's physical and social power renders him a violent or loving master according to whim or circumstance. This God is not the Lord of Hosts (or Armies). Rather, God's maternal love for Israel can be figured by women as that countermand to wanton destruction which comes of bearing the increasing weight of their creation within their own bodies, suffering to bring it safely from the tight darkness into light and air, and knowing its absolute dependence on their protective presence. The face-to-face relation of the mother and new-born child is the first form and moment of presence. And more than that, feminist spirituality and the maternalist epistemology it commonly proposes has insisted that the motherhood of God bespeaks a commonality between divine and female personality. It is this maternal commonality that redefines our trust (*emunah*) in the loving presence traditionally ascribed to God but which in post-Holocaust theology, betrayed by the desertion of its Father-God, has been substantially lost. Irving Greenberg, for example, argues that after God allowed the Holocaust and withheld his protection from Jewry he can have no moral claim on Jews' covenantal allegiance; it must now be voluntary. The covenant can no longer be commanded or enforced by reward and punishment.[64]

Israel too is the child for whom the Mother-God is covenanted to take responsibility and to share or take away its pain. But Israel is also, like all children, covenanted through the reciprocities of love to take increasing responsibility for the world given it by God. The Holocaust imposed a complex set of maternal responsibilities. We have already seen that maternal obligations often had to be reciprocated by children prematurely matured by danger and need. Mothers had responsibilities not only to their children but also to their elderly parents. This traditional duty of daughterly care further endangered women's lives; had it not been that women felt that they could not leave their parents to an unknown fate, many could have escaped before emigration became impossible. Lucie Adelsberger, for example, refused to leave her elderly mother in Germany. Although offered a visa for the United States for herself, she could not obtain one for her mother.[65]

Women's friendships could also entail mothering. Mothers mothered mothers in Auschwitz. Lying in her bunk and in great distress, Giuliana Tedeschi's friend Zilly held Tedeschi's hand in her own 'small, warm, hand'. Zilly pulled the blanket around Tedeschi's shoulders and in a 'calm, motherly voice' whispered in her ear, '"Good night dear – I have a daughter your age!"' Sleep then 'crept slowly into [her] being along with the trust that hand communicated, like blood flowing along the veins.'[66] Or again, Charlotte Delbo used to hold her friend Germaine's hand in Auschwitz to help her get to sleep. Germaine later says: '"Do you recall how you used to say, in Auschwitz, 'Let me hold your hand so I'll fall asleep. You have my mother's hands.' Do you remember saying that, Charlotte?"'[67] Once voiced in the promise of Ruth to her mother-in-law Naomi that she will go where Naomi goes, where Naomi dies she shall die; that nothing but death shall part her from Naomi (Ruth 1: 16–17), it may be that maternal presence in its multiple forms and surrogates offers a different means to trust in God than those tradition has accustomed us to.

This is not to lapse into cliché: mothers are often bored, irritated and angered by their children. Not all mothers and children like one another. Some children are frightened of their mothers. And nor are mothers and their children immunized by love. During the Holocaust, maternal power (more a fancy of nineteenth-century social and religious rhetoricians than a political force) could become an ever more necessary fiction; a way of suspending disbelief. Clara Isaacman's memories of hiding from the Nazis in occupied Belgium are illustrative of my point. During their two and a half years in hiding, Isaacman's mother would hold and comfort her, speaking confidently and with conviction of their future. It was only when the war was over that Isaacman wondered whether her mother had ever really believed her own reassurances.[68] Isaacman recalls how the expression of love had become ritualized; almost a performance of sympathetic magic. Mothers would hold their children before the latter went out on dangerous errands, willing that, if nothing else, their love would protect them.[69] Sometimes the 'strong wishing' worked and children might often not have survived were it not for the love and proximity of their parents.[70] And even when, in the great majority of cases, children did not survive, their end could be eased by a fiction that maternal or quasi-maternal presence would be their redemption.[71]

When God calls to Abraham, Jacob and Moses they answer '*hinneni*', 'I am here' or 'here I am'.[72] For Levinas this 'I am here' is the meaning of love.[73] This is also the meaning of love between God and persons. Therefore to ask the question of God's presence during the Holocaust is not only to ask 'how was God made present to us?' but also, and inseparably from that, 'how did we make ourselves present to God?' There is no divine presence without human presence – the *hinneni* or 'here I am'. Presence is transitive; God cannot be present to nothing and nowhere. Just as a mother murmurs, 'Mummy's here', when her child cries out in the night or when he is afraid because he cannot see her, to say 'here I am' is to say here with you *I am*; my being human is to find and be present to you; here, in a place, answering you.

It was not uncommon for children in the ghettos to be orphaned or to be rounded up from the streets and deported without their parents. In such an environment of sudden disappearances, the threat of maternal absence to modify children's behaviour – 'Mummy won't be with you on the transport'[74] – would have been peculiarly terrifying. But more positively, the promise of maternal or quasi-maternal presence soothed children's terror. Maternal love could take on the function and attribute of divine love. For the Warsaw ghetto orphans in Janusz Korczak's care, 'Whatever would happen, they were to know that it would not matter as long as he, the doctor, would be with them. All he asked was that they remain together. . . . And so the children set out on their journey [to the death camp, Treblinka]. . . . Nothing mattered, as long as the doctor was with them.'[75]

The redemptive loading of maternal presence is now, and was at the time, not limited to biological mothers or even a female object. Korczak refused offers of rescue from the ghetto and of a personal reprieve at the time of his deportation. He chose to accompany the children and, on his now legendary 'last walk' from the orphanage to the freight wagons, he is reputed to have carried the two smallest children in his arms – this, despite his failing health, swollen feet, and the children who walked close to his side.[76] A similarly 'maternal' attitude can be found among Hasidic men, the physical presence of whose Rebbe offered not only religious teaching, but calming words, counsel, consolation and a practical support that was reciprocated by his followers. Among numerous possible examples is the Komarner Rebbe, Rabbi Baruch Safrin, who refused two offers of rescue, insisting that he remain with his followers in their distress. The Paizesner Rebbe also refused to abandon his Hasidim, stating: 'Wherever my Hasidim are, there I shall be as well.' The Slonimer Rebbe knew that he might have been mistaken in refusing to leave Barenowich, but said, 'What can I do when my little children [his Hasidim] are dependent upon me?'[77]

Primarily, though, accounts of those who told themselves and others stories about the almost miraculous power of maternal relationships to withstand terror and annihilation are characteristic of the women's memoir literature. Eva Weiss, a Jewish nurse herself selected for death on account of her scarlet fever, attempted to calm and comfort those women around her who were terrified by their suspected fate. Knowing that they would indeed all be taken in an ambulance directly to the crematorium, she promised them that they were to be transferred to a larger hospital where some of them might find their mothers.[78] The child's sense that everything will be all right as long as they are with their mother, and even if it is not, they can hold on to her and she will not let go of their hand, was emblematized in the mass graves of Auschwitz. Ferderber-Salz and other women had to remove corpses from the graves and burn them before the liberating army reached the camp. There they sometimes found two bodies: 'a mother and a child, locked in an eternal embrace, since the mother had tried to protect the child with her body. The murderers' bullets had passed through the mother's body and entered her child's, killing both of them together.'[79]

Contemporary Jewish feminist liturgy widely expresses the faith that, 'The Lord is warmth/She will cradle me. The Wings of the Lord will cover me. Her breath will soothe me.'[80] There are, in short, important inter-textual connections to be made between scriptural words, these contemporary words and women's words about Auschwitz where the meaning and purpose of Jewish motherhood was to be destroyed and where pregnancy – motherhood of an unborn child – could not be declared. Much Jewish feminism has insisted that the motherhood of God is the undeclared, untold story still unborn from the body of Israel and it seems necessary to bring these narratives of maternal disappearance together and to reflect upon them without confusing their reasons.

A dying and deathless God

Narratives of maternal presence and disappearance thread their way through women's Holocaust memoirs, whether they write as mothers of hidden children, of children struggling to survive, of dead children, or whether they write as daughters with, or longing for, their mothers. As I read it, this narrative corpus is both a historical and theological commentary on presence and absence; appearance and disappearance. In these stories and fragments of stories, the face of Shekhinah shines dimly, almost imperceptibly, through the smoke clouds of Auschwitz. Hers was a countenance figured by the *tremendum* of divine maternal wrath at the despoilation of her love, Israel, and the *fascinans* of her divine longing, seeking and calling to what was disappearing – literally going up in smoke – before her. And it was this resistant love which Shekhinah, God-in-relation-to-the-world, could mediate to those who still inhabited the relational structures (namely those of family or its surrogates) to receive and express it.

It would seem that for many mothers, grief predominated over rage. Rage was impotent, but grief held a woman to the object of her love rather than to her grief's hated cause. Women in Auschwitz sang songs redolent of peace and safety in a place which could supply neither of these. Among other survivors, Bertha Ferderber-Salz remembers how even the memory of singing lullabies to children now dead helped mothers release their grief. Women who were forced to sew in the workshops would cry as they sewed, remembering how they would once sing lullabies to their children. Other young mothers continued to sing lullabies even though their children were dead because by doing so they remained close to their children: '"That's how I used to sing to my Sarahle when I was putting her to bed."'[81] Jacob Neusner has theorized Torah as God's song; Israel sings responsively to God. Yeshivah scholars sing to one another in sing-song chanting speech that is song when the ear is attuned to its rhythms. In answer, God's is not the voice of thunder but the thin urgent voice that pierces the silence.[82] Neusner's thesis points towards a way of calling to God and being called to by God that is well known to mothers, even mothers who, in Auschwitz, sang to the silence. Their mother-songs were songs of the Shekhinah, whose own song is the maternal song that soothes the good to sleep/death; in the tradition, the death of the righteous comes by the kiss of the Shekhinah.

As mother, Shekhinah intercepted, suffered and was extinguished by violence. As God-present-among-us she was bound by the conditions of immanence; namely by the kenosis of the transcendental divinity whose absolute incommensurability would have made her unknowable even while it would have kept her from the consequences of immanence. It is possible for the love between a mother and child to approximate the absorptive love described by Jewish mystics as *devekuth* – a cleaving to God. And when God is alongside us, it is this form of love which best describes the anguished love God bears for us, her creation, when we are not what we were created and born(e) into this world to be. (Thus Lewinska on the man she saw in Auschwitz being dragged by his legs, his dead body 'tracing a great furrow in the black mire': 'If you had seen your child so, oh mother, or you, wife, if you had seen your love and joy in such a state.')[83] Both God and human persons suffer with what we have created because, as its creator, our love, will and personality are in it. So too, where Israel loved and suffered for its children its face was transparent to the face of its God. God suffered in Auschwitz because Israel, the bearer of her creative love lay s(p)oiled and mortally wounded in the fathomless holocaustal pit; taken beyond her consolatory touch, but not beyond her love. In that place, God was diminished by the haemorrhaging of that human and divine creative love – that which makes persons, persons, and God, God. But this is not to imply a Rubensteinian or Nietzchean death of God. As Shekhinah, God suffers the conditions of finitude. But as God, she endures forever.

That God was both dying and deathless in Auschwitz was attested in the maternal love that was a manifestation of God's love. Like God's, the maternal love of the dying mother was also sometimes experienced as deathless and therefore as an antidote to death. Isabella Leitner remembers how her mother, facing imminent death on her way to Auschwitz, reassured her son and five daughters: ' "And wherever I'll be, in some mysterious way, my love will overcome my death and will keep you alive. I love you." '[84] Long after liberation, with children of her own, Leitner promises her mother, 'I will tell them to make what is good in all of us our religion, as it was yours, Mother, and then you will always be alive and the housepainter [Hitler] will always be dead.'[85] Analogically, God's immanence as the maternal Shekhinah was both infinitely strong as the presence of unconditional love and also *thereby* infinitely vulnerable to harm.

When relatively young mothers had teenage daughters and no other young children, they sometimes managed to stay together in the women's camp in Auschwitz-Birkenau (for however short a duration). However, as well as the elderly and infirm, mothers with young children were the most vulnerable of all those entering Auschwitz. By the summer of 1944 children were being torn from their mothers outside the crematoria and sent separately to the gas or burnt alive in a fire-pit near the crematoria.[86] And yet in the memoirs of some of those who had struggled to live in the women's camp that was just a short walk from those crematoria, the necessity for mothers to survive to care for their children and for daughters to survive to become mothers amounts to a female cosmological principle. In Leitner's memoir, the (violated) womb came to represent the possibility of cosmic and personal deathlessness. Forced to bury a young girl in the camp of Birnbaumel in East Germany, Leitner's memoir addresses the dead girl with the words: 'Rest in peace young girl. The flickering stars above must be the weeping children of your womb. The womb, the glorious womb, the house that celebrates life, where life is alive, where the bodies of young girls are not carried out into the night. Rest in peace, young girl.'[87] In this context, the biblical words 'love is stronger than death' are not those of merely rhetorical consolation but the statement of a moral and redemptive imperative born of Israel's carnal election. Like familial relationships, that election is neither earned nor voluntary, but passed through bodies by the union of bodies. Hence Wyschogrod: 'that is why the enemies of God destroy not only Jewish religion or culture but the Jewish body; the body of Israel.'[88]

In Psalm 121:5 God's guardianship of humanity is sometimes translated as 'God is your shadow'. This latter implies a non-ordinary, yet physical, correlation between divine and human action.[89] To adapt the words of Tehillah Lichtenstein who wrote in her immanentist sermon of 1947: 'Believing in God . . . is seeing God; seeing [Her] in the form of those attributes that you believe [Her] to possess.'[90] It is possible to see God in the practices of human maternity. If women's maternal love and grief was deathless and without consolation, then all the more so was God's. The vulnerability, futility and necessity of maternal love in a death camp maps both the obstruction of divine love and its transformatory power. With death before them, mothers arriving in Auschwitz would hold and soothe babies and children with their own bodies, seeking (and forever failing) to protect them from harm. And yet, for Hillesum (who was not a mother) there remains something that is infinitely protective or maternal about God even in a world which will destroy those God loves. Perhaps that tragedy makes God seem more like a mother, not less. Caught in the trap that was occupied Europe, Hillesum is nonetheless able to say, 'I lie suddenly against the naked breast of life and her arms around me are so gentle and so protective.'[91] In Auschwitz, women would have had several decades to wait before the words of Naomi Janowitz's prayer could have expressed for some of them precisely the way in which a woman can have exhausted her strength to care and yet be renewed by her identification with the God who also suffers as Mother:

> My body, my breasts, my womb
> have no more strength.
> Who will be our strength?
> G-d will be our strength.
> For She too has carried
> the pain of motherhood
> and seen Her children do evil
> and been rent asunder.[92]

To cast God's presence as that of a mother in Auschwitz is not, therefore, to infer that women are supernaturally strong.[93] Mothers do not hypostasize a fantastic divine omnipotence, but image the maternal face of God, which in Auschwitz was a suffering face. (And in the ghettos and freight wagons, at the end of their endurance, when women would have lost their tempers with crying babies and fretful children, it was also a wrathful face.)

In the (very dim) light of Auschwitz, such a God might be dismissed as a mere shadow passing over, a passive, useless God whose lack of the traditional attribute of omnipotence abandons Jewry to its fate, now even more frighteningly vulnerable to harm than it was before. But a maternal God leaves Israel no more vulnerable than was empirically the case under a theology of divine omnipotence for which there was, in any case, little or no evidence. As Mother-God this God *is* ethically interruptive, interceptive, protective and consoling. But this is not to attribute to God any power other than that which is productive of power in others within the conditions of a given situation: here, the power to resist violence by the spectacle of love.

Without any theological intention, Isabella Leitner's description of a mother giving birth in her barrack in Auschwitz illustrates my meaning. In her account, the women clustered around the mother cannot let her see the emergent child, let alone care for it, for had she done so she would never have consented to their separation and her life as well as the baby's would have been lost. Nonetheless, the mother is figured by Leitner in the classic posture of the Shekhinah whose wings enfold the dying, protecting what is passing beyond the capacity and need of protection. Leitner remembers how the child dropped from the womb onto the ground with its mother's thighs shielding it 'like wings of angels'.[94] Like others in Auschwitz the (by now fatherless) child lay on the ground abandoned to death but was also shielded from the extinction of its meaning by the love of God for Israel and the love of Israel for Israel – here the women gathered around the mother and the child she never saw.

But God did not self-empty God-self onto the ground of Auschwitz as this unnamed woman had done in giving birth. God weeps with Rachel for her children who are gone (Jer. 31: 15), but if God had so depleted God-self she would have lost the will to (re)create. If that had happened the whole world would have been extinguished and God, who is definitively creative, would have ceased to be God. So the pain of Israel had to be given over to God but also taken away from her so that the world and God would survive Auschwitz, as they have done.

6   The redemption of God
   in Auschwitz

Come and see how beloved Israel is before God; for wherever they went
into exile the Shekhinah went with them. When they were exiled to
Egypt, the Shekhinah went with them, in Babylon the Shekhinah was
with them, and in the future, when Israel will be redeemed, the Shekhinah
will be with them.

(Megillah 29a)

PART I

Jewry's eternal presence (or the stopping train)

The closing sequences of two recent films set during the Holocaust, *Korczac* and
Jakob the Liar,[1] are similar in one respect: both of their directors refuse to end their
stories (the former historical and the latter a fable) with the death of the Jews whose
deportation they narrate. Both films end with the train stopping before its
destination, a death camp. In *Korczac,* the orphaned children, Janusz Korczak and the
other adults caring for them, tumble in serene slow motion from the train into the
fields as if to play.[2] In *Jakob the Liar*, deliverance unfolds in just the surreal manner
Jakob had promised them it would: the liberating Soviet troops stop and surround
the train, playing exuberant American jazz from the open tops of their tanks. The
lies that were Jakob's stories of comfort and consolation become the audience's
fantastic truth. In both of these films, the audience experiences a redemption from
death, even while conscious that, historically, these particular deliverances did not
and could not have occurred. An empty train reversed out of Auschwitz.

There will be those who regard such films as taking unwarranted artistic
licence with history; as the seduction and reward of an audience about to leave
the cinema by an ending that can only uplift because the horror is left out of shot.
But in neither of these two films does the stopping train represent a facile 'happy
ending' or an admission that the terminus of the gas chambers is cinematically
unrepresentable (which is almost undoubtedly the case). Theologically, the train
had to stop to signify that there was something about the story of those Jews
which was wholly interruptive and transcendent of the means and processes of
their death.

Hirsh Goldszmit (known as Korczak) is one in whom myth and history have begun to coalesce. Related in his own diary and by artists' reading of that diary, his is one of the best-known stories of redemptive interruption. As if in a kind of triumphal counter-march, on 5 August 1942, Korczak and the Warsaw ghetto orphans in his care processed to their deportation to Treblinka under a Zionist flag. Their flag and voices raised in song signalled a defiant resistance to degradation and terror; an eternal refusal of the eternal inaudibility and invisibility of death. In dialogue with Abrasha, Korczak says,

> The murderer has *got* to believe in destruction and has got to believe that the victim believes he will be destroyed forever. But if the victim begins to sing right into the murderer's face, 'How so?' That's simple. They will make us march to the *Umschlagplatz*. When they do, then we, from the children's home, will march in step, just as if we were going on one of our hikes. . . . And we will sing.

And when they were taken out of the ghetto, all two hundred children, Korczak and nine other staff members did indeed sing together: 'Whenever the storm troopers lashed them with their whips, they drowned the pain by singing even louder. Nothing mattered as long as the doctor was with them. No power on earth was able to stop their singing.'[3]

In many ways, Jewish adults and children who met their death in Treblinka suffered more sheer uncontrolled brutality and terror before they were killed than was even customary in Auschwitz.[4] But because Korczak's diary ends before he and his orphans arrive in Treblinka the imagination cannot find them there but sees them forever walking to the *Umschlagplatz* (which is not the redemption of history, merely the arrest of time). Korczak and his children were leaving history in all senses. Treblinka would end their life but also, in them, eternalize it. This is not to mystify the horror,[5] it is to resist the reduction of its victims to that of its mere objects. Rosenzweig described Jewry as being an eternal people 'outside' history; here, in Korczak, they enter a space elsewhere to that of secular historical consciousness: not, finally and ultimately that of Treblinka, but one which stands over and against it as its judgement. In Korczak, that is, in the space he created within the ambit of his care, Jewry was deathless and redemptive of what is human.[6] It seems not uncoincidental that in Treblinka itself Korczak has not been allowed to disappear: he is the only individual now commemorated there.[7]

In Korczak and the orphans' procession towards death, finitude enters into its own eternity in that moment when there could no longer be hope for the deliverance of self but the redemption of history. These were acts with an afterlife. The eternal presence (as distinct from the immortality) of those singular, named Jews has come to stand for that of European Jewry, which has itself come to be a particular representation of the inextinguishable humanity of all persons. This return from absence into presence comes about through the passing of time. A canonical memory is mediated by the enduring texts and images of the Holocaust and its post-Holocaust representations. Without allegorizing suffering, it is the textual translation of the finite individual's acts into the collective infinite, Israel, that allows us, for a moment, to put to one side the undoubted historical fact that for large numbers of Jews suffering withered rather than nourished their souls.[8]

Etty Hillesum has become another of those in whom holocaustal erasure has been resisted, this time by a few words. Etty Hillesum's last message was written on a postcard thrown from a train as it left the transit camp of Westerbork for Auschwitz on 7 September 1943. On it were words which recall Korczak's departure for Treblinka in August 1942. She wrote: 'We left the camp singing'.[9] Even more than her diary, this textual fragment that is delivered to us over on the 'safe' other side of the Holocaust is the means by which Hillesum sends the ineradicable humanity of that 'we' back to us. As the Torah does for God, Hillesum's text – her inked words on paper – establish both her eternal presence and, as a surrogate for presence, her absence. Essentially, if not materially, her presence, like her postcard, will forever flutter towards us like a butterfly on the fresh breeze of a Dutch field in early autumn somewhere near Westerbork. And it is when the theologian kneels in the grass to retrieve that card that history and theology begin to unite – a process already underway in Hillesum's own writing.

In its turn, theological history uses the imagination to draw out from the historical record a set of meaningful connections with the faith traditions of its community. This is a recuperative distribution: the mind knowing what happened but also shifting (not jettisoning) the load the historical consciousness must bear onto the far broader shoulders of the tradition's narrative realm. In this sense alone, the train never got there. Whatever postmodern literary criticism may think of the schematic formalism of traditional narrative forms, for those participant in the Jewish theological scheme, compelling stories about God and humanity have an origin or beginning, a historical middle inhabited by the present generations, and a redemptive end which resolves the crises of the middle and in some senses returns us to the creative beginning.[10] If, then, we are to make a twenty-first century Jewish response to the Holocaust through the elaboration of its stories committed to memory, 1933–45 *must* be accommodated within the dateless schema of creation, history and redemption.

The present study has sought to make the Holocaust transmissible through its theology of image (creation), its interpretation of memory (history) and its faith in the eventual healing of Auschwitz (redemption). With this last, there is a conviction that the extermination of European Jewry was a process against which there was cosmic as well as human resistance, the latter moving the former. Here, theology encompasses and then transcends history. If humans are made in the image of God there must be something about them which, once created, endures forever. To be created in the image of a (divine) other entails that creation is necessarily relational – a face-to-face event – God making us present to one another. It follows, then, that the retrieval or even momentary restoration of a face is the restoration of presence. In the one last glimpse of a face turning back to look at us, the victims of the Holocaust did not and could not disappear.

This is not to deny history but to question how it records the holocaustal disappearance of the human image whether in death or by the disfigurations that usually preceded it. (For Fackenheim, even the resistance of one person suffices to deny evil its victory.)[11] Post-Holocaust art and literature has been at least as theologically educative as theology itself. Rather than scholarship, it is post-Holocaust art's (re)production of the human image of the dead, whose curtailed lives have necessarily taken on the dramatic depth and pathos of art, which has, through various media, best conveyed the Jewish transcendence of history by a force of ineradicable presence (not to be confused with anti-Semitism's 'Eternal Jew' who simply will not go away). One of the most striking examples of such is the fictional Ernie Levy, the *Lamedvovnik* or Just Man of André Schwartz-Bart's novel *The Last of the Just* who, after his death in Auschwitz, nonetheless remains a (compassionate) presence: 'Yesterday, as I stood in the street trembling in despair, rooted to the spot, a drop of pity fell from above upon my face; but there was no breeze in the air, no cloud in the sky . . . there was only a presence.'[12] The death of Ernie, who had wept tears of blood as he died with his dying people, is taken up into the mysteries of divine immanence which is *itself* the meaning of eternal presence. Hence Schwartz-Bart's brave closing hymn to the destruction:

> And praised be Auschwitz. So be it. Maidanek. The Eternal. Treblinka. And praised be Buchenwald. So be it. Chelmno. The Eternal. Ponary. And praised be Theresienstadt. So be it. Warsaw. The Eternal. Wilno. And praised be Skarzysko. So be it. Bergen-Belsen. The Eternal. Janow. And praised be Dora. So be it. Neuengamme. The Eternal. Pustkow. And praised be . . .[13]

There is something about the lives of dead and surviving Jews who have lived Jewishly (that is, humanely) which means that although their faces have disappeared they cannot be finally erased.[14] Their gaze is steady; we simply need to know where to look. Visiting Auschwitz or, indeed, the towns and cities of continental Europe, the story of words once spoken in a garden outside Jerusalem's city walls comes to mind. A young man asked the women who sought to anoint the violated body of the dead rabbi Jesus, why they were seeking the living among the dead: 'He is not here. . . . He is going [on] before you' (Luke 24: 5).[15] As Schwartz-Bart writes of his own Just Man, the one who takes upon himself the sufferings of the world: 'At times it is true one's heart could break in sorrow. But often too, preferably in the evening, I cannot help thinking that Ernie Levy, dead six million times, is alive, somewhere, I don't know where . . .'[16]

To say that European Jewry is not there, in Auschwitz, but *here*, is to say what, in the uttering, is almost platitudinous: that despite appearances, good is not consumed by evil; a good life is infinitely greater than its dying; that what was very good is eternally good and stands as a witness to God's creation of a good world. When Israel in Auschwitz answers the human and divine summons in the present tense, with the great *hinneni*: the 'Here I am' recorded of the biblical dialogue between God and humanity, it defies the genocidal attempt to deport Jewish existence into the past tense. It is notable that in the State of Israel, the eternal presence of European Jewry is enshrined in law; the dead are accorded a 'citizenship of remembrance'. They are not in heaven but virtual citizens of a place on earth. Religion – even civil religion – is not merely the hearing of divine words but the production of a witnessing presence in resistance to the forces of erasure.

There are holocaustal texts, then, whether autobiographical or fictional whose letters take wings of fire; which accrue some of the kind of authority Jews call Torah when they *talk over*, indeed drown out, Nazi ideology with a different kind of script: one which keeps or returns its Jewish actors on and to the stage. And if such texts (whether memoirs, diaries or post-Holocaust art) make history all right again that is because there *were* those who sought to make it all right again. In the previous chapter I examined how, in pitifully modest ways, mothers and quasi-mothers sought to retrieve the other from death by their own *hinneni* to the summons of the other; by soothing songs and stories, a little food or a comforting touch. For the post-Holocaust generations, those who were not there, photographic images of faces caught in an instant of time have offered an intimation (no more) of the redemption of presence. The image is lifted up as a prophetic judgement on disappearance, as a resurrection of the loved by love, and as a restoration of the human image, which, in that of God's, is eternal. Intelligent faces, known from photographs left behind (one thinks of the photograph of Anne Frank in a crisp, cotton summer dress taken in Amsterdam in 1941 that graces most editions of her diary) are never soiled by filth or erased by violence or the blank, silent stare of the *Muselmänner* lying in the camp bunk next to them.

But the survivor literature is different. Even though increasing numbers of the survivor generations are dead or dying of old age, the authors of Holocaust memoirs are, as such, still here in a compromised world; their presence is not transcendentalized by their eternal absence. How are we to read their texts as testaments to the restoration of a divine and human presence which, washed of history, signals the possibility of healing and peace?

Not all texts readily mediate transcendent presence. Whereas Etty Hillesum and Janusz Korczak have become textual presences whose reading redeems their authors from death as the last disappearance, most survivors' memoirs supply the reader with a burden of detail that exhausts the religious imagination, appearing to leave their authors and readers stranded knee- (or neck-) deep in history. Some of these authors, few of them well known, seem almost less alive to us than those whose own texts stop dead before their death. The survivors' memoir literature takes us into, through and out of Auschwitz. And yet, paradoxically, writers like Hillesum, Korczak and Frank survive as a more poignant presence than do the survivors themselves. The dead achieve a kind of deathless presence because we cannot or do not need to imagine their death and because we remain in a perfected readerly and emotional relationship with them. Whereas the survivor literature bears more than a trace of the messy complicities of any fortuitous survival, those who did not survive make no demand on us: we cannot hear the dead-and-eternally-alive like Korczak and Hillesum cry out for our help at the end. In short, it can be difficult to tell whether the redemptive quality of the spiritualized, textualized faces of the Holocaust is truly such, or whether it is an aesthetic intimation of redemption alone. More specifically, we need to consider how the women's memoirs used in the present study as the basis for a holocaustal theology of relation can also, truthfully, complete the task and, through tradition, yield a redemptive vision of the restoration of human and divine presence from erasure without themselves having disappeared (Hillesum) or stopped the train (Zeitlin, on Korczak).

In my Introduction I noted that this was to be a book in three movements: God's approach to, passage through, and departure from Auschwitz with Israel into an open future. It is this final post or extra-historical phase of the trajectory of divine presence that both parts of the present chapter seek to evoke. It will do so by attending to the ways in which the individual's preservation of a relationship with God (in and by that with other persons) moves towards the *telos* of collective relationship in which all individual relationships finally inhere: namely that accord or *shalom* between God and the world. Jewish theology may not account for human evil by a notion of a Fall, but it does assume estrangement by its witness to suffering and moral chaos and its complex halakhic regulations to assuage it. From a feminist perspective, the world and God are estranged by the incursion of the profane into the holy; that is, by the hubristic appropriation of creation to the patriarchal interest and the exile of its creator. The reunion of God and the world by the restoration of the holy is a gradual and recursive process, not an act of divine fiat. I have argued that in Auschwitz, in discharging the covenantal obligation to be holy as God is holy, women took themselves and the world they represented up into the drama of divine being and becoming. The redemption of God among women in Auschwitz was to return and reconcile God to the world by the restoration (*tikkun*) of her divine image in women. Revelation in Auschwitz was not the announcement of God's will but the reappearance of what has disappeared. We have seen that for Levinas, judgement is in the face. I want to say that the judgement that is in the *defiled* face is proleptical of the eschatological judgement on patriarchal alienation after which authentic relation, and therefore presence, can be restored. It has been remarked that pre-Holocaust Jews, 'always living more securely in time than space, would soon be banished to it altogether'.[17] But relation, being there for the other, is definitively a presence in space that is not necessarily bounded by time. It is therefore by relation that Jewry was redeemed from its intended temporal and spatial erasure.

The transformed state of the world to come, a world to which God has returned, has traditionally been secured and encapsulated as that of the holy walled city: Jerusalem. If history can offer a proleptical vision of the post-historical, then it is precisely because the bounded city of Auschwitz is now a mythographic antonym of Jerusalem that the theologian can look there for a refraction or reversed image of the world to come. For it was there, where Jewry sought to separate itself from evil by washing, holding, mending and carrying, that it began to achieve unity with the divine image in its own face and thus to reconcile the exiled God to God. It carried the sign of peace that is at once the product and precondition of eschatological peace. In women as well as men, Jewry was travelling onwards to the wholeness of the world (within this one) to come, summarized mythographically as Jerusalem.

In this book I have proposed a holocaustal theology of presence on the grounds of a feminist reading of its relational sustenance by women in Auschwitz. It should have become clear that a feminist theology of relation is not founded on female experience to the exclusion of men's, or on the assumption that men's religiousness was not, or was insufficiently, redemptive. Rather, it is that women as well as men were participant in the redemptive process in ways previously unarticulated by theologians of the Holocaust. In the present chapter I want to say that the redemption of relationship from brutal competition for negligible resources, mutual disgust, traumatized apathy and from death itself, prefigures the eschatological Shalom of transformed relationships that is willed by a just and loving God. This is no reversion to a form of Sabbatian heresy where the sin of Nazi Germany can be accorded an instrumental, sanctifying power because redemption is incomplete until Jewry has descended into the abyss of sin and impurity to rescue the divine sparks.[18] Rather, the sanctification of the world through the redemption and restoration of the divine image from the pit of holocaustal impurity is a revelation of God's face/presence that is also a revelation of the human face/presence because when humankind is truly human, God is known as God: the very essence of the eschaton. The face/presence of God is also the face/presence of our redeemed humanity, knowable in the world. The revelation of the human being as a divinely created person, not an object or means, reunites the creature and the creator, closing the circle between creation and redemption. The creature is restored to its original goodness in God: this is what it means to be blessed and to live forever. Perhaps this was what (male) Hasidim were anticipating when they went to their deaths with joy and gratitude.[19]

Envisioning *tikkun*

Dan Cohn-Sherbok has recently pointed out that post-Holocaust theologians have ignored traditional, if widely neglected, elements of rabbinic eschatology and have made no appeal to the Hereafter in response to Jewry's innocent suffering. God's love and justice may not have been exercised in the fate of Jewry under Nazism, but could yet be exercised in the promise of post-historical immortality. It was this promise which had sustained righteous Jews through the centuries and which sustained many to the point of death during the Holocaust.[20] And yet a feminist theology of the Holocaust would not want to defer redemption to a post-mortem Hereafter or some messianic *Endsieg*. There is in any case a strong, intramundane (if androcentric), liberative emphasis in the Jewish vision of redemption. Thus Sanhedrin 91b: all that will distinguish Messianic times from the present is the former's delivery from servitude to foreign powers.[21] It is not that the post-mortem dimension should be necessarily excluded from post-Holocaust religious feminist ideals, but that their traditionally envisaged means weakens the causal relation between women's holocaustal history and the resolution of history; or less grandly, what both women who died and survived did to effect their own intramundane redemption: their own (here)after Auschwitz.

Mine has been a phenomenological approach to theology. Differentiating between religious experience and its divine object, I have not presumed to read God's mind or to speculate on a supra-historical world to come. From the (more) knowable human sphere of what shows itself, I have instead examined the ethico-aesthetic practices which honour the central moral *telos* of religious experience, namely the sense of God's will for the restoration of the human(e) to creation so that it is properly God's and not the colony of other powers. This relation between the human and the divine will to restoration is best articulated by the notion of *tikkun olam* (the mending of the world): the means by which Judaism can, in fact, offer conceptual resources by which redemption can be conceived on *both* the intra- and extra-historical planes.

The Hebrew term *tikkun olam* is variously translated as the completion, restoration, healing or mending of the world. With the exception of its appearance in the book of Ecclesiastes, it is a largely non-biblical term that accrued its eschatological connotations more in liturgy and kabbalah than in rabbinic Judaism. Sometimes, in the sources, the restoration of this world to its original goodness becomes a sufficient end in itself; sometimes it is the precondition of a heavenly restoration of peace within God-self and bliss in the world to come (*olam ha' ba*). The conception of *tikkun* can be traced back to the biblical, prophetic vision of a God who is fiercely critical of the ways of the powerful and who wills a just socio-religious order. Rabbinic Judaism, in its turn, also strove for the establishment of such by elaborating an all-encompassing socially regulative system of law for the sake of *tikkun olam*. Late medieval and early modern Jewish mysticism was inclined to spiritualize *tikkun*, putting the good deed more to the service of the theosophical project of intra-divine reunion than to the social world. Yet while Jewish communities were often, by historical necessity, somewhat inward looking, and in some mystical quarters the notion of *tikkun* suffered from its overly esoteric framing, Judaism's universalist redemptive dynamic was never entirely lost and emerged most notably in the rationalist Jewish liberalism of the nineteenth and early twentieth centuries.

Alongside this latter repudiation of ancient notions of redemptive catastrophe and cataclysm, came secular Jewish radicalism's prophetic struggle for a universal social justice. Dispensing with orthodox messianism, this social justice was to be of political rather than supernatural origin (a foretaste of which had been the civic emancipation of Western Jewry). Where Jewish secularism was influenced by Marxism it retained some of the sense that chaotic destruction must precede the creation of a new type of society. For others, a new form of social harmony and stability was to be the consummation of the Zionist dream in the establishment of a Jewish nation state. From its biblical, rabbinic, mystical, liberal and revolutionary antecedents, the contemporary Jewish left has developed a fruitful vision and praxis of *tikkun* where theological and political consciousness are engaged as one. This is the heartland of Judaism's feminist, ecological and peace movements, all of these being more or less espoused as one, even if separately organized.[22] Indeed, as Arthur Waskow claims (in good kabbalistic style) together such movements and groupings have the transformatory potential to mend the rifts not only in the world, but in God.[23]

But it is Emil Fackenheim, himself an inmate of Sachsenhausen before leaving Germany in 1939, who has made the best known connection between *tikkun* and the Holocaust. Since my own argument bears significant resemblances to Fackenheim's, his account of *tikkun* must be presented before advancing my own. Fackenheim argued that *tikkun olam* was *already* underway in the midst of catastrophe (at least two decades before prosperous liberal Anglophone Jewish communities had begun to articulate its processes). In *To Mend the World*, published in the early 1980s, Fackenheim claims that 'the *tikkun* which for the post-Holocaust Jew is a moral necessity is a possibility because during the Holocaust itself a Jewish *tikkun* was already actual'. Holocaustal resistance 'is the ultimate ground of our own'.[24]

Of course, Fackenheim acknowledges that to speak of redemption in the context of the Holocaust is counterintuitive. The Holocaust was a 'total rupture' in the great Western social and religious institutions, compelling them to reassess their moral standing and the nature of their power. Moreover, the screams of burning children and the living death of the *Muselmänner* in whom the divine spark had been extinguished testify against the possibility of any *tikkun* or mending of the world after the Holocaust. If there is *tikkun* it is fragmentary: 'incomplete and laden with risk.'[25] For Fackenheim, the *tikkun* is both impossible and necessary; impossible because nothing can heal Jewry of the Holocaust, and necessary because without it 'we could not live at all'.[26] The burning children of Auschwitz 'will not be restored, and the question of Auschwitz will not be answered by a saving divine Presence'. Indeed, Fackenheim questions whether there could there be a Jewish acceptance of or rejoicing in such a Presence had it been manifest. Auschwitz paralyses Jewish theology. The writer 'must tremble lest he permit any light after Auschwitz to relieve the darkness of Auschwitz. He must rejoice lest he add to the darkness of Auschwitz.' For it is in 'rejoicing after Auschwitz and because of Auschwitz, [that] the Jew must be a witness to the world, preparing a way for God.'[27]

If this historical rupture could be mended in history, it was not to be by intel-lection alone but in 'flesh-and-blood action' – a Jewish *and* Gentile '*tikkun* of ordinary decency' or practical mending of the world – that ran counter to the Nazi 'logic of destruction' to which Jews were so horrifyingly subjected.[28] Fackenheim therefore wants to say that *tikkun* began in the camps themselves where some Jews, though not all, spiritually and practically demonstrated that they understood the logic of destruction – the 'excremental assault' – to which they were subjected. Such men and women willed their resistance to this assault by selfless acts and by their determination to survive or die as Jews.[29] Fackenheim acknowledges that many would not have conceived their acts within a redemptive frame, but we can and must.[30] As was non-Jewish resistance to Nazism, theirs was a new form of resistance to a phenomenon that was itself a *novum* in history. The non-Jewish Pelagia Lewinska's record of her resistance to degradation is one of Fackenheim's most important pieces of testimony. But he also cites Jewish partisan resistance, pregnant women who refused to abort their unborn children in the hope that these new lives would frustrate the Nazi attempt to eradicate the Jewish people, and those Jews who resolved to die with the dignity of a human being as contributing to and exemplifying *tikkun*. All of these performed a sanctification of God's name in life. Where Jews could still respond to the 'commanding voice of God' and live and die as Jews, life, and therefore God's name, was sanctified. As Marc Ellis notes of Fackenheim's theology of 'ordinary decency':

> The rupture of the Holocaust, ontological in its significance, creates a boundary in which the ordinary flow of life is demeaned, denigrated and made impossible. Because of this ordinary decency is a crossing of the boundary within history and beyond; it is profoundly human and much more.[31]

For Fackenheim, divine presence is a mystery mediated by history and inter- preted through human faith and commitment. It was faith and commitment that had begun to mend the holocaustal rupture just as mystics' prayers and rituals had once sought to mend the rupture of Jewry's exile and of the exile of God within God. But it is in the contemporary empowerment of the Jewish people through the establishment of the State of Israel that Fackenheim is most confident that the paradigmatic act of *tikkun* is at work. Ultimately, *tikkun is* the State of Israel: the restoration of the Jewish people in a reclaimed land, however fragmentary and risk- laden that *tikkun* might be.[32] His view that *tikkun* occurs where Jews, whether secular or religious, make a practical commitment to national Jewish survival is characteristic of its period: it is the existence of the State of Israel which ultimately, for Fackenheim, as for so many others, affirms God's presence in Jewish history.

However, as Marc Ellis points out, the Zionist conception of *tikkun* in *To Mend the World* seems almost oblivious to the actual rupture between Jews and Palestinians; the latter meriting only a footnote in Fackenheim's book. Ellis rightly wonders how Fackenheim's 'ordinary decency' has been shown to the Palestinians and is concerned that the Holocaust, dwarfing all other suffering, has blunted Jewish moral sensibility to other situations that require healing or *tikkun*. The Jewish community has voiced its anger at its own violation in the Holocaust while remaining silent at that more recent violation of Palestinian lives, bodies, rights and property. The covenant will only be renewed and the era of Auschwitz brought to a close when these great wrongs are addressed.[33]

Clearly my own position has much in common with Fackenheim's in so far as I have proposed that an ethical, embodied and practical sanctification of the world is the response to Nazism that is most translucent to divine will, agency and pre- sence. Even so, I would want to supplement Ellis's criticism. That is, Fackenheim's *tikkun* of ordinary decency is also oblivious to gender: to the abuses of female religious agency legislated by Orthodox Judaism itself. This is also, and perhaps more fundamentally, a moral rupture in the fabric of Jewish life.

Zachary Braiterman's recent discussion of Fackenheim's *To Mend the World* is also germane to the present discussion. Braiterman thinks that Fackenheim's interpretation of Jewish resistance to the Nazi assault as redemptive has lost a proper sense of balance and proportion. These stories are as much or more likely to be read with despair as hope:

Much depends on the telling. True, the stories testify to the dignity of the human spirit. Perhaps they even point to some transcendent trace. However, they also remind us that human good and divine sparks remain powerless before the face of evil. Indeed, Fackenheim makes too little, a bare minimum of revelation, mean too much. These small, isolated figures of resistance (a pregnant woman, a lonely philosophy professor . . .) prove disproportionate to the gross fissure that Fackenheim hopes to heal by their example. The future of Jewish life, the future of the world, are made to rest on an edifying but meagre stock of moral good.[34]

Undoubtedly, the coupling of holocaustal and redemptive narratives is a risky undertaking. It is easily misinterpreted as the dodging of historical truths; as attributing an instrumental purpose to a monumental crime and judging its suffering to have been a price worth paying. Theological meaning cannot be attributed to evil, only to the Jewish response to evil. I would insist from the outset that, first, the instances of care elaborated in previous chapters of the present study were, however numerous, *never enough* to assuage the depth of pain that had elicited the care and never enough to match the quality and quantity of the assault. Second, while those who died in or survived the Holocaust may have contributed to a process whereby God and creation were to be redeemed, their doing so was less a purpose than an effect. Nonetheless, Braiterman is not alone among religious and non-religious commentators in remarking upon the disproportion between the nugatory instances of moral goodness produced by the Holocaust and the redemptive efficacy some theologians (and I would include myself) have claimed for them. This critical observation can hardly be ignored. Braiterman writes: 'Some evils remain radically resistant to any frame of good. . . . There are epistemic and moral limits to the act of philosophical, theological, or artistic representation at which any act of murder or violence, much less Auschwitz, resists its strongest interpreters.'[35]

In no other area of discourse on the Holocaust is there so great a clash between secular and religious, and even intra-religious, worldviews as that of the question of its having a higher order (redemptive) meaning. Certainly, to propose that the study of Auschwitz might yield any kind of higher order meaning is to offend against Holocaust Studies' almost definitively anti-redemptive stance where no artistic or research endeavour should intend to heal the world of Auschwitz and nothing can be mended on behalf of its victims (though I wonder whether all of those victims would have wanted their deaths left theologically adrift, unassimilated into Judaism's redemptive patternings).

Less speculatively, poststructuralist hermeneutics might suggest otherwise than unbelief. Of course poststructuralism is inimical to a theological realism in so far as it dismisses the possibility of an external, universal reality as truth, arguing that meaning is produced only in the relation between given signs; the individual is not an author of meaning but a mere site of significations. Poststructuralism's postulation of the 'death' of the unified subject is also clearly hostile to Jewish feminism's distinctively modern project: the tradition's restitution of Jewish female personhood. And yet Braiterman cautiously offers a postmodern, poststructuralist hermeneutic as a means by which – 'up to a point' – theology and art can indeed reconfigure human experience. Poststructuralism has, after all, suggested that

> no signifier, including the signs that mark suffering and evil, possesses a stable significance, pre-established referent, or self-identical essence. If every 'text' points to every other 'text', if every sign points beyond itself to still other signs there is no reason why Auschwitz should only point to Auschwitz. Auschwitz can point (or be forced to point) towards its polar opposite, the resurrection of the Jewish people and the redemption of the world.[36]

And, interestingly, Braiterman does not rule out that Fackenheim's redemptive exemplars 'may, in fact, represent a profound religious truth'; that they might point to 'some transcendent trace'.[37] And this is surely the point of theological historio-graphy: that the microcosmic and the macrocosmic recapitulate one another; that the historical process is both participant in and signifier of the cosmic process. Jewish theology, rooted in the historical moments of the Exodus and Sinai, cannot and does not bypass history. Rather, it traverses history by way of a different map of time, space and causality. Theology is acclimatized to the eschatological-prophetic mode that reads history in reverse: where the injustices that grind the faces of the oppressed are righted and they are lifted up from sorrow to joy; weakness to strength. Just as the Baalshem Tov is reputed to have rejected notions of the innate sinfulness of humanity and rebuked a preacher who was denouncing his audience, saying, 'Dost [thou] not know that every Jew, when he utters ever so short a prayer at the close of day, is performing a great work before which the angels in heaven bow down',[38] so too post-Holocaust theologians may want to attach very large meanings to very small signs. In the talmudic and mystical milieu one key moment of righteousness can suffice to acquire the future world. And it is conceptual terrain such as this in which modernity has little or no foothold, though postmodernity, ironically, is regaining one. So that where commentators have justifiably questioned how resistance to Hitler's will could even begin to effect the global and cosmic restoration of which Fackenheim speaks,[39] it is only possible to answer that question by insisting that phenomena yield different meanings within different interpretative frameworks. Truth is not simply the realistic correspondence of claims with a given state of affairs existing over and above the claimant. Because we cannot know the mind of God, truth in itself may be unknowable, but is best approximated by claims in which experiential knowledge and tradition successfully cohere. This is not to renounce the possibility of truth but, more modestly, to attempt to speak truthfully through a meshing of historical and supra-historical claims in ways that are neither reductive nor arbitrary.

Signals of redemption

Nowhere are historiography and mythography more thoroughly entwined than in the attribution of redemptive causality to historical acts. In examining women's

Holocaust memoirs it is possible for the theological reader to make precisely the interpretative connections described above; here between historical female practice and the metaphors and symbols of *tikkun*. This is not a wholly unprecedented move. In her significant article 'In a World Shorn of Color', Susan Nowak has given a humanistic reading of Rena Kornreich Gelissen's memoir *Rena's Promise*. In Kornreich Gelissen's undertaking to lead other women in the gruelling task of giving fifteen women's corpses a decent, and above all individual, burial, Nowak finds a witness to *tikkun atzmi* (self-mending). *Tikkun atzmi* occurred when women resisted their degradation and brutalization, and it occurs again in so far as its reading is a critical personal and political spur to a post-Holocaust *tikkun* of the holocaustal moral rupture. Although Kornreich Gelissen is of Orthodox family and does in fact initiate silent prayer for the women they have buried, Nowak interprets her act as 'an act of human recognition'. Kornreich Gelissen's prayer 'locates the sacred in a new location: the recognition given by one human being to another.' For 'in the "kingdom of the night," the glory of humanity is no longer reflected in its creation as the *imago dei*, but in the act of recognition that arises from the choice to live as the *imago hominis*.'[40]

I am not persuaded that the restoration of the *imago hominis* is Jewishly meaningful unless it is at once that of the *imago dei*, as it is the transcendental immanence of the latter in which the inviolability of human dignity is founded. And not wishing to cede as much to 'the kingdom of the night' as Nowak does, my own theistic reading of *tikkun* from the memoir literature reads the historical text through Jewish sacred texts and through spiritual feminist texts which at once critique and celebrate traditional female practice. Each type of text, though politically incommensurate, can point towards the other so as to accrue a density of meaning and reference that cuts across boundaries of Jewish time and place.

To illustrate and substantiate my point: *tikkun* – the mending or ravelling up of an unravelled world – finds its analogue in the traditional restorative skills of women, namely patching, darning, and the bandaging of wounds. It is well known that women sewed in the camps, both for themselves and as forced labour. (In Auschwitz the *Weberei* were forced to use the hair of women deportees to make thread.) Clearly, a distinction must be made between forced labour and the sewing which, though hardly the work of leisure, women undertook for themselves and loved others. In Ravensbrück a number of small embroidered items that women made for their children are now on display. It was there in Ravensbrück that Maya Nagy's mother sewed her a coat from scraps of material to protect her from the biting north wind.[41] In Auschwitz, even in the better conditions of one its satellite camps, Charlotte Delbo recalls that it took complex manoeuvres to obtain even 'the tiniest tatter, or bit of wool'.[42] Nevertheless, Giuliana Tedeschi remembers a woman called Sara knitting a gift from a worn-out stocking for her husband, still alive at that time in the men's camp: '"It's for him, to protect his ears from the cold."'[43] Knitting and sewing could be a practical and symbolic means of renewing the connective and protective functions of love and one that bound women to their mothers and grandmothers within a female world now destroyed.[44] Of particular significance to Tedeschi was the wrap her mother had knitted for her to keep warm in prison and which was taken from her on arrival in Auschwitz. 'It was', she writes, 'something from home, something that still had the smell of drawers, soft as my bed, warm as an embrace. I had it in my hands the whole trip from Italy to Auschwitz.'[45] By now the wrap had come to represent the relationship between herself and her mother; though the comfort of both were lost to her.

Judy Chicago's stitched panels for her work *Double Jeopardy* honours women's sewing in the ghettos and camps as a way of retaining their human dignity.[46] Chicago's reading of this labour is also a spiritual one for sewing has been consistently sacralized in the writings of spiritual feminism (including my own) as that which covers, protects and celebrates the body. [47] Sewing is also a theological trope and practice. Like the *chuppah* or canopy under which a marriage contract is sealed, sewn and worked cloth is a symbol of the beauty and durability of a covenant of protective love made between persons and between God and persons. As with the traditional practice of knitting, sewing or collecting clothes in the months before a baby is born, domestic sewing signals a lifelong commitment; a promise to care for the created body. (And conversely when the body is taken forever from human care by death or the body of Israel suffers a historical calamity, garments are rent as a sign of mourning.)[48] Ezek. 16: 6–37 figures the covenant as God's love covering Israel's female naked, rejected, unbathed, bleeding body:

> So I spread my robe over you and covered your nakedness, and I entered into a covenant with you . . . thus you became Mine. I bathed you in water, and washed the blood off you, and anointed you with oil. I clothed you with embroidered garments, and gave you sandals of leather to wear, and wound fine linen about your head, and dressed you in silks.
>
> (Ezek. 16: 4–10)

But in Auschwitz, the Nazis' 'uncovering of the nakedness' of women replicated the patriarchal biblical figuration of Israel's punitive humiliation by God where, in exile and defeat, God's countenance is turned from her. The Hebrew word for the exilic situation (*galut*) is both grammatically feminine and is figured by the uncovering of women. Lamentations 1: 9 describes Israel's dereliction as that of a peculiarly female degradation: 'Her uncleanness clings to her skirts. . . . She has sunk appallingly, With none to comfort her.' The text goes on, 'Her elect were purer than snow, Whiter than milk; Their limbs were ruddier than coral, Their bodies were like sapphire. Now their faces are blacker than soot, They are not recognized in the streets' (Lam. 4: 7–8; cf. Isaiah 47: 1–3). In Jeremiah 13: 22 Israel is cast as a violated woman; her femaleness is the site and means of her punishment: 'It is because of your great iniquity that your skirts are lifted up, Your limbs exposed.'

And yet the anguished patriarchal text also gestures towards the means of its own healing. For while in Ezekiel, Jeremiah, Hosea and Isaiah Israel is cast as a woman whose infidelities tear the covenant, it is also possible to figure Israel as a woman in Auschwitz who, setting the misogynistic prophetic trope into reverse, was darning the canopy that is the symbol and function of covenant at the very moment its fabric was being ripped apart. Here, darning as practice and metaphor no longer connotes an antiquated inconsequential fire-side chore or a tedious expedience of poverty. Nor is it merely a properly womanly skill once acquired by girls to equip them for marriage. It is what mends, renews and therefore ultimately *changes* the structure and fabric of very old things. A midrash tells us that apart from the High Priest, only those who were engaged in the work of repair could enter the Holy of Holies. Lynn Gottlieb notes: 'the work of repair permits one to enter the most sacred places.'[49] Gottlieb's gloss points towards the re-positioning of women in relation to the covenant after the Holocaust. In the camps, the old masculinist covenant made between sovereign divine and human powers was in tatters. Like the torn prayer shawls profaned as rags, the covenant could no longer keep Israel warm. But what is mended is returned to its owner with a changed substance and tension. Not only was their mending or *tikkun* beginning the work of mending the Holocaust (sometimes described as 'a kind of hole in the cosmos'),[50] the covenant between God and Israel was forever altered by women's restorative labours.

Pelagia Lewinska recalls those women in Auschwitz who sought to cover the bodies of other women with warming cloth: 'I will never forget you, Jeanne, the school teacher, nor you, Salome, the laundress from Cracow; sometimes you came late in the evening, most often when it was very dark outside, bearing a warm slip for someone, stockings for other women and me.'[51] Where bodies were exposed to extreme heat, cold and derision, women's holocaustal covering and protection of absolutely vulnerable, damaged and broken bodies/souls/minds (these are only linguistically distinct) mended, warmed and renewed the world. For the world is made an interconnected whole through an ecology of relationship where the violation or reconsecration of one is that of all. In her memoir, Giuliana Tedeschi described relationship as a form of knitting. As she put it, 'prison life' in the women's camp in Auschwitz-Birkenau was 'like a piece of knitting whose stitches are strong as long as they remain woven together; but if the woollen strand breaks, the invisible stitch that comes undone slips off among the others and is lost.'[52]

Where the communal fabric of the world was being torn apart, human love was anticipating its renewal. That there were those, men and women, who stopped the world unravelling is, after all, the meaning of the word religion, from *religare*, to bind up. And more than this: when mothers covered their daughters' bodies by giving or sewing together (by then, precious) rags and pieces of cloth, they also took the first halting steps of Jewry's return from exile – from Jerusalem, the holy. For the holy is what is appointed by God to be God's own, it comes from and belongs in an-other place and must be covered and protected from the profane touch or gaze. In re-covering bodies from the filth, women undertook what was both an ordinary and, here, an exceptionally difficult task and by doing so entered into the *illud tempus* of redemptive story or myth. The body transfigured by sight and touched is a resurrected body; that is, it is made eternally present. Within a religious conceptual frame, it is not extravagant to claim that women's (largely gestural) restoration of human dignity in Auschwitz and other sites re/covered the holy from demonic space and time, carrying it from Auschwitz to Jerusalem: the eschatological journey home.

And there are other ways too, in which the record of female activity in the camps can be read mythopoetically as both anticipating and carrying forward the long work of *tikkun* – the end of exile, where exile is a metonym for separation from the holy – the state of being in and of God. As we have seen in other parts of this study, vestigial replications or suggestions of home in Auschwitz carry a wealth of theological signification. The open boundaries of a home signify welcome and shelter; the closing of its boundaries around the body signify sanctuary. Enclosing the clean, the home invites the holy and as such can be a foretaste of the redeemed world, the holy mountain where all God's creation can flourish safe from harm (Is. 65: 25). And, like Jerusalem, the walled city, home is a metonym for the end of exile.

In Auschwitz, never further from home, 'home' could still be carried on the body within the portable dimensions of the 'beggar bundle' known in the women's camp as a *pinkly*. The *pinkly* consisted of a scrap of rag, a sock, stocking or old cap tied into a bag in which women kept their bread, margarine, or perhaps, if very fortunate, an object such as an almost toothless comb. Although owned on pain of death, the *pinkly* was a woman's '"hand-bag," "closet," and "pantry"'.[53] Sometimes the pinkly was no more than a piece of rag wrapped around some bread or a broken comb and tied to a woman's belt.[54] When Olga Lengyel made a toothbrush and handkerchief out of two scraps of rag she felt her human dignity to have been partially restored: 'These new acquisitions filled me with pride. I felt that I had become a rich woman in the camp.'[55] Maya Nagy remembers that almost all the women had little bundles: 'you'd find a piece of cloth and then put something in it and then you could carry it. A little potato peeling maybe; maybe somebody found a needle – the little treasures.' When the Red Cross removed these after liberation, fearing that they carried typhus, there was great distress among the women.[56] After the war, when Nagy was hospitalized, she 'started to build up a little side table next to the bed of my new belongings. That was very important, picking up life by having belongings. . . . My new bundle started to take shape.'[57]

The *pinkly* represented what could be kept back of women's humanity from Nazism. In Auschwitz, 'belongings'[58] were not so much possessions as the means to carry on belonging to another space and time than that of Auschwitz and to carry on belonging to others than those in command of Auschwitz. The *pinkly* could be a sign and practical means of women still carrying and collecting meaning and personhood; fragments and scraps of other possibilities, other worlds; remnants of the past to be reassembled from its detritus. As Bertha Ferderber-Salz left Belsen, she re-membered or resurrected the dead body of European Jewry by taking with her from the warehouses of stolen possessions a few small, personal items of the dead, not for herself, 'but as a reminder of a people that had been destroyed'. Taking the things that would have once helped to groom, feed and protect bodies from day to day, Ferderber-Salz hid a pair of reading glasses, a toothbrush, a child's shoe and a comb beneath her dress.[59] Between August 1945 and March 1946, she left her children once more, this time to journey through Poland looking for her relatives, friends and possessions; the world of eastern European Jewish women. Finding no one, these women were present only in the signs of their absence; in what they had left behind: a pillow; a bridal eiderdown with a coin sewed by a Jewish mother into the corner as a good luck talisman for her daughter; Ferderber-Salz's own embroidered depiction of a biblical scene now hanging in a Gentile woman's house; and, most saturated of all the objects, her mother, grandmother and great-grandmother's Sabbath head scarf, threaded with pearls, now adorning the statue of the Madonna in a church in Podgorze, Krakow. She did not take back her scarf, and when she looked back at it as she left the church, the pearls gleamed in the darkness as they once had at her mother's Sabbath table.[60]

It is as if collections of lost (or rather, stolen) women's property could summon their owners' presence back from history if only one knew the secret words by which to do so.[61] These objects may have marked the absence of European Jewry; but, *still there*, they anticipated return. I experienced this sense of presence myself several years ago, walking between the great heaps of shoes, cases, pots and pans that the dead carried with them to Auschwitz, now on display in the museum at Auschwitz I. It was in these 'valleys of dry bones' that the post-Holocaust Jew could gain powerful access to the particular humanity of European Jewry, not in abstraction from life as a quantity of death or as emblematic of the heroic or the pitiful, but in the accumulated domestic quiddities that situate persons in a particular time and space. Among the vast pile of footwear, an occasional vividly coloured women's fashion shoe stood out from the rest. One of these was almost animate in its red and blue insistence on the personhood of its owner and her ordinary female pleasures. The Jewish poet and child survivor Irena Klepfisz once wrote that she had come to believe that 'ordinariness is the most precious thing we struggle for.' The tragedy of Anne Frank is the loss of the 'ordinary anonymous life' of a girl and woman, not the world's loss of a potentially great writer.[62]

It may be that women's restoration of erased presence begins in the ordinary places most associated with female presence, namely among familiar domestic and personal objects (like the red and blue appliquéd shoe) that they acquired on the way through their own and Israel's history. Not only persons disappeared but also the objects they chose to identify and situate their personhood. In Germany today, domestic objects still raise the question of their provenance. They are a part of the post-Holocaust after-image in the eye of continental Europe. As James Young is aware, not only is there the implied question, '"Where were you in the war?" but also "to whom did that [antique] table belong before the war?"'[63]

Nearly fifty years after Bertha Ferderber-Salz retrieved small personal items from Belsen and her former home, the artist Rachel Lichtenstein, working with materials from the remains of the Polish ghettos for her 1993 installation *Shoah*, 'would let nothing go, not an envelope, not a lock of hair. . . . [She] would have filled albums from corners of curtain, cabinets of splinters.' For as Iain Sinclair put it, 'Lichtenstein's art was inspired by a love of these indestructibles, residual whispers. From the temperature that remained in found objects, she constructed new ceremonies.'[64] Found objects are not fetishes but transmitters, concentrations of reference. Lichtenstein then went on to resurrect the reclusive, vanished kabbalist and scholar (of sorts) David Rodinsky from his attic room above Princelet Street Synagogue in Spitalfields in the East End of London. By then, after their migration to more prosperous parts, Spitalfields was all but empty of Jews. So it was not only Rodinsky who was retrieved by his possessions. From a heap of what Sinclair called 'manic accumulations of holy junk', [65] Lichtenstein resurrected an entire generation of an Anglo-Jewish community that Rodinsky's own disappearance embodied. What Sinclair does not notice is that this 'holy junk' is domestic and therefore (associatively) *female* junk. Lichtenstein does not merely retrieve Rodinsky's words – his notebooks – but a configuration of personal possessions in his room. The whole is in the fragment. As with Ferderber-Salz's (re)collections, Lichtenstein's is perhaps a female way of sanctifying a name and a life: by carrying out of a dead space into a living space some of the practical objects or remnants of the self that turn absence into presence. To reassemble Israel from the domestic clues she has left behind is to signal towards the eschatological resurrection of presence. But whereas a grand resurrection from a Mount of Olives translates a lived life into a purified sacred place away from the body's (maternal) home, a 'female' resurrection restores personal presence by the things that persons have touched, using them over and over again in the sustenance of relation that is the purpose of creation; why there is some-thing rather than no-thing.

But perhaps it is not, finally, enough to pick over the historical rubble for allusions and symbols of the restoration of human faces and ultimately, the face of God. Theology is not to be confused with archaeology. For a theologian, it is unified, narrated systems of meaning, not a postmodern accumulation of reference, which provide a comprehensive structure by which to contemplate the enormity of the Nazi crime and propose a Jewish response. And it is to one such narrative structure: that offered by Jewish mystical theology, that I now turn as a means of further elucidating the redemptive process from which Auschwitz could not be exempt.

PART II

Jewish mysticism and the narration of redemption

Visual and literary texts contemporary with and produced after the Holocaust can talk to theology by talking through and over Nazism and the Nazi scripting of history. There are also older resources by which theology can engage the Holocaust and these can be found in the Jewish mystical tradition. It is not uncommon for Jewish theologians to draw upon the mystical corpus. In the second half of the twentieth century particularly, in the work of writers such as Martin Buber, Abraham Heschel, Arthur Green, Arthur Waskow, Richard

Rubenstein and Emil Fackenheim, Jewish mystical theology has been adapted (often from Gershom Scholem's not uncontested reading of kabbalah)[66] to supply a mythico-temporal narrative whereby cosmology and history – not only that of the Holocaust – have been brought together in a dynamic fusion. Kabbalah has offered contemporary theology an imaginary; a literary, not a literal, scheme.

For the present purposes, kabbalistic schemata can offer a heuristic model of the redemptive process of which Auschwitz was a part (though not a necessary instrument). In so far as Auschwitz was an assembly of Israel, it was a place of revelation and therefore participant in the redemption of history: a mystery intuited by what Rudolf Otto called the *sensus numinis*. The *sensus numinis* is a non-rational intuition of an awesome mystery and so needs rational elaboration before it can mediate ethical and religious meaning. It is my contention that Auschwitz can be contemplated by post-Holocaust theology in the light of kabbalism's redemptive narrative in just such a fashion, for kabbalism is itself an accomodation of the non-rational and the rational; the mystery and its exposition.

To juxtapose Auschwitz and a mythical narration is not to imply that Auschwitz's horrors were imagined, that the Jewish mystical corpus is itself an evidential source, or that its original authorial intentions are decisive. Lurianic kabbalah's preoccupation with the reunification of divine being may, for example, have been a response to the trauma of exile following the expulsion from Spain in 1492, but it is not useful to speculate on what Isaac Luria might have taught about the Holocaust (supposing that we could reconstruct his own thinking, as distinct from those who spoke and wrote in his name).[67] Even should one wish to use the Jewish mystical corpus as authoritative in and of itself, its ascetic derogation of female sexuality and the traditional exclusion of women from its practice make it an inhospitable environment for the feminist theologian. Moreover, the specialized exegetical skills required to read the corpus in the original are only now beginning to be acquired by women within the still predominantly male Jewish academy.

Kabbalism had, of course, long been disapproved of by Jews in non-Hasidic Orthodox communities and, since the nineteenth century, in those of the Reform movement as well. Each with their distinctive rationalisms, both were suspicious of its role in the development of the heretical Shabbatean messianic movement and fearful of its supposed departure from monotheism.[68] (Not surprisingly, Jews with Pagan and New Age leanings also favour kabbalism's esoteric approach.) However vogueish it is today, kabbalistic theology has informed Jewish spirituality and practice since the early medieval period, through the history of Hasidism and up to the present day where it remains highly influential in the contemporary Jewish theological academy. What (post)modern Jews find above all congenial in kabbalism is its view of *tikkun* as a reconciliation, healing or completion in God above and in the world below which can be initiated by human agency.

Recent theology has not, however, comprehensively adopted the kabbalistic worldview. Mystical themes have rather been used in ways that corroborate what is by now a postmodern commonplace, namely that theory is metaphorical in character and that its elaboration is dependent on the models or imaginaries (rather than universal truths) by which local meanings are yielded. In my turn, I want to use the Jewish mystical repertoire as precisely that: an imaginary through which a contemplation of holocaustal texts can pass and gather meaning in its passing, not as a complex esoteric system by which history is explained. The kabbalistic scheme is too riddled with gnosticism, dualism and misogyny to be helpful to a feminist theology of relation of its own accord. It also does not question the validity of halakhic and social orthopraxis (including those injustices to women, the disabled, and others which make orthopraxis inimical to *tikkun*).[69] Certainly, Hasidism went some way to deschematize and democratize the Lurianic mysteries,[70] but there is little doubt that the kabbalistic/Hasidic redemptive scheme to which the present chapter is indebted seems profoundly inimical to the religious feminist project. The kabbalist would view the liberation of the holy within the here and now as being also an annihilation of the here and now; what matters to the mystic is what is *hidden* in the largely irrelevant garments of the immanent realm. The life of God is distilled or extracted from the experiential realm and lifted up towards abstraction and transcendence. The Hasidic neo-kabbalistic contemplation of human action 'destroys' the here and now, according to Scholem (and contra Buber),[71] rather than realizes it. It is the reduction of things to nothingness that is the restoration of their true nature.[72]

To elaborate on the traditional kabbalistic cosmological drama in so far as it serves as a theory of the historical one: at the moment of creation, God ceased to be the All but contracted from a space within God-self to make room for creation (*tsim tsum*). God then emerged from concealment as a self-revelatory emanation of light (*atzilut*). At this the vessels of the seven lower emanations of the divine (*sefirot*) shattered because they could not contain the divine light that filled them. In Lurianic kabbalah, then, the cosmic breakage to be mended took place at creation itself where the outpouring of God cracked the vessels that were to hold it. A stream of spilled light ran down from world to world until, catastrophically, it reached the 'Other Side', where the *kelipot* or 'shells' could not hold the light and its holy sparks scattered all about, falling into the 'impure' material world. The Shekhinah or divine presence has been imprisoned within creation since the breaking of the vessels, especially since *Adam Kadmon*, primordial man, could not stem the power of evil and impurity and ever more divine light was lost. Evil fed upon good and Adam's fall was replicated in the human sphere as his soul was that of all humankind.

What contemporary Jewish theology has taken from this cosmology is not its world-denying gnosticism but its perception that the turbulence, fragmentation and rupture of world and cosmos are a function of one another and that humanity has an active role to play in righting the wrongness. The redemption of the world and God from evil is brought about when Jews consecrate the world by their goodness, if necessary by descending into the very abyss of impurity to rescue the hidden or imprisoned sparks, and, by their elevation, return them to God.[73] Aspects of the human character are traditionally figured as earthly reflections of entities in the sefirotic realm. By demonstrating a trait such as loving kindness a person manifests or brings down the *sefirah* of *hesed* to the benefit of the whole of creation. Here the imitation of God becomes a performative revelation of ultimately cosmic repercussion.[74] Human efforts to reunite God with God by the elevation of the sparks initiate a unification within God. Here gender comes into theological play for these human efforts enable the female Shekhinah (also known as *Sefirah Malkhut* – God's sovereignty over creation and the emanation of God closest to humanity) to be reunited with the male, kingly *Sefirah Tiferet* (beauty, also called 'The Holy One, Blessed be He'). Theirs is a sacred marriage bringing peace and harmony to the *sefirot* and enabling the free flow of divine grace to the world.

If it proves possible to put its arcane and misogynistic baggage to one side, how might the kabbalistic scheme assist a feminist theology of redemption in Auschwitz? One answer lies in the Lurianic redemptive claim that human good deeds liberate the divine sparks dispersed and imprisoned in the *kelipot* or 'shells' of impurity that parasitize the good: good deeds return God to God and therefore eschatologically close the circle of creation. God's being is, as it were, re/collected as fallen sparks by her own creation. It is this historico-cosmic redemptive drama which can take on the work of a structuring metaphor for a feminist theology of the redemptive processes at work in, but not a product of, the Holocaust.

Here, reflection on women's resistance *as* relationality can be accommodated in a basic redemptive narrative frame: that is, each relational act elevated the profaned spark of the divine image in the self and other and reunited that spark with God. Where Auschwitz almost stamped out the divine spark, Israel could reignite it by tending the body, the sanctuary of the divine spark. Even at the most obliterative extremity of patriarchal domination over the subjected other, the fouled, loved body could be a tabernacle whose surface properly reflected the glory of God and shielded the sparks from the 'shells' or forces of impurity. The reconsecration of the sanctuary; the return of God's Shekhinah to God's own place meant that the redemptive process was going on in a manner all the more mysterious and powerful to contemplate *because* it happened there, in a place precisely organized for the profane to cover and extinguish the spark of the divine in persons. This is not to allow Auschwitz itself an instrumental role in the resolution of history. This *tikkun* was not an eschatological climax but a donation towards it that was all the more powerful in being that of a people who had nothing left to give.

The kabbalistic notion that the catastrophes that befall the Jews are also catastrophes for God, tearing God apart from God-self can help us (who stand at an admittedly comfortable distance from Auschwitz) to understand relationality within it as a token of the reconciliation or *tikkun* in God and in the world, brought about as kabbalah urges, namely by good deeds. For it is a yearning for wholeness in the world below which ascends to bring wholeness in that above. Despite the Lurianic breaking of the vessels and scattering of the sparks, good deeds hold a spark which, in the ascent of the good deed, is lifted up and reunited with God. In zoharic mysticism,[75] there is holiness even in the world that is alienated from God; good and evil are intermingled, and it is the individual's duty to separate them. Indeed, this resolution of cosmic and intramundane alienation is dependent on human effort to separate the good from the evil by the practices of holiness. If this is so, where Auschwitz had broken God's heart, female good deeds (no less than male ones) were not only for the suffering other, but also for God so that, in their image, God's own wounds could heal. The theology of image, like the mystical theology of the redemptive gathering of the holy sparks, is a reciprocal or recursive one.[76] In Auschwitz, women's humanity was completed in the restoration of God's image in their own face just as God's female face was restored and completed by taking on the suffering face of women. Perhaps God created humanity in her own image so as to bear some of its burdens.

Jewish feminism and the redemptive process

To better understand why this mystical view of redemption from cosmic rupture should be intrinsic to a feminist theology of the Holocaust we need to attend first to Jewish feminism's diagnosis of the social and theological malfunctioning of which Auschwitz is an (admittedly aberrant) part. Jewish and Christian feminist theologians have agreed that the dehumanization of women is the cause and the result of the patriarchal de-divinization of God. Patriarchy has been theorized as a power founded in human alienation from the divine, where what is worshipped in its place is a masculine numen; an idol whose name and will is perceived and articulated by the projections of the patriarchal interest. Nonetheless, patriarchy is also redeemable, often by those of its own practices and traditions that countermand it. Although few Jewish communities have taken the full measure of feminist criticism, or indeed countenanced its hearing, the notion of redeeming the divine in the redemption of the human is not a new one. Long ago the Baalshem Tov taught that 'the true believer, recognising the reflection of God in every man, should hopefully strive, when that reflection was obscured by sin, to restore the likeness of God in man'.[77] So too, when Jewry comes to honour women's divine image, obscured as it has been by the sin of patriarchy, it is engaged in a restorative struggle – the very process of *tikkun*.

There is some way to go. Mainstream Judaism's resistance to Jewish feminism, perhaps recognizing the systemic transformation it entails, has alienated many women (and some men) from the tradition over the past thirty years. In its academic setting, and before its political energy was defused by the interests of its own specialisms, second wave Jewish feminism was moved by a common notion that 'under patriarchy women are in *galut*. We are a community in exile' from our womanhood and our divinity.[78] Although Jewish feminists may now want to make more nuanced, less sweeping claims, Rita Gross remains right that 'God, as well as women, has been imprisoned within patriarchal imagery'.[79] On mysticism's territory, Gross's contention is grounded in both feminism's emancipatory project and the zoharic conviction that God suffers creation's suffering while, conversely, God's own suffering is experienced in the body of creation.

Traditionally, the suffering of the immanent God is figured as the suffering of the exiled Shekhinah. Shekhinah's exile 'denotes a fundamental sense of alienation and lostness in the divine self as a result of human sin'.[80] In kabbalah, the exile of the Shekhinah is interpreted as meaning that a part of God is exiled from God.[81]

Once, in the tradition, Shekhinah was united with God in the Garden as a wife is to her husband – but it was human sin that separated them. Arthur Green notes that Shekhinah, for the kabbalists, is 'the bride of God within God, mother of the world and feminine side of the divine self, in no way fully separable from the male self of God. Indeed the root of all evil, both cosmic and human, is the attempt to bring about such a separation.'[82]

First Jewish mysticism and then Jewish feminism have, each in their own way, yearned for the unification of the male and the female in God. The kabbalists and their successors, the Hasidim, understood the human task to be that of reuniting the Shekhinah with God and with Israel, as it had been before the cosmic catastrophe of their separation. Without this reunion evil would continue unabated.[83] For a feminist thinking and imagining in Lurianic mode, God's alienation from God must be understood not as the product of some generalized cosmic and human flaw, but as the result of specifically patriarchal religious discourse and practice. The division in God is first an intramundane division. As Elyse Goldstein puts it, if mainstream Judaism were to restore the harmony between God and Shekhinah – between the masculine and feminine in God and in the world – that would be 'an important step' towards a return to the original wholeness and peace of the Garden of Eden.[84] Rita Gross noted this crucial connection between feminism and redemption some time ago, although Jewish feminist theology has not pursued her point with much rigour. (Perhaps because, like Gottlieb, Jewish feminists prefer to find their spiritual resources in women's stories, poems and prayers rather than recondite theosophies.)[85] Gross's point is, however, worth quoting in full:

> The most profound, intriguing, and inviting of all Jewish theologies – the *Kabbalah* – teaches us that *galut* – exile – is the fundamental reality and pain of present existence. It teaches us that one of the causes of *galut* is the alienation of the masculine from the feminine in God, the alienation of God and the *Shekhinah*. Now that the masculine and the feminine have been torn asunder and the feminine dismembered and banished, both from the discourse about divinity and from the human community, such a *tikkun* [reparation] is obligatory, is a *mitzvah*. When the masculine and feminine aspect of God have been reunited and the female half of humanity has been returned from exile, we will begin to have our *tikkun*. The world will be repaired.[86]

I have chosen to look for a restoration of the female in God in the restoration of God to women in Auschwitz. For it seems to me that the socio-theological shift sought by second wave Jewish feminism is a trans-historical redemptive process, not a theological and historical *non sequitur*. I have traced that redemptive process back through Auschwitz not least because, being the place least hospitable to the redemptive process, its contribution would be the greatest.

In Auschwitz, God was at once imprisoned in and exiled from the world. Women's acts of restoration both returned God to Auschwitz and liberated her from Auschwitz. For women to have called God back into the world was to know her name(s). But women in Auschwitz had almost no words of their own with which to call God, God (into Auschwitz). Under patriarchy, Shekhinah, God's presence in the world, is exiled from the world and from God-self. She has been veiled to the point of disappearance under a welter of patriarchal names that, whatever their intrinsic merit, obscure her female face from women's religious thought and experience. Yet to create a space in the situation of persons next to and around other persons was to trace out an open, boundless circle within the closed circle of the perimeter fences. Where the world was sanctified for the coming of the Shekhinah, her presence held open the circle to any who could or would enter. Each gesture of care retrieved a spark of the humanity/divinity that had been trodden into the mud. Each gesture gathered into itself the humanity/divinity dispersed by evil and was as such a redemption of both God in humanity, and in humanity, God.

In Hasidic theology redemption is *kimah kimah*, bit by bit: a continuous process, not a sudden once-and-for-all act of God. This is the understanding of redemption at work here. So that, after Auschwitz, this redemptive, restorative process continues wherever religious feminist resistance rescues the sparks of female divinity from the *kelipot* of patriarchal oppression by their invocation of Shekhinah and other (subordinated or denied) Jewish female images and names of the divine. No theologian could claim that a redemptive process ascribed to the past is not also at work in the present, if differently mediated. And it seems to me that contemporary religious feminists' struggle to restore the erased female image of God describes a redemptive process that is continuous with the entire history of women's resistance to the patriarchal dehumanization and demonization of subjected persons, including that at the time of the Holocaust.

Much of women's struggle against religious patriarchy has focused on the re-naming of God. The non-canonical story of Lilith, Adam's ill-fated first wife, tells us much about women and the naming of God. The Alphabet of Ben Sira 23 tells us that Lilith knew the secret name of God. Empowered by her knowledge, she insisted on her sexual equality with Adam; indeed, her knowing God's name was its guarantor. When equality was denied her, Lilith pronounced God's secret, world-destroying name as she flew off into the air, demonized and banished into exile by a patriarchal Adam and the God he had fashioned in his own image. Perhaps the name Lilith had uttered was God's female name, as unutterable then as it is now. The punishment of its first utterance marked the beginning of the history of patriarchal theology and since that history began God has heard few in creation call her name. Gradually, the world's original lustre diminished because the divine names summon presence: the radiant glory by which God sees and knows her creation to be good. Just as in Genesis 2: 19 where men assume dominion over the animals because they have named them, patriarchy assumes dominion over God by naming God. But to assume dominion over God is to profane God. It is to rob God of ultimacy and render what is holy the merely ordinarily powerful: under patriarchy, a dominant hierarchical male. For a woman in Auschwitz, as for a contemporary Jewish feminist, to sanctify God's female name(s) by female religio-ethical acts, is also to name the profanity of patriarchy as that power which fouls the world in and by the alienation of persons from one another. In the colonization of the divine sparks, the glory dims and what was once 'very good' (Gen. 1: 31), is no longer.

While the world was created by the (over)flowing of God's love, patriarchal structures of alienation have set up divisive barriers that have damned (up) God's love in which we might be washed. And yet over half a century ago the effort to mend the relational connections torn apart by Nazism not only bound up and mended the broken heart of God, it staunched the flow of God's love through the cosmic fissure that was Auschwitz. As Rachel Feldhay Brenner notes, both Anne Frank and Etty Hillesum were convinced that kindness was redemptive. Kindness was a precondition of the world's moral restoration: the 'cure' or 'new order' of which Hillesum writes in her diary and which she intended to help to inaugurate in Westerbork, even as her world collapsed around her.[87] A Jewish feminist may, then, interpret acts of kindness (*hesed*) between women in the camps as being 'ordinary' in the natural, practical sense, but in another, as non-ordinary because their cleaning or restoration of the (female) divine image pointed towards the metapatriarchal dimension of divine and human becoming that *tikkun* or mending engages.

Wherever *hesed* sanctified God's name outside the camps, then *a fortiori* it did so inside them where the assault on human decency and life itself incapacitated the body and will. But the sanctification of God's name was also a deposition of evidence. To say the name of God by words and acts (even those without explicitly religious intent) was to make God's name unname evil: so that in time it would be excised and erased from her heart and the dead would rest in her peace. To say the name of God in acts that named the abjected as human was to sanctify both; by doing so it was to summon the infinite good that is loving presence. One such female name of God which precisely denotes such presence is, of course, that of Shekhinah. I have used this divine name throughout the present study in order to elucidate the possibility of divine presence in Auschwitz – that which Holocaust theologians have been unable to deny but have also found so difficult to affirm. To understand the redemptive character of such a presence in ways other than that of the jubilant deliverance often associated with the term redemption, we need to look a little more closely at how mysticism's figuration of Shekhinah's presence to Israel informs an interpretation of women's presence to Israel as the body of the suffering other in Auschwitz.

Shekhinah: God going with us

It was during the late twelfth and thirteenth centuries that kabbalistic literature rendered the Shekhinah a separate feminine hypostasis; a manifestation of God in the world.[88] In the *Zohar*, the Shekhinah is not only 'God's face turned toward creation', it is 'God's interface with the universe, the *sefirah* through which the flow of divine complexity touches the world'.[89] Religious activity in the world below restores balance to the sefirotic world, enabling the Shekhinah to receive an influx of light from the higher *sefirot* that renders the whole world translucent to God.

Each subsequent Shekhinah tradition builds upon that of its predecessor. Where the rabbis saw Shekhinah as God's presence, the kabbalists saw her as a female element within God – the *sefirah* through which God interacts with the world. While Jewish medieval philosophers, with Maimonides, had separated humanity from an unknowable, non-personal, un-nameable God, kabbalists wanted to restore the divine–human relationship by postulating a God who, in divine immanence, could be known under ten aspects. By the thirteenth century, mystical texts had imaged the Shekhinah as the Bride of God, the Sabbath Bride or, reflecting the social hierarchies of the day, as a princess or queen. Significantly for our purposes, she was also to be figured as a mother or daughter. As the final sphere of the divine emanation she was the closest point of divine contact with the world and at the furthest remove from the unknowable *En Sof*. By this time, the Shekhinah no longer indicated so much God's presence in a particular holy place but a (subordinated) divine hypostasis in her own right and a representation of Israel as a collective body.[90]

There were those who claimed that the Shekhinah's presence was exiled with the destruction of the second Temple and would not return until the coming of the Messiah. But for most she remained a source of consolation, both in and with Israel in their exile. By the seventeenth century Shekhinah had been figured as a woman mourning for and comforting her people.[91] In eighteenth- and nineteenth-century Hasidic theology she suffers not only with the whole Jewish people, but with each Jewish soul. Without her sharing their suffering, humanity could not endure.[92]

Contemporary liberal Jews – especially those with Jungian sympathies – are well disposed to perceiving the Shekhinah as the 'feminine' aspect of God, reunion with whom brings psycho-spiritual completion. In particular, Jewish feminists have incorporated a politically remythologized Shekhinah tradition into their theology and liturgy, especially where the trope of her exile is used to signal a rupture in the female and male elements of the divine brought about by ideological sin. Jewish feminists have used the name Shekhinah to denote not a separate God(dess) but the maternal intimacy of the divine presence as an aspect of the one God which can be reclaimed from patriarchal theology and which should no longer be metaphysically and erotically subordinated (as it has been) to male interests or the masculine roles of God.[93] Jewish feminists are, of course, disinclined to attribute to Shekhinah the feminine passivity and moral ambiguity that has typified her masculinist characterization.[94] In many cases the dangerous charge of the Shekhinah's independent femaleness (conveying on her the title of a *niddah* or menstruant) is absorbed into the masculinity of God by her becoming his bride.[95] Jewish feminists, by contrast, want to accord Shekhinah the status of a divine subject. Above all, (the) Shekhinah bridges Jewish women's spiritual past and future: 'The many [female] images associated with the Shekhinah can become a source for women's encounter with the divine today as well as a bridge to our past. Women yearn for this possibility. When women speak of God-She, we can finally picture ourselves as created in God's image.'[96]

It will have become clear from this brief discussion that the figure of the Shekhinah in mystical (as well as rabbinic traditions)[97] can be reclaimed in such a way as to become central to a feminist theology of the Holocaust. Not only do those traditions provide a set of female images of divine care, they have also shown themselves to be adept in negotiating the exilic situation (one which, for those who do not see the establishment of the State of Israel as a theological resolution of history, can amount to a definitively Jewish historico-spiritual condition).

In Auschwitz, in her grief, Shekhinah would have drawn her scorched, blackened wings around her and seemed, therefore, to disappear. But she was still there, because there is no place where she is not. If the Shekhinah is a (female) image of the presence of God whose presence precisely entails female care for and intimacy with her people in exile then Auschwitz must be definitively both her place and not her place. The 'places of communion we establish with our bodies', as Rachel Adler writes, 'bespeak our likeness to the God the rabbis called *Ha-Makom*, the Place. The capacity to create intersubjective space, which we and God share, is what makes covenant possible.'[98] Auschwitz kept God outside the gate because it was not the home of Jewry but its intended terminus. Yet in the space created in and by the communion of embodied care, those gates also opened onto the possibility of redemptive liberation.

This is, of course, to write after, not during the catastrophe. But it is not to write in abstract hope. Religion's acts of consecration are, as acts, open to a kind of historical scrutiny. Buber, in his remarks on Hasidic theology, recognizes that redemption is performative; it is a practice:

> the Divine is dormant in all things, and . . . it can be awakened only by him who, in sanctification, conceives these things and consecrates himself through them. Corporeal reality is divine, but it must be realized in its divinity by him who truly lives it. The *shekhinah* is banished into concealment; it lies, tied, at the bottom of every thing, and is redeemed in every thing by man, who, by his own vision or his deed, liberates the thing's soul. Thus every man is called to determine, by his own life, God's destiny; and every living thing is deeply rooted in the living myth.[99]

Once, as the Sabbath came in, sixteenth-century kabbalists would go out joyfully into the Galilean fields to meet the Sabbath Bride. Another traditionally masculine way of inviting the Shekhinah into the world was by the encircling of male bodies around a sacred text. Women would invite the Shekhinah into the home by their preparations to welcome the divine guest. Similarly, in the camps, women singing together, remembering their homes, their families and their Sabbath and festival recipes, allowed them, as Myrna Goldenberg notes, to affirm their skills, their community, and their commitment to the future.[100] And in the intentionality of these moments as the re-call of home, Shekhinah was beckoned into the circle of these camp sisters as it were their home.

One body bent over or towards another became a space in which the Shekhinah could dwell and could therefore anticipate the properties of a tent of healing. The notion of the female body as a canopy, wall or curtain of flesh under or within which transformations in state occur is not a new one and may derive from the sacral capacity of the womb as a quasi-alchemical vessel and shelter of emergent life.[101] Remembering the light of the Shekhinah which hovered as a cloud of glory over the matriarch Sarah's tent and within which the Sabbath lights burned all week long,[102] contemporary Jewish women have mediated the sacral power of the tent through a variety of rituals. The feminist artist Edith Altman sought to heal her father's experiences in Buchenwald using the symbol of a tent/womb/furnace of life before which she placed photographs of the camp.[103] Marcia Cohn Spiegel also describes contemporary Jewish women's symbolic use of the healing female tent. In one rite of passage, when a woman takes a new name of her own choosing, Cohn Spiegel and other women will hold her grandmother's hand-worked tablecloth over the woman in order to mark and initiate her experience of renewal. Or when a woman is in need of healing she can be ritually wrapped in the comforting folds of Cohn Spiegel's grandfather's prayer shawl – a shelter for divine–human intimacy which here becomes a *sukkat shalom* or tent of peace.[104]

To refer to the spiritual self-expression of women in contemporary America in the same breath as the dire physical needs of women dying in Auschwitz is not to trivialize the almost fathomless pain of these latter. It is to say that there can be a proper phenomenological commonality of signification and meaning between Jewish women's practice, not of circumstance. In the barrack blocks of Auschwitz, sacral cloths, both domestic and ritual, had long since been taken, destroyed or profaned. But the raised and bent arm could still take one woman under the shelter of another. Here God's outstretched arm was not that of biblical vengeance but of community in suffering; an arm leading out to another place; motioning towards Jerusalem.

Levinas once remarked in an interview that 'this business of Auschwitz did not interrupt the history of holiness. God did not reply, but he has taught that love of the other person, without reciprocity, is a perfection in itself.'[105] In Auschwitz, the history of holiness; the process and possibility of redemption: our going out from evil, was continuous with that of pre- and post-Holocaust Jewish life because it consisted in relationality, the love of the other without exacting a price. But it was not to go out in triumph. That 'God himself is a refugee in the world'; that 'in all their [Jewry's] affliction he is afflicted', is a significant element of the tradition.[106] God, as Shekhinah, is a homeless, wandering God.[107] For God to be present in the patriarchal world is also to be damaged by the world; her going with us is also, tragically, again her exile. Auschwitz's assault on the Jewish body – the sanctuary of the divine spark – recapitulated the destruction of the Second Temple, the dwelling place of God, which first sent Shekhinah into exile.

And yet while God's holocaustal exile from the world left God further from Jerusalem than God had ever been, that exile was also being overcome wherever the encircling female body/wall represented home. As a place of exile, Auschwitz, denotes what, in another context, Lodahl calls, 'a site *between* presence and absence'.[108] So that where God's presence as Shekhinah was at once expelled and imprisoned in Auschwitz, that presence could also be liberated by acts of sanctification which restored her to Jerusalem, where Jerusalem is both an ontic destination and always a way of going. Jerusalem came a little closer in women's welcome of the other as sister or daughter or friend; it was embodied and enacted by the mothers, daughters, sisters and aunts (familial or surrogate) who saw, touched, covered and cleaned the other. And as they did so, the Shekhinah comforted those travelling with her as she had always done since the destruction of the Temple. In kabbalistic theology Shekhinah is central to the restorative process, figured, as it often is, as the labour of overcoming her exile from Jerusalem and its violated sanctuary. So too, her return to Jerusalem describes the trajectory of the present theology as it begins its journey out of Auschwitz. Shekhinah, in deep mourning, was on her way back to Jerusalem.

It may be asked what purpose was served by the maternal, grieving presence of Shekhinah if it could not offer actual deliverance from evil *then*, not in a time to come. But within the logic of the model of God I am proposing it is not meaningful to ask why God did not protect us at that time because it is not the nature or function of God to be reduced to that of a fortification against particular suffering. God is not a supernatural arsenal. Rather, it should be asked how we could and can protect God's presence as it is this which makes it possible to know God in the other and for God to know God-self in creation. And it is in this mutual knowing that both God and humanity will come to experience the blessings consequent upon the reconciliation within self and world traditionally described as *tikkun*. Because women are made in the image of God, Shekhinah suffered in the suffering of women. So that what has been called the 'gender wounding' of Jewish women in the death and concentration camps was also a wounding of God. But conversely, when women's acts of care restored in one another that profaned spark of the divine which rendered them a reflection of God, they also restored God to God. In this sense, the redemption of both women and God from patriarchy was occurring as together they fell into the holocaustal pit.

The human face turned towards the other summoned the excluded, profaned God from her place by the gates – each redeemed spark lighting God's way back into the world; a God who, once having entered into the conditions of the world is not of a nature to alter them by fiat. Here she was shut out and shouted down, and against this was simply, silently, *there*. It may be that there are places of individual powerlessness and despair where, finally, all the other can do is to stand (spiritually if not physically) immovably by, like the women in black who have stood patiently in front of the government buildings of oppressive regimes holding up images of their dead or missing children. As Mother, God could not be cut off from Israel, her child. She could not remain outside the gates of the city of death while her children were within.[109] In an early seventeenth-century letter, Shlomo Dresnitz recorded a dream of Rabbi Abraham Halevi. While in Jerusalem, Halevi dreamt that he saw the Shekhinah standing with her back to him, above the wailing wall. She was half-naked and the reader infers that she has been raped. Halevi was distraught at seeing her thus, but she turned and touched his face and wiped away his tears, comforting him with words of a better future.[110]

God hides her glory and comes hidden in the rags and filth of her suffering. She is, as it were, smuggled into Auschwitz: this is, or what should be, meant by the hiddenness of God. And yet, within its gates, she is also held aloft by the women who carry other women, who lift them up. It is not that the *tremendum* of her presence is deferred by her abjection; *in* her abjection she comes as eschatological comforter, witness and judge.

To hold up another woman, to raise her face from the ground, as has been recorded of women in Auschwitz,[111] was to raise God's standard in Auschwitz. To drag or carry another along was not only to save her from death; it was to carry Shekhinah through the camp as she went in her ragged, blood and mud-spattered tent on her way to Jerusalem. According to tradition, where there is peace, Shekhinah returns to Jerusalem. These women lifted up the face of God and carried it as a sign of peace. They bound up her wounds (a definitive act of *tikkun*) and sent her on her way. Although Auschwitz can never be justified as its instrument, relationality constituted a redemptive moment of human presence: a *staying there* against erasure. It is that staying there that signals towards the liberation of God from the demonic attempt to remove or dis-appear the human(e) and the divine in the establishment of its own space, supremacy and possession. If anything about female moral practice in Auschwitz was messianic it was this. As Levinas proposes, where the suffering self is given over to the other's demand, then the self, in breaking through the violence of history to another way of being, is him or herself the Messiah.[112]

In this and the previous chapter I have outlined several connected means (some of them apparently negligible in proportion to the scale of the dying) by which it is possible to speak of an/other redemption in Auschwitz, without, again, saying that Auschwitz was itself redemptive. This book has been concerned with the means by which God and humanity see and bless by their seeing. In transforming the unseen, disregarded, disfigured face into an image – that which is seen and knowable – persons and God are revealed as present to one another. This making God visible to God is the theological summation of the redemptive process to which I now turn.

The vision of God in Auschwitz

If Auschwitz's function was to de-face the human image to the point of disappearance it was also to make God invisible to God because humanity images God. But the blinding of God and the disappearance of God are theological possibilities before they are historical ones. To understand this we need to revisit the kabbalistic account of the beginning, for in theology we cannot talk of the eschatological end without returning to the beginning: to creation.

We have seen that Lurianic kabbalah describes a primordial creative process (*tsim tsum*) whereby God withdraws or contracts into God-self in order to leave space and freedom for finite creation. In the beginning, God withdraws from the world so that humanity can be a free co-partner in creation; so that creation can take place. The space left by God nonetheless bears the impression of God much as (to use the customary metaphor) a bottle holds its form after the liquid has been poured out. In this sense God is both present in the world but is not identical with the world. God's immanence and transcendental absence are also traditionally figured as a tidal ebb and flow rather than as polar distinctions.

Auschwitz was a demonic dis-creation that set creation into reverse. It was so comprehensive an affront to God's creativity that the divine glory contracted into itself (*tsim tsum*) until it was no more than a pin-prick of light that was almost snuffed out by the engulfing, extinguishing darkness. But this is not to say that God's face was hidden or averted. It is rather that if, with mystical theology, we see God's creative presence as a flow, then Auschwitz reversed the glorious wash of creation which carried new and beautiful things on its tide. In Auschwitz, God's holiness, previously poured out to order the world so that the world could partake in God's love, was being poured into the pit – a cosmological and historical black hole sucking creation down into a vortex of chaos and pain. The voiding of the holy from the world left God almost no space; her presence contracted, though not as in her creative birth pangs (also known as *tsim tsum* by kabbalists), but in the recoil of the definitively holy from the definitively profane. In that apocalyptic contraction of light into its source, the skies darkened, the moon and stars disappeared, God was left almost unable to see her way, and creation was left stranded in the mud by the pull of the outgoing tide.

And yet the oral tradition of the kabbalah claims that God brought the world into existence because 'God wished to behold God'.[113] It is difficult to be sure what that phrase means but it suggests that the relational dynamic of creation is also an aesthetic one.[114] Scripture urges us to 'Seek [God's] presence constantly' (1 Chron. 16: 11). This is the ground of the Jewish ethical episteme: that we will know the good because the good is not only an act of will; it is the state of being present to God – not hiding from God as Adam and Eve did in the Garden (Gen. 3: 9–10), or being hidden from God as Nazism attempted to do to when it deported Jewry into the camps and ghettos. And we can only be before God in the state of ethical cleanness by which God knows the world to be a good image of God-self who is good. When God can see God-self in creation she will know that it is good just as she did in the beginning, where in Genesis 1: 31 'God saw all that [S]He had made, and found it very good'. That is, a world in which God can see a sharp, clean image of her face is one which is blessed because it is ordered as God intended it to be.[115] A mirror to the beauty of divine holiness, the world was once, visibly, very good. God saw God in creation so the expressive purpose of creation was fulfilled. In her emanation as a creator, God could touch the world and the world was touchable to God.

So that for a feminist theologian the tragedy of rupture is not, as the gnostic mystical temper would have it, the creation of matter as such. Rather the estrangement of the world from God occurred and continues to occur *within* the course of patriarchal history, which is a history of making one thing invisible and untouchable to another. Patriarchy has ranked and used up creation, leaving it struggling under a burden of what tradition calls sin and against whose power its great ethico-legal codes have too often proved ineffectual. God has been exiled by the violent refusal of her peace and the world has dropped below the horizon of her vision. If Auschwitz meant that God could no longer behold God on earth then her being and her reason for creation was close to destruction. She would become blind to herself. This was the case when God seemed so dispersed by absolute atrocity to have disappeared altogether. But if God could behold her image even in the smoke blackened mirror of Auschwitz, then God's original creative purpose was not utterly thwarted. In those moments when God *could* behold God in the midst of Auschwitz, through the thick scale of Jewry's profanation, these were moments of *tikkun* – the restoration of God's first vision and sight of the world in the days when it was new.

To speak of *tikkun* in a holocaustal context is not to minimize or magically reverse the destruction. Auschwitz all but extinguished the human spark that was once the illuminating glory of creation so that there God could hardly know creation as her own. Auschwitz sought to dis-appear God's image in creation by hunger, fire and mud. It would take generations of spiritual restoration – begun by those within Auschwitz and continued by those outside it – before God would know that the image was God's and could contemplate it with joy. That is what is meant by the eschatological end: the completion (*tikkun*) of God's work; the moment when it is finished and God and all those who have shouldered the (re)creative task with her can rest and enjoy the sabbath that also returns us to the new beginning. Auschwitz was an end but not the end. Wherever Jewry, living or remembered, was restored within its fences, it could also motion towards a beginning, for a restored image is one which is revealed in its original clarity.

Against those who speak of the Holocaust as a unique, qualitative break with what has gone before, many feminist theorists would argue it to be one possible (though aberrant and excessive) culmination of dominatory forces already at work in any patriarchal culture. While Auschwitz was a blotting out of God and God's name (in that sense Buber and, later, Cohen were right to speak of the eclipse of God) this was part of a longer and larger history of such. A primary factor in God's alienation from the world has been the theological erasure of the female character of God. It is this which has denied women the religious recognition as subject by self and others. The refusal of female subjecthood and its subjection to the masculine has also blinded God from the female dimension of God-self over the patriarchal millennia. Because women are made in the image of God, in denying the full personhood and visibility of women, namely the moral and rational agency of subjects, the female personality of God is obstructed and God cannot see God-self in half of her creation: the window through which God surveys God-self. The outworking of God's original creative purpose has been occluded and therefore God cannot be fully God.

We have seen that kabbalism offers an imaginary by which to envisage the restoration of God. And it is by means of this that a feminist theology of the Holocaust can respond to Gross and those other Jewish feminists who have lamented the rupture of the male and female dimensions in God (if only our concept of God) and who have looked to God's *tikkun* as a precondition of societal *tikkun*. I have argued that when women resisted the holocaustal degradation of their female humanity then the female face of God was restored to God, and thereby to Israel and creation as a whole, because then God could behold and know her face reflected in those that she loves. For God to seek God's image or likeness in Auschwitz, the place where it had been so thoroughly defaced, is not, then, to be compared to Narcissus gazing into a clouded pool. The likeness between women or men and God consists not in some literal incarnation (we are also of dust and ash) but in a likeness of moral and spiritual agency – precisely the agency which was all but prohibited to Jewry in Auschwitz.

There, the ethical and the aesthetic dimensions of the holy were brought together in a place repellent to both. In Judaism, the aesthetic is not a concern for material beauty. The beautiful is not reified as such lest it become an idol; it is a quality of good deeds, thoughts or prayer. Here, then, I use the aesthetic to refer to an ethical judgement of perception: the image-ination of the other as of absolute value. And it is in the perception of the absolute value of the human as itself a perception of the divine made present in the other through sight and touch that makes redemption an aesthetic as well as ethical moment. When one woman *saw* or recognized the humanity of the degraded other and responded to its ethical claim upon her, God was made visible to God in the facing image. God knew her femaleness and was therefore reconciled to her estranged self.[116] Where God has been reunited with her own female subjecthood she is no longer in exile from her own personality and can be fully God. For God to be reunited with God is the completion of God and the inauguration of a divine and human reign of peace.

Of course, as a matter of phenomenological observation, female divinities do not guarantee social peace. Patriarchally accommodated female divinities often stand at the helm of warlike cultures. But this is not what is meant by the restoration of female attributes to the divine. Jewish feminism does not confuse God-She with ancient goddesses from predominantly masculine pantheons and its notion of femaleness is not to be confused with a compliant femininity in service to its own oppressors.[117] Rather, the female attributes of God constitute definitively moral attributes that transform the whole and without which femaleness is not such.

The Hebrew verb *shalem*, to be complete or perfect, shares its root with the word *shalom*, a state of wholeness, and therefore peace, which is one of the traditional names of God. The (re)integration of femaleness and divinity is to make God whole and at peace with God-self, and women whole and at peace with the world. It is to restore God's power to God after its hubristic arrogation: the very essence of *tikkun*. Its moral and spiritual ultimacy, its being at the end of what has become customary may be what is meant by Exodus 33: 20 where God says that we may not see him and live. That is, we cannot know the fullness of God's personality *and* continue to exist in the patriarchal mode. Those holocaustal moments when the human and divine female face was cleaned of its patriarchal (dis)figuration constituted at once a judgement on all forces of alienation and a sign and moment of the post-patriarchal possibility. God and the world experienced at-onement because it is at the moment that the female human face can hold up a mirror to God that patriarchy has failed in its intention to cover God's face so that she cannot see and judge what it has done to her and to her creation. There were those who could lift the mirror, and those who could not. May the memory of all of them be a blessing.

The princess and the city of death

A feminist *maaseh*, after Rabbi Nachman of Bratslav

The Jewish people is a nation of fabulists. Jewishness is about knowing how to thread stories together on very long strings. Jewish religious thought is not solely an exercise in law or philosophy, but is often aggadhic or narrative in form[1] From the biblical stories of Esther and of David and Goliath, the talmudic tales of the Witches of Ashkelon and Solomon and Asmodeus, to the tales of enchantment and wonder attributed to the nineteenth-century hasidic master, Rabbi Nachman of Bratslav,[2] imaginative, often allegorical interpretations of biblical texts and the use of universal motifs of folklore are an integral part of Judaism's sacred and secular cultural tradition. It is a maaseh *— a traditional Jewish tale, often in the form of an allegory, combining universal fairy-tale, magical and religio-mythical elements[3] — that I now offer by way of a conclusion to the preceding chapters. Theology is a work of the religious imagination presented as an argument both supported by tradition and challenging tradition. In this book about seeing and presence it seems right that the imagination — the factory of images — should be given the last words.*

One cold, silent winter's day a princess was out walking in her garden when a bird flew over the wall, alighted on a branch and began to sing to her. His song told the princess that in many of the lands where her scattered people lived, their holy places and books were alight and they themselves killed, imprisoned or in hiding. At this the princess wept for her people and for herself because she knew that she must leave the castle and its beautiful gardens and travel through the mountains and forests to find them.

Her betrothed — a long-widowed king — loved her dearly and refused to let her go. They quarrelled for a day and a night. She accused the king of turning his back on the people in their hour of greatest need and of forgetting their centuries of loyalty to his causes. She begged him not to abandon them but to remember the days of old when, little more than a boy, he would travel through the land in a tent: a nomad king always in the midst of his wandering people. He, in turn, warned her that for a woman of her standing to journey alone through the villages and fields would dishonour the glory and prestige of the royal house. He begged her to first let his ministers see what they could do. She was too young and too tender-hearted to worry her head with such horrors. She must forget that she ever heard the song the bird had sung to her in the garden. The princess did not answer but turned her face from him and, standing at the window, looked out over the frozen lands below.

When at last she turned to speak to the king she saw that his hair was turning white in front of her eyes. The fires in the great hearths had gone out, the fine plate no longer shone, the lustrous jewels in his crown had dulled and the priceless mirrors had so tarnished that the king could no longer see his own face in them. The princess knew at once that this had come about because the king had locked them both away from the people – those who had always carried with them lights lit from the royal brazier that had once stood within the castle walls. Now their journeys were so very long and so very far that their lights could no longer be seen from the castle windows. Only if she could find them would light return to the royal house. The king would be able to see his own face in the mirrors and once more know his glory.

The princess vowed to herself that she would escape from the castle that very night, disguised in an old black coat she had found with a yellow star sewn on its back and front. Before she left, the princess sought to mend her quarrel with the king. She went to embrace him, but he would not hold her. Nightfall came and, unknown to her, the king stood at a window above the empty courtyard and watched her pass through the castle gates. He watched her walk out across the deep snow, a tiny, thin figure, shrouded in black and carrying only a small cloth bundle under her arm. He despaired of ever seeing her again. His heart was about to break for love and he began to run down the great staircase and across the courtyard, calling to her that he would go with her. But at that moment a great blizzard covered her footprints with snow and blew her into the darkness. He turned back to his dark castle and slowly closed its heavy gates.

The princess travelled for many days and nights until she came to the gates of the city of death where her people had been taken and were being killed all the day long. From the gates she was carried along by a great crowd to a place where there were only women to be seen. There she sat looking about her until at last she was stripped of her clothes. What remained of her jewels were torn from her neck and ears and all she was given against the cold were a summer dress and two right shoes.

The princess could not sleep in that place. Through the long nights she followed the Angel of Death and watched her cruel swoop and her gentle enfolding. She saw her old friend Lilith whom the king had banished from the castle because he both feared and desired her. Here, Lilith, clad only in old red evening dress that hung long and loose on her scarecrow body, was goading women to forget their loss for a moment and love and laugh while they could. Now, in the city of death, Lilith was losing far more than the hundred of her children a day that the king had once pronounced as her punishment for disobeying him and her husband, Adam. But Lilith was not giving in, even here.

Her thin fingers numbed blue by the icy cold, the princess worked ceaselessly, gathering together in her bundle of rags the few weak sparks of light that she could see around her; sometimes even in those who spat when they heard the name of the king. She found the sparks in the fleeting reflections of her face in women's eyes, in the Sabbath lights that women sometimes found ways to kindle, in the small loyalties to the promise of blessings the king and his long dead queen had once made to their people.

The horror of that place made her long to return home to the fountains and rose gardens of the royal house. But she knew that the castle was in darkness; all light was here, fuelling the ovens that burnt the dead, and sometimes the living, for hour upon hour, day after day in the city of death. The princess could not return to the castle until her bundle was full of light. And even though there were women there who helped her in her task when they could, the bundle seemed to empty almost as fast as it was filled. The cloth was torn and she had no needle or thread with which to mend the holes. All day and night, starved and thirsty, she wandered through the city, stroking a child's face here and humming a melody there, blowing gently on the candles that still flickered in her people's hearts.

But many were too sick or blinded by their hunger, fear and loss to know that she was there. Some pushed her aside and she was regularly beaten, sworn at and attacked by the soldiers' dogs. She often fell in the mud and filth as she bent to look for fallen sparks and few had the strength to pull her from it. And there were some whom she herself could not but pass by: those who, no longer believing the king's promises to them, had cursed not only the king but also his people who suffered beside them.

There were a few in that city of death who had heard whispers that the princess was among them and had searched for her on their way to and from their endless labours. But they were looking for a princess and all they saw were lice-ridden women in rags. Many said that it was another of the rumours and lies that circulated in that city, often to torment them. Most despaired of finding the princess. Few could have recognized her. But some thought that when they came together with the other women to share scraps of food, to sing, and to share dreams of the past and the future, they would later catch a glimpse of her – perhaps far across a field of mud or breaking rocks at the very bottom of a quarry.

One day a large number of pregnant women were taken from their quarters and surrounded by those who guarded the city of death from life. They beat the women with whips and clubs, kicked their stomachs, and dragged them over the ground by their hair. They set their ferocious dogs upon the women to tear at their flesh. And when the women fell unconscious, they and their unborn children were thrown alive into the devouring fires.[4] At some distance away, the princess stood watching, her face moon-white and her body twisted with pain. For a while afterwards she could not remember why she had come to this city and what she had come to do. Her heart all but broken, dimly aware that the wet ash and snow were extinguishing the sparks in her bundle, she stumbled off into the starless night.

All the while, the king was growing ill and blind in his dark, silent, ice-cold castle and he feared that he would die. At last he called his ministers to him and told them to send an emissary to travel through all the lands where his people dwelled. The princess was to be found and brought home to make him well again.

But wherever the emissary went he could find no one who had seen her. It was on the day that he turned to make his way back to the castle that he met an old woman collecting firewood in the forest. The old woman told him that she had given a young woman food and a bed some time past and that she had said that she was on her way to the city of death. The emissary hastened there but when he got through the gates, the soot, grease and smoke that filled the air choked him, and each emaciated woman's face he looked into was both like and unlike the face of the woman he sought. He could not bear to stay in that place and with a heavy heart he began his journey back to the castle without her.

Several years passed and the princess was still alive. But on the day her bundle of sparks had become as heavy as her broken body could carry, she too was selected for death. As she and a great crowd of women were driven with curses and blows towards the place of execution she dropped her bundle of light in the mud. A little girl picked it up and gave it back to her with the slow stare of the very young. She tucked the bundle inside her dress, kissed the child, took hold of her hand and walked with her into the noisy darkness.

A short while later the tall chimney flared and the princess, clothed in flame, flew out into the night on wings of light. Her bundle had been lifted and opened by the fire and its heap of sparks was drifting outward across the night sky.

It was not long afterwards that peace was declared in the lands where her people had once dwelled. But few were left alive in the city of death and those that were had not been healed of their great sorrow. The princess no longer wished to return to the castle and live as a wife within its walls. More and more she sighed to herself at the thought of the pomp of the royal house and the clamour of men arguing among themselves as to who among them were to be appointed ministers and keepers of its tradition.

Instead she began to wander from house to house, bringing her light and peace to all who sought it; to all who lit their candles in her name. Sometimes, on days when the spring sunshine broke through the clouds, she would sit a while on rocks and logs by the railway tracks near the towns and villages, forests and ravines where her people had suffered and died, collecting the stories of the dead and the dead at heart to bring as evidence against the evil ones at the time when they would be brought before her.

Years passed and one day she heard that the old king had died, and that his son who wished to make her his bride had himself grown old while seeking her. But she hid from him because some of the daughters and grand-daughters of the dead had begun to call to her and to one another. She smiled when she heard their new teachings and knew that they needed her as she needed them and that for a while longer she must make this place of exile her home. Sometimes she thought of the king's son and hoped that one day their marriage as two equals in friend-ship and love would bring peace and justice to all lands forever. But such a marriage could not be celebrated while there were still so many among her people who banished her from their houses as soon as the Sabbath candles went out. And inside the castle the candles flickered, the fires smoked and the great mirrors were shrouded in dust and soot. For there were still too many there who hated the princess for neglecting her duties to the king and his son. They were plotting against her. It was not safe for her to return.

And now it is a wet, foggy winter night. The princess is hastening towards a small house at the end of a winding, dark alleyway on the very edge of a city. She finds the house and looks in at the window. Through the raindrops rolling down the glass she sees the reflection of her face in a room crowded with women. Each one is lighting her own Sabbath candle and the room glows with myriad lights. The princess slips in silently through the open door.

Notes

Preface

1 Arthur Cohen, 'Some Theological Implications of the Death Camps', in David Stern and Paul Mendes-Flohr (eds), *An Arthur A. Cohen Reader: Selected Fiction and Writings on Judaism, Theology, Literature and Culture*, Detroit, Wayne State University Press, 1998, p. 235, and *idem, The Tremendum: A Theological Interpretation of the Holocaust*, New York, Continuum, 1993, p. 2.

2 *After Tragedy and Triumph: Essays in Modern Jewish Thought and the American Experience*, Cambridge, Cambridge University Press, 1990, p. 3.

3 Michael Goldberg has expressed fears that a cult of the Holocaust is supplanting Judaism itself. (*Why Should Jews Survive? Looking Past the Holocaust Toward a Jewish Future*, New York, Oxford University Press, 1995, p. 49). The 'Americanization' of the Holocaust refers to the colonization of the Holocaust, rendering it palatable for American consumption and deployable in the promotion of specific political and ideological agendas. See e.g. Hilene Flanzbaum, 'The Americanization of the Holocaust', *Journal of Genocide Research* 1 (1999), pp. 91–104; Berenbaum, *After Tragedy and Triumph*, pp. 8–16.

4 See further Anne Michaels' novel, *Fugitive Pieces*, London, Bloomsbury, 1998, pp. 159–60.

5 Cohen, *The Tremendum*, p. 23.

6 *Love's Work*, London, Vintage, 1997, pp. 10–11.

7 Cohen, *The Tremendum*, p. 107. He concludes, 'I find this no reason to despair of theological discourse, no reason to dismiss its findings' (ibid.).

Introduction

1 Joan Ringelheim, 'The Split between Gender and the Holocaust', in Dalia Ofer and Lenore J. Weitzman, (eds), *Women in the Holocaust*, New Haven and London, Yale University Press, 1998, pp. 346–9.

2 This enumeration of holocaustal factors affecting women, and mothers in particular, is indebted to Miriam Gillis-Carlbach, 'Jewish Mothers and Their Children During the Holocaust: Changing Tasks of the Motherly Role', in John K. Roth and Elizabeth Maxwell (eds), *Remembering for the Future: The Holocaust in an Age of Genocide*, Basingstoke, Hampshire, Palgrave, 2001, pp. 230, 237–8. There is now too considerable a literature on women's 'double jeopardy' to cite in the present note. See e.g. Myrna Goldenberg, 'Different Horrors, Same Hell: Women Remembering the Holocaust', in Roger S. Gottlieb (ed.), *Thinking the Unthinkable: Meanings of the Holocaust*, New York, Paulist Press, 1990, pp. 150–66 and ' "From a World Beyond": Women in the Holocaust', *Feminist Studies* 22 (1996), pp. 667–87; Marion A. Kaplan,

Between Dignity and Despair: Jewish Life in Nazi Germany, Oxford, Oxford University Press, 1999, esp. pp. 50–73; Claudia Koonz's discussion of the predicament of Jewish women in Nazi Germany in *Mothers in the Fatherland: Women, the Family and Nazi Politics*, New York, St Martin's Press, 1987, chs 10 and 11; Joan Ringelheim, 'Women and the Holocaust: A Reconsideration of Research', *Signs, Journal of Women in Culture and Society* 10 (1985), pp. 741–61. Reprinted with additions as 'Women and the Holocaust: A Reconsideration of Research' in Carol Rittner and John Roth (eds), *Different Voices: Women and the Holocaust*, New York, Paragon Press, 1993, pp. 373–418.

3   The relation of Jewishness to femininity is a complex one. The feminization of Jewry is by no means confined to anti-Semitic caricature. In Judaism itself, Israel is cast as God's (sometimes adulterous) wife. Popular American and British Jewish humour has often revelled (as have Woody Allen and the New York rabbi turned comedian, Jackie Mason) in the Jewish husband's indifference to *goyische* machismo and the acquisition of practical expertise. However, the derogatory feminization of Western Jewry is a phenomenon dating from antiquity and includes the medieval superstition that Jewish men menstruated. The feminization of male Jews in popular anti-Semitic culture continued at least into the late nineteenth century (see Amy-Jill Levine, 'A Jewess, More and/or Less' in Miriam Peskowitz and Laura Levitt (eds), *Judaism Since Gender*, New York, Routledge, 1997, p. 153). See also Daniel Boyarin's reclamation of the Jewish 'sissy' in 'Justify My Love', in Peskowitz and Levitt (eds), *Judaism Since Gender*, pp. 131–7; Harry Brod (ed.), *A Mensch Among Men: Explorations in Jewish Masculinity*, Freedom, CA, Crossing Press, 1988. Ronit Lentin, in *Israel and the Daughters of Shoah*, New York and Oxford, Berghahn Books, 2000, has argued that the macho, secular Israeli military establishment has defined its rights of occupation and domination by stigmatizing Ashkenazic diaspora Jews as 'female' victims of the Nazis. In 'Interarticulations: Gender, Race and the Jewish Question', in Peskowitz and Levitt (eds), *Judaism Since Gender*, p. 51, Ann Pellegrini asks, 'If all Jews are womanly, are any women also Jews? The collapse of Jewish masculinity into a kind of femininity appears to "disappear" Jewish women.'

4   *Post-Holocaust Dialogues: Critical Studies in Modern Jewish Thought*, New York, New York University Press, 1983, p. 169.

5   To avoid confusion, I have used the masculine pronoun for God in its own traditional context and the feminine pronoun when intending to move outside it. Although the Jewish God is always referred to in the masculine (Hebrew lacks a gender neutral form), I refer to God as 'she' when I am speaking of God imaged in women; of a divine mutuality between women and God that is socially, spiritually and imaginally distinct from that usually obtaining between men and God. I take seriously Judith Plaskow's view that Jewish theology is not properly monotheistic until its naming of God is sexually inclusive. While feminist talk of 'God-She' is not a literal account of God-in-God's-self who is not a possible object of ordinary knowledge, neither is it a mere provocation. To use a feminine pronoun for God is to properly name and include bio-cultural modes of being traditionally (but not exclusively) associated with women and valued as telling us something important about relationality, both human and divine. The female pronoun is *not* used because women in the camps may or may not have experienced or intended God as female in character.

6   'Mother Love, Child Death and Religious Innovation: A Feminist Perspective', *Journal of Feminist Studies in Religion* 12 (1996), p. 20.

7   Ibid., p. 22.

8   *Women as Ritual Experts: The Religious Lives of Elderly Jewish Women Living in Jerusalem*, New York, Oxford University Press, 1992, p. 140.

9   As is customary, this book uses the German name Auschwitz in two senses. First in its particular sense as the name of a large complex of camps (including the death camp Auschwitz-Birkenau) and a town in Poland. Second, and less often, I use the name as a holocaustal generic. The sense should be clear in context. Because not all Jews

survived or died in Auschwitz, some commentators object to the use of the name Auschwitz as a holocaustal generic whose gates, railway tracks and gatehouse have become visually emblematic of all other places and times of the Holocaust. Although not uncontroversial, where I have used the word Auschwitz as a generic it has been to remember that the catastrophe is not an abstract philosophical problem but happened – took (a) place – somewhere in a world which cannot be absolved from its happening. The term 'Holocaust' is also contested. The Hebrew *Shoah* (destruction) is doubtless a better and more accurate term than the anglicized New Testament Greek 'Holocaust' which translates the Hebrew *olah* – an offering consumed by fire. I use the term 'Holocaust' because it is simply more familiar and accessible to the non-Jewish readership whose sense of involvement this book warmly invites.

10   This set of points summarizes the basic Jewish feminist critique of the tradition. However, there are various types of Jewish feminism. See e.g. Nurit Zaidman, 'Variations of Jewish Feminism: The Traditional, Modern and Postmodern Approaches', *Modern Judaism* 16 (1996), pp. 47–65. Zeidman elucidates the three main types of Jewish feminism as the traditional or Orthodox Jewish feminism which adapts Torah in women's interests but only so far as Torah might permit; 'modern' Jewish feminism which seeks equality with Jewish men through the ethical reform of tradition; and ultra-liberal or 'postmodern' Jewish feminism whose eclectic approach might also involve celebrating the Goddess within alternative Jewish communities or those on the fringes of the liberal ones to which they are allied. This typology is, however, more schematic than the practice and thought it describes, allowing some Jewish feminists to have sympathies with elements of all three types.

11   Emil L. Fackenheim, *Quest for Past and Future: Essays in Jewish Theology*, Boston, Beacon Press, 1970, p. 17.

12   'Voluntary Covenant', in Steven L. Jacobs (ed.), *Contemporary Jewish Religious Responses to the Holocaust*, Lanham, MD, New York and London,, University Press of America, 1993, pp. 97–8, 101–2.

13   'Foreword' to Rabbi Elyse Goldstein, *ReVisions: Seeing Torah Through a Feminist Lens*, Woodstock, Vermont, Jewish Lights Publishing, 1998, p. 13.

14   Contemporary feminism is, of course, highly diverse. The term 'patriarchy' has been justly criticised by some contemporary feminists themselves as generalizing or suppressing difference in the form, degree and context of oppression. A post-ideological, postmodern unease with grand narratives and ambitious ideas has seen many feminist theorists relinquish the term 'patriarchy', or at least to temper its rebuke by using it in the plural. To call Jewish theology 'patriarchal' is, of course, to generalize. Emancipatory, prophetic theological counter-traditions exist in complex relationship with the dominant tradition, and are produced (and often revered by) the very cultures they judge. In the sense that patriarchy is geographically, culturally, economically and historically diverse it may indeed be proper to speak of patriarchies in the plural. But carefully nuanced, the noun and its adjective, patriarchal, remain a central tool of religious feminist criticism. Whether or not 'patriarchy' is one of a number of hierarchies (race, ethnicity, economic privilege and so forth) or refers to a common, primary gender hierarchy that precedes, produces and encompasses all other inequalities is an open question. In this book, patriarchy denotes an alienated social ordering that allows a powerful subject to harness the energies of the subjected object to its own end. To criticize social orderings and religious orientations which privilege the masculine posture is not, however, to make essentialist statements about what men *are*. For this reason, the term 'masculinist' has also been used to indicate that it is not masculinity as such, but a set of norms and values associated with masculine practices that are religiously problematic. Men have been the primary agents of this social (dis)ordering – even men who, in their turn, are subjected to other more powerful men, but it has also been in the interests of some women to have adopted masculinist values and practices.

15 Cited in Naomi Shepherd, *A Price Below Rubies: Jewish Women as Rebels and Radicals*, London, Weidenfeld & Nicolson, 1993, p. 68.

16 Unfortunately Jewish theological discussion, like other forms of patriarchal scholarship, is not always dialogical. Commentators seek to dispose of theologies rather than see what they can learn from them. Radicalism is a risk – even in times more intellectually liberal and experimental than our own, Richard Rubenstein's radical approach to Holocaust theology left him subjected to 'an unprecedented torrent of personal abuse, so that he has nearly been driven out of Jewish public life. He has been called a Nazi and compared to Hitler!' (Jacob Neusner, 'The Implications of the Holocaust' in *idem* (ed.), *Understanding Jewish Theology: Classical Issues and Modern Perspectives*, New York, Ktav Publishing House/Anti-Defamation League of B'nai Brith, 1973, p. 184).

17 Steven Katz, *Post-Holocaust Dialogues: Critical Studies in Modern Jewish Thought*, New York, New York University Press, 1983, p. 168.

18 Cohen, *The Tremendum*, p. 78.

19 Rudolf Otto, *The Idea of the Holy. An Inquiry into the Non-rational Factor in the Idea of the Divine and its Relation to the Rational*, London, Oxford University Press, 1958, pp. 62, 152.

20 *Engendering Judaism: An Inclusive Theology and Ethics*, Philadelphia, The Jewish Publication Society, 1988, p. 96.

21 *Seek My Face, Speak My Name: A Contemporary Jewish Theology*, Northvale, NJ and London, Jason Aronson, 1992, p. 37.

22 Lawrence L. Langer, *Versions of Survival: The Holocaust and the Human Spirit*, Albany, State University of New York Press, 1982, p. 72.

23 *Holocaust Testimonies: The Ruins of Memory*, New Haven and London, Yale University Press, 1991, pp. 26, 37, 2.

24 Ibid., pp. 204, 7, 41.

25 Ibid., p. 48.

26 Eliezer Schweid, 'Faith, Ethics, and the Holocaust: The Justification of Religion in the Crisis of the Holocaust', *Holocaust and Genocide Studies* 3 (1988), p. 404.

27 Lawrence L. Langer, 'Gendered Suffering? Women in Holocaust Testimonies', in Ofer and Weitzman (eds), *Women in the Holocaust*, p. 362.

28 *Auschwitz: A Doctor's Story*, trans. Susan Ray, London, Robson Books, 1996, p. 105.

29 Fuchs has demonstrated that even the better films about the Holocaust have represented women as politically naive: oblivious of the political causes of their situation. These women win our sympathy not only by their plight, but by their gaunt beauty, asexuality and triumphant moral goodness. Fuchs raises the question: 'What about ugly women, and what about mundane women, or rough, insensitive, and untalented women? What about unsophisticated women, and illiterate women, and disabled women, or selfish and cowardly women, or pessimistic and depressed women?' ('The Construction of Heroines in Holocaust Films: The Jewess as Beautiful Soul', in *idem* (ed.), *Women and the Holocaust: Narrative and Representation*, Studies in the Shoah, vol. xxii, Lanham, MD, University Press of America, 1999, p. 98).

30 In his novel *Wartime Lies* (London and Basingstoke, Picador, 1992, p. 122), Louis Begley's narrator asks 'Why do we find it so difficult to admire those who are tormented and make no defiant gesture? Suppose they are neither meek nor proud, only frightened.'

31 Cited by David Stern in 'The Natural and the Supernatural. Arthur Cohen: An Introduction', in Stern and Mendes-Flohr (eds), *An Arthur A. Cohen Reader*, p. 30.

32 Rachel Feldhay Brenner has asked to what extent femaleness or 'feminine sensibilities' determined women's confrontation with the Holocaust. She has found that while it is impossible to prove that particular sensibilities are peculiar to gender, it is also impossible to deny the significance of gender-consciousness in her research subjects' mode of resistance to dehumanization and annihilation. *Writing as Resistance.*

Four Women Confronting the Holocaust: Edith Stein, Simone Weil, Anne Frank, Etty Hillesum, University Park, Pennsylvania, Pennsylvania State University Press, 1997, pp. 147–8.

33 *Ghetto Diary*, trans. Jerzy Bachrach and Barbara Krzywicka, New York, Holocaust Library, 1978, p. 74.

34 Cf. Michael Wyschogrod, *The Body of Faith: Judaism as Corporeal Election*, New York, Seabury Press, 1983, p. xv.

35 Hilkka Pietila, quoted in Mary Mellor, *Breaking the Boundaries: Towards a Feminist Green Socialism*, London, Virago, 1992, p. 249.

36 Jean-François Lyotard argues that Auschwitz is 'the experience of language that brings speculative discourse to a halt', and questions the legitimacy of names and narratives. (*The Differend: Phases in Dispute*, trans. Georges van Den Abbeele, Manchester, Manchester University Press, 1989, pp. 88, 155). See also Susan Shapiro, 'Hearing the Testimony of Radical Negation' in Elisabeth Schüssler Fiorenza and David Tracy (eds), *The Holocaust as Interruption, Concilium* 175 (1984), pp. 3–10; *eadem* 'Failing Speech: Post-Holocaust Writing and the Discourse of Post-modernism', *Semeia* 40 (1984), pp. 65–91; George Steiner, 'The Hollow Miracle', in *idem, George Steiner: A Reader*, Harmondsworth, Penguin, 1984, pp. 211–13. Aahron Appelfeld's *For Every Sin*, trans. Jeffrey M. Green, London, Weidenfeld & Nicolson, 1989, is a powerful account of how a (fictional) survivor, Theo, has to relearn the forms, tone and content of bourgeois European speech after his 'liberation'.

37 I particularly appreciated this on a visit to Auschwitz. At dusk, the rabbi accompanying my group stood on the damp rubble at the edge of the former crematorium at Auschwitz-Birkenau and blew the shofar for peace and justice. The blasts of the ram's horn pierced the falling darkness to ineffably numinous effect and persuaded me that now, as then, the performances of the holy return the most powerful answer to the radical profanation of Jewry in Auschwitz.

38 See Sara Nomberg-Przytyk, trans. Roslyn Hirsch and edited by Eli Pfefferkorn and David H. Hirsch, *Auschwitz: True Tales from a Grotesque Land*, Chapel Hill and London, The University of North Carolina Press, 1985; Olga Lengyel, *Five Chimneys: The Story of Auschwitz*, New York, Howard Fertig, 1995; Isabella Leitner, Irving A. Leitner (ed.), *Fragments of Isabella: A Memoir of Auschwitz*, New York, Thomas Y. Crowell, 1978; Giuliana Tedeschi, trans. Tim Parks, *There Is a Place on Earth: A Woman in Birkenau*, London, Minerva, 1994; Bertha Ferderber-Salz, *And the Sun Kept Shining . . .*, New York, Holocaust Library, 1980.

39 *Auschwitz and After*, trans. R.C. Lamont, New Haven, Yale University Press, 1995, p. 26.

40 For example, Rena Kornreich Gelissen's book, *Rena's Promise: A Story of Sisters in Auschwitz* (Boston, Beacon Press, 1996) used a literary assistant, Heather Dune MacAdam. The names of Mirjam Pressler and James Skofield appear alongside that of Schoschana Rabinovici in her *Thanks to My Mother*, trans. Shoshanah Rabinovits, London, Puffin, 2000.

41 James Young, *Writing and Rewriting the Holocaust: Narratives and the Consequences of Interpretation*, Bloomington and Indianapolis, Indiana University Press, 1988, pp. 44–5; Lawrence L. Langer, *Admitting the Holocaust: Collected Essays*, New York, Oxford University Press, 1995, pp. 101–3.

42 E.g. Frida Michelson, trans. and ed. Wolf Goodman, *I Survived Rumbuli*, New York, Holocaust Library, 1979.

43 *Facing the Abusing God: A Theology of Protest*, Louisville, KY, Westminster/John Knox Press, 1993, p. 3.

44 When the Auschwitz survivor, Kitty Hart, received her honorary doctorate from my own University in November 1999, I took the opportunity to ask her whether she had any objections to my deriving feminist theology from, amongst others, her own non-feminist, non-theological testimony. She was friendly but dismissive in her

answer, having no apparent interest in Jewish theology in general or mine in particular. She said that everyone had done what they wanted with her memoirs and I need be no exception. Perhaps, in a crowded hotel bar, it was not the moment to ask. Nonetheless, I felt that a permission of sorts had been granted.

45 'No Heroes, No Martyrs', in Jeanette Copperman *et al.* (eds), *Generations of Memories: Voices of Jewish Women*, London, The Women's Press, 1989, p. 167.

46 Louis Jacobs, *A Jewish Theology*, London, Darton, Longman & Todd, 1973, p. vii. Note that he signals this tentativeness in the use of the indefinite article in the title of his own study.

47 James Young, *Writing and Rewriting the Holocaust*, pp. 6–7, 8.

48 Ibid., p. 95.

49 Ibid., p. 26.

50 Ibid., p. 90.

51 Ibid., p. 10 and *passim*.

52 Ibid., pp. 22, 36.

53 *At Memory's Edge: After Images of the Holocaust in Contemporary Art and Architecture*, Yale University Press, New Haven and London, 2000, pp. 4, 5, 42. See further, ibid., pp. 1–5, 10.

54 Jacobs, *A Jewish Theology*, p. 131.

55 See Miriam Peskovitz, 'Engendering Jewish Religious History', in Peskowitz and Levitt (eds), *Judaism Since Gender*, pp. 26–9.

56 *On Judaism*, Nahum N. Glatzer (ed.), New York, Schocken Books, 1967, p. 22.

1 Reading post-Holocaust theology from a feminist perspective

1 Cohen, *The Tremendum*, p. 24.

2 Brenner, *Writing as Resistance*, pp. 8, 9, 55.

3 Cohen, *The Tremendum*, p. xvi; Jacobs, *A Jewish Theology*, pp. 6, 11.

4 Julia Neuberger, *On Being Jewish*, London, Mandarin, 1996, p. 255.

5 Brenner, *Writing as Resistance*, p. 55

6 Ibid., pp. 55, 30, 34–45.

7 *Etty: A Diary 1941–43* , trans. Arnold J. Pomerans, London, Grafton Books, 1985, pp. 234, 232.

8 See, however, Susan E. Nowak, 'In a World Shorn of Color: Toward a Feminist Theology of Holocaust Testimonies', in E. Fuchs (ed.), *Women and the Holocaust*, pp. 33–46. This article, which seems more humanistic than theological, will be discussed in Chapter 6 of the present study.

9 In Britain, key contributors to a growing body of Jewish feminist theological literature have been rabbis whose theology has predominantly emerged from the hermeneutical, ritual and pastoral situation. These include Elizabeth Tikvah Sarah, Alex Wright, Marcia Plumb, Sybil Rothschild and Sybil Sheridan. In the United States, Judith Plaskow, Rachel Adler and Ellen Umansky are well-known practitioners of Jewish feminist theology. To the left of these, Rabbi Lynn Gottlieb's work has connections with the Goddess feminism to be found in neo-Pagan and post-Christian circles to the left of the Jewish feminist community. (See my 'Goddess Religion, Postmodern Jewish Feminism and the Complexity of Alternative Religious Identities', *Nova Religio* 1 (1998), pp. 198–215.)

10 See the significant exchange between Cynthia Ozick and Judith Plaskow on this point. Their respective anti-theological and theological positions are set out in Ozick's, 'Notes toward Finding the Right Question' and Plaskow's, 'The Right Question is Theological' in Susannah Heschel (ed.), *On Being a Jewish Feminist: A Reader*, New York, Schocken Books, 1983, pp. 120–51 and pp. 223–33. See also, Judith

Plaskow, 'Jewish Theology in Feminist Perspective', in Lynn Davidman and Shelly Tenenbaum (eds), *Feminist Perspectives on Jewish Studies*, New Haven and London, Yale University Press, 1994, pp. 62–84.

11   It seems no coincidence that Judith Plaskow's and my own interest in Jewish theology has developed from an initial academic training in Protestant theology.

12   Jewish feminist responses to suffering will, of course, differ to those of Christian feminists because they have not had to negotiate the traditional glorification of suffering in the service and imitation of Christ. However, contrary to both Christians and Jews who have believed non-natural suffering to be a consequence of personal sin, all religious feminists have identified the chief causes of suffering as the institutional sins of, amongst others, sexism, racism and militarism. Those social and religious ideologies of femininity that have both valorized female passivity and powerlessness and held womankind responsible for primal sin (more typical of Christian than Jewish theology) have been unanimously rejected.

13   Richard Rubenstein's *After Auschwitz: Radical Theology and Contemporary Judaism*, New York, Bobbs-Merrill, 1966, is no longer representative of his view. However, the book remains a historically and conceptually significant element of the post-Holocaust theological corpus.

14   The present discussion does not require a comprehensive survey of the post-Holocaust theological canon. In different ways, that task has been undertaken more than competently by others. See e.g. Dan Cohn-Sherbok, *Holocaust Theology: A Reader*, Exeter, Exeter University Press, 2002; *idem, God and the Holocaust*, Leominster, Herefordshire, Gracewing, 1996; Steven L. Jacobs (ed.), *Contemporary Jewish Religious Responses to the Holocaust*; Katz, *Post-Holocaust Dialogues*.

15   Cohn-Sherbok, *God and the Holocaust*, p. i.

16   Ozick, 'Notes Towards Finding the Right Question', pp. 133–8.

17   I would like to emphasize that my using Dan Cohn-Sherbok's *God and the Holocaust* in this way does in no sense constitute an *ad hominem* criticism of its author. Nor does my discussion intend to demean the male suffering Cohn-Sherbok's chapter properly relates.

18   Ibid., p. 5.

19   Noting that the majority of women engaged in ghetto resistance activities undertook to care for Jewish children, Andrea Dworkin asks 'how long [it will be] before women are honoured for their values of care and consoling' (*Scapegoat: The Jews, Israel and Women's Liberation*, London, Virago, 2000, p. 202).

20   Cf. e.g. Meed, *On Both Sides of the Wall*; Nechama Tec, 'Women among the Forest Partisans', in Ofer and Weitzman (eds), *Women in the Holocaust*, pp. 223–64.

21   Cohn-Sherbok, *God and the Holocaust*, p. 10.

22   Judy Chicago notes that Jewish women's 'survival tactics' during the Holocaust were 'often derived from the very basis of [theirs and] our oppression' (*Holocaust Project: From Darkness into Light*, New York, Viking, 1993, p. 27). The deliberate reclamation and reversal of oppressive phenomena and texts by their transposition into another interpretative context has been methodologically characteristic of feminist theology. If such is itself a religious phenomenon, adaptation of Jewish practice and values to meet the challenges of the time would have obtained during the Holocaust period as well.

23   Cohn-Sherbok, *God and the Holocaust*, p. 12.

24   Ibid., p. 12.

25   Lynn Gottlieb remarks of Judaism in general: 'to be male is to be remembered. To be female is to be penetrated, to leave behind a famous son if possible, and then to disappear from the story.' (*She Who Dwells Within: A Feminist Vision of a Renewed Judaism*, San Francisco, HarperSanFrancisco, 1995, p. 204). For a graphic illustration of how women have been incidental to the sacred grand narrative of Jewish history see Marek Halter's monumental *The Book of Abraham*, London, Collins, 1986, where

women appear only fleetingly in their sole function as wives and mothers who will supply the ancestral line.

26 Cited in Pesach Schindler, *Hasidic Responses to the Holocaust in the Light of Hasidic Thought* , New Jersey, Ktav Publishing House, 1990, p. 61. See also ibid., pp. 59–65. There are a number of such cases recorded in the theological literature. Hillel Zeitlin, for example, arrived for deportation wearing his prayer shawl and tefillin (cited in Marc H. Ellis, *O Jerusalem! The Contested Future of the Jewish Covenant*, Minneapolis, Augsberg/Fortress, 1999, p. 22).

27 Modesty may not always have served ultra-Orthodox Jewish women well. Their long, shapeless, dark dresses could make them appear older than they were and so more likely than secularized women to be selected by the SS for immediate death rather than slave labour. See Judith Tydor Baumel, *Double Jeopardy: Gender and the Holocaust*, London, Vallentine Mitchell & Co., 1998, p. 22.

28 *With God in Hell: Judaism in the Ghettos and Deathcamps*, New York and London, Sanhedrin, 1979, pp. 75, 112.

29 See Dan Kurzman, *The Bravest Battle*, Los Angeles, Pinnacle, 1978, p. 98.

30 Compare Aviva Cantor's liturgical remembering of named Jewish women resistance fighters (Hannah Senesh, Haviva Reik, Chaika and Frumka Plotinski, Rosa Robota, Tosia Altman, Zofia Yamaika, Niuta Teitelboim are just a few of these) as part of her feminist Seder (Aviva Cantor, 'A Jewish Woman's Haggadah' in Carol P. Christ and Judith Plaskow (eds), *Womanspirit Rising: A Feminist Reader in Religion*, New York, HarperSanFrancisco, 1992, p. 190). It is notable, though, that even here women are being remembered for their secular rather than immediately religious contribution to Jewish resistance.

31 See Otto, *The Idea of the Holy*, Appendix VIII, 'Silent Worship', pp. 211–12.

32 See further my 'Feminism, Constructivism and Numinous Experience', *Religious Studies* 30 (1994), pp. 511–26.

33 Cohn-Sherbok, *God and the Holocaust*, pp. 13–14.

34 Ibid., p. 14.

35 See Rachel Adler, 'The Jew Who Wasn't There: *Halakhah* and the Jewish Woman' in Heschel (ed.), *On Being a Jewish Feminist*, p. 13.

36 See Judith Romney Wegner, *Chattel or Person? The Status of Women in the Mishnah*, New York, Oxford University Press, 1988; Gottlieb, *She Who Dwells Within*, p. 3.

37 'Jewish Ethics after the Holocaust', in Elliot N. Dorff and Louis E. Newman (eds), *Contemporary Jewish Ethics and Morality: A Reader*, New York, Oxford University Press, 1995, p. 195.

38 Morgan, 'Jewish Ethics after the Holocaust', p. 201.

39 Ibid., p. 202.

40 Ibid., p. 205.

41 Ibid., p. 206.

42 'The Right Question is Theological', p. 231.

43 Cynthia Ozick, 'Notes toward Finding the Right Question', p. 150.

44 See Blu Greenberg, *On Women and Judaism: A View from Tradition*, Philadelphia, Jewish Publication Society of America, 1981.

45 This is the argument of Plaskow's *Standing Again at Sinai: Judaism from a Feminist Perspective*, New York, HarperSanFrancisco, 1990.

46 Rabbi Joel Teitelbaum, the leader of the Satmar Hasidim and a survivor of Bergen-Belsen, drew upon the biblical texts in which suffering is a consequence of Israel's disobedience to declare the Holocaust a punishment for sins, particularly the sin of Zionism in anticipating the exercise of divine will and prematurely returning to Israel from exile. Menachem Harton has taken the opposite view and seen the Holocaust as a punishment for anti-Zionism and Jewry's comfortable accommodation with those lands of exile which, like Germany, offered emancipation in return for assimilation. (See Jonathan Sacks, *Faith in the Future*, London, Darton, Longman & Todd, 1995, p. 239.)

47   Berkovits, *Faith After the Holocaust*, p. 136; Cohn-Sherbok, *God and the Holocaust*, pp. 127–9. It would be difficult for Jewish feminism to defend God's providence by these means. Jewish feminists would not be much inclined to defer the victims' happiness to a post-mortem state of disembodied spiritual bliss as such forms of transcendentalism devalue embodied, female modes of mediating God's covenantal love in and by the giving of life. For the sake of the created world and its creator, God's presence cannot be postponed to, and therefore for, eternity. Judaism, in its cultic, prophetic and legal theology of holiness, makes God's presence a possibility in life which can be achieved through the right ordering of the holy and the profane in the world and by the ethico-political transformation that can and should imply. (See my *Rudolf Otto and the Concept of Holiness*, Oxford, Clarendon Press, 1997, ch. 7.)

48   Zachary Braiterman, *(God) After Auschwitz: Tradition and Change in Post-Holocaust Jewish Thought*, Princeton, New Jersey, Princeton University Press, 1998, pp. 4, 10. Eliezer Schweid has contended that the Holocaust sets not so much a theodical problem as a problem for the justification of religion. Christianity contributed significantly to the possibility of the Holocaust and, differently, failures of vision and leadership in the Orthodox and liberal Jewish communities had exposed Jewry to danger and ultimately, annihilation. ('Faith, Ethics and the Holocaust: The Justification of Religion in the Crisis of the Holocaust', *passim*.)

49   Ibid., p. 11.

50   *After Auschwitz*, pp. 136–7.

51   Emil Fackenheim, 'The Holocaust and the State of Israel: Their Relation', in Fleishner (ed.) *Auschwitz: Beginning of a New Era*, p. 211. See also the first chapter of Fackenheim's *Quest for Past and Future: Essays in Jewish Theology*, Boston, Beacon Press, 1970; and *idem, God's Presence in History: Jewish Affirmations and Philosophical Reflections*, New York: Harper & Row, 1972, chs 1 and 3.

52   Fackenheim, *Quest for Past and Future*, p. 18.

53   *Book of Remembrance*, Great Portland St, London, Central Synagogue, 1997/5758, p. 46.

54   *Faith in the Future*, p. 241.

55   'Between the Fires' in Jacobs (ed.), *Contemporary Jewish Responses to the Holocaust*, p. 176.

56   Sacks, *Faith in the Future*, p. 240.

57   *God's Presence in History: Jewish Affirmations and Philosophical Reflections*, New York, Harper & Row, 1972. This book represents but one aspect of Fackenheim's contribution. His later study, *To Mend the World: Foundations of Future Jewish Thought*, will be discussed in Chapter 6.

58   *God's Presence in History*, p. 92. See esp. pp. 84–95. Fackenheim's proclamation that Jewry was and is commanded by God to refrain from giving Hitler a posthumous victory by ceasing to be Jews was not primarily addressed to the academy. As one condescending reviewer wrote, it became the popular slogan of 'Jewish shoe-salesmen, accountants, policemen, cab-drivers [and] secretaries' (Cited by Fackenheim in *To Mend the World*, p. 229).

59   *God's Presence in History*, p. 84.

60   Somewhat literalistically, many have questioned how Fackenheim's thesis of a divine commanding voice in Auschwitz could be tested: who has claimed or could claim to have actually heard this commandment? Michael Goldberg disparagingly refers to it as Fackenheim's 'new *mitzvah* for modern Jews – "Survive to spite the *goyim*"'. For Goldberg, this commandment is devoid of any real content or rationale. The theology amounts to no more than '"Just be Jewish!"' (*Why Should Jews Survive? Looking Past the Holocaust Toward a Jewish Future*, New York, Oxford University Press, 1995, pp. 89, 91). Ironically, the group who have most steadfastly observed Fackenheim's assertion of a divine command to survive as Jews have been ultra-Orthodox Jews. But it is they who would most object to Fackenheim's insistence on the survival of the Jewish

people, irrespective of the survival of Jewish piety (Sacks, *Faith in the Future*, p. 241). Michael Wyschogrod denies that Judaism can be circumvented by Auschwitz or indeed promoted by it: 'no new reason for the continuation of the Jewish people can be found in the Holocaust'. Yet under Fackenheim's interpretation of the Holocaust, 'amazing as this may appear, Judaism has gotten a new lease on life' ('Faith and the Holocaust: A Review Essay of Emil Fackenheim's *God's Presence in History*', *Judaism* 20 (1971), pp. 294, 290). Most serious of all objections is that which notes how profoundly unfortunate it is that Fackenheim's theology of the commanding voice casts all those who did not or would not hear it in the role of wilful accomplices of Hitler (Richard L. Rubenstein and John K. Roth, *Approaches to Auschwitz: The Legacy of the Holocaust*, London, SCM Press, 1987, p. 320). In Auschwitz, Fackenheim says, there were Jews who heard God's commanding voice and Jews who 'stopped their ears' (*The Jewish Return into History: Reflections in the Age of Auschwitz and a New Jerusalem*, New York, Schocken Books, 1978, p. 31).

61 *Standing Again at Sinai*, pp. 25–6.
62 See Julia Neuberger, 'Woman in Judaism: The Fact and the Fiction' and Jonathan Webber, 'Between Law and Custom: Women's Experience of Judaism', in Pat Holden (ed.), *Women's Religious Experience*, London, Croom Helm, 1983, pp. 132–42 and 143–62 respectively.
63 'The Holocaust and the State of Israel: Their Relation', p. 212.
64 For Berkovits' view of the significance of Zionism in relation to post-Holocaust Jewish theology see *Faith After the Holocaust*, pp. 144–69.
65 Ibid., p. 134. It could reasonably be objected that God could equally have chosen to show his face in, say, 1942 when the 'Final Solution' was named and accelerated.
66 *Faith After the Holocaust*, p. 156.
67 See Plaskow, *Standing Again at Sinai*, pp. 107–19. See also e.g. Adrienne Baker, *The Jewish Woman in Contemporary Society: Transitions and Traditions*, Basingstoke and London, Macmillan, 1993, pp. 209–11; Dworkin, *Scapegoat, passim*. Although Dworkin is both a Jew and a feminist her critique would not accurately be described as Jewish feminist since her sexual politics appear separable from her cultural and religious identity.
68 *Why Should Jews Survive?*, p. 70. See also p. 107.
69 Ibid., pp. 73, 83, 85, 164, 165.
70 *The Face of God After Auschwitz*, Amsterdam, Polak and Van Gennep, 1965.
71 Ibid., pp. 66–8.
72 Ibid., p. 32.
73 Ibid., p. 67.
74 See Katz, *Post-Holocaust Dialogues*, pp. 255–6.
75 *Modernity and the Holocaust*, Cambridge, Polity Press, 1989, *passim*.
76 See John Armstrong, *The Idea of the Holy and the Humane Response*, London, Allen & Unwin, 1981, *passim*.
77 Cited in Ellis, *O Jerusalem!*, p. 69.
78 See e.g. David Blumenthal, *Facing the Abusing God: A Theology of Protest*, Louisville, Kentucky, Westminster/John Knox Press, 1993, pp. 228–30.
79 *After Auschwitz*, p. 46. Philosophically, this argument is something of a blunt instrument and not surprisingly has failed to persuade the theological establishment. Rubenstein would have had to prove that the Holocaust was unique and unprecedented in Jewry's history to reject its God on these grounds alone.
80 Jantzen makes this point of Western theodicy in general, *Becoming Divine: Towards a Feminist Philosophy of Religion*, Manchester, Manchester University Press, 1998, p. 260.
81 The golem appeared in the popular mythology of the fifteenth and sixteenth centuries, though the figure can be traced back to scripture and talmudic aggadah. A number of great esoteric scholars claimed to have created golems, but the most famous of these was Rabbi Loew of Prague. See Gershom Scholem, *On the Kabbalah*

176 *Notes*

and Its Symbolism, trans. Ralph Manheim, New York, Schocken Books, 1996, pp. 200–1.

82 See ibid., p. 201.
83 *After Auschwitz*, pp. 128–9.
84 Ibid., p. 49.
85 Goldberg, *Why Should Jews Survive?*, p. 81.
86 Oliver Leaman, *Evil and Suffering in Jewish Philosophy*, Cambridge, Cambridge University Press, 1995, p. 210.
87 Ibid., p. 201.
88 *Auschwitz*, p. 39.
89 *And the Sun Kept Shining*, pp. 194, 154–5, 229, 232.
90 *The Body of Faith*, p. 36. See also ibid., p. 57. Judith Plaskow points out that Wyschogrod's understanding of Israel's corporeal election is exclusive of women in its central assumption that circumcision is the mark of election (*Standing Again at Sinai*, pp. 83–4).
91 Chicago, *Holocaust Project*, p. 10.
92 Ibid., pp. 25, 62, 5.
93 See Plaskow, *Standing Again at Sinai*, pp. 128–34.
94 'A Different Power', in Rittner and Roth (eds), *Different Voices*, pp. 359–62. Wendy Farley also affirms, again, from a Christian perspective, that creation is structured by compassionate love. Evil is a resistance to God, but love is a deathless, resilient power which will finally overcome it (*Tragic Vision and Divine Compassion: A Contemporary Theodicy*, Louisville, KY, Westminster/John Knox Press, 1990, pp. 32, 62, 65). For a discussion of pregnancy and birth-giving as acts of female Jewish resistance to Nazism see Katharina von Kellenbach, 'Reproduction and Resistance during the Holocaust', in Fuchs (ed.), *Women and the Holocaust*, pp. 19–32.
95 Note that to criticize the attribute of omnipotence is not to prohibit divine intervention. Arthur Cohen has explained the non-intervention of God in the Holocaust by making that non-intervention an attribute of God. But this is equally unhelpful. Cohen's theology veers towards the heretically deistic; his God is so indifferent, so detached from human affairs that the Holocaust must be something for which humanity was solely responsible. Cohen's God may indeed be, as Rubenstein and Roth have suggested, 'functionally irrelevant.' (*Approaches to Auschwitz: The Legacy of the Holocaust*, p. 332). Why should anyone wishing to do evil need to take this God into account? In the absence of anything more than scriptural and legal prohibition (to the unbeliever, just so much paper) evil is effectively permitted because there need be no fear that God will actually intervene to thwart or punish it. By and large, however, Jewish tradition does envisage an interruptive, redemptive, loving God whose creation of the world entails concern and responsibility for its fate.
96 Leaman, *Evil and Suffering in Jewish Philosophy*, p. 197.
97 *ReVisions: Seeing Torah Through a Feminist Lens*, Woodstock, Vermont, Jewish Lights Publishing, 1998, p. 171.
98 *The Idea of the Holy*, pp. 12–24.
99 Cf. Greenberg: 'Cloud of Smoke, Pillar of Fire', pp. 42, 44.

2 The hiding of God's face in Auschwitz

1 *Faith After the Holocaust*, pp. 102–7, 124. In *With God in Hell*, esp. pp. 7, 74–6, Berkovits offers a less well-known account of the preservation of masculine freedom in the ghettos and camps. He describes male Orthodox Jews' radical indifference to their suffering and to the prohibition of their observance. Their religious *apatheia* imitated that of the God of classical Jewish philosophy: they were both spiritually autonomous and free of the fear that would diminish their freedom. What Berkovits does not say is

that they were 'free' because they were not subject to the practical constraints of caring for the bodily needs of others. Freedom, in other words, is gendered.

2　'The Price of (Masculine) Freedom and Becoming: A Jewish Feminist Response to Eliezer Berkovits's Post-Holocaust Free Will Defence of God's Non-Intervention in Auschwitz', in Pamela Sue Anderson and Beverley Clack (eds), *Feminist Philosophy of Religion: Critical Perspectives*, London and New York, Routledge, forthcoming.

3　'Women's Agency and Survival Strategies During the Holocaust', *Women's Studies International Forum* 22 (1999), pp. 333–4, 343, 344.

4　Schweid notes that apart from a 'minority of ultra-pious believers', 'most of the believing public agrees that it is possible to understand the Holocaust only as a "Concealment of the Countenance" (*Hester Panim*), and that this concealment is beyond comprehension' ('Faith, Ethics and the Holocaust: The Justification of Religion in the Crisis of the Holocaust', p. 396). It will be evident from my discussion that I do not consider that concealment entirely mysterious; it is in some senses at least a theo-political construction.

5　Foreword to Ferderber-Salz, *And the Sun Kept Shining*, p. 9.

6　Cf. Ps. 13: 2–4: 'How long will You hide Your face from me? . . . Look at me, answer me, O Lord, my God!' See also, Ps. 44: 25; Ps. 69: 18. In biblical theology the experience of God's hiddenness is integral to the challenge of faith in a God who is both near and far, hidden but present. (See Samuel E. Balentine, *The Hiding of the Face of God in the Old Testament*, Oxford, Oxford University Press, 1983, p. 172.) Balentine notes that the biblical phrase *hester panim* functions differently in different contexts (p. 79). Humanity too, can turn from the afflicted (Tob. 4: 7; Sir. 4: 4, 5). Post-biblical Judaism prefers the terminology of 'turning' to that of the 'hiding' of God's face.

7　*Faith After the Holocaust*, p. 107.

8　Ibid., pp. 109, 106.

9　Ibid., p. 101.

10　'Loving the Torah More than God', in Zvi Kolitz, *Yosl Rakover Talks to God*, trans. C. Brown Janeway, from the edition established by Paul Badde, London, Jonathan Cape, 1999, pp. 83, 86, 87. Although I will draw heavily on Levinas' phenomenological theology of the human face in Chapter 4 of this book, this is not to adopt his theology in its entirety. Chapter 5 argues the precise opposite of Levinas' account of holocaustal divine absence.

11　Ibid., p. 85.

12　Ibid., p. 86.

13　*The Eclipse of God: Studies in the Relation Between Religion and Philosophy*, New York: Harper & Brothers, 1952, pp. 50, 91. Cf. *The Prophetic Faith*, New York, Harper Torchbooks, 1960, p. 177, where even God's self-revelation is 'nothing but a different form of hiding His face'.

14　*On Judaism*, Nahum N. Glatzer (ed.), New York, Schocken Books, 1967, pp. 224, 223.

15　Ibid., pp. 223–5.

16　Cohen finds Buber's notion of the eclipse of God theologically anaemic, but finally adopts a similar position, claiming that humanity has the power to 'obscure, eclipse, burn out the divine filament' – the divine life within the historical realm (*The Tremendum*, pp. 97–8). On the dovetailing between Buber and Cohen, see Michael E. Lodahl, *Shekhinah/Spirit: Divine Presence in Jewish and Christian Religion*, Mahwah, NJ, Paulist Press, 1992, pp. 131–2. Another customary move has been to reject not God but 'man' as in Deuteronomy 32: 4–5 where God is pronounced just; the corruption is his children's who are unworthy of him. After Buber, a question often asked is not where was God in the Holocaust, but where was 'man'?

17　See Buber, *Pointing the Way: Collected Essays*, trans. Maurice Friedman, New York, Harper, 1957, pp. 237–9. Where feminists would differ from Buber is in arguing that women's orientation to the other has not been that of an I/It. A relational posture – spiritually, biologically or socially produced – has been both morally attractive and practically necessary. The alienation to which Buber refers belongs to the political milieu that produced it. The causal relation between political and existential failure is a circular one.

18 In Micah 3: 4, God will not answer his suffering people and will turn his face from them in accordance with the wrongs they have done. In Deuteronomy 31: 16–18, God threatens that he will punish Israel by hiding his countenance from those who forsake him for other gods. (See also Job 13: 24.) See further, Leon Wieseltier, 'A Privation of Providence', in Zvi Kolitz, *Yosl Rakover Talks to God*, pp. 94–5.

19 *Faith in the Future*, pp. 239–40.

20 'A Privation of Providence', p. 98.

21 Michaels, *Fugitive Pieces*, p. 107.

22 See Deborah Dwork, *Children With a Star: Jewish Youth in Nazi Europe*, New Haven, Yale University Press, 1991; Helen Epstein, *Children of the Holocaust*, New York, Viking Penguin, 1988.

23 A theology that likens God to a mother who will not countenance the suffering of her children can be found in religious feminism's first as well as second waves. See e.g. Debra Campbell, 'Hannah Whitall Smith (1832–1911): Theology of the Mother-hearted God', *Signs* 15 (1989), pp. 79–101.

24 See also Ps. 104: 29.

25 Vladka Meed, trans. Steven Meed, *On Both Sides of the Wall: Memoirs from the Warsaw Ghetto*, New York, Holocaust Library, 1993, pp. 111, 112–13.

26 *Facing the Abusing God: A Theology of Protest*, Louisville, KY, Westminster/John Knox Press, 1993, p. 247.

27 Ibid., p. 262.

28 Ibid., p. 243.

29 Ibid., p. 267.

30 Ibid., pp. 245–6.

31 Ibid., esp. pp. 223, 249–56. See further, Anson Laytner, *Arguing With God: A Jewish Tradition*, Northvale, NJ, Jason Aronson, 1990.

32 *Facing the Abusing God*, p. 256.

33 *With God in Hell*, pp. 124–5

34 *Facing the Abusing God*, p. 262.

35 Ibid., p. 285. Michael Goldberg remarks caustically of Blumenthal's theology: 'One can only wonder: Does God need to go through a 12-step program? or do we?' (*Why Should Jews Survive?*, p. 125).

36 *Facing the Abusing God*, p. 263.

37 Ibid., pp. 258, 259.

38 *Facing the Abusing God*, p. 265.

39 There is now an extensive literature on domestic abuse in Jewish communities. See e.g. Naomi Graetz, *Silence is Deadly: Judaism Confronts Wife Beating*, Northvale, NJ, Jason Aronson, 1998; Julie Ringold Spitzer, *When Love is not Enough: Spousal Abuse in Rabbinic and Contemporary Judaism*, New York, Women of Reform Judaism, Federation of Temple Sisterhoods, 1995; Mimi Scarf, 'Marriages Made in Heaven? Battered Jewish Wives', in Heschel (ed.), *On Being a Jewish Feminist*, pp. 51–64. Marcia Cohn Spiegel speaks for herself and other Jewish women survivors of abuse in making a significant connection between women's recovery from abuse and their struggle to reshape Judaism. She writes of herself: 'I had to reinvent God for myself so that I could awaken each day with a sense of purpose and joy.' She continues, 'We have difficulty praying to a transcendent God who rules over the world and acts in history. Where was he while we suffered? Why didn't he take care of us? Why did he abandon us? We need a God of immanence, a nurturing, caring, protecting deity who is present in our daily lives – a God we can trust in, who helps us find peace. Some contemporary Jewish women seeking these qualities in God have found them embodied in the ancient concept of *Shekhinah*, the indwelling presence' ('Spirituality

for Survival: Jewish Women Healing Themselves', *Journal of Feminist Studies in Religion* 12 (1996), p. 126).

40 *Facing the Abusing God*, p. 205. In a Christian feminist context, Joanne Carlson Brown and Rebecca Parker accuse God of child abuse in '"For God So Loved the World"?' in Joanne Carlson Brown and C.R. Bohn (eds), *Christianity, Patriarchy and Abuse: A Feminist Critique* , New York, Pilgrim Press, 1989, pp. 1–30.

41 *Facing the Abusing God*, p. 212.

42 Ibid., p. 217.

43 Ibid., p. 218.

44 Ibid., pp. 220–2.

45 *The Tremendum*, pp. 96–7.

46 Cohn-Sherbok, *God and the Holocaust*, pp. 65–6. It is notable that the Exodus, the conquest of Canaan and the Monarchy have equated covenantal loyalty with prosperity. Judaism has not regarded suffering as its normal state (Wyschogrod, *The Body of Faith*, p. 35).

47 Martin Buber, trans. Olga Marx, *Tales of the Hasidim: The Early Masters*, New York, Schocken, 1947, p. 122.

48 'The Modern Pietà: Religious Imagery in the Construction of Gendered Embodiment', a paper given at the Annual Conference of the British Sociological Association, Sociology of Religion Study Group, Plater College, Oxford, 11 April 2001. Utriainen's book, whose title can be translated as *Present, Naked, Pure: A Study of the Anthropology of Religion on Women by the Side of the Dying*, Helsinki, Finnish Literature Society, 1999, is shortly to appear in English.

49 *In Bluebeard's Castle*, p. 38.

50 *The Tremendum*, p. 77.

51 Ibid.

52 This is not to renounce the central moment and idea of Jewish salvation history: the Exodus and its revelation of an accompanying God of liberation from oppression.

53 The Holocaust was, of course, to play a significant role in the American 'death of God' theological movement of the 1960s. See further, Stephen R. Haynes and John K. Roth (eds), *The Death of God Movement and the Holocaust: Radical Theology Encounters the Shoah*, Westport, CT and London, Greenwood Press, 1999, esp. Thomas J.J. Altizer, 'The Holocaust and the Theology of the Death of God', pp. 17–23.

54 Cited in Gillian Rose, *Judaism and Modernity: Philosophical Essays*, Oxford, UK, and Cambridge, MA, Blackwell, 1993, p. 244.

55 Some believe that the entire post-biblical period is a time of the silence of God since that of the direct prophetic encounter with God has passed (Wyschogrod, *The Body of Faith*, p. 85).

56 Naomi Seidman, 'Theorizing Jewish Patriarchy *in Extremis*' in Peskowitz and Levitt (eds), *Judaism Since Gender*, p. 45. Seidman is using Bluma Goldstein's research here.

57 See further Hyman E. Goldin, *The Jewish Woman and Her Home*, New York, Hebrew Publishing Co., 1978, pp. 235, 239.

58 See Theo Richmond, *Konin: A Quest*, London, Vintage, 1996, pp. 37–40. Girls did not normally go to *cheder* at an early age. Older girls could, however, receive a rudimentary Jewish education premised on their domestic and familial religious responsibilities.

59 Adrienne Baker, *The Jewish Woman in Contemporary Society: Transitions and Traditions*, London, Macmillan, 1993, p. 90.

60 Buber, *Early Masters*, p. 97.

61 Jewish feminists who wish to make Shekhinah less an attribute of God than a name of God tend to omit the definite pronoun before Shekhinah's name.

62 See Isidore Epstein, *Judaism: A Historical Presentation*, Harmondsworth, Middx., Penguin Books, 1959, pp. 137–8.

63 *The Body of Faith*, pp. 25, 212, 103. 'Hashem' (literally, the Name) is a reverent circumlocution most often used by Hasidic and other ultra-Orthodox Jews.

64   *Auschwitz and After*, p. 37.
65   E.g. Delbo writes of a young woman who, literally dying of thirst, breaks rank during a roll-call to eat snow from a ditch and is stranded there, too skeletally weak to move and only moments from her death at the jaws of an SS dog: 'I no longer look at her. I no longer wish to look. If only I could change my place in order not to see her. . . . Why does she stare at us? Isn't she pointing at me? Imploring me? I turn away to look elsewhere. Elsewhere' (*Auschwitz and After*, p. 26).
66   Wyschogrod helps us to elucidate the nature of God's presence. God is not incarnated in Israel, 'No, that would be going too far. . . . But God certainly dwells in the midst of his people in some special way. Perhaps it would be best to say that he does not dwell *in* the people of Israel but among or alongside them.' God's immanence is akin to how a person dwelling in a city has not actually fused with its walls (*The Body of Faith*, p. 11).
67   Trans. R.A. Wilson and J. Bowden, *The Crucified God: The Cross of Christ as the Foundation and Criticism of Christian Theology*, London, SCM Press, 1974, p. 274.
68   *Etty: A Diary*, pp. 193, 192.
69   Ibid. p. 198.
70   *I and Thou*, trans. Walter Kaufmann, New York, Charles Scribner's Sons, 1970, p. 130.
71   See further my article, 'The Face of God in Every Generation: Jewish Feminist Spirituality and the Legend of the Thirty-Six Hidden Saints', in Ursula King (ed.) *Spirituality and Society in the New Millennium*, Brighton, Sussex Academic Press, 2001, pp. 234–6, from which some of the present discussion of the Just Man is drawn.
72   The legend of the Just Man (in Yiddish, the *Lamedvovnik*) originates in the Babylonian Talmud (Sanhedrin 97b; Sukhah 45b) and is accredited to the fourth-century teacher Abbaye. The Just Man is not to be confused with the Suffering Servant of Isaiah 53 who, though similarly despised, suffers sacrificially and intercessively for Israel's sin. The legend of the Just Man has gained currency only among Ashkenazic Jews where it is found in kabbalistic and hasidic folklore and, in the early twentieth century, in the Yiddish and Hebrew literature of modernist writers such as I. L. Peretz and Moyshe Kulbak. Orthodoxy has expressed some reservations about the twentieth-century literary evolution of the legend – particularly that of André Schwartz-Bart's characterization of his fictional Ernie Levy as the last of a dynasty of Just Men. Schwartz-Bart's renowned *The Last of the Just*, (trans. Stephen Becker, London, Secker & Warburg, 1962), may, in Orthodoxy's view, owe more to Schwartz-Bart's imagination and to Christian theological influence than to the original Jewish sources of the legend.
73   Martin Buber, *Tales of the Hasidim: Later Masters*, New York, Schocken, 1961, p. 65.
74   'The Face of God in Every Generation', p. 239.
75   *And the Sun Kept Shining*, pp. 143–4.
76   *There Is a Place*, p. 86. See also my discussion of the nameless, hidden woman who saved Sara Nomberg Przytyk's life in Chapter 5 of the present study.
77   Cited by Berkovits, *With God in Hell*, p. 19.
78   *Man's Search for Meaning*, p. 69.

3   Feminist intimations of the holy in Auschwitz

1   Rebecca Chopp, *The Power to Speak*, New York, Crossroad, 1989, p. 119; Mary Grey, *Redeeming the Dream: Feminism, Redemption and the Christian Tradition*, London, SPCK, 1989, p. 44. See also my, 'Feminism, Constructivism and Numinous Experience', pp. 511–26.
2   The work of the eighteenth-century Moses Hayyim Luzzatto typifies such an approach to holiness. See his *Mesillat Yesharim: The Path of the Upright*, trans. and ed. Mordecai M. Kaplan, Philadelphia, Jewish Publication Society of America, 1966.

3   T. Drorah Setel, 'Roundtable Discussion: Feminist Reflections on Separation and Unity in Jewish Theology', *Journal of Feminist Studies in Religion* 2 (1986), pp. 113–18. In the same discussion, Marcia Falk suggests that both relationship and separation are dialectically linked, and both 'necessary to human life' (p. 121). As Rita Gross points out, the problem with the holy/profane distinction is not so much duality since mutuality may result from duality, but dualism (p. 130).

4   Rachel Hyman insists that women should not be duped into thinking that the transmission of Jewish culture lies in their cleaning the home, lighting candles or urging children to be good Jews ('The Jewish Family: Looking for a Usable Past' in Heschel (ed.), *On Being a Jewish Feminist*, p. 22).

5   *God in Search of Man*, New York, Farrar, Straus & Cudahy, 1956, p. 113.

6   *Difficile Liberté*, pp. 28–9.

7   Cohen, *The Tremendum*, p. 17 and 'Thinking the Tremendum', in Stern and Mendes-Flohr, *An Arthur A. Cohen Reader*, p. 244.

8   *On Judaism*, p. 9.

9   It is the task of a Jewish phenomenological theology to focus on the meanings of Jewish practice. I am not, thereby, dismissing the religious intentionality of non-Jewish women's practice; I simply do not wish to subsume their experience into a Jewish interpretative frame.

10 *On Judaism*, p. 111.

11 Greenberg makes this key point in a number of works including 'Voluntary Covenant', pp. 101–2.

12 On these mutual assistance groups see Judith Tydor Baumel, 'Social Interaction among Jewish Women in Crisis during the Holocaust', *Gender and History* 7 (1995), pp. 64–84.

13 Rejecting a world-denying Jewish spirituality of martyrdom, Senesh writes: 'What is a heroic death? Is it possible to consecrate God's name in a manner divorced from life itself? Is anything more holy than life itself?' Hannah Senesh, trans. Marta Cohn, *Hannah Senesh: Her Life and Diary*, London, Vallentine Mitchell & Co., 1971, p. 103.

14 See Buber, *On Judaism*, pp. 9, 84.

15 Rose, *Judaism and Modernity*, p. 256.

16 *Auschwitz*, p. 115.

17 Nagy, 'No Heroes, No Martyrs', p. 172.

18 In the film *La Vita é Bella* (*Life is Beautiful*, dir. Roberto Benigni, 1998) Guido, the main protagonist, is sent to a death camp with his young son. He does everything he can to comfort his son by a series of explanations for the horror that reverse the Nazis' reversal of ordinary reality. Despite, indeed because of, his attempt to represent the non-ordinary as the ordinary, Guido's audience refuses to be fooled but is also disoriented to the point of appalled, incredulous laughter.

19 Lewinska's account of the degradation of women in Auschwitz has influenced both Fackenheim's and Berkovits' post-Holocaust theology. Berkovits called her 'an honorary Jew'. In *To Mend the World*, p. 25, Fackenheim uses Lewinska's testimony as exemplifying resistance to the Nazi 'logic of destruction.'

20 *Faith After the Holocaust*, pp. 78–9.

21 Cited in Berkovits, *With God in Hell*, p. 92.

22 *Akedat Treblinka: Gedanken un Refleksen* cited in Gershon Greenberg, 'The Death of History and the Life of Akeda: Voices from the War', in Haynes and Roth (eds), *The Death of God Movement and the Holocaust*, p. 103.

23 *With God in Hell*, p. 92.

24 Cf. Michaels, *Fugitive Pieces*, p. 166.

25 Cited in Berkovits, *With God in Hell*, pp. 90–1.

26 Michelson, *I Survived Rumbuli*, trans. and ed. Wolf Goodman, New York, Holocaust Library, 1979, p. 38. See also e.g. Gillis-Carlebach, 'Jewish Mothers and Their Children During the Holocaust', p. 232.

27   Shimon Huberband, *Kiddush Hashem: Jewish Religious and Cultural Life in Poland During the Holocaust*, trans. David E. Fishman; Jeffrey S. Gwock and Robert S. Hirt (eds), Hoboken, NJ, and New York, Yeshiva University Press, Ktav Publishing House, 1987, p. 438.

28   To be 'cut off' or excommunicated was the Israelite God's own punishment for (usually) private, unwitnessed legal infringement of the codes of the holy. Offences carried the penalty of *kareth* – a 'cutting off' from the presence of God (see e.g. Lev. 20: 3, 17–18).

29   Frida Michelson's memoir, *I Survived Rumbuli*, pp. 62–3, conveys how the isolation was effected. In the words of her friend Sonia, 'From the first days of the Nazi occupation [of Riga] an invisible wall of isolation was erected around the Jews. It was forbidden for Jews to move from their living places. The Aryans were forbidden all communication with Jews.' See also Livia Bitton-Jackson's description of living under the Nazis' exclusionary ban in *I Have Lived a Thousand Years: Growing Up in the Holocaust*, London, Simon & Schuster, 1999, p. 34.

30   *I Survived Rumbuli*, p. 54; Kornreich Gelissen, *Rena's Promise*, pp. 257, 265.

31   See Michelson, *I Survived Rumbuli*, pp. 65, 69, on the humiliations of this ordinance.

32   Accessed 22 November 1999 <www.interlog.com/~mighty/'personal reflections'>

33   *Five Chimneys*, p. 14

34   *Auschwitz and After*, pp. 151–2. Delbo was a non-Jewish Frenchwoman who was deported to Auschwitz in January 1943 on account of her activity in the Resistance.

35   *Five Chimneys*, p. 21.

36   'Twenty Months at Auschwitz', in Rittner and Roth (eds), *Different Voices*, p. 87. See further, Delbo, *Auschwitz and After*, p. 140. It may be that the grossly insanitary conditions in the women's and men's barracks in Auschwitz-Birkenau owed their existence to a lack of foresight that resulted in a great deal of unplanned death. For a detailed discussion of the organizational dimension of Auschwitz see Deborah Dwork and Robert Jan van Pelt, *Auschwitz: 1270 to the Present*, New York, W.W. Norton & Co., 1997; Israel Gutman *et al.* (eds), *Anatomy of the Auschwitz Death Camp*, Bloomington, Indiana University Press, 1998.

37   *Auschwitz and After*, pp. 150–1. After liberation Delbo would bathe twice a day, scrubbing with fine soap even though she had long ceased to smell unwashed (ibid., p. 151).

38   *Return to Auschwitz*, St Albans, Herts., Granada Publishing, 1983, pp. 107, 135.

39   *I Have Lived a Thousand Years*, p. 93.

40   Lewinska, 'Twenty Months at Auschwitz', pp. 90, 91, 88.

41   Lengyel, *Five Chimneys*, pp. 44–6, 22. (Lengyel's use of the term 'swarm' conveys some apparent internalization of the Nazis' ideological identification of Jewish personhood with vermin.) For further accounts of the degradation of Jewry through bodily and environmental filth see Des Pres, *The Survivor: An Anatomy of Life in the Death Camps*, Oxford, Oxford University Press, 1976, pp. 53, 57, 66; Tedeschi, *There is a Place*, pp. 4, 8.

42   Hart, *Return to Auschwitz*, pp. 100–1.

43   Tedeschi echoes others in observing that the cessation of menstruation as a result of shock and starvation deprived women in Auschwitz of a feminine identity (*There is a Place*, p. 97).

44   Ferderber-Salz, *And the Sun Kept Shining*, p. 150.

45   See e.g. Bitton-Jackson, *I Have Lived a Thousand Years*, pp. 83, 92.

46   See e.g. Des Pres, *The Survivor*, pp. 53, 57, 66; Lengyel, *Five Chimneys*, pp. 22, 44–6; Lewinska, 'Twenty Months at Auschwitz', pp. 85–93.

47   While bodily cleanliness is a practical precondition of normal human relationship, in the camps, where almost no inmates were clean, the maintenance of relationship often took precedence over that of bodily cleanliness. In Auschwitz, Kitty Hart was pleased to be put to work on the *Scheisskommando*, digging out the mess from the

latrines and carrying it in buckets to the pits because this enabled her to maintain relationships with other women to a far greater degree than did other work details (*Return to Auschwitz*, p. 106). That the stench from the latrine often kept guards away, making it a place which could sustain relation is also confirmed by Bitton-Jackson (*I Have Lived a Thousand Years*, p. 91).

48 The almost initiatory sexual degradation of women set apart for labour upon arrival at Auschwitz is well known. They were subject to an intimate examination and shaving of body hair in front of leering, often drunken, male Nazi guards (see e.g. Lengyel, *Five Chimneys*, p. 19). However, feminist scholars of the Holocaust have pointed out that both memoirs and androcentric historical studies of the camps are either reticent about, or in the latter case, oblivious of, other experiences of sexual defilement peculiar to women. Some survivors interviewed by Joan Ringelheim told her about their rape and other forms of sexual humiliation and abuse but often regarded such details as having 'no significance within the larger picture of the Holocaust' (personal letter to Judy Chicago, *Holocaust Project*, p. 125). While the sexual abuse of Jewish women was not permitted in the camps and ghettos and may not have been the most prevalent form of degradation, it did occur. One mother told Lengyel how she had been forced to undress her daughter and watch while the girl was violated by dogs 'whom the Nazis had specially trained for this sport'. This abomination was also inflicted on young girls who dropped from exhaustion when working in the quarries for twelve to fourteen hours a day (*Five Chimneys*, pp. 185–6). See further, Helen Fein, 'Genocide and Gender: The Uses of Women and Group Destiny', *Journal of Genocide Research* 1 (1999), p. 53; Sara R. Horowitz, 'Mengele, the Gynecologist, and Other Stories of Women's Survival', in Peskowitz and Levitt (eds), *Judaism Since Gender*, pp. 207–11.

49 Lidia Rosenfeld Vago, 'One Year in the Black Hole of Our Planet Earth: A Personal Narrative', in Ofer and Weitzman (eds), *Women in the Holocaust*, p. 281.

50 *The Idea of the Holy*, pp. 51, 10.

51 Lengyel, *Five Chimneys*, p. 83. See also Kornreich Gelissen, *Rena's Promise*, pp. 257, 265.

52 Langer, *Holocaust Testimonies*, p. 70.

53 *Auschwitz: A Doctor's Story*, p. 107. In the event, the effectiveness of Miriam's labours earned her extra rations and saved her life.

54 *Auschwitz*, p. 19.

55 See Langer, *Holocaust Testimonies*, p. 70.

56 Hart, *Return to Auschwitz*, p. 107.

57 Lewinska, 'Twenty Months at Auschwitz', p. 88.

58 Ibid., p. 97.

59 *Muselmänner* is a figurative term, somewhat offensive to Muslims, which describes those who had given up the will to live and were no longer concerned about their fate. They were the 'walking dead'.

60 Lewinska, 'Twenty Months', pp. 90, 92. Fackenheim analyses the Nazis' 'excremental assault' in *To Mend the World*, p. 26.

61 See e.g., Itka Frajman Zygmuntowicz with Sara Horowitz, 'Survival and Memory' in Ellen Umansky and Dianne Ashton (eds), *Four Centuries of Jewish Women's Spirituality: A Sourcebook*, Boston, Beacon Press, 1992, p. 289; Delbo, *Auschwitz and After*, p. 83.

62 Delbo, *Auschwitz and After*, p. 200.

63 *There is a Place*, p. 179. When moved from Birkenau to a new women's block in Auschwitz, Tedeschi rejoiced in its facilities for maintaining bodily hygiene (ibid., p. 138).

64 Many Jewish feminists have reclaimed the mikvah as a symbolic and practical means to their spiritual and emotional regeneration. See e.g. Gottlieb, *She Who Dwells Within*, pp. 220–3; Mierle Laderman Ukeles' powerful interpretation of the mikvah as 'a square womb of living waters' in 'Mikva [*sic*] Dreams: A Performance

(1978)', in Umansky and Ashton (eds), *Four Centuries of Jewish Women's Spirituality*, pp. 218–20.

65   Rivkah Slonim, 'Mikveh: Gateway to Purity', in Sarah Tikvah Kornbluth and Doron Kornbluth (eds), *Jewish Women Speak Out about Jewish Matters*, Southfield, MI, Targum, 2000, pp. 73–81, esp. p. 80. Slonim articulates the customary ultra-Orthodox view of what are referred to positively as the laws of family purity.

66   Although female holiness might be said to have transcended the radical corruption of Auschwitz, this is not to equate holiness with the patriarchal transcendence of the (female) natural. Alan Unterman, for example, conforms to the classic patriarchal denigration of the natural in observing that the holy is that which transcends the natural, 'corrupt' environment, in *Jews: Their Religious Beliefs and Practices*, London, Routledge & Kegan Paul, 1981, p. 136.

67   Adelsberger, *Auschwitz*, p. 60.

68   *Auschwitz and After*, p. 105.

69   Lewinska, 'Twenty Months at Auschwitz', p. 87.

70   *I Have Lived a Thousand Years*, p. 146.

71   Lengyel, *Five Chimneys*, p. 123.

72   Ibid., p. 135.

73   Adelsberger, *Auschwitz*, p. 51.

74   *There is a Place*, p. 23.

75   See e.g. Anna Eilenberg (ed.) Penina Soloveitchik, *Sisters in the Storm*, New York, London and Jerusalem, CIS, 1992; Pearl Benisch, *To Vanquish the Dragon*, Jerusalem and New York, Philip Feldheim, 1991, *passim*.

76   Hart, *Return to Auschwitz*, pp. 153–4.

77   The view that a space fit for God's presence can be established wherever people remain under a sense of moral obligation can be found in Berkovits' *Faith After the Holocaust*, p. 77. He records the moment when a woman, Sonya, ran forward to save the Gestapo officer who was about to be killed by the man with whom she had been hiding. This was, for Berkovits, a sign that the Holocaust could not banish the holy, nor, in retrospect, its vocabulary: 'At that moment there was no place on earth holier than that dark and dusty corner in that attic in the Warsaw ghetto. It was the Holy of Holies on earth, sharing the very majesty of Sinai, when God descending upon it, proclaimed His "Thou shalt not kill!".'

78   Some might prefer to interpret these acts psychologically as expressions of a basic survival instinct. However, while Judaism is a practical religion designed to preserve life, the religious anthropology of the present study suggests that human acts can also point to values, intentions and meanings that both encompass and transcend (but do not devalue) bodily survival.

79   See e.g. Irving Rosenbaum, *The Holocaust and Halakhah*, New York, Ktav Publishing House, 1976; Berkovits, *With God in Hell*.

80   Jonathan Sacks, *Faith in the Future*, p. 241.

81   In his *Hasidic Responses to the Holocaust*, pp. 99–105, Pesach Schindler gives a six-page account of Hasidic men's spiritual resistance in the camps and ghettos by the maintenance of forbidden Jewish practices such as circumcision, Jewish burial rites, the baking of *matzot* (unleavened bread), the wearing of Hasidic dress and so forth. Schindler notes that descriptions of Hasidic women's 'activities', as he puts it, are rare. He cites only the resistance of one woman, Perele Perlow, the wife of the Koidenever Rebbe, who organized women's prayer and study sessions in the Vilna ghetto.

82   Buber, *Early Masters*, p. 308.

83   E.g. Pirke Avot 3: 2; 3: 6. See further, Kunin, *God's Place in the World*, pp. 53–5; *idem*, 'Judaism', in Jean Holm (ed.), with John Bowker, *Sacred Space*, London, Pinter, 1994, p. 140. Kunin's points in both texts are general and none cited here are made in relation to the Holocaust. See also, Ephraim Urbach, *The Sages: Their Concepts and Beliefs*, Jerusalem, Magnes Press, 1979, p. 42.

84 *With God in Hell*, p. 22.
85 Ibid., p. 65.
86 Ibid., p. 25.
87 See Kunin, *God's Place in the World*, pp. 55–6.
88 In Judaism, the religious status of the secular public sphere is broadly that of the private sphere. The public sphere is that of (male) communal study and devotion. Therefore the 'masculine' world of trade was not prohibited to women and was culturally far from alien to eastern European Jewish women in particular.
89 Cited in Sacks, *Faith in the Future*, p. 241.
90 Technically women are exempt from wearing these, but, culturally, exemption amounts to prohibition.
91 Schindler, *Hasidic Responses to the Holocaust*, p. 99.
92 Irving Greenberg notes that 'the fact that the central symbol of the covenant is only carried by men creates some moral and cultural problematic, i.e., it is gender-linked'. Nonetheless, he points out that although women of the Holocaust period did not carry the mark of the covenant they too experienced 'the inescapability of being Jewish as a determinant of their fate' ('Voluntary Covenant', n. 10, p. 196).
93 *Faith After the Holocaust*, p. 59.
94 See e.g. Burton M. Leiser 'The Sanctity of the Profane: A Pharisaic Critique of Rudolf Otto', *Judaism* 20 (1971), pp. 87–92.
95 Note that for Reform Judaism the abolition of gender difference in matters of observance entails that the female mediation of God need not be at issue. This study rejects the injustices against women wrought by traditional Judaism's rigid gendered divisions of religious labour but wants to preserve and revise its notion of female difference on religious feminist terms and without rendering women, in effect, honorary men.
96 *There is a Place*, p. 40.
97 Kunin, 'Judaism', p. 141.
98 A divine command is understood here not as an order from God but as the sense of being under the particular moral and spiritual obligations of love arising from humanity's responsibilities to creation and its creator.
99 David S. Shapiro, 'The Ideological Foundations of the Halakhah', in Jacob Neusner (ed.), *Understanding Jewish Theology: Classical Issues and Modern Perspectives*, New York, Ktav Publishing House/Anti-Defamation League of B'nai Brith, 1973, p. 108.
100 Rachel Biale, *Women and Jewish Law: An Exploration of Women's Issues in Halakhic Sources*, New York, Schocken Books, 1984, p. 8.
101 Alex Wright, 'An Approach to Jewish Feminist Theology', in Sybil Sheridan (ed.), *Women Rabbis Tell Their Stories*, London, SCM Press, 1994, p. 152.
102 See Yaffa Eliach's account of this gendered division of the sacred and secular in the pre-war shtetl, *There Once Was a World: A 900 Year Chronicle of the Shtetl of Eishyshok*, Boston, New York and London, Little, Brown & Co., 1998, pp. 334–41. However, Eliach demonstrates that women enjoyed a degree of female empowerment through their limited control of the domestic sphere.
103 Wyschogrod argues that it is the embodied character of election which compels the 'enemies of God' to deny not only Jewish teaching, but to murder the Jewish body (*The Body of Faith*, p. xv).
104 Ellen Umansky, 'Piety, Persuasion, Friendship: A History of Jewish Women's Spirituality', in *idem* and Dianne Aston (eds), *Four Centuries of Jewish Women's Spirituality*, p. 1 and *passim*.
105 *The Jewish Woman and Her Home*, New York, Hebrew Publishing Co., 1978, pp. 71–2.
106 See further, Hayyim Schneid (ed.), *Family*, Philadelphia, Jewish Publication Society of America, 1973, p. 94. On the 'femaleness' of Jewish religious virtue see Jacob Neusner, *Androgynous Judaism: Masculine and Feminine in the Dual Torah*, Macon, Georgia, Mercer University Press, 1993, esp. pp. 83–123.

107 Schneid (ed.), *Family*, p. 94.
108 See Paula E. Hyman, 'Gender and the Jewish Family in Modern Europe', in Ofer and Weitzman (eds), *Women in the Holocaust*, pp. 25–38.
109 Dworkin, *Scapegoat*, pp. 9, 14.
110 Much of contemporary Orthodoxy would deny that this is the purpose and effect of the laws of menstrual purity. According to Hyman Goldin, *The Jewish Woman and Her Home* (p. 285), the purpose of these laws is to demonstrate that a man 'must abstain from his lust and control his desires during certain periods of his wife's life, because she is not at his back and call'. In more recent years Orthodox commentators have avoided speaking of the *niddah* with traditional disgust as unclean or impure. They have instead emphasized the marital benefits of separation during women's 'unclean' days. (See Jonah Steinberg, 'From a "Pot of Filth" to a "Hedge of Roses" (and Back): Changing Theorizations of Menstruation in Judaism', *Journal of Feminist Studies in Religion* 13 (1997), pp. 5–26. While Steinberg might have given an accurate picture of the rhetorical and apologetic aspects of the Jewish discourses on purity, contemporary women's positioning in Jewish sacred space in Orthodox synagogues is once more demonstrating the prevalence of quasi-cultic, intrinsic notions of female impurity as opposed to rabbinic notions of women's extrinsic pollution as a sexual distraction to male worshippers. See Kunin, *God's Place in the World*, pp. 116–35, esp. pp. 129–30.
111 Although popular perception might have suggested otherwise, menstruants cannot pollute the scrolls of the Torah by touch, nor need they abstain from attending synagogue.
112 See further e.g. Rivka Haut, 'The Presence of Women', in Susan Grossman and Rivka Haut (eds), *Daughters of the King: Women and the Synagogue. A Survey of History, Halakhah, and Contemporary Realities*, Philadelphia, Jewish Publication Society, 1992, pp. 276–7.
113 See also, for example, rabbinic texts stating that women are inclined to witchcraft (Sanhedrin 67a); are gluttonous eaves-droppers, lazy and jealous (Genesis Rabbah 58: 2); that they need perfume because they were taken from Adam's bone and are therefore meat which rots where the earth from which Adam was made does not (Genesis Rabbah 17: 8); that it would be better for the words of Torah to be cast into the fire than imparted to a woman (Sotah 19a), and that women are not to be called to read Torah for the sake of 'the dignity of the community' (Megillah 23a).
114 For an account of women's pre-war Sabbath purifications see Eliach, *There Once Was a World*, pp. 408–9. Leah Kohn offers a women's ultra-Orthodox configuration of the Sabbath motifs of light, the transformation of the material, and divine presence in her meditation on the matriarch Sarah in 'Sarah: Finding the Spiritual in the Mundane', in Kornbluth and Kornbluth (eds), *Jewish Women Speak Out*, pp. 85–9, esp. pp. 86–7.
115 Cf. Kathryn Allen Rabuzzi's *The Sacred and the Feminine: Toward a Theology of Housework*, New York, Seabury Press, 1982, which argues that all housework reenacts the primordial creation of order out of chaos.
116 *And the Sun Kept Shining*, p. 143. Like many in the women's camp at Auschwitz-Birkenau, Ferderber-Salz was evacuated to Belsen towards the end of the war.
117 Ibid., p. 163. Cf. Frida Michelson's account of how she and her friend Sonia worked for several days to make their tiny apartment within the verminous filth of the Riga ghetto into a home of sorts: 'Somehow we fashioned curtains for the windows, hung some pictures on the walls, put a clean cloth on the table, and it became home' (*I Survived Rumbuli*, pp. 71–2).
118 *And the Sun Kept Shining*, pp. 24, 37–8.
119 Ibid., pp. 147, 160, 163.
120 *There is a Place*, pp. 129, 193. Cf. Hillesum, *A Diary*, p. 227, where she writes of Westerbork, 'I feel at home'. Her writing is more consciously mystical in content and expression than that of the Auschwitz memoirs used here.

121 Tedeschi, however, notes that as a starving woman, food fantasies could be an added torture and, with dry camp humour, told her friend Bianca that she would rather discuss pulmonary tuberculosis than good food (*There is a Place*, p. 208). See also Myrna Goldenberg, 'Food Talk: Gendered Responses to Hunger in Concentration Camps', in Roth and Maxwell (eds), *Remembering for the Future*, pp. 248–57.

122 *Triumph of Hope: From Theresienstadt and Auschwitz to Israel*, trans. M. Bettauer Dembo, New York, John Wiley and Sons, 1988, p. 122. Tara DeSilva's edited collection *In Memory's Kitchen: A Legacy from the Women of Terezín*, (Northvale, NJ, Jason Aronson, 1996), has been harshly criticized by Hilene Flanzbaum as being an ill-researched 'pseudo-cookbook' whose publication 'posthumously humiliates these women who so painstakingly labored when starvation had robbed them of every clear thought' ('The Americanization of the Holocaust', p. 95). But Flanzbaum may have misunderstood the book, which, however ill-advised, intends to establish a female continuum through the passing on of recipes and cooking skills that is transgenerational, a significant element of Jewish women's history, and allows Jewish women, spiritually and emotionally, to take the women of Terezín with them into the future rather than leaving them forever in a camp.

123 Delbo, *Auschwitz and After*, pp. 68, 60–1. The white muslin curtains later ceased to symbolize peace and security when Delbo realized that the house belonged to a member of the SS.

124 Ibid., pp. 77–8.

125 Ibid., p. 102.

126 Compare childhood games where any space in a playground can be designated 'home'. There, in a space without visible boundaries, the child finds temporary refuge from her captor: 'it'.

127 The Hebrew *kipper* (atonement) can also connote covering.

128 *Facing the Abusing God*, pp. 7, 31.

129 Ibid., pp. 8, 43.

130 *With God in Hell*, p. 33.

131 David Roskies, *Against the Apocalypse: Responses to Catastrophe in Modern Jewish Culture*, Cambridge, Mass. and London, Harvard University Press, 1984, p. 35 (emphasis mine).

132 The numbers of people murdered in Auschwitz upon their arrival was subject to certain variables, principal among these being the camp's capacity to accommodate and use slave labourers. If the camp could not accommodate labour, most or all of a transport might be gassed on arrival. Otherwise, about 10 per cent of a transport might be judged fit for work.

133 Cf. Greenberg, 'Cloud of Smoke, Pillar of Fire', pp. 41–2: 'To talk of love and of a God who cares in the presence of [the] burning children [of Auschwitz] is obscene and incredible; to leap in and pull a child out of a pit, to clean its face and heal its body, is to make the most powerful statement – the only statement that counts.'

134 Jacobs, *A Jewish Theology*, p. 63. The presence of the Shekhinah is also promised as a reward of righteousness in the hereafter where 'the righteous sit with their crowns on their heads feasting on the brightness of the Shekhinah' (Berakhot 17a).

135 See e.g. Ex. 29: 46; Deut. 23: 15; Zech. 2: 14–17.

136 See Lodahl, *Shekhinah/Spirit*, pp. 51–4.

137 See Pirke Avot 3.2 where Rabbi Hanina ben Tradion opines that when two people (men) sit together and the words of the Torah pass between them, there the Shekhinah is in their midst. See also Lodahl, *Shekhinah/Spirit*, p. 54; Elliot Wolfson, *Through a Speculum That Shines: Vision and Imagination in Medieval Jewish Mysticism*, Princeton, NJ, Princeton University Press, 1994, pp. 41, 122, 347, 356.

138 Lodahl, *Shekhinah/Spirit*, p. 53.

139 Kunin, 'Judaism', pp. 121, 129.

140 The eighteenth-century Hasidic Rebbe, Hayim Hackel of Amdur, taught that the

body is a home for the Holy One (this is the meaning of Ps. 132: 5, 'Until I find a place for the Lord'). God lives where he is allowed to enter (Louis Jacobs, *Hasidic Thought*, New York, Behrman House, Inc., 1976, p. 157).

141   On the significance of *mishkan* symbolism in contemporary Jewish feminist spirituality see Gottlieb, *She Who Dwells Within*, pp. 123–9, 134.

142   See Deut. 41: 41–2.

143   In Belsen, before its liberation, Jews lay dying in makeshift tents (the anti-type of the biblical encampment). And even the tents were blown away by the wind. See e.g. Ferderber-Salz, *And the Sun Kept Shining*, p. 142.

144   In *Ritual and Morality: The Ritual Purity System and its Place in Judaism*, Cambridge, Cambridge University Press, 1999, Hyam Maccoby argues that the sanctuary does not require protection from demonic power nor the offices of the priesthood.

145   Epstein, *Judaism*, p. 136.

146   Blumenthal, *Facing the Abusing God*. p. 19. See also, Tsvi Blanchard, 'The Search for the Holy in a Consumer Society', in Rodney Clapp (ed.), *The Consuming Passion: Christianity and the Consumer Culture*, Downers Grove, IL, InterVarsity Press, 1998, pp. 93–4.

147   Schechter, *Studies in Judaism,* p. 180.

4   Face to face (with God) in Auschwitz

1   *Holocaust Project*, p. 125.

2   Lesbianism in the camps is commonly divided by historians and survivors into three categories: first, that of women who were already lesbians; second, a type of non-sexual emotionally supportive bonding between women; and third, a sexually coercive type in which women of higher status in the inmate or camp hierarchy predated on other women. However, it must be noted that Jewish women's memoirs tend to be either reticent about, or openly hostile to, lesbianism in the camps. Unhelpfully, Holocaust scholars have tended to subsume lesbian experience with that of gay men or chosen to interpret it as the result of emotional deprivation rather than as a sexual inclination and identity – a supposition not made of homosexual men (see e.g. Chicago, *Holocaust Project*, p. 109; R. Amy Elman, 'Lesbians and the Holocaust', in Fuchs (ed.), *Women and the Holocaust*, pp. 9–17; Lengyel, *Five Chimneys*, p. 184).

3   Des Pres defines a survivor as 'anyone who manages to stay alive in body and spirit, enduring dread and hopelessness without the loss of will to carry on in human ways. That is all.' (*The Survivor*, p. 6). His analysis of survival emphasizes 'forms of social bonding and interchange, of collective resistance, of keeping dignity and moral sense active' (p. vii).

4   E.g. Brenner notes that Hillesum found meaning in giving her whole attention to others: their suffering became 'the liberating raison d'être of her own existence' (*Writing as Resistance*, p. 45). Not uncoincidentally, Hillesum's writing has become attractive to many Christians.

5   Although some Jews have written about their determination to survive, Adelsberger found that 'The problem for us in Auschwitz was not whether [death] but when and how. No Jewish prisoner reckoned on ever leaving Auschwitz alive' (*Auschwitz*, p. 65).

6   Shepherd, *A Price Below Rubies*, pp. 19–20, 212.

7   Tzvetan Todorov, trans. Arthur Denner and Abigail Pollack, *Facing the Extreme: Moral Life in the Concentration Camps*, London, Weidenfeld & Nicolson, 1999, p. 81.

8   Sacks, *One People?*, p. 45.

9   It is notable that both Judith Tydor Baumel and Rachel Feldhay Brenner theorize women's holocaustal relationships in the light of Gilligan's and other maternalist philosophers' conclusions. Tydor Baumel has used Carol Gilligan's and Nancy

Chodorow's studies of women's moral development within a nexus of relationships of care to support her observations on female caring in the camps (see also n. 86 of the present chapter; Tydor Baumel, 'Social Interaction among Jewish Women in Crisis during the Holocaust', esp. pp. 78–9). Carol Gilligan's position is still contested, but if she and others are right that women's ethical behaviour is less rule- and principle-bound than that of men, many Jewish women's moral and spiritual inclination may not have been to turn to halakhic modes of negotiating the crisis even had their circumstances enabled them to do so. Therefore in developing a Jewish feminist theology of care in relation to the Holocaust – that is, a theology *for a time of catastrophe* – to take an exclusively halakhic approach would not only dismiss many women's experiences, it may not be congruent with the female religio-ethical mode.

10   Kitty Hart notes: 'I had already grasped the value of being invisible. Not being around when the hunters came. Having an unidentifiable face. There were thousands and thousands of women in the various sections of the camp, and even the *Kapos* were unable to tell one from the another. With shaven heads, ravaged faces and ill-fitting garments, everybody looked so much alike. . . . As long as numbers tallied, nobody cared about faces' (*Return to Auschwitz*, pp. 100–1).

11   *The Body of Faith*, p. 213. Some Orthodox commentators would deny that Israel is a comprehensively inclusive category regardless of merit or observance or that it is a synonym for the Jewish people, religious and secular alike.

12   *Auschwitz*, p. 104. Similarly, Tedeschi, *There is a Place*, p. 13.

13   *Kiddush Hashem*, pp. 239–43, esp. p. 240. Huberband and others set themselves the task of recording the events and conditions of the Warsaw ghetto. The essay cited here is the only surviving fragment of his larger study of Jewish women in the ghetto.

14   *I Survived Rumbuli*, pp. 75, 96–7.

15   Cited in Langer, *Holocaust Testimonies*, pp. 12–13.

16   Adelsberger, *Auschwitz*, p. 22.

17   The age of Jews selected for labour varied according to their appearance and skills and the camp's needs and capacity for slave labour.

18   Ibid., p. 100.

19   Lengyel, *Five Chimneys*, p. 106.

20   Adelsberger, *Auschwitz*, p. 30.

21   *Five Chimneys*, p. 19.

22   Nagy, 'No Heroes, No Martyrs', p. 166.

23   Ibid., p. 169.

24   Tedeschi, *There is a Place*, p. 29.

25   Nomberg-Przytyk, *Auschwitz*, p. 64.

26   Ibid., p. 21. The bleakest accounts of inmate behaviour (see e.g. Primo Levi, *Survival in Auschwitz*, trans. Stuart Woolf, New York, Collier Macmillan, 1961) may also be shaped by an accepted patriarchal worldview in which the ideology of competition for survival can filter out some or all of the evidence for more cooperative 'female' gestures.

27   Nomberg-Przytyk, *Auschwitz*, pp. 4–5; Ferderber-Salz, *And the Sun Kept Shining*, p. 137.

28   Nomberg-Przytyk, *Auschwitz*, p. 18.

29   *Five Chimneys*, pp. 26, 30–31, 45, 46, 96, 212.

30   Lengyel records that in 1944, when the gasoline used to burn children alive had become scarce, the Germans decided that the children should be 'bathed'. Barefoot and in rags, the children were whipped along a snow- and ice-coated road, 'bathed' in icy water and left to stand to attention for five hours until they froze to death. 'Few of the children of Birkenau survived that roll call.' Lengyel was involved in carrying out this atrocity. Although she mourns these 'innocents of Birkenau', or 'the snow-men' as she calls them, 'at Birkenau one did not discuss an order. One carried it out no matter how revolting it might be' (*Five Chimneys*, pp. 209–10).

31   It should be noted that despite the danger of ripped, burnt skin and, indeed, death itself, inmates returned again and again to the wires in order to exchange words, notes and food (Adelsberger, *Auschwitz*, pp. 111–12).

32   Nomberg-Przytyk, *Auschwitz*, p. 27.

33   Adelsberger, *Auschwitz*, pp. 127–8. Women were not always healed of the trauma of non-relation after liberation. By 1945, women and men customarily found themselves alone, with many or all of their relatives dead. Married Jewish women could be left as *agunot* ('anchored' or 'chained' women) if evidence of their husband's death was not found. According to most Orthodox legal authorities, they would have been unable to remarry.

34   Nagy, 'No Heroes, No Martyrs', p. 165. See also Brenner, *Writing as Resistance*, p. 106.

35   Adelsberger, *Auschwitz*, p. 45.

36   Nagy, 'No Heroes, No Martyrs', p. 174.

37   *Fragments of Isabella*, p. 37. On the same page she continues, 'Yet the insanity of Auschwitz must be imbued with meaning if *living* is to be continued, and the only meaning of living has to be for the four of us . . . All of us. Together.' See also ibid., pp. 35–6, 63–4, 68.

38   Nomberg-Przytyk, *Auschwitz*, p. 19. Cf. Joseph Roth, trans. Michael Hoffman, *The Wandering Jews*, London, Granta, 2001, pp. 122–3.

39   *Auschwitz*, p. 13.

40   Ibid., p. 17.

41   See Lengyel, *Five Chimneys*, pp. 42–4.

42   *Auschwitz*, p. 20.

43   Ibid., pp. 17, 21, 20.

44   Ibid., pp. 75–6. See also Tedeschi, *There is a Place*, p. 12. In *Making Stories, Making Selves: Feminist Reflections on the Holocaust* (Columbus, Ohio State University Press, 1993, p. 100), Ruth Linden points out that symbiotic relationships could be established between privileged prisoners and the SS. The latter would disobey camp rules by taking goods stolen from deportees and the prisoners would look the other way in return for tacit permission to eat the food deportees had brought into the camp.

45   *There is a Place*, p. 56. Sephardic and Ashkenazic women inmates would have come from distinct religious and historical cultures. Tedeschi's observations, however, are made not of women's Jewish, but national, identities.

46   Nomberg-Przytyk, *Auschwitz*, p. 38.

47   See Linden, *Making Stories, Making Selves*, pp. 97–8.

48   Langer, *Holocaust Testimonies*, p. 91.

49   *Facing the Extreme*, pp. 76–82.

50   Nomberg-Przytyk, *Auschwitz*, p. 69. Numerous others testify to this crime.

51   Adelsberger, *Auschwitz*, pp. 100–1; Ferderber-Salz, *And the Sun Kept Shining*, pp. 158–9; Lengyel, *Five Chimneys*, p. 60; Nomberg-Przytyk, *Auschwitz*, pp. 69–70. Similarly, for nurses in the Warsaw ghetto, the final sign of their commitment to the babies and children in their care was to take their lives just before the arrival of the SS and deportation (Todorov, *Facing the Extreme*, p. 19).

52   The psychotherapist and writer Alix Pirani once said to me that she thought Lilith as well as Shekhinah was there in the camps. She did not elaborate and I never did find out precisely what she meant. But her words stayed with me for a number of years until I made my own sense of them. Lilith represents the (female) *yetzer hara* – that 'evil inclination' or erotic drive which, according to the rabbis, not only leads people into sexual temptation, but is also a necessary element of their creative energy. Maybe some women's furious will to live was expressive of Lilith's energy – and was therefore both of God and not of God. As for Shekhinah, most of this book is my own response to a point which, at that moment, was expressed as no more than a chance remark.

53 Gisella Perl witnessed this atrocity in Auschwitz. See *idem*, 'A Doctor in Auschwitz', in Rittner and Roth (eds), *Different Voices*, p. 113. Perl also witnessed how 292 pregnant women were forced onto a single truck, on Josef Mengele's orders, and taken to the crematoria to be burnt alive (p. 115, ibid.).

54 *Five Chimneys*, pp. 100–1.

55 Ibid., p. 212.

56 'Women's Agency and Survival Strategies During the Holocaust', pp. 345, 343.

57 Ibid., p. 341.

58 Ibid. See further *idem* Kolot Mikommando Kanada, *Voices from the 'Canada' Commando*, Jerusalem, Emunah, 1989, pp. 1–7.

59 See Erna F. Rubenstein's *The Survivor in Us All: A Memoir of the Holocaust* (Hamden, CT, Archon Books, 1984) for an account of how the camp sisterhood she was a part of assisted one another for four years.

60 See Deborah R. Weissman, 'Beis Yaakov: A Historical Model for Jewish Feminists', in Elizabeth Koltun (ed.), *The Jewish Woman: New Perspectives*, New York, Schocken Books, 1976, pp. 139–48.

61 Judith Tydor Baumel, 'Social Interaction among Jewish Women in Crisis during the Holocaust', *Gender and History* 7 (1995), pp. 72–6.

62 *Auschwitz and After*, pp. 72, 73.

63 Ibid., pp. 74, 105, 104.

64 *Faith After the Holocaust*, p. 77. Feldhay Brenner's research concludes that the women writers she studied (who were either not, or not yet, in camps) created meaning from the horror of their situations by their insistence that they would not surrender their obligations, responsibilities and dignity as human beings to a struggle for survival at any cost. Indeed, they sought to improve and strengthen their humanity; to actualize the self, at the very historical moment the Jewish self was under greatest pressure to disintegrate (*Writing as Resistance*, pp. 21–2 and *passim*).

65 Linden's phenomenology of female survival in *Making Stories, Making Selves*, pp. 84–112, lists these and other factors as contributing to survival. She, like others, notes that survival was only a social possibility; it could not be done alone (p. 99).

66 Myrna Goldenberg's reading of women's memoirs of Auschwitz supports the present one. See 'Memoirs of Auschwitz Survivors: The Burden of Gender', in Ofer and Weitzman (eds), *Women in the Holocaust*, pp. 327–39, esp. pp. 336–7.

67 Adelsberger, *Auschwitz*, pp. 96, 97.

68 Ibid., pp. 99–100.

69 Ibid., p. 71. Not everyone who was offered the role of *kapo* or overseer either accepted or exploited it (see Leitner, *Fragments of Isabella*, pp. 56–7).

70 *Auschwitz*, p. 39.

71 Ibid., pp. 139, 141.

72 Ruth Adler, 'Woman of the Eighties', interviewed and edited by Ruth Swirsky, in Copperman *et al.* (eds), *Generations of Memories*, p. 39.

73 Lengyel, *Five Chimneys*, p. 139.

74 *And the Sun Kept Shining*, pp. 152, 156, 212.

75 Judith Tydor Baumel, 'Women's Agency and Survival Strategies During the Holocaust', p. 329. See also Todorov, *Facing the Extreme*, esp. pp. 71–90. Todorov's is an argument against the view that the death and concentration camps wholly prohibited moral choice. Drawing on a wealth of testimony he demonstrates that the 'ordinary', non-heroic virtues of caring and compassion and the preservation of human dignity were a possibility of camp existence.

76 After concluding that the idealizing cultural feminist context of her research had led her to pay insufficient attention to women inmate's actual psychological and physical oppression, Ringelheim revised her thesis in 'Women and the Holocaust: A Reconsideration of Research', *Signs: Journal of Women in Culture and Society* 10 (1985), pp. 741–61. See her earlier 'The Unethical and the Unspeakable: Women and the

Holocaust', in *Simon Wiesenthal Center Annual*, (1984), pp. 69–87. See also, Linden, *Making Stories, Making Selves*. Linden's phenomenology of survival rejects the notion of a specifically female or feminine ethic of care having characterized women's relationships during this period.

77   Baumel, 'Women's Agency and Survival Strategies during the Holocaust', p. 330.

78   Ibid., p. 330. This gendered difference can be read in a number of ways. Todorov's *Facing the Extreme*, p. 20, regards heroic virtue in the camps as the province of men, while 'ordinary virtues [were] equally if not more characteristic of women'. This distinction seems to me to be a false one. The ordinary can be heroic even if it is not daring. As Anne Michael's protagonist Jakob puts it: 'What is the smallest act of kindness that is considered heroic? In those days, to be moral required no more than the lightest flicker of movement – a micrometre – of eyes looking away or blinking, while a running man crossed a field. And those who gave water or bread! They entered a realm higher than the angels' simply by remaining in the human mire' (*Fugitive Pieces*, p. 162).

79   'Memoirs of Auschwitz Survivors: The Burden of Gender', p. 337.

80   See Todorov, *Facing the* Extreme, pp. 17, 18.

81   'Women's Agency and Survival Strategies During the Holocaust' p. 338. In 'Social Interaction Among Jewish Women in Crisis', pp. 80–4, Tydor Baumel finds that when women's groups grew too large (at the risk of compromising invisibility) they became liable to hierarchy, territoriality and inter-group competition. (On inmate hierarchy in the men's camp see e.g. Frankl, *Man's Search for Meaning*, p. 63.)

82   Ringelheim, 'Women and the Holocaust', pp. 378–9. Tydor Baumel, 'Social Interaction among Jewish Women in Crisis', p. 78.

83   From a letter to Judy Chicago, *Holocaust Project*, p. 125.

84   Tydor Baumel, 'Women's Agency and Survival Strategies During the Holocaust', p. 342.

85   Drawing upon the work of feminist theorists Nancy Chodorow and Carol Gilligan, Tydor Baumel and others have regarded their subjects' cooperative, maternalist ethic as integral to women's moral and psychological development – in distinction to that of men whose moral development would have been, and remains, more separative, hierarchical and less adaptive ('Women's Agency and Survival Strategies During the Holocaust', pp. 342–3). Gilligan's research on women's moral development finds its dynamic to be that of care and relationality (as opposed to that of men, who suppose that the highest moral development is to have subordinated relational considerations to abstract, universalized values such as justice and rights). She criticizes this masculinist evolutionary hierarchy and valorizes the particularities of women's moral development. Gilligan's theory has been subject to vigorous criticism from ethical theorists, including feminists who are uncomfortable with apparently essentialist accounts of difference. See further, Carol Gilligan, *In a Different Voice: Psychological Theory and Women's Development*, Cambridge, MA, Harvard University Press, 1982. Nancy Chodorow's *The Reproduction of Mothering: Psychoanalysis and the Sociology of Gender* (Berkeley and Los Angeles, University of California Press, 1978), examines the production of relational values through the mother–daughter bond. For representative critical debate on the ethic of care generated by Gilligan's work, see Mary Jeanne Larrabee (ed.), *An Ethic of Care: Feminist and Interdisciplinary Perspectives*, London, Routledge, 1993, esp. Linda K. Kerber, 'Some Cautionary Words for Historians', ibid., pp. 102–6.

86   See Ellen M. Umansky, 'Piety, Persuasion, and Friendship', in *idem* and Ashton (eds), *Four Centuries of Women's Spirituality*, pp. 16–18. Female communal networks remain central to contemporary religious women's lives. Maurie Sacks' study of contemporary Orthodox women in suburban New York has shown that religious women do not feel diminished or threatened by men's public religious status but understand Jewish community life to consist in an empowering network of reciprocal relation-

ships mediated from the home and by women's committees and social networks. Their exchange is that of a woman's world yet represents the entire community in being derived from traditional Ashkenazic religious values. Women's activities sometimes involve self-legislated modifications of Jewish law in order to give practical and emotional support to other women when they are in need of childcare and at times of sickness and bereavement. See 'Computing Community at Purim', *Journal of American Folklore* 102 (1989), pp. 275–91.

87 Baumel, 'Women's Agency and Survival Strategies During the Holocaust', pp. 333–45.
88 Ibid., p. 340.
89 See Ringelheim, 'Women and the Holocaust: A Reconsideration of Research', pp. 374–405.
90 Ibid., p. 336.
91 Foreword, Ferderber-Salz, *And the Sun Kept Shining*, p. 8.
92 Tydor Baumel, 'Social Interaction among Jewish Women in Crisis', pp. 70, 74, 78.
93 Ibid., p. 79. Bertha Ferderber-Salz and her sister also cite this Talmudic dictum as having been of spiritual nourishment in the Krakow ghetto (*And the Sun Kept Shining*, p. 40). Even today, Sue Levi Elwell's, 'Rosh Hashanah Sermon' cites this dictum as 'what being a Jew, and a human being, is all about' (Umansky and Ashton, (eds), *Four Centuries of Jewish Women's Spirituality*, p. 270).
94 Cited in Tydor Baumel, 'Social Interaction Among Jewish Women in Crisis', p. 79.
95 Ibid., p. 74.
96 Itka Frajman Zygmuntowicz with Sara Horowitz, 'Survival and Memory' in Umansky and Ashton (eds), *Four Centuries of Women's Spirituality*, pp. 288–90.
97 *A Mother's Shoah: The Holocaust Diary of Susan Kaszas*, 20 November 2001 <http://www.remember.org/mother>
98 See Paul Mendes-Flohr, 'Law and Sacrament: Ritual Observance in Twentieth-Century Jewish Thought', in Green (ed.), *Jewish Spirituality*, p. 323.
99 Jacobs, *A Jewish Theology*, p. 242. See also ibid., p. 268.
100 Horowitz, 'Mengele, the Gynecologist, and Other Stories of Women's Survival', p. 211.
101 This approximates David Blumenthal's translation of the term *hesed* (*Facing the Abusing God*, p. 109).
102 *On Judaism*, pp. 109, 110, 113. For Buber, Sinai, Judaism's root experience, was, above all, a religious experience of divine presence – an I–Thou encounter, not a revelation of law as such. Here God was revealed as the eternal You (*On the Bible*, New York, Schocken Books, 1967, pp. 77–8). This is a 'You' who is always present to us: 'it is we only who are not always there' (*I and Thou*, trans. Ronald Gregor Smith, New York, Charles Scribner's Sons, 1958, p. 99). In an I–It relation a person stands apart, detached from the other in a subject–object relation. But in the I–Thou mode, the relation is one of total involvement; an interpersonal engagement that is at once a meeting with God who is the eternal Thou of every particular Thou. Buber's distinction in *I and Thou* between the I–It and the I–Thou relation is well known to the point of cliché but cannot but be entirely foundational to a Jewish feminist theology of relation. Feminists have noted Buber's subtle masculinism where the solitary 'I' moves towards, rather than beginning in, relation, as most women have done. From a maternal perspective, women's lives are not, on the whole, characterized by the atomistic 'I–It' relation Buber critiques but are already and immediately engaged by 'I–Thou' relations with their children and others.
103 *The Tremendum*, pp. 72–3.
104 For a recent discussion of Judaism and visual representation see Anthony Julius, *Idolizing Pictures: Idolatry, Iconoclasm and Jewish Art*, London, Thames & Hudson, 2000, esp. pp. 33–58.
105 Wyschogrod, *The Body of Faith*, pp. 115–16. Wyschogrod's comments on the visuality of the *tselem* are not made with specific reference to the Holocaust.

106 'Encountering the Divine Presence', in Umansky and Ashton (eds), *Four Centuries of Women's Spirituality*, p. 246.
107 While Levinas acknowledges his debt to Buber, Levinas' work importantly supplements Buber's in two ways. First, Buber's notion of reciprocity in relationship constitutes more an ontological connection than an ethical demand. For Levinas, it is in our response to the face of the other (rather than merely 'knowing' the other) that we are presented with ethical responsibility. See Andrius Valevičius, *From the Other to the Totally Other: The Religious Philosophy of Emmanuel Levinas*, New York, Bern, Frankfurt am Main and Paris, Peter Lang, 1988, p. 144; Tamra Wright *et al.* trans. Andrew Benjamin and Tamra Wright, 'The Paradox of Morality: An Interview with Emmanuel Levinas' in Robert Bernasconi and David Wood (eds), *The Provocation of Levinas: Rethinking the Other*, London and New York, Routledge, 1988, p. 169. Second, although Buber's notion of relationship seems to be informed by an egalitarian reciprocity that is far less pronounced in Levinas' notion of the asymmetricality of relations of care, this latter may be interpreted not as an inequality of power but, in the present case, as how women in Auschwitz could take varying degrees of responsibility for the other without demanding the same.
108 See *Difficile liberté*, pp. 28–9. See also Valevičius, *From the Other to the Totally Other*, pp. 119–21, 129. Wyschogrod dismisses Levinas' ethical reading of Judaism as the inadequately Jewish Judaism of the assimilated (*The Body of Faith*, p. 181). I cannot agree with him, but this is not the place to pursue the argument.
109 Séan Hand (ed.) *The Levinas Reader*, Oxford, Blackwell, 1989, p. 83.
110 *Totality and Infinity: An Essay on Exteriority*, trans. Alphonso Lingis, Pittsburgh, Duquesue University Press, 1969, p. 244. See also ibid., p. 215. The feminization of Levinas' 'other' is my own.
111 *Otherwise than Being, or Beyond Essence*, trans. Alphonso Lingis, The Hague, Martinus Nijhoff, 1981, p. 55.
112 Wright *et al.*, 'The Paradox of Morality', p. 177. Rosenzweig also insisted that love of neighbour is the 'embodiment of all commandments'. That arch-commandment, the 'primal "love me!"', can command love because it proceeds from the mouth of God: the lover (*The Star of Redemption*, trans. from the second edition of 1930 by W.W. Hallo, Notre Dame, IN, Notre Dame Press, 1985, p. 205).
113 *The Second Sex*, trans. and ed. H.M. Pashely, Harmondsworth, Penguin, 1972, p. 16.
114 'Feminism and the Other', in Bernasconi and Wood (eds), *The Provocation of Levinas*, p. 36.
115 *Becoming Divine*, p. 238.
116 Susan A. Handelman, *Fragments of Redemption: Jewish Thought and Literary Theory in Benjamin, Scholem, and Levinas,* Bloomington and Indianapolis, Indiana University Press, 1991, p. 178.
117 See Levinas, 'Useless Suffering', trans. Richard Cohen, in Bernasconi and Wood (eds), *The Provocation of Levinas*, pp. 156–67; Jantzen, *Becoming Divine*, p. 238.
118 Feldhay Brenner, *Writing as Resistance*, pp. 176–7; Catherine Chalier, 'Ethics and the Feminine' in Robert Bernasconi and Simon Critchley (eds), *Re-reading Levinas*, Bloomington, Indiana University Press, 1991, pp. 119–30.
119 *Auschwitz and After*, p. 30.
120 Ibid., pp. 94, 89.
121 Ibid., pp. 84, 85, 86.
122 *There is a Place*, pp. 11, 113, 180, 103, 13.
123 *Auschwitz and After*, p. 254.
124 Wright *et al.*, 'The Paradox of Morality', p. 171.
125 Ibid., p. 172.
126 See *Totality and Infinity*, pp. 62, 75, 78, 168.
127 Buber, *Early Masters*, p. 102.
128 Chanter, 'Feminism and the Other', pp. 35–6. See Levinas, 'Le Judaïsme et le féminin'

in *Difficile liberté*, pp. 51–62; trans. Edith Wyschogrod as 'Judaism and the Feminine Element', *Judaism*, 18 (1969), pp. 30–8. I have worked from Wyschogrod's translation.
129   'Judaism and the Feminine Element', trans. Edith Wyschogrod, p. 33.
130   See ibid., p. 32.
131   Interview with Raoul Mortley, in Raoul Mortley, *French Philosophers in Conversation: Levinas, Schneider, Serres, Irigaray, Le Doeuff, Derrida*, London, Routledge, 1991, p. 22.
132   Ibid., p. 37.
133   Ibid., pp. 35, 58.
134   Buber, *Early Masters*, p. 77.
135   *Through a Speculum that Shines: Vision and Imagination in Medieval Jewish Mysticism*, Princeton, NJ, Princeton University Press, 1994, pp. 13–51.
136   Cf. Levinas' interview with Raoul Mortley in *French Philosophers in Conversation*, pp. 15–16. Levinas's phrasing is not made with direct reference to the Holocaust or God.
137   Handelman, *Fragments of Redemption*, p. 180.
138   Ibid., p. 209.
139   Rachel Adler follows Levinas in regarding the otherness of God and of persons as the precondition of relation: 'Only if there is an Other can there be mirroring and reciprocity.' God, then, is imagined as 'continually pregnant with, delivering, rearing, and separating from the world. . . . The world is inside God, outside God, part of God as in halakhah the unborn infant is "part of its mother's body," and separate from God, as the emancipated child is separate from a parent who still watches its story unfold, sometimes with pride, sometimes with pain' (*Engendering Judaism*, p. 93). However, for Adler, Levinas' ethic of the face as the locus of moral obligation is undermined by what she alludes to as 'his treatment of women' (ibid., p. 221 n. 8).

5   A mother/God in Auschwitz

1   I acknowledge, but have omitted, the subsequent verse: 'her iniquity is expiated – the Lord has given her double punishment for her sins' (Is. 40: 2).
2   Susan Starr Sered, '"She Perceives Her Work to Be Rewarding": Jewish Women in a Cross-Cultural Perspective', in Davidman and Tenenbaum (eds), *Feminist Perspectives on Jewish Studies*, pp. 174, 175, 186. Sered is using the anthropologist Robert Redfield's distinction between local, non-literate 'little' and transregional, literate, elite 'great' traditions.
3   'Mother Love, Child Death, and Religious Innovation', *Journal of Feminist Studies in Religion* 12 (1996), p. 7.
4   Judy Chicago, for example, found that women survivors' video-taped testimonies consistently emphasized family connection above all others (*Holocaust Project*, p. 17).
5   'Mengele, the Gynecologist, and Other Stories of Women's Survival', in Peskowitz and Levitt (eds), *Judaism Since Gender*, pp. 203–4.
6   Dayan Yisroel Yaakov Lichtenstein, 'A Voice . . . But Not the Vote', *Hamaor* Pesach 5755/1995, p. 23.
7   Andrea Dworkin, writing of women in the Holocaust, reminds us that if you are a woman the children need not be your own to also be yours: 'women are a group with a relationship to children not their own.' (*Scapegoat*, p. 200).
8   'The Bride to Be' from 'A Document of Roses', *Feminist Studies* 22 (1996), p. 657.
9   *Holocaust Project*, p. 23.
10   See e.g. Ellen Frankel, *The Five Books of Miriam: A Woman's Commentary on the Torah*, New York, HarperSanFrancisco, 1998, pp. 191–2.
11   Cited in Baker, *The Jewish Woman*, p. 100. In the washroom at Krakow airport, on my return from a one-day visit to Auschwitz, I heard a group of Jewish women who had been on the trip agree among themselves that their experience at the site had made them, above all, long to see and hold their children again.

12 Cited in their editorial commentary, Umansky and Ashton (eds), *Four Centuries of Women's Spirituality*, pp. 205–6.

13 *There is a Place*, p. 57.

14 *Auschwitz and After*, pp. 261–2.

15 Susan Starr Sered's feminist ethnography of the lives of elderly Jewish women, *Women as Ritual Experts: The Religious Lives of Elderly Jewish Women Living in Jerusalem*, is a fine example of a methodological prioritizing of the 'little' over the 'great' tradition.

16 Judy Chicago's book *Holocaust Project* exemplifies a feminist methodological approach to the mediation of the Holocaust. The first half of this book is a reflexive account of her preparatory studies for a series of collaborative paintings, needleworks and photomontages that were later exhibited throughout America. Central to her project is the narration of her own response to the research: how it made her want to sleep; how she would read without comprehension, or if with comprehension, feel suicidal (see ibid., pp. 7, 21 and *passim*).

17 *Holocaust Project*, p. 10

18 This aspect of the Holocaust is distinctive to its period. Previous Jewish catastrophes, such as the million who died in defence of the Second Temple, left no film or photographs to haunt us and family connections cannot be traced back that far with any certainty.

19 Jantzen is citing Adriana Cavarero, *Becoming Divine*, p. 150.

20 Esther M. Broner with Naomi Nimrod, *The Women's Haggadah*, New York, HarperSanFrancisco, 1993, p. 12.

21 Naomi Janowitz and Maggie Wenig, 'Sabbath Prayers for Women', in Christ and Plaskow (eds), *Womanspirit Rising*, p. 176.

22 Cf. Is. 49: 15. See further, Phyllis Trible, *God and the Rhetoric of Sexuality*, Philadelphia, Fortress Press, 1978, esp. pp. 34, 38. The tradition is, however, ambiguous. Rabbinic Judaism also called the womb 'a place of rot' (Niddah 57b).

23 See e.g. Adelsberger, *Auschwitz*, pp. 100–1; Lengyel, *Five Chimneys*, p. 100; Gisella Perl, 'A Doctor in Auschwitz', in Rittner and Roth (eds), *Different Voices*, pp. 113–16.

24 Early Hasidism taught that, rightly conceived and executed, all acts are a manifestation of and service to the divine, to the extent that the ultimate purpose of Torah is 'that man should become a Torah himself' (Solomon Schechter, *Studies in Judaism: Essays on Persons, Concepts, and Movements of Thought in Jewish Tradition*, New York, Atheneum, 1970, pp. 174–5).

25 *Auschwitz*, pp. 135–6. I have used Nomberg-Przytyk's first name here as being more appropriate to her own narrative form.

26 Tedeschi, *There is a Place*, p. 45.

27 Ibid., pp. 198, 197. Cf. Delbo, *Auschwitz and After*, pp. 37–9.

28 Ex. 3: 14.

29 Accessed 22 November 1999 <www.interlog.com/~mighty/'personal reflections'>

30 Linden, *Making Stories, Making Selves*, p. 99. To *shlep* is to drag or pull. The Yiddish term conveys the women's almost terminal weariness.

31 *Auschwitz and After*, p. 92. It is curious that despite such passages, Lawrence Langer regards Delbo's work as exemplifying a remembering that is unredeemed and irredeemable.

32 *There is a Place*, pp. 35–6.

33 Nagy, 'No Heroes, No Martyrs', p. 173.

34 Adelsberger, *Auschwitz*, p. 48.

35 *Auschwitz and After*, pp. 66, 45. See also ibid., pp. 79, 287.

36 Rena Kornreich Gelissen, *Rena's Promise*, p. 152. Dworkin also cites this passage in her book *Scapegoat*, p. 253, noting that 'this grace wins women nothing in the post-Holocaust world'.

37 *Otherwise Than Being*, pp. 75, 77; *Totality and Infinity*, p. 267.

38 *Clara's Story* as told to Joan Adess Grossman, Philadelphia, The Jewish Publication Society of America, 1984, p. 103.
39 *Fragments of Isabella*, p. 21.
40 Adelsberger, *Auschwitz*, p. 40.
41 'No Heroes, No Martyrs', p. 165.
42 On the ultra-liberal Jewish feminist reclamation of Shekhinah as 'Lady of the Moon' and keeper of the natural cycles, see Gottlieb, *She Who Dwells Within*, p. 135. See also Goldstein, *ReVisions*, p. 167.
43 Ferderber-Salz, *And the Sun Kept Shining*, p. 101. See also, Tedeschi, *There is a Place*, p. 18.
44 *Fragments of Isabella*, p. 81.
45 Brenner, *Writing As Resistance*, p. 10
46 *A Diary*, pp. 195, 223–4.
47 Brenner, *Writing As Resistance*, pp. 108–9.
48 Hillesum, *A Diary,* p. 219.
49 Brenner, *Writing as Resistance*, pp. 111–13.
50 Ibid., p. 113.
51 Ibid., p. 109.
52 'Beginning a Religious Response to Mastectomy' in Sylvia Rothschild and Sybil Sheridan (eds), *Taking Up the Timbrel: The Challenge of Creating Ritual for Jewish Women Today*, London, SCM Press, 2000, p. 183. See also Elizabeth Tikvah Sarah, 'Our Jewish Wedding', ibid., p. 139.
53 See also Isaiah 42: 14.
54 'The Gifts of First Fruits (1988)', in Umansky and Ashton (eds), *Four Centuries of Women's Spirituality*, p. 284.
55 Penina V. Adelman, 'A Drink from Miriam's Cup: Invention of Tradition Among Jewish Women', *Journal of Feminist Studies in Religion* 2 (1994), p. 165.
56 Harmondsworth, Penguin, 1986.
57 See Leo Rosten, *The Joys of Yiddish*, Harmondsworth, Penguin, 1968, pp. 451, 436–7, 433 respectively.
58 See Joyce Antler (ed.), *Talking Back: Images of Jewish Women in American Popular Culture*, Brandeis, Waltham, MA, Brandeis University Press, 1997, on Jewish women as not only the objects of stereotyping, but also as those who shape their own representation. See also Faye Moskowitz (ed.), *Her Face in the Mirror: Jewish Women on Mothers and Daughters*, Boston, Beacon Press, 1995.
59 Asphodel Long notes the necessary energy, intelligence, resourcefulness and dependability of the Anglo-Jewish immigrant mother of the early twentieth century. Long's mother ran a small shop, took care of her children and did all the housework. Her father '(like many immigrants) expected a woman to do everything, including make the money. He expected to sit and *daven*, go out with his mates and pretend to be learned but really, as far as I can make out, just do nothing in particular' ('A Pinhole in the Darkness', interviewed and edited by Ruth Swirsky, in Copperman *et al.* (eds), *Generations of Memories*, p. 190).
60 *Letters from Westerbork*, trans. Arnold J. Pomerans, London, Grafton Books, 1988, p. 132.
61 'Reproduction and Resistance During the Holocaust', in Fuchs (ed.), *Women and the Holocaust*, pp. 19–32.
62 Trudi Birger and Jeffrey M. Green, *A Daughter's Gift of Love: A Holocaust Memoir*, Philadelphia, Jewish Publication Society, 1992; Sara Tuvel Bernstein *et al.*, *The Seamstress: A Memoir of Survival*, New York, Putnam Publishing Group, 1997. This memoir tells of how Bernstein survived Ravensbrück by banding together with her sister Esther and two friends. See also Rena Kornriech Gelissen, *Rena's Promise*; Kitty Hart, *Return to Auschwitz*; Schoschana Rabinovici *et al.* trans. Shoshanah Rabinovits, *Thanks to My Mother*, London, Puffin, 2000. This book describes how Rabinovici's mother enabled her and many other women to survive the camps. See further, Brana

Gurewitsch and Leon J. Weinberger (eds), *Mothers, Sisters, Resisters: Oral Histories of Women Who Survived the Holocaust*, Tuscaloosa, University of Alabama Press, 1999; Roger A. Ritvo and Diane M. Plotkin, *Sisters in Sorrow: Voices of Care in the Holocaust*, Austin, Texas University Press, 1998.

63   Accessed 19 November 1999 <www.interlog.com/~mighty/'personal reflections'>

64   'Voluntary Covenant' in S.L. Jacobs (ed.), *Contemporary Jewish Religious Responses to the Holocaust*, Lanham, MD, New York and London, University Press of America, 1993, pp. 92–3 and *passim*.

65   Adelsberger, *Auschwitz*, p. 12.

66   *There is a Place*, pp. 9–10.

67   *Auschwitz and After*, p. 310.

68   Isaacman, *Clara's Story*, p. 37. Cf. Hanna Mortkowicz Olczakowa's account of Korczak's assuring his children of a future in which he does not believe ('Janosz [*sic*] Korczak's Last Walk', in Jacob Glatstein *et al.* (eds), *Anthology of Holocaust Literature*, New York, Atheneum, 1985, p. 135).

69   See e.g. Isaacman, *Clara's Story*, p. 60.

70   See e.g. ibid., p. 97.

71   Cf. André Schwartz-Bart's fictional account of this phenomenon in his novel, *The Last of the Just*, trans. Stephen Becker, London, Secker & Warburg, 1962, pp. 337–45.

72   See Gen. 22: 1, 31: 11, 46: 2; Ex. 3: 4. See also Is. 6: 8. Cf. Cohen *The Tremendum*, p. 95.

73   *Otherwise than Being*, pp. 113, 147.

74   Hillesum, *Letters from Westerbork*, p. 121.

75   Aaron Zeitlin, 'The Last Walk of Janusz Korczak', trans. Hadassah Rosensaft and Gertrude Hirschler, in Korczak, *Ghetto Diary*, pp. 56–7.

76   Hanna Mortkowicz Olczakowa, 'Janosz [*sic*] Korczak's Last Walk', p. 135.

77   Schindler, *Hasidic Responses to the Holocaust*, pp. 74–9.

78   Lengyel, *Five Chimneys*, p. 64. This moment is, I hope, unrepeatable, and ungeneralizable. It is not presented here as a means of advocating that women should be spared difficult knowledge.

79   Ferderber-Salz, *And the Sun Kept Shining*, p. 102.

80   Maggie Wenig, cited in Blumenthal, *Facing the Abusing God*, p. 79.

81   *And the Sun Kept Shining*, pp. 122, 117; See also Nomberg-Przytyk, *Auschwitz*, p. 181, n. 17.

82   *Judaism's Theological Voice: The Melody of the Talmud*, London and Chicago, University of Chicago Press, 1995, pp. 13, 1.

83   'Twenty Months at Auschwitz', p. 87.

84   *Fragments of Isabella*, p. 17.

85   Ibid., p. 95.

86   A Polish guard testified to this crime at Nuremberg. The testimony is drawn upon by both Greenberg and Fackenheim ('Cloud of Smoke, Pillar of Fire', p. 11 and *To Mend the World*, pp. 212–13, respectively).

87   *Fragments of Isabella*, p. 59.

88   *The Body of Faith*, pp. 175–6. By using the phrase 'carnal election' I do not, myself, infer that Israel enjoys an exclusive and privileged relation with God. I use the phrase to denote a particular, historical, intimate and embodied relation between one human family and God. Other faith traditions will conceive of their relationship with God by different and equally legitimate means.

89   Tanakh translates the words as 'The Lord is your guardian'.

90   'God in the Silence', reprinted in Umansky and Ashton (eds), *Four Centuries of Women's Spirituality*, pp. 180–4 (p. 182). For clarity in the present context, I have replaced Lichtenstein's 'Him' with 'Her'.

91   *A Diary*, p. 153.

92   Naomi Janowitz, cited in Blumenthal, *Facing the Abusing God*, p. 79.

93 See Isaacman, *Clara's Story*, pp. 64–5 on her mother as made both strong and vulnerable by her predicament.
94 *Fragments of Isabella*, p. 31.

6 The redemption of God in Auschwitz

1 *Korczac* (dir. Andrzej Wajda, 1990); *Jakob the Liar* (dir. Peter Kassovitz, 1999).
2 The director was interpreting Aaron Zeitlin's imagining of 'The Awakening' of Korczak, the orphans and their carers 'on the other side of that which is called life': a pure place where 'there was a breeze, which was spirit at the same time – just like the wind that had hovered above the waters at the time of Creation' (Zeitlin, 'The Last Walk of Janusz Korczak', in Korczak, *Ghetto Diary*, p. 58). Here Zeitlin depicts a God who cares for the intimate details of each and every person's life and who resurrects Korczak, his assistant Stefa and a child, Abrasha, as one new family (ibid., pp. 62–3).
3 Zeitlin, 'The Last Walk of Janusz Korczak', pp. 50, 56, 57. The *Umschlagplatz* was the railway siding where deportees were loaded onto trains bound for Treblinka and Majdanek.
4 See e.g. Yankel Wiernik, 'One Year in Treblinka Horror Camp', in Glatstein *et al.* (eds) *Anthology of Holocaust Literature*, pp. 178–85. Unlike Auschwitz, Treblinka functioned only as a death camp.
5 See Wieseltier, 'A Privation of Providence', in Kolitz, *Yosl Rakover Talks to God*, p. 92.
6 See Mortkowicz Olczakowa, 'Janosz [sic] Korczak's Last Walk', pp. 136–7. Mortkowicz Olczakowa refers to the march as crossing 'a bridge between now and eternity'.
7 James E. Young, *The Texture of Memory: Holocaust Memorials and Meaning*, New Haven and London, Yale University Press, 1993, p. 192.
8 See Linda Grant's novel, *When I Lived in Modern Times*, London, Granta, 2000, p. 211, where a young Anglo-Jewish woman, Evelyn, arrives in the Palestine of 1946 from Britain and is surprised to find that the Jews who had emigrated there after the war were callous rather than compassionate. Evelyn reports, 'It was a country of so-what people. So-what you are cold and hungry? You want to know about cold and hunger? Let me tell you where *I* have been. *I* know cold and hunger. So-what you miss your mother? My mother was gassed. And my father and my grandparents and my sisters and brothers. . . . Suffering rarely ennobles. I know that now.' See further, Hanna Yablonka, trans. Ora Cummings, *Survivors of the Holocaust: Israel after the War*, Basingstoke, Hampshire, Macmillan Press, 1999. Yablonka points out that, apprehensive of the influx of large numbers of new immigrants, Israel was often hostile to the Holocaust survivors. These latter then found that Israel could not match their idealization of a Jewish homeland.
9 *Letters from Westerbork*, p. 146.
10 It should be noted that, as a legal scheme, Judaism cannot be wholly accommodated within a narrative framework as crisis is more continuously resolved by legal judgement than by historical eventuality.
11 *To Mend the World*, p. 301. Cf. Sanhedrin 37a.
12 *The Last of the Just*, p. 350.
13 Ibid., pp. 349–50.
14 Shimon Attie's European installations powerfully illustrate my point. Between 1991 and 1996 he used a high-intensity projector to cast images of former Jewish residents back into the places they had once lived. His sense of the haunting presence of their loss led him to project them back into the present by light and air alone. The rebuke of their (re)appearance was redoubled as they disappeared all over again after a short exposure to the world of the visible. Attie's photographs of the slide projections became the after-images of after-images, the traces of traces. See further, Young, *At Memory's Edge*, pp. 62–89. For an account of the re-tracing of Jewish presence see

Martin Gilbert, *Holocaust Journey: Travelling in Search of the Past*, London, Weidenfeld & Nicolson, 1997.

15   See also Mark 16: 1–8; Matt. 28: 1–7. These verses were a particularly poignant commentary on my visit to Anne Frank's almost deserted house in Amsterdam on a late afternoon in December 1980.

16   *The Last of the Just*, p. 350.

17   Michael Hoffman, 'Translator's Preface' to Roth, *The Wandering Jews*, p. xv.

18   Gershom Scholem, trans. Michael A. Meyer and Hillel Halkin, *The Messianic Idea in Judaism And Other Essays on Jewish Spirituality*, New York, Schocken, 1971, pp. 94, 95, 109. This Sabbatian form of kabbalistic theology (sometimes accompanied by belief in a female messiah) was in currency for about one hundred and fifty years. See Scholem, *Major Trends in Jewish Mysticism*, London, Thames & Hudson, 1955, p. 323.

19   Some Torah observant Jews clearly rejoiced in their impending death, believing their suffering to be the birth pangs of the Messiah; their death would purify Israel and hasten the eschatological end (see Fackenheim, *To Mend the World*, p. 256).

20   *God and the Holocaust*, pp. 120–9.

21   Although Judaism enjoys a plurality of Messianic models, classically it is left to one man of high office and exceptional strength and wisdom to appear at a time of great need to destroy and judge Israel's enemies and, under his rule, usher in a reign of peace, prosperity, international reconciliation and universal recognition of the sovereignty of God.

22   Organizations working towards the liberative ideals of *tikkun* have included groups such as the American ecological activists, Shomrei Adamah (Guardians of the Earth), the New Jewish Agenda with its support for gay rights and its anti-racist platform, the Israeli Oz VeShalom movement's struggle for a non-aggressive, ethical Zionism in which Jews peacefully share land with the Palestinians, the Jewish Peace Fellowship, and Jewish feminist spirituality groups such as the highly influential American B'not Esh which Judith Plaskow helped to found in 1981. All these and many others, as well as progressive writers like Arthur Waskow and Marc Ellis, have made a significant practical, intellectual and spiritual contribution towards the realization of *tikkun olam*. See further Plaskow, *Standing Again at Sinai*, pp. 211–38.

23   See *These Holy Sparks: The Rebirth of the Jewish People*, San Francisco, Harper & Row, 1983.

24   *To Mend the World*, pp. 300, 302.

25   Ibid., pp. 256, 312.

26   Ibid., p. 254.

27   *Quest for Past and Future*, p. 26. Irving Greenberg develops a similar point. Talk of redemption takes place in 'moment faiths' when both the Redeemer and a vision of redemption are present to faith ('Cloud of Smoke, Pillar of Fire', p. 27). If we did not have such moments we would never have children: 'having the child makes the statement of redemption.' But these 'moment faiths' are interspersed with times when the smoke rising from the burning children almost extinguishes such faith (ibid., pp. 42, 27). Fackenheim also regards the decision to have Jewish children as a commitment to healing (*To Mend the World*, p. 216).

28   *To Mend the World*, p. 307.

29   Ibid., pp. 248, 25.

30   Ibid., p. 254.

31   *O Jerusalem! The Contested Future of the Jewish Covenant*, Minneapolis, Augsberg/Fortress, 1999, p. 81.

32   *To Mend the World*, p. 312.

33   *O Jerusalem!*, p. 174, n. 13, and pp. 75, 78, 73, 25.

34   *(God) After Auschwitz*, p. 150.

35   Ibid., p. 83.

36   Ibid.

37 Ibid., p. 150.
38 Schechter, *Studies in Judaism*, p. 169. The Baalshem Tov was the eighteenth-century founder of Hasidism.
39 Cohn-Sherbok, *God and the Holocaust*, pp. 54–5.
40 'In a World Shorn of Color', pp. 42–5.
41 'No Heroes, No Martyrs', p. 171.
42 *Auschwitz and After*, p. 163.
43 *There Is a Place*, p. 149. See also Leitner, *Fragments of Isabella*, p. 81.
44 *There is a Place.*, p. 16.
45 Ibid., p. 176.
46 *Holocaust Project*, pp. 130–1.
47 See my *Thealogy and Embodiment: The Post-Patriarchal Reconstruction of Female Sacrality*, Sheffield, Sheffield Academic Press, 1996, pp. 148–53.
48 See Gen. 37: 29, 34.
49 *She Who Dwells Within*, p. 185.
50 Badde, 'Zvi Kolitz', p. 75.
51 'Twenty Months at Auschwitz', pp. 92–3.
52 *There Is a Place*, p. 124.
53 Lengyel, *Five Chimneys*, pp. 136–7.
54 Tedeschi, *There Is a Place*, p. 4.
55 Lengyel, *Five Chimneys*, p. 47.
56 Nagy, 'No Heroes, No Martyrs', p. 174.
57 Ibid., p. 176.
58 On the importance of acquiring what she calls 'belongings' in Auschwitz, see Delbo, *Auschwitz and After*, p. 196.
59 *And the Sun Kept Shining*, p. 145.
60 Ibid., pp. 192–217.
61 Jacob Beer, the protagonist of Anne Michaels' novel *Fugitive Pieces*, p. 50, looking at photographs of these mountains of personal possessions, 'imagined that if each owner of each pair of shoes could be named, then they would be brought back to life. A cloning from intimate belongings, a mystical pangram.'
62 *Dreams of an Insomniac: Jewish Feminist Essays, Speeches and Diatribes*, Portland, OR, Eighth Mountain Press, 1990, p. 134.
63 *At Memory's Edge*, p. 82.
64 Rachel Lichtenstein and Iain Sinclair, *Rodinsky's Room*, London, Granta Books, 1999, p. 57.
65 Ibid., p. 56.
66 Susan Handelman notes that Scholem's romanticism may have led him to make too forceful a distinction between a rabbinic Judaism which triumphed over gnosticism, and theosophical kabbalism. Halakhah is also permeated by elements of myth and reciprocity. Scholem's reading of kabbalah may have provided 'a new postmodern "myth" for alienated Jews who, like their historical precursors in medieval Spain and modern Germany, [have] lost their faith in rational philosophy, progressive history, and the covenant' (*Fragments of Redemption*, pp. 101, 109, 164).
67 Rabbi Isaac Luria (1534–72) was a leading sixteenth-century Jewish mystic associated with the kabbalistic community in Safed, a small city in upper Galilee. One of the best short accounts of Luria's thought remains Scholem's essay, 'Isaac Luria and his School', in *Major Trends in Jewish Mysticism*, pp. 244–86.
68 Kabbalism's doctrine of the ten divine emanations (*sefirot*) led many to suppose it guilty of decatheism. In their defence, kabbalists insisted that the ten emanations of God are each a distinct revelation of the one unknowable *En Sof* to whom all worship is offered.
69 Kabbalists have traditionally taught that the redemption of the world and the restoration of divine unity can only be achieved by men in highly focused prayer,

study, the observance of the 613 mitzvot, and a number of technical ascetic practices of self-purification.

70   Scholem agrees with Buber's view that Hasidism strove to 'de-schematize' the kabbalistic mystery and purify the principle that the meeting with God depends on 'man's' good deeds (see Scholem, *The Messianic Idea*, pp. 237–8).

71   Arguably, Hasidic immanentism or panentheism has been somewhat exaggerated by Buber who neglected the powerful strain of Neoplatonic dualism that was introduced to Hasidism through the Kabbalah.

72   Scholem, *The Messianic Idea*, pp. 240–2.

73   See Schindler, *Hasidic Responses to the Holocaust*, p. 53.

74   Jacobs, *A Jewish Theology*, p. 234.

75   The *Zohar* or *Book of Splendour* is a foundational thirteenth-century allegorization of the Torah written in Aramaic by the Spanish Jewish mystic Moses de Leon. Sixteenth-century Lurianic mysticism is grounded in Luria's meditation on the *Zohar*.

76   This recursive element is not confined to a few specific facets of Jewish theology; it is also found in the biblical text. As Fackenheim notes in *Quest for Past and Future*, p. 39, rabbis interpret Isaiah 43: 2, 'Ye are my witnesses, saith the Lord, and I am God', as meaning that 'when humanity does not witness to God, God, ceases, as it were, to be God'. (Similarly, in the rabbinic midrash on Psalm 123: 1 and Lamentations 1: 6.) In consequence, Fackenheim observes that the relation of God and humankind is fully mutual: 'the free actions and reactions of finite men make a difference to the infinite God.' In stressing human responsibility 'they even make the omnipotent God dependent on impotent man'. In *To Mend the World*, p. 331, Fackenheim tempers his remarks of *Quest for Past and Future* and says that a greater burden should fall on the rabbinic 'as it were'. This book, however, supports Fackenheim's earlier view.

77   Schechter, *Studies in Judaism*, p. 170.

78   Batya Bauman, 'Women-identified Women in Male-identified Judaism', in Heschel (ed.), *On Being a Jewish Feminist*, pp. 88–95. Lynn Gottlieb makes the same point in *She Who Dwells Within*, p. 6.

79   Gross, 'Steps toward Feminine Imagery of Deity in Jewish Theology', in Heschel (ed.), *On Being a Jewish Feminist*, pp. 246–7.

80   Lodahl, *Shekhinah/Spirit*, p. 136.

81   See Scholem, *On the Kabbalah and Its Symbolism*, p. 107.

82   Arthur Green, 'Bride, Spouse, Daughter: Images of the Feminine in Classical Jewish Sources', in Heschel (ed.), *On Being a Jewish Feminist*, p. 255.

83   For that reason, before performing a precept Hasidim commonly recite the formula based on that of Zohar III. 51b, 'For the sake of the unification of the Holy One, Blessed be He, and His Shekhinah'.

84   *ReVisions*, p. 169.

85   *She Who Dwells Within*, p. 7.

86   'Steps toward Feminine Imagery of Deity in Jewish Theology', p. 234. Gross also makes this point to introduce her article, 'Female God Language in a Jewish Context', in Christ and Plaskow (eds), *Womanspirit Rising*, p. 167. Judith Plaskow likewise insists that 'the long-suppressed femaleness of God, acknowledged in the mystical tradition, but even here shaped and articulated by men, must be recovered and reexplored and reintegrated into the Godhead' ('The Right Question Is Theological', in Heschel (ed.), *On Being A Jewish Feminist*, pp. 231–2).

87   *Writing as Resistance*, p. 16.

88   Chani Smith, 'The Symbol of the Shekhinah – the Feminine Side of God', in Alix Pirani (ed.), *The Absent Mother: Restoring the Goddess to Judaism and Christianity*, London, Mandala, 1991, p. 6.

89   Lodahl, *Shekhinah/Spirit*, p. 87.

90   See Smith, 'The Symbol of the Shekhinah', p. 6.

91   Helen Freeman, 'Chochmah and Wholeness: Retrieving the Feminine in Judaism', in

Sybil Sheridan (ed.), *Hear Our Voice: Women Rabbis Tell Their Stories*, London, SCM Press, 1994, p. 187. On the Shekhinah's role in the redemption of the soul see Buber, *The Origin and Meaning of Hasidism*, New York, Harper & Row, 1960, pp. 202–18. See further, Goldstein, *ReVisions*, pp. 167–70; Ephraim Urbach, *The Sages: Their Concepts and Beliefs*, Jerusalem, Magnes Press, 1979, pp. 37–65.

92 Schindler, *Hasidic Responses to the Holocaust*, p. 26.

93 The subordination of Shekhinah should not be underestimated. Elliot Wolfson has discussed the (homo)eroticization of the figure of Shekhinah in medieval Jewish mysticism where her femininity – far from that of the feminist vision – is thoroughly absorbed by a (literally) phallocentric vision of divine revelation (*Through a Speculum That Shines*, *passim* and summarized pp. 395–7).

94 Certain acts, such as the practice of male circumcision, uncover the Shekhinah so that she can receive the influx of divine light, for the Shekhinah, according to patriarchal conception, is something of a channel. Like the moon, she has no light of her own but shines by the light she reflects. For this reason, and because she is the 'lowest' rung of the divine ladder, she is sometimes held to be closest to the powers of evil and can be colonized by those as well as by beneficent powers. Her passivity leaves her available to sexual colonization as well. Some early Hasidic documents, in the fervour of their love for God, describe the spiritual arousal and swaying motion of prayer as a form of sexual intercourse (*zivvug*) with the Shekhinah; the *Zohar* claims that Moses had intercourse with the Shekhinah and that the Shekhinah substitutes for the body of a wife when she is menstruating or when the husband is away or studying (Jacobs, *Hasidic Prayer*, pp. 60–1).

95 See further, Elliot R. Wolfson, *Circle in the Square: Studies in the Use of Gender in Kabbalistic Symbolism*, Albany, State University of New York Press, 1995.

96 Gottlieb, *She Who Dwells Within*, p. 22.

97 For an outline of the role of the Shekhinah in rabbinic tradition see Chapter 3 of the present study.

98 *Engendering Judaism*, pp. 118–19.

99 *On Judaism*, p. 106.

100 'Memoirs of Auschwitz Survivors', p. 335.

101 See my *Thealogy and Embodiment*, pp. 288–96.

102 See Frankel, *The Five Books of Miriam*, p. 37.

103 Gloria Orenstein, *The Reflowering of the Goddess*, New York, Pergamon Press, 1990, pp. 100–1.

104 'Spirituality for Survival', pp. 132–3.

105 Mortley, *French Philosophers in Conversation*, p. 21.

106 Berkovits, *Faith After the Holocaust*, pp. 124, 127.

107 Buber, *The Origin and Meaning of Hasidism*, p. 28.

108 *Shekhinah/Spirit*, p. 136.

109 Cf. Isaiah 63: 9: 'In all their troubles He was troubled, and the angel of His Presence delivered them. In His love and pity He Himself redeemed them, Raised them, and exalted them all the days of old.'

110 Cited without a reference in Freeman, 'Chochmah and Wholeness', p. 187.

111 See e.g. Lewinska, 'Twenty Months at Auschwitz', pp. 87–8.

112 *Difficile liberté*, pp. 122, 123. It should be noted that Levinas insists that the moral law of the face does not promise a happy ending; faith is believing in responsibility and love without victory or reward. See also Mortley, *French Philosophers in Conversation*, p. 21.

113 See Z'ev ben Shimon Halevi, *Kabbalah: Tradition of Hidden Knowledge*, London, Thames & Hudson, 1979, p. 5.

114 Similarly Arthur Green points out that the self-revelation of God requires an other to whom God can be revealed. The flow of divine energy which is experienced as God's love for the world needs witness and response. Indeed, the divine had to withdraw

some way from being (*tsim tsum*) in order to be seen and so that we could be the other who is witness to God (*Seek My Face, Speak My Name*, pp. 161–2).

115 See also Gen. 1: 4, 10, 12, 18, 21, 25.

116 For a non-holocaustal discussion of this redemptive struggle, again in mystical idiom, see my '"Refresh me with Apples for I am Faint with Love" (Song of Songs 2.5): Jewish Feminism, Mystical Theology and the Sexual Imaginary', in Lisa Isherwood (ed.), *The Good News of the Body: Sexual Theology and Feminism*, Sheffield, Sheffield Academic Press, 2000, pp. 54–72, esp. pp. 63–72.

117 Jewish Goddess feminism is a phenomenon of the far Jewish left, but this too is not an uncritical adoption of ancient paganisms. See my 'Goddess Religion, Postmodern Jewish Feminism and the Complexity of Alternative Religious Identities', *Nova Religio* 1 (1998), pp. 198–215.

The princess and the city of death

1 *Aggadah* is an Aramaic word from the Hebrew *haggadah*, itself from the root 'to tell' or 'relate'. In Jewish tradition, *aggadah* comprises biblical tales, rabbinical midrashic elaborations of biblical stories, legends of post-biblical figures and rabbinic sages, and theological, philosophical and ethical material. There is a complex relation between the aggadic and the halakhic material in rabbinic literature, though the two are usually regarded as distinct from one another. *Aggadah*, with its more popular emphasis on miracles and legends, is not a basis for halakhic judgements. However, the ethical material in the *aggadah* can nonetheless inform the spirit of halakhah, sensitizing it to human needs and feelings (Chaim Pearl, *Theology in Rabbinic Stories*, Peabody, MA, Hendrickson, 1997, p. 3 and ibid., p. 2, on the distinctive ethical truths of rabbinic fictions). See also David Stern and Mark Jay Mirsky's edited anthology, *Rabbinic Fantasies: Imaginative Narratives from Classical Hebrew Literature*, London, Yale University Press, 1998.

2 Some of the finest of these tales of enchantment and wonder are attributed to the nineteenth-century Hasidic master, Rabbi Nachman of Bratslav. Rabbi Nachman's allegories of the Shekhinah – the Bride of God – who, as the lost, exiled or imprisoned princess, will be freed with the coming of the Messiah, were not only stories about the business of the heavenly court, but also allegories about how each individual can seek their own 'lost princess' or soul in order to bring about a microcosm of the macrocosmic redemption. (Howard Schwartz, *Elijah's Violin and Other Jewish Folktales*, Harmondsworth, Penguin, 1983, p. 21). I am conscious that religious feminism is not well served by perpetuating the hierarchical motif of 'princess' which connotes hyper-privilege and, as an accessory of power, sexual and genetic commodification. However, it seems to me that the transformation of tradition requires a measure of continuity with traditional imaginal frameworks and forms of numinous experience early established in childhood. Monarchical imagery may be antiquated and oppressively hierarchical, but it can also signal in a highly accessible manner what is numinously other to or discontinuous with the (here, patriarchal) norm.

3 Schwartz, 'Introduction' to *idem, Elijah's Violin*, pp. 11–13.

4 Gisella Perl witnessed this atrocity in Auschwitz. See *idem*, 'A Doctor in Auschwitz', in Rittner and Roth (eds), *Different Voices*, p. 113.

Select glossary of Hebrew and Yiddish terms

aggadah	(Aramaic) from the Hebrew *haggadah*, itself from the root 'to tell' or 'relate'. Aggadah comprises biblical tales, rabbinical midrashic elaborations of biblical stories, legends of post-biblical figures and rabbinic sages, and theological, philosophical and ethical material.
Ashkenazic	referring to Jews from western, central and eastern Europe
avodah begashmiut	service to God through the ordinary conditions of life
avodah halev	religious 'service of the heart'
The Baalshem Tov	the eighteenth-century founder of Hasidism, a mystical, pietistic sect of Orthodox Judaism
baleboosteh (Yiddish)	bourgeois Jewish housewife
cheder	religious school
devekuth	the mystical experience of cleaving to God
emunah	trust, sometimes weakly translated as 'faith'
En Sof	the unknowable God-in-God's-self
galut	exile
halakhah	Jewish law
hesed	translatable as loving kindness, faithfulness, or gracious love
hester panim	the hiding of God's face. A traditional term used to evoke the withholding of God's power to avert human suffering
'hinneni'	the 'I am here' or 'here I am' attributed to key biblical protagonists when responding to the summons of God
kabbalah	broadly, the Jewish mystical tradition
kavannah	spiritual focus and intentionality
kavod	divine radiance or glory
kedushah	holiness (*kadosh* – holy)
Kiddush ha' hayim	the sanctification of God's name in life
Kiddush Ha' Shem	the sanctification of God's name, often through martyrdom
kipper	commonly translated as 'to atone', but cognate with 'rubbing off' or decontamination and 'covering'
kittel	a white robe worn by observant male Jews on Yom Kippur that symbolizes their spiritual and bodily purity as well as denoting human mortality
Lamedvovnik (Yiddish)	Just Man or one of the Thirty-Six Hidden Saints who, according to Jewish legend, are concealed in every generation and upon whom the fate of the world depends

maaseh	a traditional Jewish tale, often in the form of an allegory, combining universal fairy-tale, magical and religio-mythical elements
menschlekheit (Yiddish)	a humane attitude and code of behaviour
midrash	rabbinic commentary or, more generally, a new religious story told to interpret an old one
mikvah	ritual bath
mishkan	'Tent of Meeting', the portable desert shrine that was eventually replaced by the Jerusalem Temple
niddah	menstruant
olam ha' ba	the world to come
Rebbe	a Hasidic master whose learning, wisdom and spiritual charisma attracts loyal disciples
sefirah (pl. *sefirot*)	a kabbalistic term denoting an emanation of God
shalem	to be complete or perfect (cf. *shalom*, a state of wholeness, and therefore peace)
(The) Shekhinah	the indwelling presence of God, traditionally figured as a 'female' hypostasis or attribute, but one nonetheless subordinated to the masculinity of God. Contemporary Jewish feminists have reclaimed the Shekhinah, often dropping the definite article and using the name Shekhinah to denote the female character of the divine personality, instead of, or in complementary relation to, God's masculine attributes.
shtetl (Yiddish)	small east European Jewish townships, many of which were in decline before the Holocaust eradicated them altogether
tallit	prayer shawl
tikkun atzmi	the mending or healing of the self
tikkun olam	the redemptive healing, mending or restoration of the world
tselem Elohim	the image of God
tsim tsum	God's creative contraction from a space within God-self to make space for the world
yeshivah	rabbinic seminary
The *Zohar*	or *Book of Splendour* is a foundational thirteenth-century allegorization of the Torah written in Aramaic, probably by the Spanish Jewish mystic Moses de Leon. Sixteenth-century Lurianic mysticism is grounded in Rabbi Isaac Luria's meditation on the *Zohar*.

Bibliography

Adelman, Penina V., 'A Drink from Miriam's Cup: Invention of Tradition Among Jewish Women', *Journal of Feminist Studies in Religion* 2 (1994), pp. 151–66.

Adelsberger, Lucie, *Auschwitz: A Doctor's Story*, trans. Susan Ray, London, Robson Books, 1996.

Adler, Rachel, 'The Jew Who Wasn't There: *Halakhah* and the Jewish Woman', in Heschel (ed.), *On Being a Jewish Feminist*, pp. 12–18.

—— *Engendering Judaism: An Inclusive Theology and Ethics*, Philadelphia, The Jewish Publication Society, 1988.

Adler, Ruth, 'Woman of the Eighties', interviewed by Ruth Swirsky, in Copperman *et al.* (eds), *Generations of Memories*, pp. 25–47.

Altizer, Thomas J.J., 'The Holocaust and the Theology of the Death of God', in Haynes and Roth (eds), *The Death of God Movement and the Holocaust*, pp. 17–23.

Altman, Rita, 'Conflicts and Contradictions', interviewed by Ruth Swirsky, in Copperman *et al.* (eds), *Generations of Memories*, pp. 104–32.

Antler, Joyce (ed.), *Talking Back: Images of Jewish Women in American Popular Culture*, Brandeis, Waltham, MA, Brandeis University Press, 1997.

Appelfeld, Aahron, *For Every Sin*, trans. Jeffrey M. Green, London, Weidenfeld & Nicolson, 1989.

Armstrong, John, *The Idea of the Holy and the Humane Response,* London, Allen & Unwin, 1981.

Badde, Paul, 'Zvi Kolitz', in Kolitz, (ed.), *Yosl Rakover Talks to God*, pp. 27–77.

Baker, Adrienne, *The Jewish Woman in Contemporary Society: Transitions and Traditions*, Basingstoke and London, Macmillan, 1993.

Balentine, Samuel E., *The Hiding of the Face of God in the Old Testament*, Oxford, Oxford University Press, 1983.

Baskin, Judith, R., 'Rabbinic Judaism and the Construction of Woman', in Peskowitz and Levitt (eds), *Judaism Since Gender*, pp. 125–30.

Bauman, Batya, 'Women-identified Women in Male-identified Judaism', in Heschel (ed.), *On Being a Jewish Feminist*, pp. 88–95.

Bauman, Zygmunt, *Modernity and the Holocaust*, Cambridge, Polity Press, 1989.

Baumel, Judith Tydor, *Kolot Mikommando Kanada* (Voices from the 'Canada' Commando), Jeusalem, Emunah, 1989.

—— 'Social Interaction among Jewish Women in Crisis during the Holocaust', *Gender and History* 7 (1995), pp. 64–84.

—— 'Gender and Family Studies of the Holocaust', *Women: A Cultural Review* 7 (1996), pp. 114–24.

—— *Double Jeopardy: Gender and the Holocaust*, London, Vallentine Mitchell & Co., 1998.

—— Women's Agency and Survival Strategies During the Holocaust', *Women's Studies International Forum* 22 (1999), pp. 329–47.

Beauvoir, Simone de, *The Second Sex*, trans. H.M. Pashely, Harmondsworth, Middx., Penguin, 1972.

Begley, Louis, *Wartime Lies*, London and Basingstoke, Picador, 1992.

Benisch, Pearl, *To Vanquish the Dragon*, Jerusalem and New York, Philip Feldheim, 1991.

Berenbaum, Michael, *After Tragedy and Triumph: Essays in Modern Jewish Thought and the American Experience*, Cambridge, Cambridge University Press, 1990.

Berkovits, Eliezer, *Faith After the Holocaust*, New York, Ktav, 1973.

—— *With God in Hell: Judaism in the Ghettos and Deathcamps*, New York and London, Sanhedrin, 1979.

Bernasconi, Robert and David Wood (eds), *The Provocation of Levinas: Rethinking the Other*, London and New York, Routledge, 1988.

Bernstein, Sara Tuvel, Louise Toots Thornton and Marlene Bernst Samuels, *The Seamstress, A Memoir of Survival*, New York, Putnam, 1997.

Biale, Rachel, *Women and Jewish Law: An Exploration of Women's Issues in Halakhic Sources*, New York, Schocken Books, 1984.

Birger, Trudi and Jeffrey M. Green, *A Daughter's Gift of Love: A Holocaust Memoir*, Philadelphia, Jewish Publication Society, 1992.

Bitton-Jackson, Livia, *I Have Lived a Thousand Years: Growing Up in the Holocaust*, London, Simon & Schuster, 1999.

Blanchard, Tsvi, 'The Search for the Holy in a Consumer Society', in Rodney Clapp (ed.), *The Consuming Passion: Christianity and the Consumer Culture*, Downers Grove, IL, InterVarsity Press, 1998, pp. 91–106.

Blumenthal, David, *Facing the Abusing God: A Theology of Protest*, Louisville, KY, Westminster/John Knox Press, 1993.

Bondy, Ruth, 'Women in Theresienstadt the Family Camp in Birkenau', in Ofer and Weitzman (eds), *Women in the Holocaust*, pp. 310–26.

Boyarin, Daniel, 'Justify My Love' in Peskowitz and Levitt (eds), *Judaism Since Gender*, pp. 131–7.

Braiterman, Zachary, *(God)After Auschwitz: Tradition and Change in Post-Holocaust Jewish Thought*, Princeton, NJ, Princeton University Press, 1998.

Brenner, Rachel Feldhay, *Writing as Resistance: Four Women Confronting the Holocaust. Edith Stein, Simone Weil, Anne Frank, Etty Hillesum*, University Park, PA, Pennsylvania State University Press, 1997.

Brod, Harry (ed.), *A Mensch Among Men: Explorations in Jewish Masculinity*, Freedom, CA, Crossing Press, 1988.

Broner, Esther M. with Naomi Nimrod, *The Women's Haggadah*, New York, HarperSan Francisco, 1993, p. 12.

Brown, Joanne Carlson and Rebecca Parker, '"For God So Loved the World"?' in Joanne Carlson Brown and C.R. Bohn (eds), *Christianity, Patriarchy and Abuse: A Feminist Critique*, New York, Pilgrim Press, 1989, pp. 1–30.

Buber, Martin, *Tales of the Hasidim: The Early Masters*, trans. Olga Marx, New York, Schocken, 1947.

—— *The Eclipse of God: Studies in the Relation Between Religion and Philosophy*, New York, Harper & Brothers, 1952.

—— *Pointing the Way: Collected Essays*, trans. Maurice Friedman, New York, Harper and Brothers, 1957.

—— *I and Thou*, trans. Ronald Gregor Smith, New York, Charles Scribner's Sons, 1958.

—— *The Prophetic Faith*, New York, Harper Torchbooks, 1960.

—— *The Origin and Meaning of Hasidism*, New York, Harper & Row, 1960.

—— *Tales of the Hasidim: Later Masters*, New York, Schocken, 1961.

—— *On Judaism,* ed. Nahum N. Glatzer, New York, Schocken Books, 1967.

—— *On the Bible*, New York, Schocken Books, 1967.

—— *I and Thou*, trans. Walter Kaufmann, New York, Charles Scribner's Sons, 1970.

Campbell, Debra, 'Hannah Whitall Smith (1832–1911): Theology of the Moher-hearted God'. *Signs* 15 (1989), pp. 79–101.

Cantor, Aviva, 'A Jewish Woman's Haggadah', in Christ and Plaskow (eds), *Womanspirit Rising*, pp. 185–92.

Chalier, Catherine, 'Ethics and the Feminine', in Robert Bernasconi and Simon Critchley (eds), *Re-reading Levinas*, Bloomington, Indiana University Press, 1991, pp. 119–30.

Chanter, Tina, 'Feminism and the Other', in Bernasconi and Wood (eds), *The Provocation of Levinas*, pp. 32–56.

Chicago, Judy, *Holocaust Project: From Darkness into Light*, New York, Viking, 1993.

Chodorow, Nancy, *The Reproduction of Mothering: Psychoanalyisis and the Sociology of Gender*, Berkeley and Los Angeles, University of California Press, 1978.

Chopp, Rebecca, *The Power to Speak*, New York, Crossroad, 1989.

Christ, Carol P. and Judith Plaskow (eds), *Womanspirit Rising: A Feminist Reader in Religion*, New York, HarperSanFrancisco, 1992.

Cohen, Arthur, A., *The Tremendum: A Theological Interpretation of the Holocaust*, New York, Continuum, 1993.

—— 'An Autobiographical Fragment, The Holocaust', in Stern and Mendes-Flohr (eds), *An Arthur A. Cohen Reader*, pp. 250–3.

—— 'Thinking the Tremendum, Some Theological Implications of the Death Camps', in Stern and Mendes-Flohr (eds), *An Arthur A. Cohen Reader*, pp. 234–49.

Cohen, Shaye J.D., 'Purity and Peity: The Separation of the Menstruant from the Sancta', in Grossman and Haut (eds), *Daughters of the King*, pp. 103–16.

Cohn-Sherbok, Dan, *Jewish Mysticism: An Anthology*, Oxford, Oneworld Publications, 1995.

—— *God and the Holocaust*, Leominster, Herefordshire, Gracewing, 1996.

—— *Modern Judaism*, Basingstoke, Hampshire, Macmillan, 1996.

—— *Holocaust Theology: A Reader*, Exeter, Exeter University Press, 2002.

Copperman, Jeanette, Hannah Kanter, Judy Keiner and Ruth Swirsky (eds), *Generations of Memories: Voices of Jewish Women,* London, The Women's Press, 1989.

Davidman, Lynn and Shelly Tenenbaum (eds), *Feminist Perspectives on Jewish Studies,* New Haven and London, Yale University Press, 1994.

Davidman, Lynn and Shelly Tenenbaum, 'Toward a Feminist Sociology of American Jews' in *idem*, (eds), *Feminist Perspectives on Jewish Studies*, pp. 140–68.

Delbo, Charlotte, *Auschwitz and After*, trans. R.C. Lamont, New Haven, Yale University Press, 1995.

DeSilva, Tara (ed.), *In Memory's Kitchen: A Legacy from the Women of Terezín*, Northvale, NJ, Jason Aronson, 1996.

Dorff, Elliot N. and Newman, Louis E., *Contemporary Jewish Theology: A Reader*, New York and London, Oxford University Press, 1999.

Dwork, Deborah, *Children With a Star: Jewish Youth in Nazi Europe*, New Haven, Yale University Press, 1991.

—— and Robert Jan van Pelt, *Auschwitz: 1270 to the Present*, New York, W.W. Norton & Co., 1997.

Dworkin, Andrea, *Scapegoat: The Jews, Israel and Women's Liberation*, London, Virago, 2000.

Eilenberg, Anna, ed. Penina Soloveitchik, *Sisters in the Storm*, New York, London and Jerusalem, CIS, 1992.

Eliach, Yaffa, *There Once Was a World: A 900 Year Chronicle of the Shtetl of Eishyshok*, Boston, New York and London, Little, Brown & Co., 1998.

Elias, Ruth, *Triumph of Hope: From Theresienstadt and Auschwitz to Israel*, trans. M. Bettauer Dembo, New York, John Wiley & Sons, 1988.

Ellis, Marc H., *Toward a Jewish Theology of Liberation*, London, SCM Press, 1987.

—— *O Jerusalem! The Contested Future of the Jewish Covenant*, Minneapolis, Augsberg/Fortress, 1999.

Elman, Amy, 'Lesbians and the Holocaust', in Fuchs (ed.), *Women and the Holocaust*, pp. 9–17.

El-Or, Tamar, *Educated and Ignorant: Ultraorthodox Women and Their World*, trans. Haim Watzman, Boulder, CO and London, Lynne Reinner Publishers, 1994.

Epstein, Helen, *Children of the Holocaust*, New York, Viking Penguin, 1988.

Epstein, Isidore, *Judaism: A Historical Presentation*, Harmondsworth, Penguin Books, 1959.

Exum, Cheryl, J., *Plotted, Shot and Painted: Cultural Representations of Biblical Women*, Sheffield, Sheffield Academic Press, 1996.

Fackenheim, Emil, L., *Quest for Past and Future: Essays in Jewish Theology*, Boston, Beacon Press, 1970.

—— *God's Presence in History: Jewish Affirmations and Philosophical Reflections*, New York, Harper & Row, 1972.

—— 'The Holocaust and the State of Israel: Their Relation', in Fleishner (ed.), *Auschwitz: Beginning of a New Era?*, pp. 205–15.

—— *The Jewish Return into History: Reflections in the Age of Auschwitz and a New Jerusalem*, New York, Schocken Books, 1978.

—— *To Mend the World: Foundations of Future Jewish Thought*, New York, Schocken Books, 1982.

Farley, Wendy, *Tragic Vision and Divine Compassion: A Contemporary Theodicy*, Louisville, KY, Westminster/John Knox Press, 1990.

Fein, Helen, 'Genocide and Gender: The Uses of Women and Group Destiny', *Journal of Genocide Research* 1 (1999), pp. 43–64.

Ferderber-Salz, Bertha, *And the Sun Kept Shining . . .*, New York, Holocaust Library, 1980.

Flanzbaum, Hilene, 'The Americanization of the Holocaust', *Journal of Genocide Research* 1 (1999), pp. 91–104.

Fleischner, Eva, (ed.), *Auschwitz: Beginning of a New Era? Reflections on the Holocaust*, New York, Ktav, 1977.

Frankel, Ellen, *The Five Books of Miriam: A Woman's Commentary on the Torah*, New York, HarperSanFrancisco, 1998.

Frankl, Victor E., trans. Ilse Lasch, *Man's Search for Meaning: An Introduction to Logotherapy*, Boston, Beacon Press, 1962.

Freeman, Helen, 'Chochmah and Wholeness: Retrieving the Feminine in Judaism', in Sybil Sheridan (ed.), *Hear Our Voice, Women Rabbis Tell Their Stories*, London, SCM Press, 1994, pp. 179–89.

Fuchs, Esther (ed.), *Women and the Holocaust: Narrative and Representation*, Studies in the Shoah, vol. xxii, Lanham, MD, University Press of America, 1999.

—— 'The Construction of Heroines in Holocaust Films: The Jewess as Beautiful Soul', in *idem* (ed.), *Women and the Holocaust*, pp. 97–112.

Gelissen, Rena Kornriech with Heather Dune MacAdam, *Rena's Promise: A Story of Sisters in Auschwitz*, Boston, Beacon Press, 1996.

Gilbert, Martin, *Holocaust Journey: Travelling in Search of the Past*, London, Weidenfeld & Nicolson, 1997.

Gilligan, Carol, *In a Different Voice: Psychological Theory and Women's Development*, Cambridge, Mass., Harvard University Press, 1982.

Gillis-Carlbach, Miriam, 'Jewish Mothers and Their Children During the Holocaust: Changing Tasks of the Motherly Role', in Roth and Maxwell (eds), *Remembering for the Future*, pp. 230–47.

Glatstein, Jacob, Israel Knox and Samuel Margoshes (eds), *Anthology of Holocaust Literature*, New York, Atheneum, 1985.

Goldberg, Michael, *Why Should Jews Survive? Looking Past the Holocaust Toward a Jewish Future*, New York, Oxford University Press, 1995.

Goldenberg, Myrna, 'Different Horrors, Same Hell: Women Remembering the Holocaust', in Roger S. Gottlieb (ed.), *Thinking the Unthinkable: Meanings of the Holocaust*, New York, Paulist Press, 1990, pp. 150–66.

—— ' "From a World Beyond": Women in the Holocaust', *Feminist Studies* 22 (1996), pp. 667–87.

—— 'Memoirs of Auschwitz Survivors: The Burden of Gender', in Ofer and Weitzman (eds), *Women in the Holocaust*, pp. 327–339.

—— 'Food Talk: Gendered Responses to Hunger in Concentration Camps', in Roth and Maxwell (eds), *Remembering for the Future*, pp. 248–57.

Goldhagen, Daniel Jonah, *Hitler's Willing Executioners: Ordinary Germans and the Holocaust*, London, Abacus, 1997.

Goldin, Hyman E., *The Jewish Woman and Her Home*, New York, Hebrew Publishing Co., 1978.

Goldstein, Elyse, *ReVisions: Seeing Torah Through a Feminist Lens*, Woodstock, VT, Jewish Lights Publishing, 1998.

Gottlieb, Lynn, *She Who Dwells Within: A Feminist Vision of a Renewed Judaism*, San Francisco, HarperSanfrancisco, 1995.

Graetz, Naomi, *Silence is Deadly: Judaism Confronts Wife Beating*, Northvale, NJ, Jason Aronson, 1998.

Grant, Linda, *When I Lived in Modern Times*, London, Granta, 2000.

Green, Arthur, 'Bride, Spouse, Daughter: Images of the Feminine in Classical Jewish Sources', in Heschel (ed.), *On Being a Jewish Feminist*, pp. 248–60.

—— (ed.), *Jewish Spirituality from the Sixteenth-Century Revival to the Present*, London, SCM Press, 1989.

—— *Seek My Face, Speak My Name: A Contemporary Jewish Theology*, Northvale, NJ and London, Jason Aronson, 1992.

Greenberg, Blu, *On Women and Judaism: A View from Tradition*, Philadelphia, Jewish Publication Society of America, 1981.

Greenberg, Gershon, 'The Death of History and the Life of Akeda: Voices from the War', in Haynes and Roth (eds), *The Death of God Movement and the Holocaust*, pp. 99–109.

Greenberg, Irving, 'Cloud of Smoke, Pillar of Fire: Judaism, Christianity, and Modernity after the Holocaust', in Fleischner (ed.), *Auschwitz: Beginning of a New Era?*, pp. 7–55.

—— 'Voluntary Covenant', in Jacobs (ed.), *Contemporary Jewish Religious Responses to the Holocaust*, pp. 78–105.

Grey, Mary, *Redeeming the Dream: Feminism, Redemption and the Christian Tradition*, London, SPCK, 1989.

Gross, Rita M., 'Steps toward Feminine Imagery of Deity in Jewish Theology', in Heschel (ed.), *On Being a Jewish Feminist*, pp. 234–47.

——— 'Female God Language in a Jewish Context', in Christ and Plaskow (eds), *Womanspirit Rising*, pp. 167–73.

Grossman, Susan and Rivka Haut (eds), *Daughters of the King: Women and the Synagogue. A Survey of History, Halakhah, and Contemporary Realities*, Philadelphia, Jewish Publication Society, 1992.

Gurewitsch, Brana and Leon J. Weinberger (eds), *Mothers, Sisters, Resisters: Oral Histories of Women Who Survived the Holocaust*, Tuscaloosa, University of Alabama Press, 1999.

Gutman, Israel, Michael Berenbaum and Raul Hilberg (eds), *Anatomy of the Auschwitz Death Camp*, Bloomington, Indiana University Press, 1998.

Halevi, Z'ev ben Shimon, *Kabbalah: Tradition of Hidden Knowledge*, London, Thames & Hudson, 1979.

Halter, Marek, *The Book of Abraham*, London, Collins, 1986.

Hand, Séan (ed.), *The Levinas Reader,* Oxford, Blackwell, 1989.

Handelman, Susan A., *Fragments of Redemption: Jewish Thought and Literary Theory in Benjamin, Scholem, and Levinas,* Bloomington and Indianapolis, Indiana University Press, 1991.

Hart, Kitty, *Return to Auschwitz,* St Albans, Herts., Granada Publishing, 1983.

Hauptman, Judith, *Rereading the Rabbis: A Woman's Voice*, Boulder, CO, Westview Press, 1998.

Haut, Rivka, 'The Presence of Women', in Grossman and Haut (eds), *Daughters of the King*, pp. 274–8.

Haynes, Stephen R. and John K. Roth (eds), *The Death of God Movement and the Holocaust: Radical Theology Encounters the Shoah*, Westport, CT and London, Greenwood Press, 1999.

Hertzberg, Arthur and Aron Hirt-Manheimer, *Jews: The Essence and Character of a People*, San Francisco, HarperCollins, 1998.

Heschel, Abraham Joshua, *God in Search of Man*, New York, Farrar, Straus & Cudahy, 1956.

——— *The Prophets*, New York, HarperCollins, 1975.

Heschel, Susannah (ed.), *On Being a Jewish Feminist: A Reader*, New York, Schocken Books, 1983.

Hilberg, Raul, *Perpetrators, Victims, Bystanders: The Jewish Catastrophe 1933–1945*, New York, HarperCollins, 1992.

Hillesum, Etty, *Etty: A Diary 1941–43,* trans. Arnold J. Pomerans, London, Grafton Books, 1985.

——— *Letters from Westerbork,* trans. Arnold J. Pomerans, London, Grafton Books, 1988.

Holden, Pat (ed.), *Women's Religious Experience*, London, Croom Helm, 1983.

Horowitz, Sara R., 'Mengele, the Gynecologist, and Other Stories of Women's Survival', in Peskowitz and Levitt (eds), *Judaism Since Gender*, pp. 200–12.

Huberband, Shimon, *Kiddush Hashem: Jewish Religious and Cultural Life in Poland During the Holocaust*, trans. David E. Fishman; Jeffrey S. Gwock and Robert S. Hirt (eds), Hoboken, NJ and New York, Yeshiva University Press, Ktav Publishing House, 1987.

Hyman, Paula E. 'Gender and the Jewish Family in Modern Europe', in Ofer and Weitzman (eds), *Women in the Holocaust*, p. 228.

Hyman, Rachel. 'The Jewish Family: Looking for a Usable Past', in Heschel (ed.), *On Being a Jewish Feminist*, pp. 19–26.

Isaacman, Clara, as told to Joan Adess Grossman, *Clara's Story*, Philadelphia, The Jewish Publication Society of America, 1984.

Jacobs, Louis, *A Jewish Theology*, London, Darton, Longman & Todd, 1973.

——— *Hasidic Thought*, New York, Behrman House, Inc., 1976.

——— *Hasidic Prayer*, London, The Litman Library of Jewish Civilization, 1993.

Jacobs, Steven L. (ed.), *Contemporary Jewish Religious Responses to the Holocaust,* Lanham, MD, New York and London, University Press of America, 1993.

Jacobson, Jane, 'A Document of Roses', *Feminist Studies* 22 (1996), pp. 657–66.

Janowitz, Naomi and Maggie Wenig, 'Sabbath Prayers for Women', in Christ and Plaskow (eds), *Womanspirit Rising,* pp. 174–8.

Jantzen, Grace M., *Becoming Divine: Towards a Feminist Philosophy of Religion,* Manchester, Manchester University Press, 1998.

Julius, Anthony, *Idolizing Pictures: Idolatry, Iconoclasm and Jewish Art,* London, Thames & Hudson, 2000.

Kaplan, Marion A., *Between Dignity and Despair: Jewish Life in Nazi Germany,* Oxford, Oxford University Press, 1999.

Katz, Steven, *Post-Holocaust Dialogues: Critical Studies in Modern Jewish Thought,* New York, New York University Press, 1983.

—— 'The Holocaust. Jewish Theological Responses', in Mircea Eliade (ed.), *The Encyclopedia of Religion,* New York, Macmillan, 1987, vol. 6, pp. 423–31.

—— *The Holocaust in Historical Context,* vol. 1, *The Holocaust and Mass Death Before the Modern Age,* New York and Oxford, Oxford University Press, 1994.

Kellenbach, Katharina von, 'Reproduction and Resistance during the Holocaust', in Fuchs (ed.), *Women and the Holocaust,* pp. 19–32.

Klepfisz, Irena, *Dreams of an Insomnniac: Jewish Feminist Essays, Speeches and Diatribes,* Portland, OR, Eighth Mountain Press, 1990.

Kolitz, Zvi, *Yosl Rakover Talks to God,* trans. C. Brown Janeway, from the edition established by Paul Badde, London, Jonathan Cape, 1999.

Koonz, Claudia, *Mothers in the Fatherland: Women, the Family and Nazi Politics,* New York, St Martin's Press, 1987.

Korczak, Janusz, trans. *Ghetto Diary,* Jerzy Bachrach and Barbara Krzywicka, New York, Holocaust Library, 1978.

Kornbluth, Sarah Tikvah and Doron Kornbluth (eds), *Jewish Women Speak Out about Jewish Matters,* Souhfield, MI, Targum, 2000.

Kunin, Seth D., 'Judaism', in Jean Holm (ed.), with John Bowker, *Sacred Space,* London, Pinter, 1994, pp. 115–48.

—— *God's Place in the World: Sacred Space and Sacred Place in Judaism,* London and New York, Cassell, 1998.

Kurzman, Dan, *The Bravest Battle,* Los Angeles, Pinnacle, 1978.

Laderman Ukeles, Mierle, 'Mikva Dreams: A Performance', in Umansky and Ashton (eds), *Four Centuries of Jewish Women's Spirituality,* pp. 218–20.

Langer, Lawrence, *Versions of Survival: The Holocaust and the Human Spirit,* Albany, State University of New York Press, 1982.

—— *Holocaust Testimonies: The Ruins of Memory,* New Haven and London, Yale University Press, 1991.

—— *Admitting the Holocaust: Collected Essays,* New York, Oxford University Press, 1995.

—— 'Gendered Suffering? Women in Holocaust Testimonies', in Ofer and Weitzman (eds), *Women in the Holocaust,* pp. 351–63.

Larrabee, Mary Jeanne (ed.), *An Ethic of Care: Feminist and Interdisciplinary Perspectives,* London, Routledge, 1993.

Laytner, Anson, *Arguing With God: A Jewish Tradition,* Northvale, NJ, Jason Aronson, 1990.

Leaman, Oliver, *Evil and Suffering in Jewish Philosphy,* Cambridge, Cambridge University Press, 1995.

Leddy, Mary Jo, 'A Different Power', in Rittner and Roth (eds), *Different Voices,* pp. 359–62.

Leiser, Burton M., 'The Sanctity of the Profane: A Pharisaic Critique of Rudolf Otto', *Judaism* 20 (1971), pp. 87–92.

Leitner, Isabella, *Fragments of Isabella: A Memoir of Auschwitz*, ed. Irving A. Leitner, New York, Thomas Y. Crowell, 1978.

Lengyel, Olga, *Five Chimneys: The Story of Auschwitz*, New York, Howard Fertig, 1995.

Lentin, Ronit, *Israel and the Daughters of Shoah*, New York and Oxford, Berghahn Books, 2000.

Levi, Primo, *Survival in Auschwitz*, trans. Stuart Woolf, New York, Collier Macmillan, 1961.

Levinas, Emmanuel, *Difficile liberté: Essais sur le Judaïsme,* Paris, Albin Michel, 1963.

—— 'Judaism and the Feminine Element', trans. Edith Wyschogrod, *Judaism* 18 (1969), pp. 30–8.

—— *Totality and Infinity: An Essay on Exteriority*, trans. Alphonso Lingis, Pittsburgh, Duquesue University Press, 1969.

—— *Otherwise than Being, or Beyond Essence*, trans. Alphonso Lingis, The Hague, Martinus Nijhoff, 1981.

—— 'Useless Suffering', trans. Richard Cohen, in Bernasconi and Wood (eds), *The Provocation of Levinas*, pp. 156–67.

—— *Difficult Freedom: Essays on Judaism,* trans. and ed. Seàn Hand, London, Athlone Press, 1990.

—— 'Loving the Torah More than God', reprinted in Badde (ed.), Zvi Kolitz, *Yosl Rakover Talks to God*, pp. 79–87.

Levine, Amy-Jill, 'A Jewess, More and/or Less', in Peskowitz and Levitt (eds), *Judaism Since Gender*, pp. 149–57.

Lewinska, Pelagia, 'Twenty Months at Auschwitz', in Rittner and Roth (eds), *Different Voices*, pp. 84–98.

Lichtenstein, Rachel and Iain Sinclair, *Rodinsky's Room*, London, Granta Books, 1999.

Lichtenstein, Dayan Yisroel Yaakov, 'A Voice . . . But Not the Vote', *Hamaor* Pesach 5755/1995, pp. 21–3.

Linden, Ruth R., *Making Stories, Making Selves: Feminist Reflections on the Holocaust*, Columbus, Ohio State University Press, 1993.

Lodahl, Michael E., *Shekhinah/Spirit: Divine Presence in Jewish and Christian Religion,* Mahwah, NJ, Paulist Press, 1992.

Long, Asphodel, 'A Pinhole in the Darkness', interviewed by Ruth Swirsky, in Copperman *et al.* (eds), *Generations of Memories*, pp. 188–216.

Luzzatto, Moses Hayyim, *Mesillat Yesharim: The Path of the Upright*, trans. and ed. Mordecai M. Kaplan, Philadelphia, Jewish Publication Society of America, 1966.

Lyotard, Jean-François, *The Differend. Phases in Dispute.* trans. Georges van Den Abbeele, Manchester, Manchester University Press, 1989.

Maccoby, Hyam, *Ritual and Morality: The Ritual Purity System and its Place in Judaism,* Cambridge, Cambridge University Press, 1999.

Maybaum, Ignaz, *The Face of God After Auschwitz*, Amsterdam, Polak and Van Gennep, 1965.

Meed, Vladka, *On Both Sides of the Wall: Memoirs from the Warsaw Ghetto*, trans. Steven Meed, New York, Holocaust Library, 1993.

Mellor, Mary, *Breaking the Boundaries: Towards a Feminist Green Socialism*, London, Virago, 1992.

Mendes-Flohr, Paul, 'Law and Sacrament, Ritual Observance in Twentieth-Century Jewish Thought', in Green (ed.), *Jewish Spirituality*, pp. 317–45.

Michaels, Anne, *Fugitive Pieces*, London, Bloomsbury, 1998.

Michelson, Frida, *I Survived Rumbuli*, trans. and ed. Wolf Goodman, New York, Holocaust Library, 1979.

Moltmann, Jürgen, *The Crucified God: The Cross of Christ as the Foundation and Criticism of Christian Theology*, trans. R.A. Wilson and J. Bowden, London, SCM Press, 1974.

Morgan, Michael L., 'Jewish Ethics after the Holocaust', in Elliot N. Dorff and Louis E. Newman (eds), *Contemporary Jewish Ethics and Morality: A Reader*, New York, Oxford University Press, 1995, pp. 194–211.

Mortley, Raoul, *French Philosophers in Conversation: Levinas, Schneider, Serres, Irigaray, Le Doeuff, Derrida*, London, Routledge, 1991.

Moskowitz, Faye (ed.), *Her Face in the Mirror: Jewish Women on Mothers and Daughters*, Boston, Beacon Press, 1995.

Nagy, Maya, 'No Heroes, No Martyrs', interviewed by Hannah Kanter with Frances Carter, in Copperman *et al.* (eds), *Generations of Memories*, pp. 155–87.

Neuberger, Julia, 'Woman in Judaism: The Fact and the Fiction', in Pat Holden (ed.), *Women's Religious Experience*, pp. 132–42.

—— *On Being Jewish*, London, Mandarin, 1996.

Neusner, Jacob, 'The Implications of the Holocaust' in *idem* (ed.), *Understanding Jewish Theology*, pp. 179–93.

—— (ed.), *Understanding Jewish Theology: Classical Issues and Modern Perspectives*, New York, Ktav Publishing House/Anti-Defamation League of B'nai Brith, 1973.

—— *Method and Meaning in Ancient Judaism*, Missoula, Mont., Scholars Press, 1979.

—— *Androgynous Judaism: Masculine and Feminine in the Dual Torah*, Macon, Georgia, Mercer University Press, 1993.

—— *Judaism's Theological Voice: The Melody of the Talmud*, London and Chicago, University of Chicago Press, 1995.

Noddings, Nel, *Caring: A Feminine Approach to Ethics and Moral Education*, Berkely, CA and London, University of California Press, 1986.

Nomberg-Przytyk, Sara, trans. Roslyn Hirsch; Eli Pfefferkorn and David H. Hirsch (eds), *Auschwitz: True Tales from a Grotesque Land*, Chapel Hill and London, The University of North Carolina Press, 1985.

Novak, David, *Jewish Social Ethics*, New York, Oxford University Press, 1992.

Nowak, Susan E., 'In a World Shorn of Color: Toward a Feminist Theology of Holocaust Testimonies', in Fuchs (ed.), *Women and the Holocaust*, pp. 33–46.

Ofer, Dalia and Lenore J. Weitzman (eds), *Women in the Holocaust,* New Haven and London, Yale University Press, 1998.

Olczakowa, Hanna Mortkowicz, 'Janosz Korczak's Last Walk', in Glatstein *et al.* (eds), *Anthology of Holocaust Literature*, pp. 134–6.

Orenstein, Gloria, *The Reflowering of the Goddess*, New York, Pergamon Press, 1990.

Otto, Rudolf, *The Idea of the Holy. An Inquiry into the Non-rational Factor in the Idea of the Divine and its Relation to the Rational*, London, Oxford University Press, 1958.

Ozick, Cynthia, 'Notes Towards Finding the Right Question', in Heschel (ed.), *On Being a Jewish Feminist*, pp. 120–51.

Pearl, Chaim, *Theology in Rabbinic Stories*, Peabody, MA, Hendrickson, 1997.

Pellegrini, Ann, 'Interarticulations: Gender, Race and the Jewish Question', in Peskowitz and Levitt (eds), *Judaism Since Gender*, pp. 49–55.

Perl, Gisella, 'A Doctor in Auschwitz', in Rittner and Roth (eds), *Different Voices*, pp. 106–18.

Peskowitz, Miriam, 'Engendering Jewish Religious History', in Peskowitz and Levitt (eds), *Judaism Since Gender*, pp. 17–39.

Peskowitz, Miriam and Laura Levitt (eds), *Judaism Since Gender,* New York, Routledge, 1997.

Plaskow, Judith, 'The Right Question is Theological', in Heschel (ed.), *On Being a Jewish Feminist* pp. 223–33.

—— *Standing Again at Sinai: Judaism from a Feminist Perspective*, New York, HarperSan Francisco, 1990.

—— 'Jewish Theology in Feminist Perspective', in Davidman and Tenenbaum (eds), *Feminist Perspectives on Jewish Studies*, pp. 62–84.

Pres, Des, *The Survivor: An Anatomy of Life in the Death Camps*, Oxford, Oxford University Press, 1976.

Rabinovici Schoschana, Mirjam Pressler and James Skofield, trans. Shoshanah Rabinovits, *Thanks to My Mother*, London, Puffin, 2000.

Rabuzzi, Kathryn Allen, *The Sacred and the Feminine: Toward a Theology of Housework*, New York, Seabury Press, 1982.

Raphael, Melissa, 'Feminism, Constructivism and Numinous Experience, *Religious Studies* 30 (1994), pp. 511–26.

—— *Thealogy and Embodiment: The Post-Patriarchal Reconstruction of Female Sacrality*, Sheffield, Sheffield Academic Press, 1996.

—— *Rudolf Otto and the Concept of Holiness*, Oxford, Clarendon Press, 1997.

—— 'Goddess Religion, Postmodern Jewish Feminism and the Complexity of Alternative Religious Identities', *Nova Religio* 1 (1998), pp. 198–215.

—— 'When God Beheld God: Notes Towards a Jewish Feminist Theology of the Holocaust', *Feminist Theology* 21 (1999), pp. 53–78. Reprinted in Susan Frank Parsons (ed.), *Challenging Women's Orthodoxies in the Context of Faith*, Aldershot, Hants and Burlington, VT, Ashgate Press, 2000, pp. 73–87. Reprinted in a shortened form as 'The Holocaust and Jewish Feminism' in Dan Cohn-Sherbok (ed.), *Holocaust Theology: A Reader*, Exeter, Exeter University Press, 2002, pp. 245–8;

—— ' "Refresh me with Apples for I am Faint with Love" (Song of Songs 2.5): Jewish Feminism, Mystical Theology and the Sexual Imaginary', in Lisa Isherwood (ed.), *The Good News of the Body: Sexual Theology and Feminism*, Sheffield, Sheffield Academic Press, 2000, pp. 54–72.

—— 'The Face of God in Every Generation: Jewish Feminist Spirituality and the Legend of the Thirty-Six Hidden Saints', in Ursula King (ed.), *Spirituality and Society in the New Millennium*, Brighton, Sussex Academic Press, 2001.

—— 'Holiness *in Extremis*: Jewish Women's Resistance to the Profane in Auschwitz', in Stephen Barton (ed.), *Holiness Past and Present*, Edinburgh, T. & T. Clark, forthcoming.

—— 'The Price of (Masculine) Freedom and Becoming: A Jewish Feminist Response to Eliezer Berkovits's Post-Holocaust Free Will Defence of God's Non-Intervention in Auschwitz', in Pamela Sue Anderson and Beverley Clack (eds), *Feminist Philosophy of Religion: Critical Perspectives*, London and New York: Routledge, forthcoming.

Richmond, Theo, *Konin, A Quest*, London, Vintage, 1996.

Ringelheim, Joan, 'The Unethical and the Unspeakable: Women and the Holocaust', in *Simon Wiesenthal Center Annual* (1984), pp. 69–87.

—— 'Women and the Holocaust: A Reconsideration of Research', *Signs, Journal of Women in Culture and Society* 10 (1985), pp. 741–61. Reprinted with later additions as 'Women and the Holocaust: A Reconsideration of Research', in Rittner and Roth (eds), *Different Voices*, pp. 373–418.

—— 'The Split between Gender and the Holocaust', in Ofer and Weitzman (eds), *Women in the Holocaust*, pp. 340–50.

Rittner, Carol, and John K. Roth (eds), *Different Voices: Women and the Holocaust*, New York, Paragon Press, 1993.

Ritvo, Roger A. and Diane M. Plotkin, *Sisters in Sorrow: Voices of Care in the Holocaust*, Austen, Texas University Press, 1998.

Rose, Gillian, *Judaism and Modernity: Philosophical Essays*, Oxford and Cambridge, Mass., Blackwell, 1993.

—— *Love's Work*, London, Vintage, 1997.

Rosenbaum, Irving, *The Holocaust and Halakhah*, New York, Ktav Publishing House, 1976.

Rosenzweig, Franz, *The Star of Redemption*, trans. W.W. Hallo, Notre Dame, IN, Notre Dame Press, 1985.

Roskies, David, *Against the Apocalypse: Responses to Catastrophe in Modern Jewish Culture*, Cambridge, Mass. and London, Harvard University Press, 1984.

Rosten, Leo, *The Joys of Yiddish*, Harmondsworth, Penguin Books, 1968.

Roth, John K. and Elizabeth Maxwell (eds), *Remembering for the Future: The Holocaust in an Age of Genocide*, Basingstoke, Hampshire, Palgrave, 2001.

Roth, Joseph, trans. Michael Hoffman, *The Wandering Jews*, London, Granta, 2001.

Rothschild, Sylvia, 'Beginning a Religious Response to Mastectomy', in Rothschild and Sheridan (eds), *Taking Up the Timbrel*, pp. 182–5.

Rothschild, Sylvia and Sybil Sheridan (eds), *Taking Up the Timbrel: The Challenge of Creating Ritual for Jewish Women Today*, London, SCM Press, 2000.

Rubenstein, Erna F., *The Survivor in Us All: A Memoir of the Holocaust*, Hamden, CT, Archon Books, 1984.

Rubenstein, Richard L., *After Auschwitz: Radical Theology and Contemporary Judaism*, New York, Bobbs-Merrill, 1966.

—— and John K. Roth, *Approaches to Auschwitz: The Legacy of the Holocaust*, London, SCM Press, 1987.

Sacks, Jonathan, *One People? Tradition, Modernity, and Jewish Unity*, London, The Littman Library of Jewish Civilization, 1993.

—— *Faith in the Future*, London, Darton, Longman & Todd, 1995.

Sacks, Maurie, 'Computing Community at Purim', *Journal of American Folklore* 102 (1989), pp. 275–91.

Sarah, Elizabeth Tikvah, review of Judith Hauptman, *Rereading the Rabbis* in *Hochmah* newsletter no.14, September 1998/Rosh Ha Shanah 5759, pp. 17–19.

—— 'Our Jewish Wedding', in Rothschild and Sheridan (eds), *Taking Up the Timbrel*, pp. 134–46.

Scarf, Mimi, 'Marriages Made in Heaven? Battered Jewish Wives', in Heschel (ed.), *On Being a Jewish Feminist*, pp. 51–64.

Schechter, Solomon, *Studies in Judaism: Essays on Persons, Concepts, and Movements of Thought in Jewish Tradition*, New York, Atheneum, 1970.

Schindler, Pesach, *Hasidic Responses to the Holocaust in the Light of Hasidic Thought*, New Jersey, Ktav Publishing House, 1990.

Schneid, Hayyim, (ed.), *Family*, Philadelphia, Jewish Publication Society of America, 1973.

Scholem, Gershom, *Major Trends in Jewish Mysticism*, London, Thames & Hudson, 1955.

—— *The Messianic Idea in Judaism And Other Essays on Jewish Spirituality*, trans. Michael A. Meyer and Hillel Halkin, New York, Schocken Books, 1971.

—— *On the Kabbalah and its Symbolism*, trans. Ralph Manheim, New York, Schocken Books, 1996.

Schwartz, Howard, *Elijah's Violin and Other Jewish Folktales*, Harmondsworth, Penguin, 1983.

Schwartz-Bart, André, *The Last of the Just*, trans. Stephen Becker, London, Secker & Warburg, 1962.

Schweid, Eliezer, 'Faith, Ethics, and the Holocaust: The Justification of Religion in the Crisis of the Holocaust', *Holocaust and Genocide Studies* 3 (1988), pp. 385–412.

Seidman, Naomi, 'Theorizing Jewish Patriarchy *in extremis*', in Peskowitz and Levitt (eds), *Judaism Since Gender*, pp. 40–8.

Senesh, Hannah, *Hannah Senesh: Her Life and Diary*, trans. Marta Cohn, London, Vallentine Mitchell & Co., 1971.

Sered, Susan Starr, *Women as Ritual Experts: The Religious Lives of Elderly Jewish Women Living in Jerusalem,* New York, Oxford University Press, 1992.

——— ' "She Perceives Her Work to Be Rewarding", Jewish Women in a Cross-Cultural Perspective', in Davidman and Tenenbaum (eds), *Feminist Perspectives on Jewish Studies*, pp. 169–190.

——— 'Mother Love, Child Death and Religious Innovation: A Feminist Perspective', *Journal of Feminist Studies in Religion* 12 (1996), pp. 5–23.

Setel, T. Drorah, with Catherine Keller, Marcia Falk, Anne M. Solomon and Rita Gross, 'Roundtable Discussion: Feminist Reflections on Separation and Unity in Jewish Theology', *Journal of Feminist Studies in Religion* 2 (1986), pp. 113–30.

Shapiro, David S., 'The Ideological Foundations of the Halakhah', in Neusner (ed.), *Understanding Jewish Theology*, pp. 107–20.

Shapiro, Susan, 'Failing Speech: Post-Holocaust Writing and the Discourse of Postmodernism', *Semeia* 40 (1984), pp. 65–91.

——— 'Hearing the Testimony of Radical Negation', in Elisabeth Schüssler Fiorenza and David Tracy (eds), *The Holocaust as Interruption, Concilium* 175 (1984), pp. 3–10.

Shepherd, Naomi, *A Price Below Rubies: Jewish Women as Rebels and Radicals*, London, Weidenfeld & Nicolson, 1993.

Slonin, Rivkah, 'Mikveh: Gateway to Purity', in Kornbluth and Kornbluth (eds), *Jewish Women Speak Out about Jewish Matters*, pp. 73–81.

Smith, Chani, 'The Symbol of the Shekhinah – the Feminine Side of God', in Alix Pirani (ed.), *The Absent Mother: Restoring the Goddess to Judaism and Christianity*, London, Mandala, 1991, pp. 5–13.

Spiegel, Marcia Cohn, 'Spirituality for Survival: Jewish Women Healing Themselves', *Journal of Feminist Studies in Religion* 12 (1996), pp. 121–37.

Spitzer, Julie Ringold, *When Love is not Enough: Spousal Abuse in Rabbinic and Contemporary Judaism*, New York, Women of Reform Judaism, Federation of Temple Sisterhoods, 1995.

Steinberg, Jonah, 'From a "Pot of Filth" to a "Hedge of Roses" (and Back): Changing Theorizations of Menstruation in Judaism', *Journal of Feminist Studies in Religion* 13 (1997), pp. 5–26.

Steiner, George, 'The Hollow Miracle', in *George Steiner: A Reader*, Penguin, Harmondsworth, Middx., 1984, pp. 207–19.

——— *In Bluebeard's Castle: Some Notes Towards the Re-definition of Culture*, London, Faber & Faber, 1971.

Stern, David, 'The Natural and the Supernatural. Arthur Cohen: An Introduction', in Stern and Mendes-Flohr (eds), *An Arthur A. Cohen Reader*, pp. 11–25.

Stern, David and Paul Mendes-Flohr (eds), *An Arthur A. Cohen Reader: Selected Fiction and Writings on Judaism, Theology, Literature and Culture*, Detroit, Wayne State University Press, 1998.

Stern, David and Mark Jay Mirsky (eds), *Rabbinic Fantasies: Imaginative Narratives from Classical Hebrew Literature*, London, Yale University Press, 1998.

Tec, Nechama, 'Women among the Forest Partisans', in Ofer and Weitzman, (eds), *Women in the Holocaust*, pp. 223–64.

Tedeschi, Giuliana, *There Is a Place on Earth: A Woman in Birkenau*, trans. Tim Parks, London, Minerva, 1994.

Todorov, Tzvetan, *Facing the Extreme: Moral Life in the Concentration Camps*, trans. Arthur Denner and Abigail Pollack, London, Weidenfeld & Nicolson, 1999.

Trible, Phyllis, *God and the Rhetoric of Sexuality*, Philadelphia, Fortress Press, 1978.

Umansky, Ellen, M. and Dianne Ashton (eds), *Four Centuries of Jewish Women's Spirituality: A Sourcebook*, Boston, Beacon Press, 1992.

Unterman, Alan, *Jews: Their Religious Beliefs and Practices*, London, Routledge & Kegan Paul, 1981.

Urbach, Ephraim, *The Sages: Their Concepts and Beliefs*, Jerusalem, Magnes Press, 1979.

Utriainen, Terhri, *Present, Naked, Pure: A Study of the Anthropology of Religion on Women by the Side of the Dying*, Helsinki, Finnish Literature Society, 1999.

Vago, Lidia Rosenfeld, 'One Year in the Black Hole of Our Planet Earth: A Personal Narrative', in Ofer and Weitzman (eds), *Women in the Holocaust,* pp. 273–84.

Valevičius, Andrius, *From the Other to the Totally Other: The Religious Philosophy of Emmanuel Levinas*, New York, Bern, Frankfurt am Main and Paris, Peter Lang, 1988.

Waskow, Arthur, *These Holy Sparks: The Rebirth of the Jewish People*, San Francisco, Harper & Row, 1983.

—— 'Between the Fires', in Jacobs (ed.), *Contemporary Jewish Religious Responses to the Holocaust*, pp. 174–79.

Webber, Jonathan, 'Between Law and Custom: Women's Experience of Judaism', in Holden (ed.), *Women's Religious Experience*, pp. 143–62.

Wegner, Judith Romney, *Chattel or Person? The Status of Women in the Mishnah*, New York, Oxford University Press, 1988.

Weissler, Chava, 'The Traditional Piety of Ashkenazic Women', in Green (ed.), *Jewish Spirituality from the Sixteenth-Century Revival to the Present*, pp. 245–75.

Weissman, Deborah R., 'Beis Yaakov: A Historical Model for Jewish Feminists', in Elizabeth Koltun (ed.), *The Jewish Woman: New Perspectives*, New York, Schocken Books, 1976, pp. 139–48.

Wiernik, Yankel, 'A Year in Treblinka Horror Camp', in Glatstein *et al.* (eds), *Anthology of Holocaust Literature*, pp. 178–85.

Wiesel, Elie, *Night*, trans. Stella Rodway, New York, Avon Books, 1960.

—— *Legends of Our Time*, New York, Holt, Rinehart & Winston, 1968.

—— *The Trial of God*, New York, Schocken Books, 1979.

Wieseltier, Leon. 'A Privation of Providence', in Badde (ed.), Zvi Kolitz, *Yosl Rakover Talks to God*, pp. 89–99.

Wolfson, Elliot R., *Through A Speculum That Shines: Vision and Imagination in Medieval Jewish Mysticism*, Princeton, NJ, Princeton University Press, 1994.

—— *Circle in the Square: Studies in the Use of Gender in Kabbalistic Symbolism*, Albany, State University of New York Press, 1995.

Wright, Alex, 'An Approach to Jewish Feminist Theology', in Sybil Sheridan (ed.), *Women Rabbis Tell Their Stories*, London, SCM Press, 1994, pp. 152–61.

Wright, Tamra, Peter Hughes and Alison Ainley, trans. Andrew Benjamin and Tamra Wright, 'The Paradox of Morality: An Interview with Emmanuel Levinas' in Bernasconi and Wood (eds), *The Provocation of Levinas*, pp. 168–80.

Wyschogrod, Michael, 'Faith and the Holocaust: A Review Essay of Emil Fackenheim's *God's Presence in History*', *Judaism* 20 (1971), pp. 286–94.

—— *The Body of Faith: Judaism as Corporeal Election*, New York, Seabury Press, 1983.

Yablonka, Hanna, *Survivors of the Holocaust: Israel after the War*, trans. Ora Cummings, Basingstoke, Hampshire, Macmillan Press, 1999.

Young, James, *Writing and Rewriting the Holocaust: Narratives and the Consequences of Interpretation*, Bloomington and Indianapolis, Indiana University Press, 1988.

—— *The Texture of Memory: Holocaust Memorials and Meaning*, New Haven and London, Yale University Press, 1993.

—— *At Memory's Edge: After Images of the Holocaust in Contemporary Art and Architecture*, New Haven and London, Yale University Press, 2000.

Zaidman, Nurit, 'Variations of Jewish Feminism: The Traditional, Modern and Postmodern Approaches', *Modern Judaism* 16 (1996), pp. 47–65.

Zeitlin, Aaron, 'The Last Walk of Janusz Korczak', trans. Hadassah Rosensaft and Gertrude Hirschler, in Korczak, *Ghetto Diary*, pp. 7–63.

Zygmuntowicz, Itka Frajman, with Sara Horowitz, 'Survival and Memory', in Umansky and Ashton (eds), *Four Centuries of Jewish Women's Spirituality*, pp. 286–90.

Index